Public Administration, Governance and Globalization

Volume 14

Series Editor

Ali Farazmand
Florida Atlantic University, Fort Lauderdale, Florida, USA

Public Administration, Governance and Globalization

The aim of Public Administration, Governance and Globalization (PAGG) is to publish primary research and theoretical contributions as well as practical reports on fieldwork to help advance the knowledge and understanding about public, nonprofit, private, and nongovernmental organizations and institutions. The governance, administration, and management of these organizations at local, national, regional, and international levels will be discussed in the context of this age of rapid change and globalization. This series on public management offers original materials that contribute to our better understanding of the critical issues as well as routine processes of governance and public administration, now more than ever because of the intricate forces of globalization that affect almost every nation-states and their policy choices at all jurisdictions across the world. The series covers a wide range of topics that address the key issues of interest to scholars, educators, practitioners, and policymakers in public administration capacities around the globe. Books in the series could be research monographs, edited volumes, textbooks, reference volumes or handbooks.

Series Editor
A. Farazmand
Florida Atlantic University, Fort Lauderdale, FL, USA

More information about this series at http://www.springer.com/series/8656

Khi V. Thai
Editor

International Public Procurement

Innovation and Knowledge Sharing

Springer

Editor
Khi V. Thai
School of Public Administration
Florida Atlantic University
Boca Raton
Florida
USA

Public Administration, Governance and Globalization
ISBN 978-3-319-13433-8 ISBN 978-3-319-13434-5 (eBook)
DOI 10.1007/978-3-319-13434-5

Library of Congress Control Number: 2015934679

Springer Cham Heidelberg New York Dordrecht London

Printed on acid-free paper

Springer is part of Springer Science+Business Media (www.springer.com).

Preface

This book is a collection of best papers that were submitted to and presented at the 5th International Public Procurement Conference (IPPC5), which was held in Seattle, USA, August 17–19, 2012, and hosted by the National Institute of Governmental Purchasing, Inc., and Florida Atlantic University Public Procurement Research Center. Initiated in 2004, IPPC has become one of the largest international networks of public procurement practitioners and researchers in the world, a very strong evidence of global interest in this emerging profession.

At its inception in 2004, IPPC began a tradition that no other professional conference could match: All conference papers were reviewed and best papers were selected for publication in special issues of the academic *Journal of Public Procurement*, and an IPPC book. Particularly, these publications are published in time for distribution at the conferences.

This year, after the Great Economic Recession, 171 paper proposals (an unprecedented number) and 105 full papers were submitted. Twelve of those submitted papers did not meet our expected standard and were not accepted for presentation at the conference. Papers published in this book were selected from the pool of 105 qualified papers after subjection of two waves of peer reviews, within 4 weeks, a very short time period for members of the Scientific Committee (listed below) to review at least eight papers (as each paper was reviewed by three peer reviewers). Without their professional services, it would have been impossible to impartially select excellent papers for this volume. As co-editors of this book, we would like to thank the IPPC5 Scientific Committee members for their professional services. We would like also take this opportunity to thank The National Institute of Governmental Purchasing, Inc. that provides generous financial support of the International Public Procurement Conference. We also thank Dublin City University for hosting the conference.

It is important to note that authors of papers selected for this book should be proud of their work as their papers have survived two waves of challenging reviews, and more importantly, their papers were selected from a large pool of papers, at an acceptance rate of 14.3 %. We congratulate these authors on their book chapters and the proven quality of their research.

Scientific Committee

Paul Davis, Dublin City University (Ireland), Co-Chair
Khi V. Thai, Florida Atlantic University (USA), Co-Chair
Gian Albano, Public Procurement Agency known as Consip (Italy)
Alessandro Ancarani, University of Catania (Italy)
Hannie Badenhorst-Weiss, University of South Africa (South Africa)
Bert Baeyens, Public Procurement Management VIB (Belgium)
Benon Besheka, Uganda Management Institute (Uganda)
Jan Braechner, Chalmers University of Technology
Ana Cristina Calderon, Inter-American Development Bank
Guy Callender, Curtin University of Technology (Australia)
Fuguo Cao, Central University of Finance and Economics (China)
Jeremy Chen, Defence Science and Technology Agency (Singapore)
Paul Davis, Dublin City University (Ireland)
Richard Doyle, University of New England (Australia)
Andrew Erridge, University of Ulster (UK)
Michael Essig, Bundeswehr University Munich (Germany)
Steve Gordon, West Virginia University (USA)
Baudouin Heuninckx, Defense Ministry, Belgium
Atsushi Iimi, The World Bank
Iiao I-ming, Kaoshung University (Taiwan)
Leslie E. Harper, Inter-American Development Bank
David Jones, University of Brunei (Brunei)
Veiko Lember, Tallinn University of Technology (Estonia)
Wendell Lawther, University of Central Florida (USA)
Anders Lunander, Örebro University (Sweden)
Sofia Lundberg, Umeå University (Sweden)
Odysseus Manoliadis, Democritus University of Thrace (Greece)
Cliff McCue, Florida Atlantic University (USA)
Teresa Medina-Arnáiz, University of Burgos (Spain)
Ari Nissinen, Finnish Environment Institute (Finland)
Joseph Ntayi, Makerere University (Uganda)
Sander Onderstal, University of Amsterdam (Holland)
Emanuele Padovani, University of Bologna (Italy)
Katriina Parikka-Alhola, Consumption and Production Centre (Finland)
Gustavo Piga, University of Rome "Tor Vergata" (Italy)
Jack Pitzer, City of Alexander, Virginia (USA)
Eric Prier, Florida Atlantic University (USA)
Sharon Purchase, University of Western Australia (Australia)
Rene Rendon, Naval Postgraduate School (USA)
David Salazar, Inter-American Development Bank
Joshua Schwartz, George Washington University (USA)
Keith Snider, Naval Postgraduate School (USA)

Edwin Tachlian, Inter-American Development Bank
Satoru Tanaka, Kobe City University of Foreign Studies, Japan
Tünde Tátrai, Corvinus University of Budape
Ioannis E. Tsolas, National Technical University of Athens (Greece)
Junsok Yang, Catholic University (South Korea)
June-Seong Yi, Ewha Woman's University (South Korea)

Khi V. Thai
Editor

Contents

International Public Procurement: Innovation and Knowledge Sharing 1
Khi V. Thai

Part I Innovation and Reforms in Public Procurement

Contract Management Innovation in Public Procurement: Costa Rica's Experience 13
Ileana Palaco, Alicia Avendaño and Waldemar Núñez

The Municipal Partnering Initiative: Mixed Contracting in Local Government Procurement 31
David Rauch

The Impact of Changing Patterns of Commercial Card Use by the US Government on Governmental Efficiency and Cost Savings 57
Richard Palmer, Mahendra Gupta and Nathan Palmer

Defense Management Research Capacities and Topics: Blind Spots in Defense Acquisition Management? 89
Christian von Deimling, Andreas H. Glas and Michael Essig

Customers' Preferences in Municipal Waste Services Procurement 129
Alessandro Ancarani, Carmela Di Mauro, Francesco Mascali and Liborio La Marca

Part II Public Procurement Transparency

Rationalising Public Procurement of Complex Construction Projects by the Price Component Selection ... 145
Pertti Lahdenperä

Pricing for Public Purchase: A Qualitative-Empirical Analysis of Public Procurement and Price Setting Practices ... 167
Michael Georgi and Sascha Kemmeter

Procurement Conspiracies and Procurement Governance: Some Lessons from Thailand ... 183
Sirilaksana Khoman

Collaborative Public Procurement: A Comparative Review of the Indian Position with International Practices on Pooled Procurement from Competition Law Perspectives ... 203
Sandeep Verma

Regulating the Pre-procurement Phase: Context and Perspectives ... 221
Willem A. Janssen

Construction Procurers' Perceptions of Value for Money ... 237
Warren Staples

Part III Preferential Public Procurement

The Reform to EU Utilities Procurement: Smart, Sustainable and Inclusive? ... 255
Eleanor Aspey

Stages of Development Towards Sustainable Public Procurement ... 271
Tünde Tátrai

Policy Implementation of Sustainable Public Procurement in China ... 287
Conghu Wang and Xiaoming Li

The Role of Small and Medium-Sized Enterprises in a Sustainable Public Procurement System ... 301
Anna Górczyńska

Index ... 323

Contributors

Alessandro Ancarani University of Catania, Catania, Italy

Eleanor Aspey University of Manchester, Manchester, UK

Alicia Avendaño Digital Government Instituto Costarricense de Electricidad, San José, Costa Rica

Christian von Deimling Bundeswehr University Munich, Neubiberg (Munich), Bavaria, Germany

Carmela Di Mauro University of Catania, Catania, Italy

Michael Essig Bundeswehr University Munich, Neubiberg (Munich), Bavaria, Germany

Michael Georgi Department of Management Accounting and Control, TU Dortmund University, Dortmund, Germany

Andreas H. Glas Bundeswehr University Munich, Neubiberg (Munich), Bavaria, Germany

Anna Górczyńska Faculty of Law and Administration, University of Lodz, Lodz, Poland

Mahendra Gupta St. Louis, USA

Willem A. Janssen Public Procurement Research Center and Utrecht Center for Regulation and Enforcement in Europe, University of Utrecht, Utrecht, Netherlands

Sascha Kemmeter Department of Management Accounting, University of Duisburg-Essen, Essen, Germany

Sirilaksana Khoman National Anti-Corruption Commission, Nonthaburi, Thailand

Liborio La Marca University of Catania, Catania, Italy

Pertti Lahdenperä VTT Technical Research Centre of Finland Ltd, Tampere, Finland

Xiaoming Li Department of Business Administration, Tennessee State University, Nashville, USA

Francesco Mascali University of Catania, Catania, Italy

Waldemar Núñez Procurement Division, Instituto Costarricense de Electricidad, San José, Costa Rica

Ileana Palaco Global IT Technology Program (ITTP), Korea Advanced Institute of Science and Technology (KAIST), Daejeon, South Korea

Richard Palmer Missouri, USA

David Rauch Urban Planning and Environment, Edmonton, AB, Canada

Warren Staples RMIT University, Melbourne, Australia

Tünde Tátrai Corvinus University of Budapest, Budapest, Hungary

Khi V. Thai School of Public Administration, Florida Atlantic University, Boca Raton, FL, USA

Sandeep Verma Indian Administrative Service, New Delhi, India

Conghu Wang School of Public Administration and Policy, Renmin University of China, Beijing, China

About the Editor

Khi V. Thai, Ph.D. is a Professor and Director, School of Public Administration, Florida Atlantic University. His research interest is in public budgeting, financial management and public procurement. He is editor of International Journal of Organization Theory and Behavior, Journal of Public Procurement, and Journal of Public Budgeting, Accounting & Financial Management. His publications include over 100 books, book chapters, technical reports, and refereed articles. He has been a consultant for the US government, United Nations, and for governments in US and Canada.

International Public Procurement: Innovation and Knowledge Sharing

Khi V. Thai

Introduction

Public procurement is continuing to evolve both conceptually and organizationally. That evolution accelerated since the 1990s as governments at all levels came under increasing pressures to "do more with less." Indeed, all governmental entities of rich and poor countries are struggling in the face of: unrelenting budget constraints; government downsizing; public demand for increased transparency in public procurement; and greater concerns about efficiency, fairness, and equity. In addition, public procurement professionals have faced a constantly changing environment typified by rapidly emerging technologies, increasing product choice, environmental concerns, and the complexities of international and regional trading agreements. Further, policy makers have increasingly used public procurement as a tool to achieve socioeconomic goals (Thai 2007).

In this environment, public procurement has become much more complex than ever before, and public procurement officials must deal with a broad range of issues. They have been walking on a tight rope in:

- Balancing the dynamic tension between (a) competing socioeconomic objectives and (b) national economic interests and global competition as required by regional and international trade agreements.
- Satisfying the requirements of fairness, equity, and transparency.
- Maintaining an overarching focus on maximizing competition.
- Utilizing new technology to enhance procurement efficiency, including e-procurement and purchase cards (Thai 2007).

Established in 2004, the International Public Procurement Conference (IPPC) has become a unique forum for exchange of knowledge and information in public procurement among international experts in this field. Through the five previous conferences, many experts from various backgrounds shared their views and experiences on critical issues of public procurement. The fertile mixture of experiences,

K. V. Thai (✉)
School of Public Administration, Florida Atlantic University, Boca Raton, FL, USA
e-mail: thai@fau.edu

K. V. Thai (ed.), *International Public Procurement,* Public Administration, Governance and Globalization 14, DOI 10.1007/978-3-319-13434-5_1

interests, and contributions that emerged in the last five conferences represents an important basis upon which to build the 6th International Public Procurement Conference (IPPC6).

IPPC6, held in Dublin, Ireland, has the following unique characteristics. It will deepen the interdisciplinary research on public procurement. Public procurement research can be accessed from various academic fields, including law, economics, public administration, business administration, and construction management, to name a few. It is the tradition of IPPC that experts from various academic backgrounds share their views, thus crossing barriers between academic fields. This tradition was continued and broadened in IPPC6. In addition, IPPC6 will strengthen the link between the practitioners and scholars in finding solutions to harmonize various objectives in public procurement. Public procurement has many objectives: transparency, competition, efficiency, value for money, socioeconomic objectives, among others. Because these objectives sometimes conflict with each other, it is necessary to harmonize these various objectives. To cope with this challenge, it is important for practitioners and scholars to cooperate with each other. Practitioners should give explanations of actual problems in their harmonizing efforts, and scholars should make every effort to address these problems with sound theory and analysis.

Fifteen studies or papers (hereafter called "chapters") were selected, via a rigorous peer review process, on the basis of scholarship. Thus, it is expected that they cover a variety of research issues. However, four major public procurement issues have been the focuses of fifteen chapters: Innovation in public procurement (Chapters 2–6), procurement transparency (Chapters 7–12), and preferential procurement (Chapters 13–16).

By no means do the above identified themes reflect scientifically the current trends of research interests. Actually, there are a good number of papers presented at the conference which focus on many critical procurement concerns, including procurement innovation and reforms, transparency concerns, and sustainable public procurement.

Part I. Innovation and Reforms in Public Procurement

Public procurement is one of the most challenging functions of government as public procurement practitioners have to adapt rapidly changing environment. Rapidly newly developed technology has also forced public procurement practitioners to (i) adopt new procurement methods, such as the use of e-Signature and purchase cards; and (ii) be knowledgeable in how to procure new technology. Thus, new initiatives or innovations are always needed. In "Contract Management Innovation In Public Procurement: Costa Rica's Experience," Ileana Palaco, Alicia Avendaño, and Waldemar Núñez presented an innovative solution to the procurement dilemma in Costa Rica. Prior to the implementation of the e-Procurement Platform, known as "Mer-link," Costa Rica had made several efforts to integrate procurement, but such attempts were not perceived as an effective solution to an increasingly evident problem. The Costa Rican Public Procurement Model was fragmented, full of bureaucratic processes, with a generalized lack of opportunity for define SME's and had fostered several corruption scandals. Mer-link handles the entire procurement process. But if such features are already available in other practices, why is Mer-link an innovative solution to the procurement dilemma? Mer-link has added a great value to the Costa Rican procurement cycle and has empowered citizens through a real accountability mechanism on how their taxes are being spent and how it is facilitating the management process to key institutional players.

Recently, public–private partnership has become more and more popular, particularly in Europe. In "The Municipal Partnering Initiative: Mixed Contracting in Local Government Procurement," Daivd Rauch focuses on partnership in local government. The municipal partnering initiative (MPI) is an informal partnership of more than two dozen Chicago, Illinois, the USA suburban communities which combine their purchasing power to procure contractor services. The MPI is unique among pooled purchasing groups in the USA because contractor services include complicated road services which require multiple communities to agree on common bid specifications. This chapter examines the history of pooled purchasing in the Chicago area. In addition to a survey collecting opinions of the MPI participants, the cost of three contractor services are examined in the region over a 6-year period to compare services costs before and after the program began. Analysis found that the MPI prices for the services are generally lower than non-MPI prices, but there are important administrative cost savings not being captured.

In "The Impact of Changing Patterns of Commercial Card Use by the US Government on Governmental Efficiency and Cost Savings," Richard Palmer, Mahendra Gupta, and Nathan Palmer exmine benefits of p-cards used by the US federal government. According to them, the US Government has used bank commercial card technology since the 1980s to simplify and reduce the cost of the process to acquire goods and services. The benefits derived from card use vary by type of card, manner of card use, and degree of integration with the acquisition process. In fiscal year 2013, the US Government spent US$26 billion on commercial cards and identified US$1.7 billion in administrative cost savings and cash back incentives. Notwithstanding the putative benefits, the US Government spending on all commercial cards has been in decline since 2011 and spending on purchasing cards (the card platform on which most spending is directed) peaked in 2008. Since the US Government reaps benefits from card use, the purpose of this chapter is to explore (a) potential factors driving reductions in commercial card spending, both in absolute terms and as a percentage of budgeted spending, and (b) the counter measures available to government to optimize the benefits derived from commercial card use.

In "Defense Management Research Capacities and Topics: Blind Spots in Defense Acquisition Management?" Christian v. Deimling, Andreas H. Glas, and Michael Essig examine defense research capacities and research topics in defense acquisition. According to the authors, defense research is conducted by universities and other types of research organizations, each with a specific perspective. Key topics range from politics, military strategies, and lobbying to administration and management. Defense procurement seems to be a special area of interest. Thus, this chapter aims to explore the status quo of defense procurement research. For this purpose, the content analysis method has been applied to a set of 29 research organizations working on defense topics. The findings indicate that research focuses on procurement policies and armament cooperation, whereas procurement strategy, organization, process and surprisingly, private sector participation, are less-studied fields. The results orient both researchers and practitioners to defense procurement research institutions and their topics.

In "Customers' Preferences in Municipal Waste Services Procurement," Alessandro Ancarani, Carmela Di Mauro, Francesco Mascali, and Liborio La Marca present the application of the concept of value for customer to public service provision, recommending the assessment of users' preferences for service design and procurement, in order to motivate and promote the co-production of the service. The use of discrete choice experiments is suggested as a straightforward methodology to assess customer preferences in terms of willingness to trade-off between alternative service attributes. Municipal waste service is used as an example, through the application of discrete choice experiments to two municipalities. The aim is to illustrate the insights that public buyers can derive from such analysis, and to show implications for public procurement.

Part II. Public Procurement Transparency

One of the basic principles of public procurement is transparency which can be easily violated. In government contracting, conducting major or complex construction project procurement is not easy. In "Rationalising Public Procurement of Complex Construction Projects by the Price Component Selection," Pertti Lahdenperä presents a new trend in incorporating versatile expertise in construction project planning to avoid the problems resulting from the low bid practice. Often the solution is to strive for an open process where the price (target cost) of the project is set later after a joint development phase by the owner and the selected team is involved. Such a process poses, however, a challenge to public owners due to public accountability concerns. This study tries to respond to this challenge by exploring the possibilities of awarding a contract based on capability and mere key price components combined with specific cost management methods to ensure economic efficiency. This is done by delving into the practices and experiences of four different infrastructure construction projects. The price components used in those four projects consisted of, for instance, fee, project overhead, risk and opportunity provision, preliminaries and direct costs of a certain part of the project; these items do not cover the total project price. On the whole, the experiences from cases have been positive and they also encourage considering the possibility of using the price component method more extensively in challenging future projects.

In "Pricing for Public Purchase: A Qualitative-Empirical Analysis of Public Procurement and Price Setting Practices," Michael Georgi, and Sascha Kemmeter analyze empirically the common practice of how the system for public purchase in Germany is composed and to assess if and at which point of the purchasing process problems occur. Therefore, we use a qualitative grounded theory-based approach with 20 interviews among price auditors and managers. Finally, we give recommendations for how the existing system or the habits of involved parties will have to change. The results show that significant problems occur because of the age and design of the regulation systems and also because of a lack of expertise.

In "Procurement Conspiracies and Procurement Governance: Some Lessons from Thailand," Sirilaksana Khoman addresses public procurement governance focusing on the problem of procurement conspiracies and connected dealings. The term "connected dealings" is used to refer to situations involving conflicts of interest when at least one party in a contractual arrangement in a decision-making position and at least one other party in a position benefiting from this decision are connected through business relations, family ties, school or institutional affiliation, or other previous dealings. When contracts result from connected dealings, they are deemed to be part of a procurement conspiracy, where contracts are won because of undisclosed network relationships rather than objective criteria. Public procurement provides fertile grounds for connected dealings and conspiracies. According to Khoman, although procurement regulations may be clear and strict, loopholes can be found that allow conspirators within patron–client networks to engage in wrongdoing with impunity, to the detriment of a country's development. In some instances, laws and regulations are blatantly violated because of perceived "protection" within the network. The author presents a particular case of procurement corruption and connected dealings in Thailand. She also discusses Thailand's pre-emptive, pro-active approaches to combating these procurement conspiracies and connected dealings.

Collaborative public procurement through the use of joint purchasing contracts or interagency framework agreements, has gained wide acceptance in many countries in the world. In "Collaborative Public Procurement: A Comparative Review of the Indian Position with International Practices on Pooled Procurement from Competition Law Perspectives," Sandeep Verma expresses some concern about this procurement approach. While horizontal collaboration among distinct procuring entities may result in economic efficiencies under certain circumstances, cooperative purchasing among dominant market players can sometimes raise significant antitrust and other competition concerns, especially when collaboration is enforced rather than voluntary, and when collaborating procuring entities operate in similar geographical markets. The author explores important issues of intersection between public procurement rules on the one hand with competition law issues on the other, and covers the position in the USA, European Union, China, and India, concluding with suggestions for better design of public procurement rules for anti-trust compliance.

Fifteen years ago, Thai (2001) observed that in the American public procurement process, there was a lack of focus on procurement decision stage (see McCue and Hinson 2004; McCue and Johnson 2010 for in-depth exploration of the procurement planning and decision stage). This observation is confirmed in chapter "Regulating the Pre-procurement Phase: Context and Perspectives" this volume. Willem A. Janssen states that the decision-making phase prior to public procurement is currently unregulated. Public authorities are, from a European Union public procurement law perspective, free to decide upon who is allowed, and best suited, to provide public services to the public. The newly adopted European Union public procurement directives appear to emphasize and further facilitate this freedom. The consequences of this legal context are exemplified by discussing four sectors in the Netherlands (waste collection, supportive services, public transport, and social support). Subsequently, it concludes by providing legal perspectives to regulate this pre-procurement phase by considering regulatory initiatives in the Netherlands and the USA.

In "Construction Procurers' Perceptions of Value for Money," Warren J. Staples states that value for money underpins public procurement policy in many jurisdictions, and is accepted as a logical basis for public procurement in justifying expenditure to taxpayers. However, little is known about how "value for money" is perceived by managers who procure for public organizations. In this chapter, the author uses qualitative data from interviews with project (middle) managers in Australian State government agencies to explore their perceptions of "value for money" in the context of their construction procurement work. "Value for money" is viewed primarily as comprising "economy" and "efficiency" drivers with less emphasis placed upon "effectiveness" drivers. The evidence highlights the pervasiveness of "value for money" discourse for those responsible construction procurement activities and across public organizations and state jurisdictions with Australia.

Part IV. Preferential Public Procurement

Jones (2011, p. 61) observed: "Widely accepted principles of public procurement are value for money and fairness based on equal access for all suitable suppliers. These are considered to be best guaranteed by open and non-discriminatory competition, in which the main methods of procurement of goods, services and works are the competitive quotation for low value purchases and the open tender or selective open tender for high value purchases." However, public procurement is also required to serve socioeconomic and political purposes, including economic stabilization, preferring national or local firms over firms from other countries or other geographic locations, enhancing market competition, environment protection, and social responsible purposes (Bolton 2006; Clark and Moutray 2004; Coggburn 2003; Coggburn and Rahm 2005; Enchautegui et al. 1997; Foresti et al. 2007; Gormly 2014; Hasselbalch et al. 2014; Jones 2011; McCue and Gianakis 2001; McCrudden 2007; National Association of State Purchasing Officials 1999; Nicholas and Fruhmann 2014; Prier et al. 2008; Qiao et al. 2009; Rice 1992; Rice and Mongkuo 1998; Roos 2013; Short 1993; Sadikin 2008; Thomas 1919; Thai 2001; Tammi et al. 2014; Tolley et al. 1999; UN Environment Programme 2012; U.S. Department of Justice 1995; U.S. Environmental Protection Agency 1998a, 1998b; U.S. Environmental Protection Agency 2000; Wallace 1999; Watermeyer 2000.

In "The Role of Small and Medium-Sized Enterprises in a Sustainable Public Procurement System," Anna Gorczynska examines the idea of a sustainable public procurement system enhancing the development of SMEs in the context of existing European legislation as compared with current Polish regulations and draft amendments. The main SME-friendly measures that have already been implemented include subdividing the contract into lots, subcontracting, framework agreements, functional description of the object of the contract, consortia of enterprises, abolishment of discriminating against contractors on the grounds of their qualifications, e-Procurement, and best value for money as the most important award criterion. The chapter also presents the idea of supporting small and medium-sized enterprises in the context of common market regulations. The author examines whether any forms of preference for SMEs could be justified. Based on research data, some remarks are also made on the abuse of competition by collusive arrangements, fraud, and corruption. The author presents an empirical study analyzing whether the existing legislation forms a complex system of sustainable procurement and meets the exigencies of practice. The effectiveness of the adopted measures is also discussed.

In chapter "Stages of Development towards Sustainable Public Procurement" this volume, Eleanor Aspey wonders if the current European Union utilities procurement policy is smart, sustainable, and inclusive. The European Union has recently reformed the procurement regulatory regime, setting out new directives for public sector and utilities procurement. In light of the Europe 2020 Agenda, which aims to encourage smart, sustainable, and inclusive growth in the European economy, it was hoped that these procurement reforms would clarify the law on sustainable procurement. This chapter evaluates whether or not this has been the case, focusing on the utilities sector reforms. It will show that while some areas of the regime still potentially restrict the use of sustainable procurement policies, overall the reform offers much greater flexibility to utilities and is a promising development for sustainable procurement, providing much needed clarity to the law.

In "Stages of Development towards Sustainable Public Procurement," Tünde Tátrai proposes a conceptual framework that can help implement sustainable procurement programs effectively. Sustainable public procurement has the potential to improve environmental performance, deliver financial benefits and develop markets for more sustainable goods and services. When implementing an SPP policy, several development levels have to be mastered for a government to be able to achieve sustainability objectives via public procurement. The author intends to establish a conceptual framework based on Telgen Harland, and Knight (2007) to connect development levels with implementation of sustainability. She concludes that sustainability cannot exist without sound foundations, aligning objectives, and specifying directions. Then, she formulates a critique of the modernization of the new European Public Procurement Directives whereas the general policy interpretation of sustainability has more role than the identification of the instruments that can serve sustainability in practice.

China has experienced an extraordinarily fast economic growth since the 1980s and expects to be the largest economy in the world in 2015, if not in 2014. But it has faced a lot of social and environment problems. In "Policy Implementation of

Sustainable Public Procurement in China," Cong-hu Wang and Xiaoming Li address the issue of sustainable development in the context of China's public procurement. They first summarize a suitable policy implementation model; and then examine policies, relationships between implementation agencies, and the purchasing process. Based on our empirical evaluation from practice, the authors recommend that the Chinese law and regulation should provide clear goals and specific criteria for congruent implementation; the supervisory agency needs to conduct unified and open oversight; the administrative agency should manage centralized purchasing with transparency in the whole purchasing process; and the vendor needs to register in the public procurement database and participate fairly in the transparent purchasing process.

Conclusions

There are some variations among public procurement systems, caused by

- The maturity level of the procurement systems and governance: well-established democratic systems, which have an undisputed check and balance of three branches of government (legislative, executive, and judiciary), and weak democratic systems, which are normally dominated a the executive branch or a political party;
- Cultural differences: some cultures tend to tolerate gratuities or gifts given to government officials; some others may have very strict restrictions on gratuities;
- Market conditions where many vendors exist and are willing to bid for government contracts, and some other countries do not have a competitive market; and
- The level of professionalism of procurement workforces.

Thai (2007) noted the extent of commonality in public procurement knowledge and practices across developed and developing countries around the world, despite significant variations in their procurement systems.

References

Bolton, P. (2006). Government procurement as a policy tool in South Africa. *Journal of Public Procurement, 6*(3), 193–217.

Celec, S., Voich, D., Nosari, E., & Stith, M. (2003). Measuring disparity in government procurement: problems with using census data in estimating availability. *Public Administration Review, 60*(2), 134–142.

Clark, M., & Moutray, C. (2004). The future of small businesses in the U.S. federal government marketplace. *Journal of Public Procurement, 4*(3), 450–470.

Coggburn, J. (2003). Exploring differences in the American states' procurement practices. *Journal of Public Procurement, 3*(1), 3–28.

Coggburn, J. D., & Rahm, D. (2005). Environmentally preferable purchasing: who is doing what in the United States? *Journal of Public Procurement, 5*(1), 23–55.

Enchautegui, M., Fix, M., Loprest, P., Lippe, S. v. d., & Wissoker, D. (1997). *Do minority-owned businesses get a fair share of government contracts?* Washington, DC: Urban Institute. www.urban.org/url.cfm?ID = 307416.

Foresti, L. F., Arantes, R. S., & Rossetto, V. (2007). The use of the public procurement power to promote the development of small businesses: the Brazilian experience. In G. Piga & K. V. Thai (Eds.), *Advancing public procurement: experience, innovation and knowledge sharing* (pp. 334–372). Boca Raton: PrAcademics Press.

Gormly, J. (2014). What are the challenges to sustainable procurement in commercial semi-state bodies in Ireland? *Journal of Public Procurement, 14*(3), 395–445.

Hasselbalch, J., Costa, N., & Bleckenm A. (2014). Examining the relationship between the barriers and current practices of sustainable procurement: a survey of UN organizations. *Journal of Public Procurement, 14*(3), 361–394.

Jones, D. S. (2011). Recent reforms to promote social responsibility procurement in east asian states: a comparative analysis. *Journal of Public Procurement, 11*(1), 61–94.

McCrudden, C. (2007). *Buying social justice: equality, government procurement, and legal change*. New York: Oxford University Press.

McCue, C. P., & Hinson, C. (2004). *Procurement planning, sourcing and requirement analysis*. Herndon: The National Institute for Government Purchasing, Inc.

McCue, C. P., & Johnson, B. R. (2010). *Strategic procurement planning in the public sector*. Herndon: National Institute of Governmental Purchasing, Inc.

National Association of State Purchasing Officials. (1999). *Survey of state & local government: purchasing practices* (5th ed., revised). Lexington, KY: National Association of State Purchasing Officials.

Nicholas, C, & Fruhmann, M. (2014). Small and medium-sized enterprises policies in public procurement: time for a rethink? *Journal of Public Procurement, 14*(3), 328–360.

Prier, E., McCue, C. P., & Bevis, M. E. (2008). Making it happen: public procurement's role in integrating economic development and sustainability strategies for local governments in the U.S.A. In *3rd International Public Procurement Conference Proceedings*, (pp. 637–654). www.ippa.org.

Qiao, Y., Thai, K. V., & Cummings, G. (2009). State and local procurement preferences: a survey. *Journal of Public Procurement, 11*(3–4), 371–410.

Rice, M. (1992). Justifying state and local government set-aside programs through disparity studies in the post-*Croson* era. *Public Administration Review, 52*(5), 482–490.

Rice, M., & Mongkuo, M. (1998). Did *Adarand* kill minority set-asides? *Public Administration Review, 58*(1), 82–86.

Roos, R. (2013). *Sustainable public procurement in LICs implications for the ongoing world bank procurement review*. Berlin: Deutsche Gesellschatt fur Internationale Zusammenarbeit.

Sadikin, S. R. (2008). Public Procurement Sustainability in Indonesia: Environmental, Social or Economic Tradeoffs. In *3rd International Public Procurement Conference Proceedings* (pp. 587–617). www.ippa.org.

Short, J. (1993). *Issues in public purchasing: a guidebook for policymakers*. Lexington: The Council of State Governments.

Tammi, T., Saastamoinen, J., & Reijonen, H. (2014). Market orientation and SMEs' activity in public sector procurement participation. *Journal of Public Procurement, 14*(3), 304–327.

Telgen, J., Harland, C., & Kinght, L. (2007). Public procurement in perspective. In L. Knight, C. Harland, J. Telgen, K.V. Thai, G. Callender, & K. McKen (Eds.), *Public procurement: international cases and commentary* (pp. 20–22). London: Routhledge.

Thai, K. V. (2001). Public procurement reexamined. *Journal of Public Procurement, 1*(1), 9–50.

Thai, K. V. (Ed.). (2007). Advancing public procurement: practices, innovation and knowledge sharing. Boca Raton: PrAcademics Press.

Thomas, A. (1919). *Principles of government purchasing*. New York: D. Appleton.

Tolley, G., Bernstein, P., & Lesage, M. (1999). *Economic analysis of a living wage ordinance*. Washington, DC: Employment Policies Institute.

United Nations Environment Programme (2012). http://www.unpcdc.org/media/390120/spp_brief_ en_2012-02-06.pdf.
U.S. Department of Justice (1995). Legal Guidance on the Implications of the Supreme Court's Decision in Adarand Constructors, Inc. v. Pena (U.S. Department of Justice memo from Assistant Attorney General Walter Dellenger). www.usdoj.gov/olc/adarand.htm.
U.S. Environmental Protection Agency (1998a). The city of santa monica's environmental purchasing: a case study (Report EPA742-R-98–001). www.greenercom puting.com/resources/resource/city-santa-monica%E2 %80 %99s-environmental-purchasing-a-case-study.
U.S. Environmental Protection Agency (1998b). Green spending: a case study of Massachusetts' environmental purchasing program (Report EPA742-R-98–002). www.epa.gov/opptintr/epp.
U.S. Environmental Protection Agency (2000). Environmentally preferable purchasing program: state and local government pioneers (Report EPA742-R-00–004). www.epa.gov/opptintr/epp.
Wallace, S. L. (1999). Minority procurement: beyond affirmative action to economic empowerment. *The Review of Black Political Economy,* 73–98.
Watermeyer, R. (2000). The use of targeted procurement as an instrument of poverty alleviation and job creation in infrastructure projects. *Public Procurement Law Review, 9*(5), 226–250.

Khi V. Thai PhD is a professor and director, School of Public Administration, Florida Atlantic University. His research interest is in public budgeting, financial management, and public procurement. He is editor of *International Journal of Organization Theory and Behavior, Journal of Public Procurement,* and *Journal of Public Budgeting, Accounting & Financial Management.* His publications include over 100 books, book chapters, technical reports, and refereed articles. He has been a consultant for the US government, United Nations, and for governments in the USA and Canada.

Part I
Innovation and Reforms in Public Procurement

Contract Management Innovation in Public Procurement: Costa Rica's Experience

Ileana Palaco, Alicia Avendaño and Waldemar Núñez

The Traditional Model

Costa Rica is an upper middle-income developing country, located in Central America; it has a population of approximately 5 million inhabitants and its national GDP amounts to US$ 45.13 billion. Accounting for roughly 20% of the Costa Rican national GDP, government procurement plays a very important role in ensuring effective and transparent management of public resources. According to a poll by the University of Costa Rica (UCR), public contracting has been identified as one of the government's activity having the highest perception of bribery risk (Poltronieri 2011, p. 3). This is a worldwide phenomenon. In a Public Expenditure and Financial Accountability Program Assessment (IDC-WB 2010) held in October 2010, the procurement model presented weaknesses due to its highly fragmented model, and lack of control facilitation or efficiency within the procedures. In this same assessment, Costa Rica's transparency in procurement ranked as low as D+. Transparency in government procurement, together with citizen's active involvement as government's expenditure auditors, constituted a critical need in Costa Rica.

To conduct a functional and practical analysis of the current Costa Rican public procurement model, the starting point of the case to be described in this chapter must

I. Palaco (✉)
Global IT Technology Program (ITTP)
Korea Advanced Institute of Science and Technology (KAIST),
Daejeon, South Korea
e-mail: ipalaco@gmail.com

A. Avendaño
Digital Government Instituto Costarricense de Electricidad,
San José, Costa Rica
e-mail: avendano.alicia@gmail.com

W. Núñez
Procurement Division, Instituto Costarricense de Electricidad, San José, Costa Rica
e-mail: Wnunez@ice.go.cr

K. V. Thai (ed.), *International Public Procurement,* Public Administration, Governance and Globalization 14, DOI 10.1007/978-3-319-13434-5_2

be clear: The traditional procurement model in Costa Rica, governed by red-tape and paper, was exhausted. The new innovated model based on an online procurement service must cover the whole cycle, from planning to contract management.

Starting Point and Scenario

According to World Bank's experts (IDC-WB 2009, pp. 163–164) who analyzed the country's public expenditure environment, Costa Rica's legal and institutional framework for procurement is based on best international practices. However, the country's procurement followed a fragmented model and had a series of deficiencies. The assessment stated that the public sector failed "to take full advantage of available procedures, practices and management tools." Some examples of how the model was failing to support Costa Rican efficient budget execution may be summarized through the existence of excessive amounts of paperwork, bureaucracy, and poorly integrated processes. These are some features that characterized this traditional model:

- No standardization of procurement documents and processes
- Lack to enable price-referencing, benchmarking mechanisms, or supply industry analysis, due to the use of different codifications (goods and services classification codes) and not-integrated supplier registration database
- Different procurement proceedings in each entity lack international standards such as product codification, forms, terms of reference, business documents, and transactions as a result of fanciful interpretations or ignorance of the applicable regulations
- Numerous regulations and procedure manuals, depending on each entity
- Numerous investments and disintegrated use of IT platforms
- Duplication of requirements and procedures for supplier registration through different institutions
- Purchasing processes that require multiple approvals and reviews at different levels (individuals and committees)
- Lack of process reengineering, standardization, and simplification, due to excessive requirements that must be met depending on the institution

After analyzing the country's reality, Inter American Development Bank (IDB) and World Bank (WB)[3] issued a series of recommendations, which pointed out that the country should focus on seeking greater efficiency and savings through procurement rather than implementation of the existing legislation. The recommendations stated that the country be urged to implement mechanisms to enable advanced procurement instruments, already available in the legal framework (reverse auction, joint contracting agreements, denominated "convenios marco"). The assessment estimated potential savings (between 12.6 and 17.6 %) and urged the Ministry of Finance to take certain measures to improve public procurement, such as: procurement consolidation, the definition of standards country-wide, the use of a single catalog, registered supplier data base, and the use of framework contracts.

Another important assessment on the matter, carried out by the Organization of American States (IDB-OAS 2012, p. 10) also repeatedly stated that among the major problems that affected the efforts made so far by the Costa Rican authorities was the fact that none of the initiatives could actually turn Costa Rica's procurement process into a 100% online traceable process. Public procurement efforts on the improvement of the national contracting scenario were focused on improving technical or specific procedures rather than on tackling the need to create a more complete and comprehensive public procurement system.

A joint study by INCAE Business School and the Technical Secretariat for Digital Government (TSDG) in early 2008 showed more evidence about this reality (Barahona et al. 2009, pp. 10–11). Based on the data from the General Comptroller's Office (CGR), the study estimated that in 2007 a small group of 20 companies billed the Costa Rican government 40% of their purchases, which is approximately 8% of the national GDP (Barahona et al. 2009, p. 6). The study suggests that this concentration "is mainly due to the barriers to participate in government's procurement processes representing system complexity and expensive it is for potential bidders" (Barahona et al. 2009, p. 6). Despite the progress and efforts made until 2009, the traditional model, followed by the Costa Rican procurement processes and based on paper-PDF-based procurement systems developed one by one within the public sector, fell short against the objectives of transparency, accountability, productivity, and development promotion.

National e-Procurement Platform: Mer-link

Before 2010, many attempts to improve Costa Rica's procurement model were carried out without noticeable success. They were not perceived as an effective solution to an increasingly evident problem. The challenge to modernize Costa Rica's procurement through a single-window process still remained.

As a result, the Technical Secretariat for Digital Government (TSDG), in partnership with the National Telecom Company (ICE), the Public Procurement Service (PPS) of the Republic of Korea, adapted the Korean e-Procurement System, known as KONEPS, into what is now called the Costa Rican National e-Procurement Platform, also known as Mer-link. This system began with the development and implementation of basic modules by July 2010, and its full scope was launched in January 2011.

A team of 14 public institutions, including national banks, universities, public agencies, and local governments, led by the TSDG and ICE through a strong standardization and Business Process Reengineering (BPR) process was able to shift a paradigm throughout the country's public administration. The interoperability model followed Mer-link's design led the country to build a basis to connect the government's back-office. The Mer-link system connected citizens, businesses, and government; transformed paper and red-tape-based public services to online, and established multichannel and one-stop transparency-based services.

As a result of these institutions' efforts, by 2012, Costa Rica reported several platforms used for procurement purposes. In the same year, the General Comptroller's Office (CGR is its acronym in Spanish) requested from the Governing Council a definition on the issue of public procurement. Consequently, CGR (2012, p. 22) issued a report that pointed out: "due to the large number of transactions generated by the public sector, it [was] necessary to consolidate efforts and automate the procurement process through a single channel. The channel must consolidate government goods and services transactions into a single IT e-procurement platform that integrates all the country's needs."

Given these recommendations, the Office of the President delegated to a National Public Procurement Committee constituted by the Ministry of Finance, Science and Technology, and TSDG's Director General, the integration of the National System of Public Procurement. The main objective of this committee was to implement Mer-link system as the national procurement service platform.

The Mer-link platform and these team's efforts in recruiting other autonomous agencies to use the platform and optimize its use are necessary precursors to this chapter. The detail story in its growth and development may be found across the Internet and through several international organization experts' reports, most of them in Spanish. Mer-link has been operational for 3 years with an expanding list of agencies (now 68 government agencies of over 300) conducting procurement through this national single-window platform.

As the national e-procurement system, throughout its interoperability model, Mer-link allows exchanging information with more than 50 institutions countrywide, all bidding-related information is integrated and publicly available. It has bridged the gap between a dynamic set of detailed information on government procurement and the citizenry. Costa Ricans are able to freely access and understand details of government procurement and budget expenditure, all accomplished by this platform on its purpose to enhance transparency in government procurement. At present, the system is being implemented and is expected to cover more than 90 % (by volume) (General Comptroller's Office, 2013)of national public procurement by the first semester of 2014.

One of Mer-link's strengths is that it handles the entire procurement process, which includes supplier registration, bid notice, bidding, awarding, contracting, payment, and the entire contract management process; hence, this project has become one of the most innovative government services within the national agenda. Once registered, suppliers are able to participate in all public tenders. The design contains the following main modules, which have been put into operation since 2010: supplier registration (user management), goods/services catalog (based on UNSPSC), bidding (procurement planning, online tendering, e-bond management (participation and performance), online bid submission, e-assessment, analysis and evaluation, and e-awarding), dynamic purchasing modules (e-auction, e-shopping mall, framework contracts), contracting (online contract issuance, e-signature/ digital certification), contract management (delivery, inspection, e-invoice, e-payment, supplier evaluation).

In spite of such complete functionalities, one could think that many of the described features are already available in some of the worldwide known practices, why then is Mer-link acknowledged as an innovative solution to the national procurement dilemma? In the last stage of contract management, Mer-link has added a great value to the Costa Rican procurement cycle by including within its online service scope the entire administrative and disciplinary sanctions procedure. Empowering citizens through real accountability, allowing them to follow-up on how the procurement process is executed, moreover on how their taxes are being spent. At the same time, this innovative module enables online, real-time access to all procurement profiles, including detailed management process actions to key players, such as the Comptroller's Office, legal departments, audits, and the judiciary branch.

Mer-link's Scope

According to the Organization for Economic Cooperation and Development (OECD 2013, p. 97) there is a general concern about "the lack of attention dedicated to the risks of waste in the needs assessment as well as in the contract management" in public procurement. In particular, OECD's mentioned documentation addressed the importance of accountability throughout the whole procurement cycle, including pre-bidding and post-bidding phases. In this regard, Costa Rica has made a remarkable effort including all the mentioned phases within Mer-link's functional scope.

According to the Costa Rican legal framework, procurement processes are essentially divided into three stages, namely:

- Planning. In this initial phase the need to be satisfied is determined and the works, goods, or services to be acquired for a certain purpose are identified. This initial stage ends with the accurate identification of the good or service required, the verification of budget availability, and the procurement modality to use. This phase includes having a potential supplier database and a standardized coding of the good or service to be purchased.
- Selection. This phase is where the entity must seek the best proposal (for e.g., price, quality, and experience). It can be done through several mechanisms such as direct contract, abbreviated or competitive open tendering, dynamic contracting, reverse auction, or shopping mall, which is a figure known as "convenio marco" [In English: multiple award or framework agreement]. A direct contracting mechanism is mainly used for frequently procured goods and commonly required standard features. This mechanism involves a shorter period tender contest, and high volume with low value, meaning lots of low unit value contracts. Tendering in its various forms (abbreviated, competitive, international) is an appropriate mechanism for the selection of goods of very specific characteristics, or the acquisition of higher value goods, which means this mechanism involves high economic impact. The selection process ends with the contract or purchase order issuing, in the case of direct contracting.
- Execution/Contract Management. During this phase the contractor delivers the goods or services and the recipient verifies its validity and proceeds with pay-

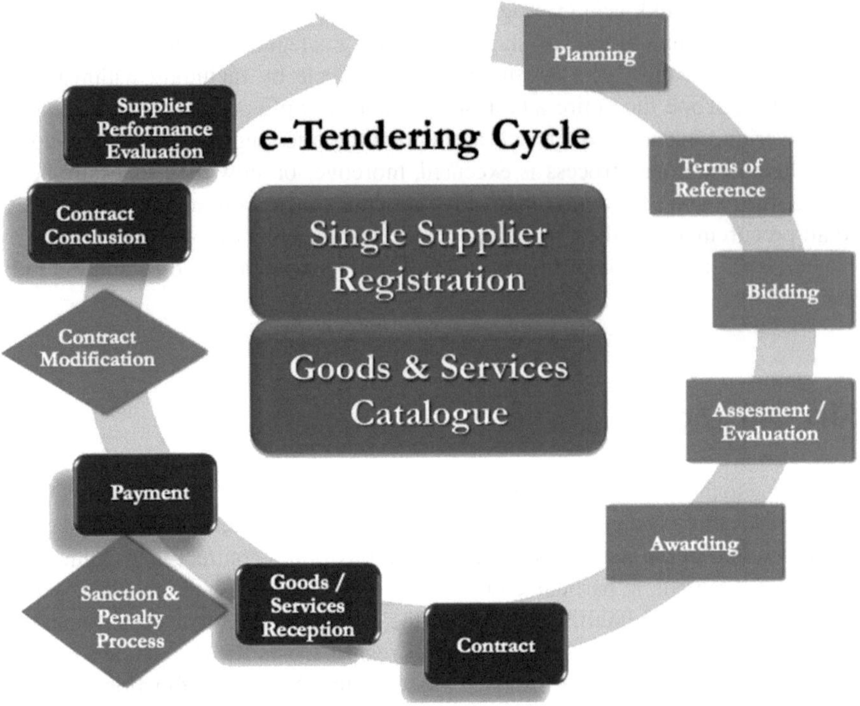

Fig. 1 e-Tendering cycle in Costa Rica and Mer-link's functional scope (Source: Self Elaboration)

ment. It ends with the final reception of all goods or services. This phase is related to the after-service for goods or services purchased. It involves any post-delivery action (such as warranty compliance) or condition stipulated in the contract or purchase order. This phase ends on the last day of the warranty.

Within all of the stages, portrayed in Fig. 1, there are a number of key features to drive characteristics such as efficiency and productivity in the procurement process, through the use of technology. At the level of a public procurement cycle in Costa Rica, the following image and related statements will provide a glimpse of Mer-link's model main features and how they constitute an innovative process.

Planning

Single Vendor Registration also known as Register of Bidders

Costa Rica's greatest weakness in terms of procurement before the implementation of the Mer-link system was the fact that potential suppliers had to go to each government procurement department (300+ institutions) and provide a series of requirements to be included and registered in the official supplier database. In a study carried out by INCAE Business School, it was determined that the cost of these requirements amounted to US$ 2000 per process. The fact that it was so complicated and expensive to register as a government supplier explains how difficult it was for an SME to actually be invited into a public tendering process.

Thanks to the extensive use of digital certification, based on public key infrastructure technology, Mer-link enabled a single nation-wide online supplier registration. This is a countrywide database, where the professional or company representative may sign in (and update information) and make sure to be invited to any potential business opportunity with the government. Through digitally signed declaration and interoperability processes, the company's data, such as legal status, capital, ownership, social security, and tax payment status may be verified online on a real-time basis. Up to date, Mer-link accounts more than 7000 potential suppliers. This massive online process has opened a very important door of opportunity for both procurement departments and potentially interested supplier companies, especially SMEs.

National Goods and Services Catalog

As the supplier registers the company in Mer-link, he/she must select from the online product catalog the goods or services that his company is in capacity to provide to the government. This catalog is based on United Nations Standard Products and Services Code (UNSPSC) classification. Once registered, the vendor will be notified (through e-mail and/or SMS) and to their inbox in the Mer-link system an official notice to participate every time there is a potential business opportunity with the government, according to the listed products and based on the related product classification.

Mer-link's organization has an expert unit trained to ensure correct classification and technical specifications of every product. Every good or service is added and classified into Mer-link's catalog through this unit and all procurement procedures base technical descriptions in this catalog. The principle behind the catalog's design is to standardize all products purchased by the government, ensuring quality in technical specifications as well as preventing bad technical interpretations and corruption practices. Another important principle is to establish a common language between private sector (vendors) and government procurement departments. The use of a unique catalog has enhanced efficiency and reduced operation costs and processing time.

One of the benefits that may be accountable to the use of the UNSPSC catalog is the enhancement of the logistics and supply chain management of public entities, thus reducing inventory levels through better management of information on available products. Additionally, it enables an accurate mechanism to compare prices of similar products and therefore speeds up the procurement selection and decision-making process. Thanks to the data collected and standardized within Mer-link's catalog, the country can use detailed statistics and important business intelligence tools for feedback about the national public procurement policy-making, and streamline organizations' operation and general management strategy.

According to several vendors' opinion surveys, Mer-link's catalog facilitates sales functions, introduces online marketplace activities between private and public sectors, ensures the quality of product technical information, streamlines the introduction of new products to the public procurement market, and facilitates collection of sales data.

Budget Management

One of the general features of Mer-link's product classification is budget/expense code classification; this allows the system to establish a seamless workflow between procurement and the accounting process. Starting from the planning phase, Mer-link will interconnect with the institution's accounting or financial system confirming budget availability to start certain contracting procedures and follow on with publication of the terms of reference.

Procurement Order/Request

The order request is the final step of the planning phase. In the traditional model (paper-based), this request was an e-mail or official letter from a certain division within any public institution addressed to the procurement division director, formally requesting the need to buy a good or service.

This platform was designed to be used by large and small institutions even one as large as ICE, whose organization accounts more than 45 working units or as small as a local government office or a public school's board. Depending on the institution, the internal process could vary, and Mer-link's standard workflow should be able to fit all working schemes. Mer-link's modeling and standardization efforts were expressed in an electronic document, a form which is filled out by an assistant/analyst, approved and digitally signed by the division's chief or director. Depending on each institution's configuration, Mer-link's flow will automatically submit this order request to procurement department users who will proceed accordingly. The form is the kick-off point of the current public e-procurement process and therefore of any procurement process e-record or transcript. The data on this e-form will feed later stages in the procurement cycle.

Selection

e-Tendering, e-Bidding

Based on the data entered and submitted on the procurement order or request, any user institution will be able to publish terms of reference (also known as RFP) and start a tendering process for any contracting mechanism established on the Costa Rican procurement legal framework. Once the user publishes the terms of reference, the system will generate a robust security mechanism based on PKI technology (using a unique encryption mechanism for each procurement process) with which, at the correct moment, the designated user will be able to open the chamber where electronic bids will be encrypted and stored. The system's functional design allows any bids to be signed at a personal, corporative level, and even at a joint bid or consortium level.

Depending on the goods or services selected on the catalog, Mer-link will send immediate notifications (through SMS or E-mail) to all potential vendors and the clock on the tendering procedure will start ticking. Any questions, remarks, or complaints on the published RFP may be managed through the platform. This step ensures that physical visits or meetings between vendors and public officers are avoided.

Similar to the previous phases, interested vendors may present their proposals. Companies fill out a form responding to their compliance with all details and specs of the RFP. Through digitally signed e-documents, each vendor's bid will be encrypted, electronically submitted, and locked-up in a chamber. The bids will not be available until the corresponding date and time selected to start the assessment and awarding phase. On the matching moment and with the key generated at the RFP publication phase, the procurement officer in charge will be able to open the chamber and proceed with the assessment phase.

A key innovation aspect in this stage is that throughout Mer-link's portal publicity the Costa Rican Government has allowed the site's publicity to substitute the obligatory publication of public bidding proceedings in the local Gazette newspaper. This decision not only generates paper- and operation-related efficiencies but also important savings in institution's printing expenses transferred to the National Gazette.

e-Bond or Collateral

Another important value added to this online process is related to the participation, warranty and performance bond issuance. In the traditional paper-based model, companies had to visit an insurance company or a bank, provide certain requirements, and issue a paper-based bond, which they had to attach to their paper-bid. Nowadays, Mer-link connects nationally to all 15 bond issuing public and private entities. Included are the National Insurance Institute, Costa Rican Bank, Scotiabank, Bansol, Promerica, and Lafise. The interoperability has streamlined the warranty-related workflow not only for potential government supplier companies but also for public procurement departments, which required a team (up to 5 resources) for bond management purposes. To this date, bonds issued in relation with any procurement process in Mer-link are issued electronically by the corresponding entities and reflected automatically in the bidding process, once the bid is opened. The system will provide to the procurement departments the necessary tools to manage the warranty issuances, amounts, valid period, expiration, and renewal dates.

Assessment/Evaluation and e-Contract

Once the procurement analyst opens the bids, Mer-link will order them automatically according to the evaluation criterion previously defined by the public institution (on the RFP). For instance, if the evaluation criteria would be 100 % based on the price, then Mer-link would display a table comparing all the received bids and place the lowest priced one in the first row and order the following ones according to the price.

The national e-procurement tool was designed in such a way that the institutions may select and define any kind of evaluation criteria or different variable combinations according to their specific needs (whether it is price, experience, quality certifications, cost effectiveness, energy efficiency, post-warranty). Mer-link will only provide important hints and efficiencies in the process; however, the procurement decision and responsibility will rely on the system's users, whether they are public officers or supplier company representatives.

Following-up with the process, the officer in charge of the corresponding contracting process will check the received bids through the table generated automatically by Mer-link (ordered according to the established criterion). The officer may review that the procurement-related conditions are covered and may forward the bids for an expert review. For example if the public institution is buying computers, then the procurement analyst may review the tenders' eligibility. The procurement officer must confirm that tenders comply with basic conditions, such as stamps, participation warranty bond, no tax and social security liens. The procurement platform will issue a bid opening summary. This is an e-document where all acts related to the chamber opening and bid review proceeding are recorded.

After the time for bid opening is issued, the procurement analyst in charge may forward the bids for technical review to a designated IT department analyst who may check that the computers offered by the bidding companies comply with the requested specs. IT analysts will check and compare the proposals and provide his technical recommendation on the best option.

Once this internal workflow is completed, procurement analysts will be able to award the best proposal and notify that winner. To make this selection official, the procurement department may request that the selected vendor submit payment of certain duties and an online presentation of a performance bond, etc. Once the awarded company fulfills these steps, the public institution will issue an e-purchase order or e-contract (depending on the contract's amount and chosen mechanism). All approval levels within the workflow described in the national legal framework to issue this contract (for example if the contract needs to be confirmed by the National Comptroller Department or by the highest level department within an institution, such as the Board of Directors or Procurement Commission) are all available features in this electronic tool. Given the fact that there is no paper involved, all these steps for internal or external approval are followed through using the system and e-signature features. The e-contract (or e-PO) will be issued by the institution and electronically submitted in an e-document to the selected vendor. This e-document will contain all legal responsibilities and rights between the parties and is as valid as a paper and manually signed one.

Contract Management/Execution

e-Reception, e-Invoice, e-Payment

From the moment the e-contract is signed by the parties and notified, the selected vendor should start working on the provision of the contracted goods or services. In this regard, Mer-link's e-procurement platform is being used in such way that the system connects with logistics and asset management systems, internal management systems allowing public entities to streamline their supply chain management. To follow-up with the previous example, the selected computer vendor will notify through Mer-link's system the amount and characteristics of the computers to be delivered, according to the contract's specifications. Thanks to Mer-link's smart catalog system and technical specifications tabs, the computers to be delivered may include important asset management features such as GTIN (Global Trade Item Number) identification or include inventory number plates. Once the vendor sends the information on partial or total delivery of the products, warehousing public officers will be able to check with the system and crosscheck the correct delivery of goods according to agreed conditions. The warehousing staff will provide a partial reception, which will always be confirmed by technical report, which in this example will be issued by the IT department. The latter will be in charge of checking the conditions of the computers and finally approving in the system the correct delivery of the products. This process is similar for services and works; however, due to the nature of professional services and public works the partial and complete dispatch and reception confirmation is done through different kinds of supervisions. All variables are included in Mer-link's system functionality and therefore in the procurement record of every process.

Once the stakeholders confirm the reception, a final acceptance e-document will be issued and the vendor may proceed to request payment. Although the Costa Rican tax system does not yet practice a general use of e-invoice, as of 2014 e-invoices will be implemented for certain industrial and professional service sectors. At present, Mer-link's design includes the use of e-invoice and also a digitalized/scanned copy of the invoice that must be physically submitted to the institution's financial and accounting authorities. When e-invoice is fully implemented, the country will issue the necessary regulation for its use. Mer-link has been already prepared for this step. Nowadays, the vendor will issue a payment request upon the goods/services reception confirmation, and submit the original copy of the invoice to the institution. Through connection with payment and financial systems, Mer-link will feed the accounting or financial system regarding that payment and through a national interbanking platform, known as SINPE, Mer-link will be able to issue payment. This means, Mer-link's system, through an interconnection with SINPE, will deduct the money from the entity's account and deposit it as the vendor had requested in a previous step. This process is most commonly used by local governments or small public entities that do not have a complex or online payment system to connect to and therefore, for them, the Mer-link system has meant a big step not only to streamline the procurement process but also for payment and the accounting process. On the other hand, the connection between Mer-link and the accounting systems may work also the other way around, which means Mer-link will only inform the institution's accounting system with all the information the vendor has provided on the payment request that a payment must be made. Following this, the internal payment system will be in charge of transferring the related funs and report to the Mer-link system that the payment was successfully made or not. Currently, big government institutions, such as ICE are using this latter procedure.

Contract Conclusion (Modification, Expansion)

The moment all contracted goods/services are delivered, paid and their warranty expires, the contract execution phase will be concluded. However, many contracts, especially in public works or complex objectives will undergo contract modifications. These changes may be caused and requested by one party or by both parties. They may include scope expansions and therefore additional payments or just an extension on the agreed duration of the contract. All these changes on the original e-contract will undergo certain requirements, which are included in the Costa Rican legislation. In this regard, all contract modifications are included in Mer-link as an appendix of the original e-contract. This appendix is represented through the numeration series of the e-document, adding to any additional or expanded contracts, for example if the original contract number is 123456789 the amended one will be 123456789-01.

e-Record

As mentioned in previous sections, Mer-link's e-Record tracking feature is one of its most important characteristics, which highly provides public procurement transparency and accountability. In this regard, it is important to emphasize that the national e-procurement platform keeps records in real time of all actions related to procurement procedures by using standard protocols to number and label each section of each phase of the procurement cycle. This enables that lawyers or judges in any dispute or trial may always find and refer to certain information in the labeled sections or procedure stages. It is Mer-link's design pillars and part of its original vision to promote traceability. This can only be accomplished by handling one single record with all actions and related information and documents of each process.

Administrative Dispute, Penalty also Known as Sanctions

Although traditional procurement IT systems worldwide basically focus on supplier registration, catalogs, tendering, direct procurement, claims, and endorsements, they generally do not get involved in the issue of contract management and execution. Commonly known systems solely handle reception, final acceptance, supplier evaluation, and payment.

In this regard, if all contract conditions were successfully and timely complied with, then the process would go directly to the vendor's performance evaluation and contract's closure. However, if any dispute regarding the contract's execution arises between the stakeholders, then the coordination of a private hearing, internal resolution committee appointment, and process resolution will be required. If this module had not been integrated into the system's scope, then public institutions would have to be forced to open a parallel paper record to follow the dispute resolution and penalty administrative process. This would highly prejudice the transparency level envisioned for Costa Rican national procurement.

The fact that Mer-link handles all this process in a seamless way, enabling the corresponding authorities to manage every detail of the contract's process management in real time and process this complicated mechanism through an efficient IT tool has set an example toward real time, totally online, zero paper e-procurement process. This innovative module, which actually represents a subsystem within Mer-link's IT architecture has being successfully implemented into the tool's scope and is known in Spanish as "Procedimiento Administrativo Sancionatorio" (or "Sanctions/Penalty and Administrative Dispute Proceeding").

This added-value module includes in its scope all actions referred to dispute resolution and sanction or penalty application toward a supplier or public officer who did not comply with public contracting regulations. The following are the specific features contained in the regulation (Public Administration Law and related ones) and therefore within Mer-link's functionalities:

- Absolute manifest nullity of a procurement procedure
- Prohibition or warning of a vendor or contractor
- Contract resolution or termination
- Fine or penalty clause application (toward the contractor who failed to comply with the contracting conditions and procurement regulations)
- Collection and payment of damage costs to a contractor, and
- Performance, participation, compliance, or collateral bond execution

With this contract management module, public institutions in Costa Rica are able to handle the necessary administrative procedures electronically with a greater value: the fact that whatever the final resolution of this process may be, the users will be able to affect the procurement process in a smart and efficient way. For example, Mer-link does not allow the contractor to request a reception or payment of a contract that is undergoing an administrative dispute procedure and its final resolution has not yet been issued. Additionally, this important subsystem within Mer-link's platform scope complies and follows all steps and procedural safeguards established by applicable legislation, such as:

- *Administrative, Dispute Management Process Initiation.* The module allows the institution to develop the statements that constitute the preliminary report in which the alleged failure of the bidder/ contractor is documented, detailing facts such as alleged damages caused to the institution, alleged unfulfilled standards, conditions or regulations, and all related proof.

- *Appointment of the Dispute Resolution Council.* Mer-link will provide special e-forms for the selection, recommendation, and appointment or the members (whether a group or individual) that will serve as referee in the process. This council will be responsible for conducting a correct and efficient dispute resolution or sanction process. If any appointed party requires to be held out from this process for any applicable reason (for example: conflict of interests), Mer-link's functionality will enable selection of a new member for the council.
- *Initial Act.* (Also referred to as Administrative Procedure Initiation) The system allows holding the initial stage of the dispute process where the stakeholders are informed of the alleged contract infringement. This stage includes information on the contractor's rights and the legal foundations for the alleged breach and the corresponding proof.
- *Bidder/Contractor Disclaimer/Evidence Presentation.* The module allows the contractor to carry out his defense, directly (personally) or through the appointment of a representative, who receives electronically the notice of the administrative procedure initiation, and may present relevant disclaimers and evidences.
- *Final Act.* Once the appointed council has analyzed all related information, the council members will input the decisions taken and register them in the system (date, time and user information will be recorded) and the system will communicate the final act to the stakeholders.
- *Appeal.* The module supports the presentation of legally valid appeals in an electronic form. These claims may be against either the initiation or final act. Mer-link's intelligence will allow the contractor to request a two-tier appeal, according to the current national regulation. In the latter case, the appeal action will be transferred to two different levels automatically: to the dispute resolution council and to the applicable judicial department.
- *Private E-Record.* According to Costa Rican regulation on this kind of procedures. The record during the administrative and dispute resolution process is private. Only the parties involved will have access to it, however the content of the final act's resolution will become automatically available once it is officially published.

Innovation in Contract Management: Mer-link's Case

Through this e-procurement tool, institutions in Costa Rica and its citizenry will have a complete electronic record available for public auditing and scrutiny. According to the Costa Rican legal framework, e-government and open government policies, this system will set an important milestone for the country's public administration practice development toward important new trends which enhance citizen's direct participation and collaboration between government and civil society.

Mer-link is a national platform; it offers advanced and complex functionalities to all users involved—whether private sector vendors or public institution users. It not only automates the entire contracting but also provides an advanced service to its users. Beginning with the capacity to overcome physical barriers of space and time, this procurement IT tool allows a more transparent and efficient flow of information and greater access to data and government accountability services. As part of its operation model, the system provides free training twice a week to vendors, as well as free e-learning courses that may be downloaded from the portal site www.mer-link.go.cr.

Mer-link as a successful government initiative has accomplished the establishment of a practical example of sustainable procurement. This statement is based on three important perspectives. First, the fact that government contracting is oriented toward an economic perspective, enabling savings of 12 % through lower prices of products due to substantial cost reductions and higher participation promotion in public, open contracts. Followed by a social vision, where Mer-link has ensured promotion and enabling small and medium enterprise's participation by accomplishing a US$ 1500 process reduction on bidding participation costs (eStrategia Publica 2014). Last but not least, this procurement initiative has followed an environmental vision, which includes a paper-less design from scratch, preventing physical transportation and visits to public institutions and promoting through an ubiquitous online service, lower-to-none procurement related visits to institutions and therefore reduced transportation effects, lower fuel consumption and gas emissions.

In this regard, the platform's organization has accomplished important growth during the past years. It was recognized in 2010 at the national level as the most innovative science and technology based innovative initiative (Ruiz 2010). In 2012, the system was granted a regional award that acknowledges excellence in e-government practices, the ExcelGob Awards(Vargas 2012). Recently being appointed as national e-procurement system, it has projected potential operating savings of US$ 165 (Ruiz 2010). Currently available real-time statistics in the Mer-link portal report that it has more than 97,000 goods and services in its national catalog, 7500 registered vendors, and has enabled contracting procedures for US$ 181 million (Mer-link, 2014).

Within government practices, Mer-link complies with basic conditions to carry out innovation. It transformed a process, which was hardly available to the citizens (due to space, time, and paper barriers) to an online, cloud-based 24/7/365 available service. It enabled dissemination of important ideas in a new context: Mer-link has made it possible for a citizen to gain trust in public expenditure and management, through its real promotion of transparency, efficiency, and procurement data democratization.

Innovation can be defined as "the process of improving, adapting or developing a product, system or service to deliver better results and create value for people" Fox, T. & Brewer, H. (2011).This definition confirms that Mer-link's case, its scope and its service platform have accomplished a no-return development process within government procurement.

References

Barahona, J. C., Elizondo, A., & Jimenez, G. (2009). Estrategia para la Adopción, Apropiación E Implementación De Un Sistema De Compras Públicas, pp. 6,10–11. http://www.gobiernofacil.go.cr/e-gob/gobiernodigital/Modernizac ioncompraspublicas/documentoscompraspublcas/Estudios%20de%20Factibilidad/Estrategia_para_la_implementacion_sistema_compras_electronicas.pdf. Accessed 20 July 2014.

eStrategia Publica. (2014). Metodología BINPS para Medir el Ahorro por la Implementación De Procesos Innovados en la Administración Pública. www.relojdelahorro-costarica.com. Accessed 20 July 2014.

Fox, T. & Brewer, H. (2011). Innovation in Government, Partnership for Public Service. http://www.ideo.com/ images/uploads/news/pdfs/ InnovationIn Government.pdf. Accessed 10 Jan 2014.

General Comptroller's Office. (2012). Informe Nro. DFOE-IFR-IF-5-2012 Informe sobre las Iniciativas que impulsan el desarrollo del gobierno digital y de una sociedad basada en la información y el conocimiento en Costa Rica. p. 22. http://www.hacienda.go.cr/docs/51dc7283c011f_DFOEIFRIF52012-DGABCA.pdf. Accessed 20 July 2014.

General Comptroller's Office, Contracting Management Information System. (SIAC for its acronym in Spanish). (2013). Procurement Volume from Total National Procurement in CRC and Percentage, for 2013, per Institution. http://cgrw01.cgr go.cr/apex/f?p=307:25:0::NO:25:P25_ANIO:2013. Accessed 20 July 2014.

Inter-American Development Bank and Organization of American States. (2012). Integración del Sistema Nacional de Compras Públicas. http://www.hacienda.go.cr/ docs/51dc72f8b02c7_Integracion_del_Sistema_Nacional_de_Compras_Public-DGABCA.pdf. Accessed 20 July 2014.

Inter-American Development Bank and World Bank. (2009). Costa Rica, Informe Sobre el Gasto Público: Hacia una Mayor Eficiencia en el Gasto. http://www.hacienda.go.cr/ cifh/sidovih/uploads/archivos/Publicacion/Informe%20sobre%20el%20Gasto%20P%C3 %BAblico-BID-2009.pdf. Accessed 20 July 2014.

Inter-American Development Bank and World Bank. (2010). Public Expenditure and Financial Accountability Program Assessment. www.pefa.org/en/assessment/cr-oct10-pfmpr-public-en. See: pp. I-19 *Indicator*. Accessed 20 July 2014.

Mer-link. (2014). Consulta Ciudadana, Estadística General. http://www.mer-link.co.cr:8082/report/EP_REJ_ COQ708.jsp. Accessed 20 January 2014.

Organisation for Economic Cooperation and Development. (2013). "Implementing the OECD Principles for Integrity in Public Procurement: Progress since 2008." OECD Public Governance Reviews. www.dx.doi.org/10.1787/978926 4201385-en. Accessed 20 July 2014.

Poltronieri, J. (2011). IV Encuesta Sobre Corrupción en la Función Pública de Costa Rica. www.cimpa.ucr.ac.cr/encuesta/Informe_de_la_encuesta_de_corrupcion_2011.pdf. Accessed 20 July 2014.

Ruiz, C. (2010). "Congreso CRInnova Escogió 12 Innovaciones más Destacadas entre el 2006 y el 2012." *El Financiero*. http://wvw.elfinancierocr.com/ef_archivo/2010/noviembre/07/tecnologia2580972.html. Accessed 20 July 2014.

Vargas, M. (2012). Mer-link Ganó Premio Internacional a la Mejor Práctica de Gobierno Electrónico. *La Nación*. www.nacion.com/archivo/Mer-Link-internacional-practica-gobierno-electronico_0_1307869271.html. Accessed 20 July 2014.

Ileana Palaco BA is Ileana Palaco, BA is a member of the Global IT Technology Program (ITTP) at KAIST, she was engaged with the e-Procurement system adoption process in Costa Rica, as well as the adaption and deployment of the Korean e-Procurement System (KONEPS) into the Costa Rican reality.

Alicia Avendaño MSITM is the Head of the Digital Government Division, formerly the Technical Secretariat for Digital Government in Costa Rica. Her research interests are in e-government, public e-procurement, and e-customs.

Waldemar Núñez PhD is a procurement director in the Instituto Costarricense de Electricidad and professor, Department of Administrative Law and Public Contracting, Costa Rican Telecommunications and Electricity Public Enterprise. His teaching and research interests are in administrative law, electronic public procurement, and supply chain management.

The Municipal Partnering Initiative: Mixed Contracting in Local Government Procurement

David Rauch

Introduction

The Municipal Partnering Initiative (MPI), which formally began in 2011 in the northern suburbs of Chicago, can be described as an instance of mixed contracting. Mixed contracting occurs when multiple public agencies jointly contract services with a nongovernmental agency for service delivery (Warner and Hefetz 2008). This is in contrast to joint contracting, which connotes a public entity contracting out some service to a private or nonprofit organization singularly. More than 24 local governments in the MPI jointly craft mutually agreed-upon bid specifications for public works, constructions, and administrative shared services through compromise and discussion. Contracts with contractors are crafted to include all of the participating communities, with contractors working with the various communities to schedule their construction season. There are no memoranda of understanding, fees, or membership to be involved in the MPI, and communities have participated from four counties as of 2013: Cook, Lake, McHenry, and DuPage County. The participating communities are listed in Table 1.

MPI services include the following: crack sealing, resurfacing, concrete, sewer lining, sewer TV, leak detection, hydrant painting, emergency contractor assistance, water meter service, cold patch, hauling and delivery, line painting, bridge inspections, janitorial, asphalt patching, tree trimming, street sweeping, sewer cleaning, generator maintenance, HVAC maintenance, utility locates, manhole rehab, valve turning, tree removal/stump grind, EAB treatment, uniforms, auditing services, inspectional services, and landscaping.

D. Rauch (✉)
Urban Planning and Environment, Edmonton, AB, Canada
e-mail: davidwrauch@gmail.com

K. V. Thai (ed.), *International Public Procurement,* Public Administration, Governance and Globalization 14, DOI 10.1007/978-3-319-13434-5_3

Table 1 MPI communities

MPI survey respondents		MPI communities—non-survey respondents
Arlington Heights	Lincolnshire	*Clarendon Hills*
Buffalo Grove	Lincolnwood	*Evanston*
Cary	Morton Grove	*Fox River Grove*
Glencoe	North Chicago	*Gurnee*
Glenview	Northbrook	*Lake Zurich*
Glenview Park District	Northfield	*Lindenhurst*
Grayslake	Skokie	*Park Ridge*
Highland Park	Vernon Hills	*Woodridge*
Kenilworth	Wheeling	
Lake Bluff	Wilmette	
Lake Forest	Winnetka	

Research Context: Region and History

Region

It will be useful to define the region in which the MPI has occurred. When compared to the 50 largest metropolitan regions according to population as of 2002, Hendrick (2011, p. 101) states that the Chicago metropolitan region contained the highest concentration of local governments (1451 local governments) within its boundaries. The second highest was the New York City metropolitan region's 1321. The number of local governments per capita is used as a measure of political fragmentation and the number of local governments per square mile as a measure of spatial fragmentation (Hendrick 2011, p. 101). The communities that make up the MPI have a median household income of $ 110,174, nearly double the US median household income of $ 52,762 and the Chicago metro region's $ 61,985 (U.S. Census 2010; CMAP 2011).

MPI Program Introduction: Logistics

MPI-bid services range from road resurfacing, crack sealing, auditing, and information technology. The service contracts are the sole binding document in the MPI. Each community in the region is free to participate or not in any MPI contracts. During annual early spring MPI meetings, communities tentatively commit to participating in any of the given services in the MPI. In an attempt to find the ideal configuration for each contract service and determine complications in the bid specifications that may be affecting the contractor's previous performance, the MPI conducts postservice interviews with communities and contractors. In the first year of the MPI, the village of Glenview took on a majority of the contract and bid specification duties. Glenview does not charge a fee for this service, nor does involvement with MPI necessitate that a community contribute to the contract administration of any contract within the MPI. However, there is an understanding among the communities that each partner will contribute in their own way when possible to contract administration tasks. Many become the main contact for a service for 1 year and lead the efforts involved with securing that particular service. For example, in 2013, the 15 joint bids issued by the construction committee were led by 11 different communities.

At the outset of awarding a bid, the contractor works with each participating community to create a schedule for service delivery. Some smaller communities have emphasized the balance they must weigh when contracting with the MPI; while contract costs may be lower due to leveraging economies of scale, it can be at the expense of being able to choose their place in the construction season schedule. Some community administrators have expressed frustration at their perception that larger municipalities get priority scheduling.

Each community is responsible for paying the contractor and monitoring its own contracts. It is important to note that joint purchasing language included in the joint bids allows other communities to participate after the bids are received, known as "piggy-backing." MPI administrators prefer that communities participate from the beginning of the bidding process because more quantity at the outset can amount to a lower unit price. The ability for communities to piggy-back on a contract can also make it difficult to know which communities are utilizing the MPI-bid services, this happens because participation is self-reported.

MPI History

In 2010, Glenview and three other communities (Morton Grove, Wilmette, and Winnetka) made a mixed-contracting trial of four communities jointly contracting for crack sealing. Crack sealing is a program designed to extend the life of streets. Crack sealing is typically performed 3–5 years after the street is resurfaced because cracks develop on the street surface due to the weather. Cracks resulting from routine wear and tear need to be sealed as they develop to prevent moisture and road salt from seeping into the base, which can lead to potholes and more serious road failures.

To construct the joint contract, members of each community, from city managers to public works technicians, convened to create a single bid specification for all four communities concerning crack sealing delivery. Each community previously had different service specifications, especially in their contract legal boilerplates. Through compromise, with some communities decreasing the strictness of their language and others increasing their contractor expectations, the four communities together created a mutual bid document. They then advertised, received bids, opened the bids publicly, reviewed them, and signed a single contract for service.

Glenview convened 18 communities in early 2011 to discuss a larger joint crack-sealing bid as well as other possibilities after sending out a survey to determine which services were routinely outsourced in the region. The survey identified roughly 40 commonly-outsourced services and commodities. These included services that each community outsourced every year. Based on that list, two committees were formed. The Public Works Committee relates to maintenance-type activities. The construction committee consists of sewer lining, road resurfacing, and other more engineering-intensive services. According to MPI administrators, the participating communities generally tended to bid the same projects every year and were in moderate fiscal shape coming out of the recession. The MPI administrators also searched for politically-stable communities. For the first year, communities were located in Lake and Cook Counties. All the Lake and Cook County communities that were chosen, shared borders.

MPI-participating communities emphasized that they wanted to maintain their current levels of service. Even in working together, stretching village or city money, services to the residents were expected to remain the same, if not improve. As Glenview was able to bring on 10 additional communities, the 2010 crack sealing contractor extended the length of the 2010 contract 2 years and also lowered its unit price from $ 1.00 to 0.99, eventually to $ 0.98 in 2012. In 2011, the MPI also added construction projects: street resurfacing, concrete, and sewer lining. These projects were chosen because they were maintenance services that nearly all of the participating communities participate in every year. One of the results of joint bidding is decreasing the amount of staff time needed in each community for each project bid. Instead of having 10–12 engineers from each community putting the bid package together, 10–12 attorneys reviewing it, 10–12 purchasing agents reviewing and advertising for it, the MPI produced 2 or 3 bid packages with only 1 or 2 engineers or attorneys.

According to Glenview staff, one of the largest hurdles to overcome was the difference in bid specifications. For example, concerning the MPI's first road resurfacing bid, one MPI administrator from Glenview said that even after working in road projects for many years previously, he had never known that there were so many different kinds of asphalt mix, with each town having its own mix. However, through compromise, communities were able to overcome some of these differences in specifications. In the first two of the MPI's yearly contracts for road resurfacing, with five communities in 2011 and eight communities represented in 2012, there were two contracts awarded each year, one each for Cook and Lake Counties, with each community within the county group having identical bid specifications. In 2013, road resurfacing has three separate contracts, and concrete services had five contracts. Concrete services for curb/gutter and sidewalk used to be bid together but are now being bid as separate services. MPI administrators have found that while some services benefit from increasing economies of scale, others benefit from geographic proximity to best economize mobilization costs.

In additional to geographic concerns, the MPI has had to accommodate communities with different budget years. Some communities operated under a January first fiscal-end year, while others ended in May or June. When appropriate, municipalities are grouped according to budget year. When division was not feasible, the MPI does insert a clause into the bid document giving, for example, 100 days to award a bid, allowing communities flexibility to award contracts when they see it as advantageous. Concerning contract scheduling, communities demonstrated trepidation about losing an element of control in choosing when the vendor would provide the service during the construction season. This requires compromise, and when services are delayed due to weather or other extenuating circumstances, scheduling conflicts between communities have been the cause for consternation. In some situations, the MPI simply picks communities' names blindly out of a hat to choose scheduling. The MPI has demonstrated flexibility for communities that change position in the schedule due to changes in street selection and other decisions.

In the first year, 2011, the MPI awarded 11 joint bids with 20 communities. Glenview administrators state that, initially, it was challenging to find an individual to lead joint bids outside of Glenview. One Glenview administrator likened it to trying to find friends to help one move, saying that there is a lot of verbal support, but when one tries to set a date, it can be a little challenging. Glenview staff says that in 2011, there were many compromises, and Glenview did take on a majority of the bid specification work and coordination. However, after the first year, many of the joint bid documents did not vary greatly from year to year. MPI communities have created a list of responsibilities for those who would be leading a joint bid such as coordinate, schedule meetings, make any minor changes, receive the bids, and distribute them at the very end. After bids are received by a community, just as if each community were doing a bid contract in their own town, it is their responsibility to award and monitor the contract as the service is delivered.

Early MPI Obstacles

Glenview staff identified obstacles early in the MPI process and has reflected on how they attempted to overcome those obstacles. Initially, other communities' municipal staff were concerned about losing or ruining relationships with contractors with whom they have had a relationship over many years. Some contractors have worked collaboratively with staff for many years, and their relationship was was valued by municipal employees. However, Glenview administrators observed that some previous contractors have been able to successfully bid for MPI contracts, scheduling an entire construction season of work with 15–20 communities with one contract. Also, municipalities have numerous smaller contracts for construction and public works projects outside of the annual main contract. Smaller contractors can still bid on these other projects. There was also concern among municipalities about the multigovernmental impact of an MPI contractor going out of business or not performing up to specifications for large MPI projects. There has been a multipronged response in order to guard against contractor failure, largely in part due to the previous failure of the Northwest Municipal League's crack sealing contractor in 2008; including provisions to allow the village and its partners to cancel a contract within 60 days of the award due to poor performance if necessary. The 2008 contract was forfeited due to the contractor not being able to complete work on schedule.

MPI Cost Savings: Current State of MPI

Cost savings calculations are left to each community within the MPI, some utilizing line item and unit price comparisons from years earlier or comparable communities or projects. The Glenview staff creates an aggregate savings presentation each year for MPI communities based on the cost savings estimates they receive and their own calculations. An example of a single service cost savings calculation is presented in Table 2.

Cost savings are calculated by Glenview staff by examining comparable line items between participating MPI prices and similar area communities' non-MPI prices, allowing for a range of savings from their calculations, depending on the scale of the projects. Savings over unit prices are multiplied by the number of communities participating. A summary of cost savings is created for a presentation to the MPI communities at the end of the construction season each year. The range reflects the combined variability incorporated into the cost savings, as calculated by Glenview staff, see Table 3.

Glenview has not attempted to calculate the *administrative* savings for the whole MPI area due to decreased staff time on bid creation and advertisement, nor have communities calculated the exact cost savings of moving from in-house production of a service to an MPI-administered outsourced service.

Variety of Intergovernmental Joint or "Mixed" Purchasing

There is variety of area pooled purchasing models listed in the following section. These pooled or mixed purchasing pools exist in various states of completion (Western Cook County at the young end of the spectrum and the Illinois Purchasing Bulletin more than 30 years old) and in varying network structures (COG-centric versus Municipality-centric versus state-centric). Comparing and contrasting these models illuminates the strengths and weaknesses inherent in each. One common

Table 2 MPI crack sealing cost savings calculation. (Source: Village of Glenview Staff Report (2011))

Crack sealing				
	Participants	Totally project value	Unit cost per pound	Vendor
MPI	14	$ 557K	$ 0.9968	North Suburban
Cook county communities		$ 35K	$ 1.15	North Suburban
MPI savings—$ 54–64K				

Table 3 Summary of cost savings—Glenview staff report. (Source: Village of Glenview Staff Report 2011)

Project	No. of communities	Total project value	Savings ($ 1000)
Crack sealing	12	$ 421,000	$ 50
Resurfacing (lake)	3	$ 2,990,000	$ 100–120
Resurfacing (cook)	2	$ 2,840,000	$ 80–100
Concrete	8	$ 966,000	$ 15–20
Sewer lining (group one)	5	$ 1,090,000	$ 3050
Sewer lining (group 2)	7	$ 945,000	$ 60–90
Sewer televising	4	$ 365,000	$ 16–26
Leak detection	5	$ 71,000	$ 3–5
Hydrant painting	6	$ 60,000	$ 8–10
Water meter testing	3	$ 20,000	$ 0.5–1.5
Emergency contractor assistance	11	$ 150,000	$ 27–37
Total savings—$ 389–529 K			

theme appears to be that many communities began their joint or mixed contracting programs with a survey to interested communities, listing services each community commonly contracted out, also asking each community to register their level of interest in jointly contracting for that service. At some point during the formation process, the groups must decide the degree to which the communities will be legally bound together, either through MOUs, letters of intent for each service, membership which may or may not include payment, or in the MPI's case, none of the above.

When considering the MPI and where it rests within the many permutations of pooled procurement, it is important to contrast it with other configurations. In some instances, the MPI was directly affected by the pooled purchasing group to be mentioned. In other instances, alternative models are proposed, which may highlight the unique qualities of the MPI.

Lake County Municipal League

Lake County Council of Government's mission is to serve as a vehicle for member municipalities to take joint action on matters affecting the Lake County area. Membership is open only for Lake County communities and costs an annual $ 500. The organization currently serves 38 communities. Besides promoting the interests of its members in the region and Illinois capital, for the first time (starting in the 2013 construction season), the COG offered three road-related joint purchasing services for joint purchasing: crack sealing, pavement marking, and street sweeping. There are currently no administrative fees for municipalities associated with joining the bids. The bid writing, advertising, and coordination was a mutual effort by the LCML executive director and Lake County community administrators.

The three services for the first year were chosen out of a dozen which were identified as possible services to be jointly bid, determined by a survey sent to interested communities in Lake County earlier in the year. At the beginning of the bid creation process, communities signed a letter of intent to be a party to the upcoming joint-bid contract in which communities include their desired quantity of service based on mutually-agreed-upon general bid specifications, with variations remaining from community to community. Communities are committed by the letter of intent to remaining with the joint bid through the process unless, after the bid prices had been received from contractors, a majority of the communities decide together not to use the bid and instead contract independently, which did not happen with any of the three contracts in the first year. Each community signs and awards its own contract with the contractor with the pre-arranged bulk price for all. This is in contrast to the MPI model where all the participating MPI communities sign the same, single contract with common boilerplate language.

Northwest Municipal Conference

The Northwest Municipal Conference (NWMC) was founded in 1958 and represents communities north and northwest of Chicago, many of which are in the MPI. Currently, 42 communities and one township belong to the Council of Government. Involved with the NWMC's mission is the Suburban Purchasing Cooperative (SPC), a joint-purchasing program. Together the SPC represents 137 municipalities and townships in the northeastern Illinois. Focusing on providing bulk purchasing goods, such as vehicles, liquid calcium chloride and natural deicing liquid (beet juice) for snow removal, and office supplies, the only road project the SPC offers wherein a contractor performs a service in the community directly is pavement marking, a service the MPI also offers.

It is important to note that the SPC did offer crack sealing joint contracts and lane marking as recently as 2008. In 2006, SPC crack sealing prices were $ 0.987 per pound with a two cent per pound administrative fee added. 2007 contractor prices came to $ 0.951 per pound with the same administrative fee, coming to $ 0.971 per pound for communities. In 2007, 29 municipalities participated with an estimated 692,000 pounds of sealant. The 2008 SPC crack sealing price for 16 communities came from Complete Asphalt Service at $ 0.987 per pound, in addition to the same administrative fee. Due to the failure of the contractor meeting contract dates in the Northwest Municipal Conference's 2008 Crack Sealing Program, the contract was forfeited before completion, after which the NWMC chose to discontinue its joint crack sealing program, leaving communities in 2009 to bid their own crack sealing programs. The NWMC vendor default made MPI communities sensitive to the impact of vendor difficulties. In 2010, the MPI began joint bidding with the four original communities.

Challenges

There were many challenges faced by MPI administrators when creating the MPI, and there are many challenges still being faced by communities both participating and otherwise. One of the perennial challenges in the region is the maldistribution of taxable resources, be they property or sales tax. This disparity results in competition in the realm particularly of economic development, which can have lasting impacts in social capital and intergovernmental relations in the area (Stephens and Wikstrom 2007, p. 94). Governments in fragmented systems, experiencing competition and perceiving the struggle as a zero-sum gain have less motivation to collaborate or to "provide goods and services that generate positive externalities, or to reduce services that generate negative externalities" (Hendrick 2011, p. 102).

Adaptation is necessary because Chicago metropolitan communities have experienced changes in their various revenue bases for many years, which creates fiscal stress or munificence for these governments (Hendrick 2011, p. 113). According to (Hendrick 2011, p. 114): "Although… many government recovered from the 2001 recession by 2005, the situation changed dramatically for them in the first 6 months of 2009… sales receipts fell by a record $ 5.8 billion, or 11.5 %, in the Chicago metropolitan region compared to the same period a year prior."

Methods

In order to understand the intergovernmental and economic dynamics that contributed to the MPI, the researcher attended and reviewed various presentations on the MPI given by Village of Glenview Staff, researched the history of joint purchasing in the Northern Illinois area, and examined other models of pooled purchasing for comparison and contrast to the MPI model. Simply comparing prices between 2010 (Pre-MPI) and 2011 (MPI years) would not result in accurate cost savings estimates, due to variations in contract size and scope that could distort price differences. Instead, tracking prices 3 years before the MPI (2008–2010) and 3 years during the MPI (2011–2013) better reflect trends in cost. Finding these figures required a survey to be generated and sent to the MPI communities. Qualitative questions were added to the survey to determine whether the MPI adapts to new information and if there are lessons to be learned from the MPI's experience.

This paper is intended to examine both the cost savings and interorganizational dynamics that influenced the MPI's creation and continuing services. The research questions are:

- What were the intergovernmental dynamics that lead to the MPI?
- Have the communities that are involved saved money as a result of their participation?
- How has the MPI evolved since its inception?
- Are there lessons to be learned from the MPI's experience?

The hypotheses are:

Hypothesis 1: All communities involved will save money on unit pricing of the three examined road services due to increased economies of scale.

Hypothesis 2: MPI service contract sizes will change the number and configuration of communities involved in each service in an attempt to find the ideal size for cost savings.

Survey

Investigation of the contract data available online going back to 2008 revealed incomplete records. A survey was needed to collect procurement data. An International Review Board-approved survey document was sent to the 24 MPI communities (as identified by the staff at Glenview) via email. The survey was sent in the summer of 2013 as a fillable form that could be filled online and sent back electronically. The researcher remained in frequent conversation with the survey recipients while surveys were being completed. See Table 1 for survey respondents.

The survey was created to collect two kinds of information: procurement and qualitative. First, the survey collected procurement data from the years 2008 to 2013 in the jointly-contracted service provision of crack sealing, concrete sidewalk replacement, and cold patch. For each service, the survey also collected quantity of services. The survey captured the variations of how services were specified and delivered before the MPI in order to determine if there were significant differences in service provision before and after the MPI that may have influenced prices and cost savings experienced by communities. The procurement questions presented for 2011–2013 are the same as for 2008–2010. A total of 12 completed surveys were returned with at least some procurement and all qualitative questions answers. An additional eight organizations responded with only qualitative questions answered, for a total of 20 responses with at least some useful information. This comes to an 83.5 % response rate for qualitative questions and 50 % response rate for quantitative questions. Further quantitative data was obtained by research from MPI community municipal minutes.

The data were used to examine how prices from MPI-area communities have changed over the 6-year period, before and after the MPI. The data indicate only line item unit prices, such as cost per ton. Contractor labor is factored into cost per pound for fiber-based crack sealing, as well as concrete sidewalk replacement, whose cost in this paper is calculated by cost per foot. Both services involve contractors supplying both material and labor, which distinguishes these MPI services from simple bulk purchasing programs (U.S. Energy Information Administration, Illinois Department of Labor, Illinois Department of Transportation). This paper will look specifically at five-feet-wide and five-inch-thick concrete sidewalk, which is a common size for which most municipalities contract. Cold patch is a product used to fill potholes and small road issues without the need for heating equipment. Cold patch is purchased in bulk in tons, and the municipalities supply the labor of patching roads spots.

The years in which data were collected (2008–2013) represent a very tumultuous time in municipal government service provision and contractor pricing, largely due to the recession. Cost changes experienced post 2008 will be impacted by the recession, which may have reduced service provision costs due to a level of desperation for contractor work regardless of the MPI's economies of scale. In order to account for the impacts of the recession and other factors, the author has aggregated various road construction-related price indices, including fuel cost, civilian employee cost per hour, bituminous asphalt (most basic and common road asphalt) price, and standard concrete price. Employee cost and the ready-mix concrete cost index data come from the Bureau of Labor Statistics. Fuel information is specific to the Midwest and comes from the U.S. Energy Information Administration. Bituminous Asphalt price indices come from IDOT's annual reports on commodity prices for road construction. Illinois Department of Transportation. (2013).

This survey attempted to collect data from communities in the MPI area that did not use the MPI for services, to provide a comparison to MPI prices. The author collected 2008–2013 procurement data from six neighboring DuPage County communities, none of which have contracted with the MPI or participated in pooled-purchasing services for the three services examined. The number of DuPage community procurement data ranges from service to service and year to year, ranging from only a single community's data in one service year to six. The small amount of data for some service's years negatively impacts the DuPage County group's usefulness as a comparison. Surveys also collected the opinions of MPI communities in short answer format.

Calculations

Procurement data were collected for each of the three services for the 18 communities over the 6 years of 2008–2013. Prices were separated into MPI and non-MPI, and averages were collected for each service each year. In order to calculate price changes in dollars in 2013, averages of previous years were altered to account for inflation. These averages were then compared across the years collected.

Due to the impact of self-selection that determined whether communities will respond to an MPI-related survey, most communities that responded with procurement data regularly contracted with the MPI post 2010, leaving the author with a small sample of non-MPI procurement figures post 2010, particularly in crack sealing services. Additionally, at least six of the communities that did not participate in the MPI crack sealing bid between 2011 and 2013 did not perform crack sealing. Another issue with self-selection that must be taken into mind when analyzing the data is the bias toward larger organizations responding with procurement data over smaller organizations. Since smaller organizations would be more likely to experience cost savings related to economies of scale, and the impact of the MPI could be more significant for smaller communities. Their experience is not as well documented in the procurement data.

It must be noted that these figures represent only three of the MPI program's many services that are jointly contracted, and they do not reflect the experience of other services. These price comparisons also do not reflect any changes in staff hours worked extra or saved due to the MPI, in addition to advertising and bid creation costs saved due to consolidated contract administration. On the other hand, much staff time was invested, especially initially, in order to create the MPI, the costs and savings of which are not reflected in this analysis.

Results

Contract Data Analysis

Figure 1 presents the average unit price of crack sealing per pound, rubber-based from 2008 to 2013 for each of the three groups, non-MPI, MPI, and DuPage County. It is possible that the MPI is affecting vendor prices in the region, possibly driving down prices for non-MPI communities in order to compete with MPI prices. Conversely, price for non-MPI communities could increase because the number of vendors might decrease as large vendors who contract with the MPI dominate the landscape.

In an attempt to demonstrate the market forces that influence the price of selected contracting services, the following costs of essential construction items have been collected below, with all figures being represented in 2013 dollars: Illinois highway

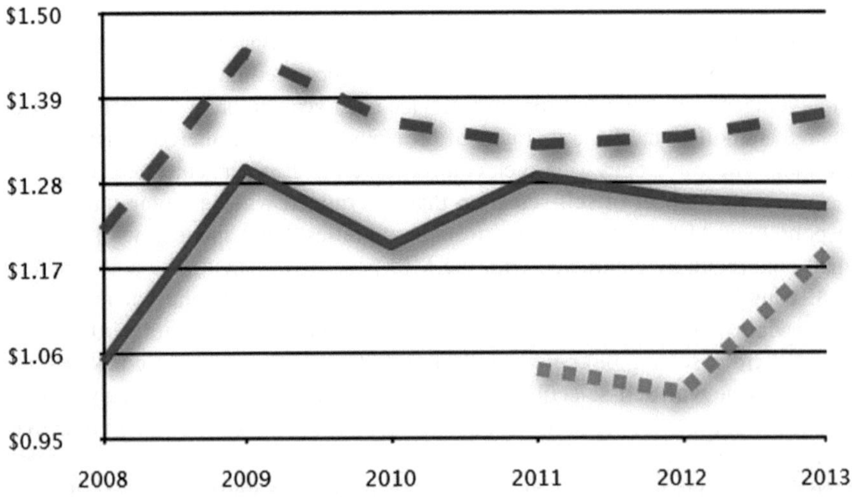

Fig. 1 Crack sealing 2008–2013 price comparison (price per pound). *Solid Line* non-MPI price, *Square Line* MPI price (2011–2013), *Rectangular Line* DuPage community price. *Note*: This graph and all below reflects inflation-corrected values to represent all values in 2013 dollars

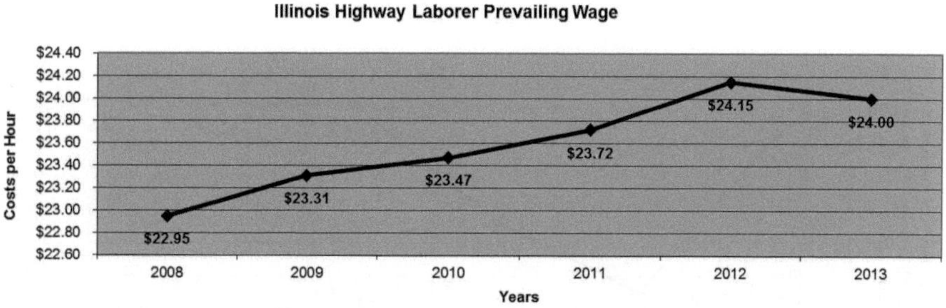

Fig. 2 Illinois highway prevailing wage 2008–2013

laborer prevailing wage, bituminous asphalt, fuel, and concrete pavement. Employer costs for employee compensation demonstrate employment costs for contractors per hour on average. Bituminous asphalt (a basic component for petroleum-based road products) figures were collected from IDOT's yearly survey of roadway-construction-material costs. Illinois Department of Transportation. (2013). Fuel information is specific to the Midwest and comes from the U.S. Energy Information Administration. Concrete prices are Bureau of Labor Statistics National Ready-Mix Concrete Index (the industry standard for concrete construction).

One can see in Figs. 2, 3, 4 and 5 that fuel, labor and asphalt (made from the same basic materials as crack sealing) have increased while MPI community prices have stayed at or below 2010 prices. As mentioned during the history of the MPI, prices fell from 2010 to 2012 due to an increasing number of communities participating in the MPI price, with administrators renegotiating the price lower each year with the same contractor as communities continued to join and MPI administrators refined the mixed-purchasing method. The sharp rise from 2012 to 2013 is the result of the MPI communities contracting with a new vendor after the MPI vendor's president, Alan M. Harris, was charged with theft of government property and mail fraud in 2012.

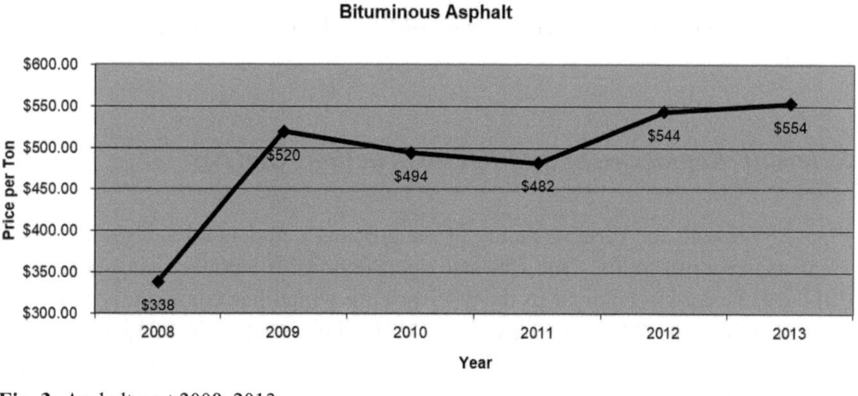

Fig. 3 Asphalt cost 2008–2013

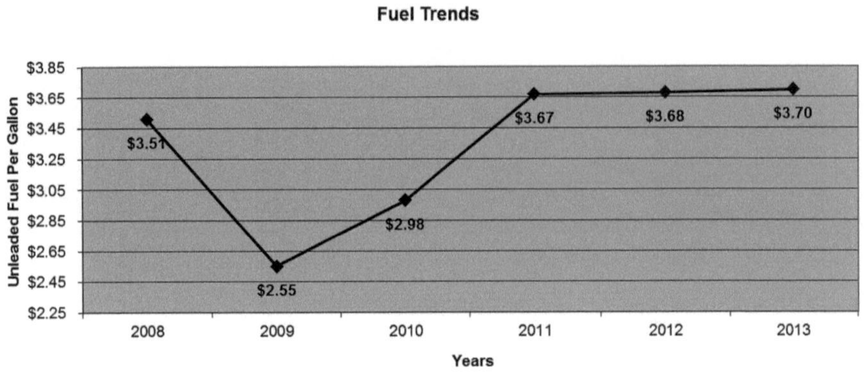

Fig. 4 Fuel cost numbers 2008–2013

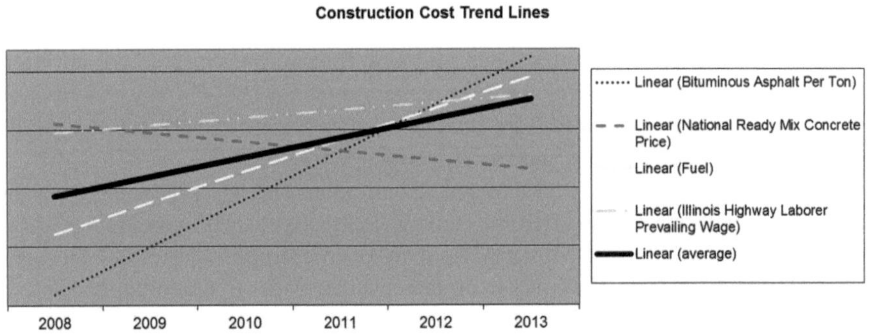

Fig. 5 Construction cost trend lines 2008–2013

One lesson taken from analyzing the crack sealing procurement data is the challenge of interpreting the collected data to explain variations in pricing alone. Each year, communities may dramatically change the scope and quantity of a service, contractors' prices may vary depending on the economic climate, and in such an interconnected area there can be many permutations of joint purchasing that impact pricing. MPI prices remain below the non-MPI or DuPage county prices from year to year.

Sidewalk Replacement and Reconstruction Analysis

Figure 6 presents the variable nature of the procurement data for sidewalk replacement and reconstruction. One can also see the non-MPI prices rising during the 2011–2013 years in contrast to the MPI pricing which has consistently remained near or below the 2008–2013 average. MPI administrators in 2013 broke concrete services into seven groups in order to achieve best costs, which follow the hypothesis that MPI contract size would continue to be adjusted in an attempt to find the best prices.

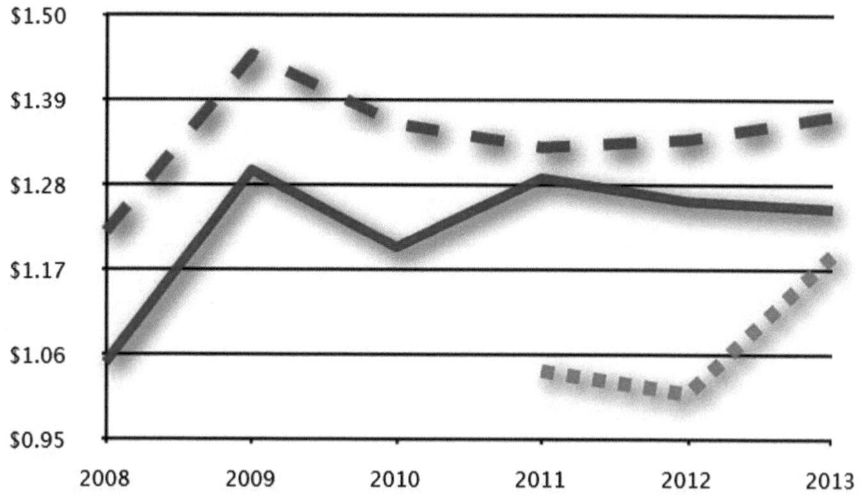

Fig. 6 Concrete sidewalk replacement (price per square foot): 2008–2013. *Solid Line* non-MPI price, *Square Line* MPI price (2011–2013), *Rectangular Line* DuPage community price

Figure 6 presents an increase in commodity prices from 2008 to 2009 followed by a decline until 2011. Despite the decline in value of concrete from 2009 to 2011, communities continue to pay increasingly more per unit (Fig. 7). This is likely due to the impact of other cost drivers in contracted service delivery including increases in fuel and labor (see Fig. 6). However, from 2011 to 2013, MPI prices came in below non-MPI and DuPage prices. Only the MPI-participating communities have been able to experience reduced costs during the 2011–2013 periods.

Cold Patch

Figure 8 above shows that cold patch prices among MPI communities and a single DuPage County community (Glen Ellyn) are lowest at the beginning of the data

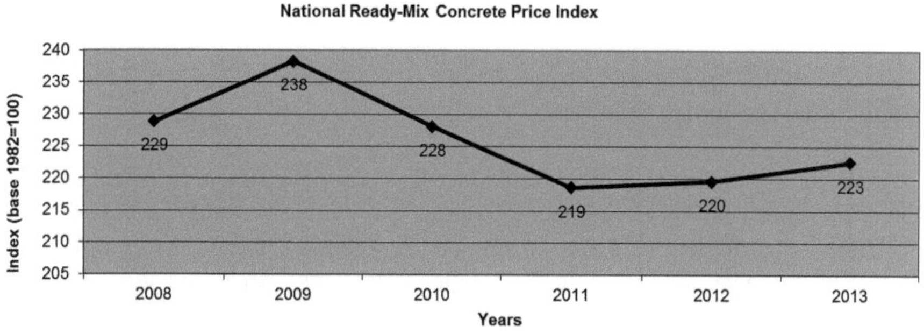

Fig. 7 Concrete pavement cost 2008–2013

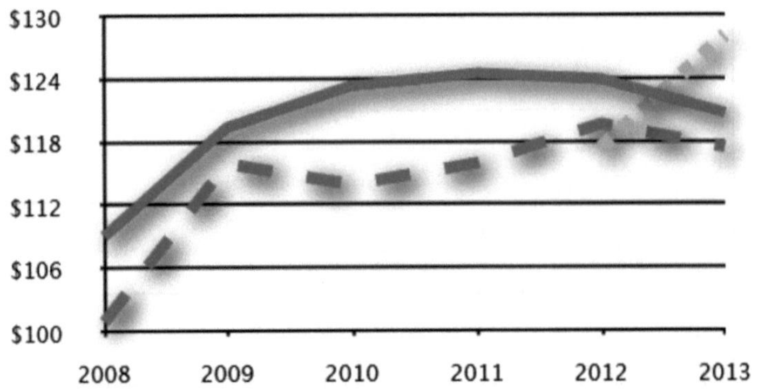

Fig. 8 Cold patch (price per ton) 2008–2013. *Solid Line* non-MPI price, *Square Line* MPI price (2011–2013), *Rectangular Line* DuPage community price

recorded for this paper in 2008, with an increase over the next 5 years followed by a drop-off in 2013. MPI-area communities encounter a small dip in price in 2012, when the MPI first began its cold patch purchasing pool. One can see the non-MPI average price of 2013 achieving a lower price than MPI.

Price Comparison for Cold Patch

One can see in Fig. 3 the climbing of asphalt cost from 2008 to 2013 mirrored by the data collected locally until 2012. When the MPI begins its cold patch service in 2012 (Fig. 2), one can see a sharp contrast between the increase from 2011 to 2012 in the asphalt cost and the MPI price's dip. The increase in the average may also be partially explained by the percent of communities using unique paving material (UPM) increased from 86 % in the pre-MPI years of 2008–2010 to 100 % from 2011 to 2013. UPM is a premium cold patch material that costs more than standard cold patch material. One would expect an increase in average price with an increase in the ratio of UPM versus cold patch in the MPI prices. While the MPI communities experienced an increase from 2012 to 2013, their cost has remained nearly the same from 2011 to 2013. The 2013 bidding process involved a single bidder which may explain a less-competitive price. It must be noted that the non-MPI communities experienced lower prices than the MPI communities, decreasing from 2012 to 2013.

Hypothesis Testing for Qualitative Analysis

Hypothesis 1: All communities involved will save money on unit pricing of the three examined road services due to increased economies of scale.

There is insufficient evidence to support Hypothesis 1 due to the complicating factors of the recession, along with changing commodity price, bid specifications, and project size. According to results from the MPI survey, for crack sealing and concrete sidewalk services, MPI prices were lower than area nonparticipating communities. For cold patch, responding non-MPI communities achieved a lower unit price compared to the MPI. This analysis does not take into account administrative costs or savings. It is also unclear what impact MPI pricing has had on prices achieved by other communities. It is likely that the pooled purchasing program has had an impact on the vendor population, creating opportunities for larger vendors and decreasing opportunities for smaller vendors less capable of fulfilling multiple-community contracts with the MPI. If smaller organizations cannot thrive or adapt in the new atmosphere of pooled purchasing, competition may decrease for contractor services. Lower unit prices for MPI communities may also influence other area communities to demand lower prices from vendors.

The MPI Experience: Questions to MPI Communities

The survey asked communities many questions concerning how they feel about the MPI. For the purpose of comparing answers based on population, municipal populations are divided according to the United States Census with small being zero through 24,999; medium being 25,000 through 64,999; and large being 65,000 and above (U.S. Census Bureau).

Why MPI Costs Are Perceived To Be Lower (If They Are)?

Respondents ranked their top three reasons why MPI prices would be lower than individually-bid contractor services: geographic proximity, economies of scale (bulk cost per unit reduction), sharing of contract administration best practices, and convenience to contractors (one contract, one bid etc.). Figure 9 suggests that communities believe, MPI savings are most significantly derived from economies of scale experienced by pooled purchasing. Geographic proximity and convenience

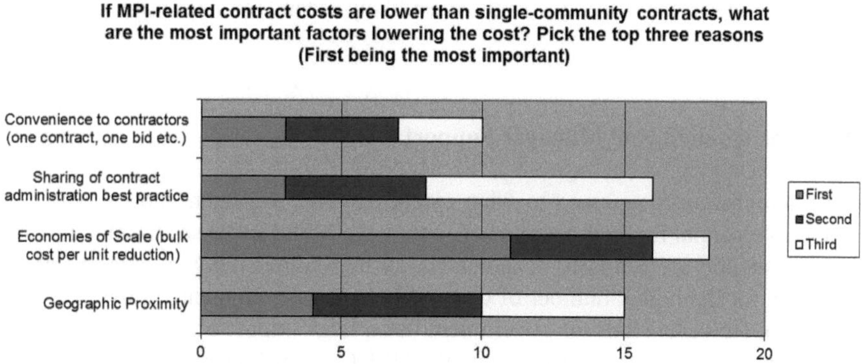

Fig. 9 Why are MPI costs lower

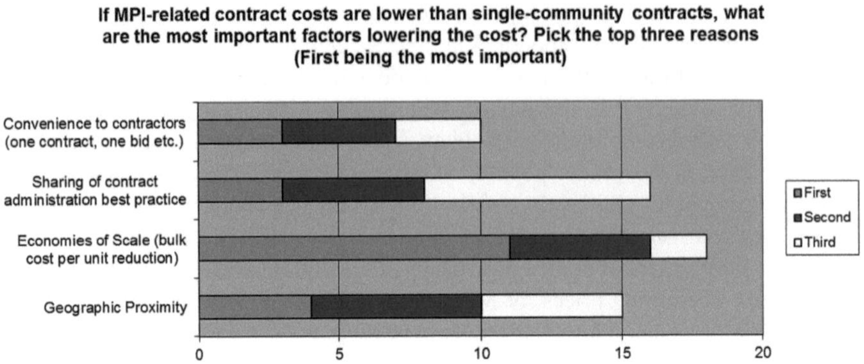

Fig. 10 Reasons for joining MPI

for contractors are similarly placed in the second choice for cost savings, while sharing of contract administration best practices has the lowest average score and number of respondents.

Why Participate in the MPI?

Communities ranked the top three reasons their organization became involved with the MPI. Communities do not officially join the MPI but rather can choose freely to participate in contracts or not. Previous experience with joint contracting was rated as the most important reason for choosing to participate in the MPI (see Fig. 10). It is rated as more important than the financial crisis. This is significant because this speaks to the suggestion in intergovernmental relations literature that an organization's likelihood to participate in ILAs or joint service contracts increases as the number of agreements increase. The recession is also highly ranked as a reason to participate in the MPI, supporting Westley and Vredenburg's (1991) theory that fiscal and environmental stress increase an organization's likelihood to work intergovernmental to find solutions to the issue. Professional associations encouraging shared service delivery was the most likely second top reason for joining the MPI.

Mayoral, Council, and Manager Support

MPI administrators assessed to what extent mayoral, manager, and council support was essential for their community joining the MPI. Responses for mayoral and council support are similarly in agreement for both forms of government when accounting for the higher number of Council-Manager governments in the MPI area (Fig. 11). However, form of government has a large impact on the importance of the manager support in partnering with the MPI. Council-Manager governments are

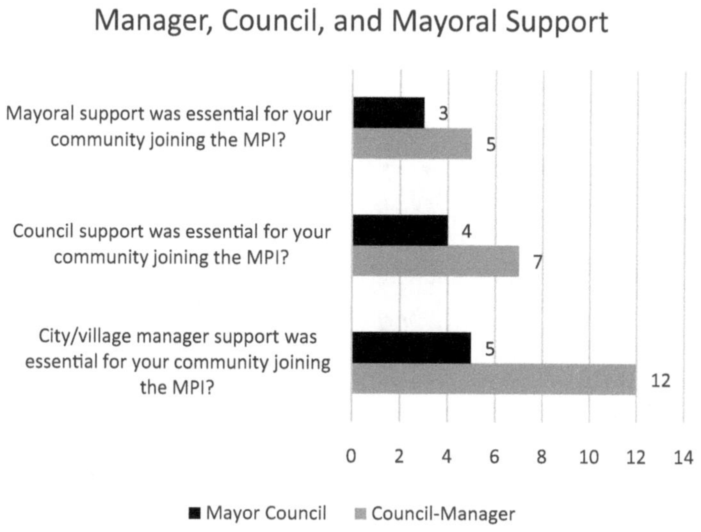

Fig. 11 Mayoral, council, and manager support

more than twice as likely to believe that manager support was essential compared to Mayor-Council governments.

Distribution of MPI-Related Duties

The question: "My community would be comfortable taking on more responsibility of MPI contract administration," is intended to find how MPI responsibilities can be distributed among the communities. Though much of the initial contract work was done by Glenview staff, 11 of the 15 contracts with the MPI in 2013 are being led by communities other than Glenview (Fig. 12). There is a clear break between small and medium communities concerning their comfort level in taking on more MPI-related responsibilities. Among small communities, the level of interest is negative, with only one community in agreement and two disagreeing. Medium-and-large-sized communities are more comfortable taking on more responsibilities. This survey was sent after the 2013 MPI contract work had already been more evenly distributed to 11 communities, so this question is assessing whether communities would be comfortable taking on even more of the workload.

While small communities respond more negatively to taking on more MPI-related responsibilities compared to large and medium-sized communities, small communities respond comparatively more favorably when asked whether they would pay a fee MPI for services (Fig. 13). Medium-sized communities lean toward disagreement, along with a single larger community. One MPI-community public works director expressed the irony that small communities often have the least to offer in terms of money or resources for joint contracting, but they often have the

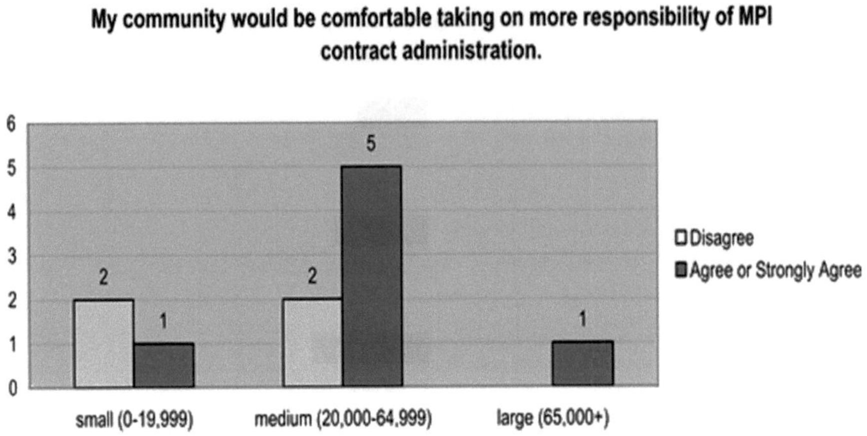

Fig. 12 Contract administration duties

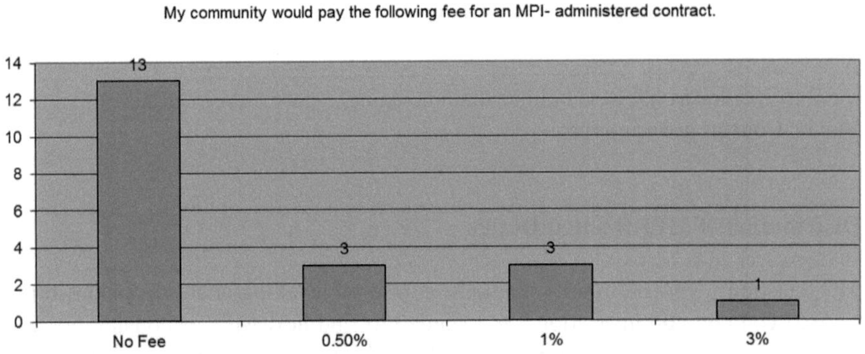

Fig. 13 MPI fees

most to gain in economies of scale. However, in this example, smaller communities are more willing to contribute a fee for MPI services, while medium-to-large-sized communities are less willing to contribute staff resources (Fig. 12).

Fee Amount

When asked what kind of fee they would be willing to pay, communities that generally responded as neutral in the previous question now indicated that no fee was acceptable. Thirteen communities responded that they would not pay any fee, with seven communities responding they would pay some fee. Of the communities that responded positively, three stated they would pay a half percent fee, three responded that they would pay a 1 % fee, and one stated it would consider paying a 3 % fee.

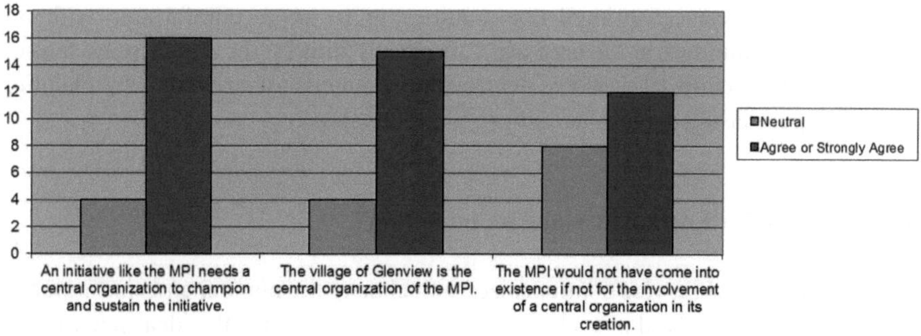

Fig. 14 Central organization

Central Organization

Communities were asked to consider the following questions:

- An initiative like the MPI needs a central organization to champion and sustain the initiative.
- The village of Glenview is the central organization of the MPI.
- The MPI would not have come into existence if not for the involvement of a central organization in its creation.

There is general agreement that something like the MPI needs a central organization, that Glenview is that central organization, and that if not for that central organization (Glenview), the MPI would not have come into existence (Fig. 14).

The Importance of Voluntary Participation

Communities feel very favorable about the voluntary nature of MPI participation, with 19 or 20 communities agreeing and one disagreeing. Many communities appreciate being able to pick which services to participate in based on their preferences, and the MPI contract's ability to realize cost savings for them. Some larger community administrators say that as long as the contract is at least the same price that they otherwise would have paid going into the contract as a single community, they choose to purchase with the MPI in order to benefit other communities, who may benefit from the increased economies of scale.

Research Questions Answered

What Were the Intergovernmental Dynamics that Lead to the MPI?

The structure of the MPI is a response to the intergovernmental dynamics in the northern Illinois area. Previous experience with pooled purchasing for contractor-provided road services primed communities to be more comfortable with the practice. Communities in the area are also closely knit by the connections formed through membership of various overlapping councils of government, planning agencies, purchasing groups, and informal partnerships.

How Has the MPI Adapted Since Its Inception?

Hypothesis 2: MPI service contract sizes will change the number and configuration of communities involved in each service in an attempt to find the ideal size for cost savings.

Since its inception in 2011, the MPI has changed dramatically in scope and size. Beginning with 20 communities and nine services in 2011, the MPI offers 23 services to 29 communities. Group sizes for individual services have also adapted during the 3 years. Some services have increased the number of communities participating in a single contract each year, such as crack sealing, while others have decreased the average number of communities per individual contract, such as concrete work. Lead contract administrators from each community work together each year to find the right size for each contract, attempting to strike a balance between size and specifications. Some services benefit from smaller contract sizes in order to decrease contractor mobilization costs. Other services benefit from dividing groups into fiscal year calendar, county, and funding source.

Are There Lessons To Be Learned from the MPI's Experience?

With many models for pooled purchasing in local government, communities should consider the pros and cons of a municipality-run program and compare them to alternative models. The MPI is a product of a single community that determined it had the capacity to create the MPI and did not want to wait for another organization to take on the task. While a municipality may have more administrative capacity for complicated engineering-related contract administration, a COG may be more regionally focused and less apt to leave peripheral communities out of discussions. Private contractors are at the center of the job-order contracting pooled purchasing model, but public organizations must consider the conflict between public and private values when contracting exclusively with private organizations for pooled purchasing.

Discussion

The variety of intergovernmental joint purchasing formulations in the Northern Illinois area is considerable. The pooled purchasing collectives can be led by a municipality, a county, a COG, a private organization (the case of a Job-Order Contractor), the state, or the federal government. Looking at Agranoff and McGuire's (2001, p. 671) four models of intergovernmental relations (top-down, donor-recipient, jurisdiction-based, and network), each form of pooled purchasing has characteristics of the models. With increased intergovernmental cooperation, horizontal links in the metaphorical picket-fence of IGR are emphasized, sometimes weakening the hold of the top-down model. As local governments increasingly act together to solve problems, relationships that used to be dominated by a central player, typically the state or federal government, will change from top-down to the more shared relationships characterized by donor-recipient, jurisdiction-based.

One of the impacts of the MPI in the region, not just within the MPI community area but the Northern Illinois area as a whole (and arguably the nation), has been to foster discussion, debate, and in some instances, variations of the MPI. A western Cook County group of communities, including Western Springs and Riverside have based their initiative heavily on the MPI, albeit without one central community doing a majority of the work in the first year. The Western Cook County initiative is possible in part because the MPI has provided a useful model, with publicly-available legal documents with their jointly-bid boilerplate, cost-savings estimates, and technical advice to those communities with questions about the mixed-purchasing process. A similar effort is beginning in DuPage County, with a group of communities forming a team to evaluate joint purchasing for commonly-outsourced services. The services are the same as the MPI in its early years, and common bid specification ideas are being borrowed from the MPI's agreements. Administrators in western Cook County have likened the MPI's impact on their process to not needing to reinvent the wheel. MPI documents already show a framework on which to base a mixed-purchasing program.

Recommendations

Based on findings and discussion of this paper, a checklist for creating a program similar to the MPI would include the following:

Examine Your Community and Region's History with Pooled Purchasing

Begin with an examination of previous joint-purchasing experiences. Ask which kind of organization was in control: the state, a COG, the county, a municipality, and consider the impacts that each central-party category has had on the performance of the joint-purchasing program. Many communities in the MPI participated in joint purchasing before the MPI (this reason was the top choice for why communities participated in the MPI). Glenview administrators preferred to create a municipality-centric program because they perceived that municipalities typically have more administrative capacity than COGs to take on the arduous task of finding compromise on bid specifications. However, with the help of municipalities in its area, the Lake County Municipal League (LCML) was able to effectively jointly purchase for three road-related services in 2013. LCML has a full-time staff of one, but if the joint-purchasing program should expand, the director has said she would consider bringing on staff to help administer the program. It is also interesting to note that in 2013, the MPI considered bidding thermoplastic road-striping services through the Northwest Municipal Conference's Suburban Purchasing Cooperative. This option did not come to pass, but it demonstrates an interesting possibility for purchasing cooperatives to work collaboratively to offer the best prices for communities.

Each configuration has benefits and potential drawbacks. There are also tradeoffs involved. While a COG may have less capacity and staff typically, COGs are by nature more regionally focused. While a central municipality may focus more locally, they exist to serve their residents. However, a question raised in public administration research is whether local governments exist only to serve *their* residents. There are many questions as to what obligations local governments have to other local governments and their residents, regionally, nationally, and internationally. Different communities have different attitudes. Thurmaier and Wood (Thumaier and Wood 2002, p. 595) write of the sentiment among communities in the Kansas City area, concerning interlocal agreements and joint purchasing (ILA):

Several of the largest jurisdictions view the system as a way to help smaller neighboring jurisdictions save costs by letting them piggyback on their large contracts. This speaks to a metropolitan culture of cooperation, repeatedly expressed by a wide range of actors across the jurisdictions.

Consider the Impetus

The second-most important reason communities chose to partner with the MPI was the financial crisis. As Westley and Vredenburg (1991) suggest, communities are more likely to collaborate when they are in fiscal distress. In tumultuous situations, entrepreneurial administrators look outside of their organization for solutions to problems (Hendrick 2011). This is to suggest that the MPI's creation may be described, at least partly, as a response to the financial crisis. It would be challenging to determine to what extent a similar program would have come into being if not for the financial crisis, but the answer to "Why did my community choose to partner with the MPI" was *firstly* "previous experience" and *secondly* "the financial crisis." It is possible to consider that a program such as the MPI would have come into being regardless of the crisis. "Professional associations encouraging pooled purchasing" is also the most-likely second choice for partnering with the MPI. As has been discussed, the financial crisis is only one of many factors impacting Northern Illinois communities' fiscal condition, so one cannot discount the changing nature of tax sources and intergovernmental aid (or lack thereof) when considering all the motivations for partnering. Hendrick (2011) also notes that communities are most likely to collaborate at the stretching phase of fiscal distress, not when they are near the breaking point of financial collapse. Glenview was in self-described moderate fiscal shape coming out of the recession. Glenview administrators looked for communities similarly stretching their dollars but not on the verge of financial collapse for initial MPI partners.

Report Intergovernmental Activities

Stephens and Wikstrom (2007, p. 273) suggest all communities should have an individual within their organization who is aware of and involved in all intergovernmental relations and that all the intergovernmental activities should be shared with the regional planning authority. If communities are considering ILAs, they would benefit from having as complete a catalogue of regional IGR efforts as possible. There is much sharing of joint-purchasing knowledge among Northern Illinois communities, but much of it is informal and not centralized. For instance, the MPI does not have a publicly-available website for those interested in examining boilerplate or bid specifications, but Glenview staff has been obliging to organizations that contact them for that purpose, and the MPI does have a shared DropBox account for all presentations, contracts, and bid specifications.

Cost Savings Calculations

If the MPI is to be touted as a model for intergovernmental joint contracting (as ICMA has done by awarding it the Community Partnership Award Winner for 2012), communities individually and as a whole should thoroughly assess cost savings, not related solely to unit prices but also contract administration costs. As practiced by the Kansas City joint purchasing arm of the regional COG, the KCRPC, fees for the joint purchasing program are justified by calculating the average cost of bid advertisement, issuing purchase orders, and other aspects of the procurement process that are largely avoided by joint purchasing. If MPI communities were interested in monitoring their administrative cost savings, they should consider doing the KCRPC's analysis. As recommended by Ammons (2008), activity-based costing may allow communities individually to determine how much staff time goes into bid creation, advertisement, and awarding. However, calculating the cost of these activities is not enough to determine cost savings because with staff-time efficiencies, the organization will not realize actual cost savings unless positions are eliminated or freed-up time is used for more value-added activities. Also, when communities go directly from in-house service provision to MPI-related service provision, there should be some form of calculation to determine the significant amount of administrative time and effort avoided by tapping into pooled experience of the MPI communities. By calculating these administrative cost savings, administrators may be able to make stronger arguments for participating with the MPI even if unit costs are similar or only slightly lower.

Acknowledgments The author wishes to thank Dr. Kurt Thurmaier, research adviser for this paper and chair of the Northern Illinois University Department of Public Administration, along with the Village of Glenview Staff for their constant assistance.

References

Agranoff, R., & McGuire, M. (2001). American Federalism and the search for models of management. *Public Administration Review, 61*(6), 671–681.

Ammons, D. N. (2008). *Tools for decision making: A practical guide for local government*. Thousands Oak: Sage Publications.

Chicago Metropolitan Planning Commission Staff. (2011). Shifts in population and household income in metropolitan Chicago. www.cmap.illinois.gov/about/updates/-/asset_publisher/UIMfSLnFfMB6/content/shifts-in-population-and-household-income-in-metropolitan-chicago. Accessed 10 Sept 2013.

Hendrick, R. M. (2011). *Managing the fiscal metropolis: The financial policies, practices, and health of suburban municipalities*. Washington, DC: Georgetown University Press.

Illinois Department of Transportation. (2013). Price indices. http://www.dot.state.il.us/desenv/asphaltpi.html. Accessed 15 Sept 2013.

Stephens, G.R., & Wikstrom, N. (2007). *American intergovernmental relations: A fragmented federal polity*. New York: Oxford University Press.

Thurmaier, K., & Wood, C. (2002). Interlocal agreements as overlapping social networks: Picket–Fence regionalism in metropolitan Kansas city. *Public Administration Review, 62*(5), 585–598.

U.S. Census Bureau. (2010). Census. http://www.census.gov/2010census/. Accessed 10 July 2013.

Warner, M.E., & Hefetz, A. (2008). Managing markets for public service: The role of mixed public–private delivery of city services. *Public Administration Review, 68*(1), 155–166.

Westley, F., & Vredenburg, H. (1991). Strategic bridging: The collaboration between environmentalists and business in the marketing of green products. *The Journal of Applied Behavioral Science, 27*(1), 65–90.

David Rauch MPA is a business analyst with the City of Edmonton, Alberta, Canada. His work and professional interests are in data analytics, public procurement, and open data.

The Impact of Changing Patterns of Commercial Card Use by the US Government on Governmental Efficiency and Cost Savings

Richard Palmer, Mahendra Gupta and Nathan Palmer

Introduction

The US Government has used bank commercial card technology since the 1980s to simplify and reduce the cost of the process to acquire goods and services. The term "commercial cards" includes purchase, travel, and fleet cards. Generally, purchase cards are used to acquire non-travel-related goods and services of lower dollar value; travel cards are used to facilitate employee travel on government business and primarily used to purchase airline tickets, hotels, and auto rentals; and fleet cards support employee purchases of fuel and other automotive services for government vehicles.

The benefits derived from card use vary by type of card, manner of card use, and degree of integration with the acquisition process. Purchasing cards are a bank commercial card product designed to increase the efficiency of the procure-to-payment cycle by the delegation of certain types of purchase decisions to employee cardholders. The government agency is obligated to pay *one* bill that summarizes monthly purchases made by *all* cardholders. The agency supports this distributed purchasing activity by assigning each cardholder a (revolving) monthly credit line. This process reduces or eliminates many activities and paperwork previously required to process these purchases, including approvals, requisitions, purchase orders, invoices, and payment while increasing days that payables are outstanding by extending the time to payment (Federal Reserve Bank of Philadelphia 2011; McHugh 2011). Estimates of government agency cost savings by use of purchase cards have ranged from $ 54 to $ 92 per transaction (Cohen 1998; U.S. GAO 1996). The General Services

M. Gupta (✉)
St. Louis, USA
e-mail: guptam@wustl.edu

R. Palmer · N. Palmer
Missouri, USA

N. Palmer
e-mail: rpalmer@semo.edu

K. V. Thai (ed.), *International Public Procurement*, Public Administration, Governance and Globalization 14, DOI 10.1007/978-3-319-13434-5_4

Administration estimates that, on an average, government agencies save about $ 70 per transaction in administrative cost savings each time a purchase card is used (instead of a paper procedure; General Service Administration 2013a).

By contrast, travel and fleet cards do not produce the same types and levels of transactional cost savings but do provide convenience to the government agency, efficiency and transparency in travel spend reporting and management, and the elimination of cash travel advances. When employees charge travel and fleet expenses the government avoids the expense and reduce risk associated with controlling cash advances while enhance visibility of spending activity. Aggregation and enhanced visibility of travel spending activity can be very important to obtain discounts on airfare, hotels, or auto rentals. Modest transactional cost savings can be obtained with the use of travel cards when paired with expense management software, reducing the time it takes to complete requests for reimbursement from the government.

Given the benefits of commercial card use, spending on commercial cards increased steadily from the 1990s through 2008 where it peaked at $ 30.8 billion. Since 2008, commercial card spending (both in dollars and as a percentage of budgeted spending) has been lower than the 2008 level and dropped sharply in 2012 and 2013. In fiscal year (FY) 2013, the US Government spent $ 26 billion on commercial cards, accumulating approximately $ 1.7 billion in administrative cost savings and card issuer refunds from their use (General Services Administration 2013b).

Since the US Government clearly recognizes benefits from card use, the purpose of this chapter is to understand (a) the factors driving reductions in commercial card spending both in absolute terms and as a percentage of budgeted spending, and (b) the countermeasures available to the government to optimize the benefits derived from commercial card use. Specifically, the chapter is broken into four sections: The first section identifies the different types of commercial cards and pinpoints the card platform primarily responsible for changes in the benefits being obtained from commercial card use (purchasing cards). The second section looks more closely at purchasing card spending and activity data. The third section breaks out the purchasing card program performance of military and civilian agencies and provides a historical timeline of events and policy changes affecting purchasing card use. The final section examines the cost and benefits of current changes to the purchasing card program and how the government can optimize the benefits derived from the use of purchasing cards.

Historical Patterns of Commercial Card Use and Benefit

Figure 1 shows that the US Government commercial card spending increased steadily from $ 17.7 billion in 2000 to its zenith of $ 30.8 billion in 2008. In 2009, commercial card spending fell to $ 29.4 billion but bounced back to $ 30.8 billion in 2011. After 2011, commercial card spending dropped by $ 1.5 billion (to $ 29.3 billion) in 2012 and dropped another $ 3.3 billion in 2013 to $ 26.0 billion. Figure 1 also shows that the US Government commercial card transactions increased from

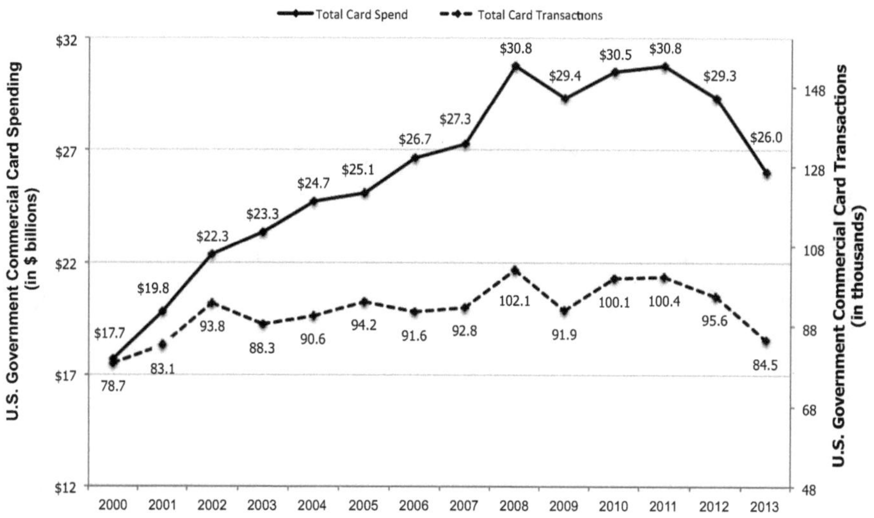

Fig. 1 Total US Government commercial card (purchasing, travel, and fleet) spending and transactions, 2000–2013

78.7 million in 2000 to the high point of 102.1 million transactions in 2008. In a pattern similar to spending, the number of commercial card transactions fell by 17.6 million transactions (to 84.5 million) by 2013.

To put commercial card spending in the larger context of the governmental operations, Fig. 2 displays commercial card spending as a percent of budgeted spend-

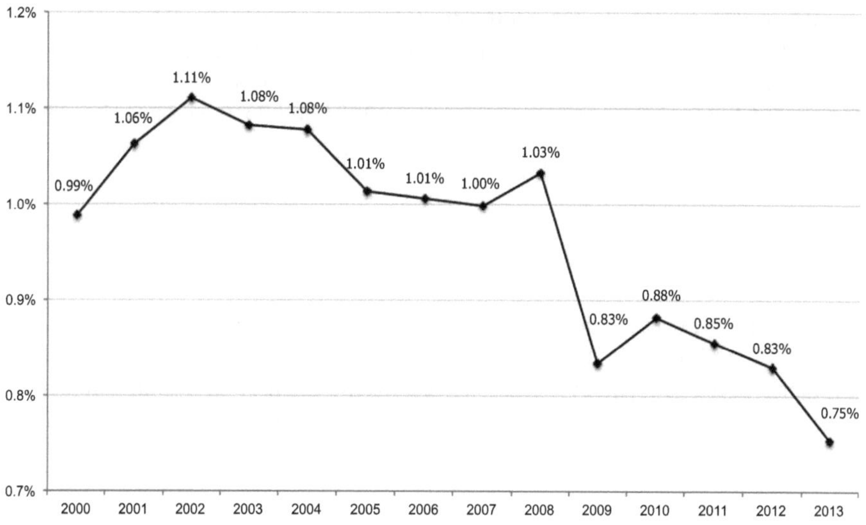

Fig. 2 Commercial card spending as a percentage of budgeted spending by the US Government, 2000–2013

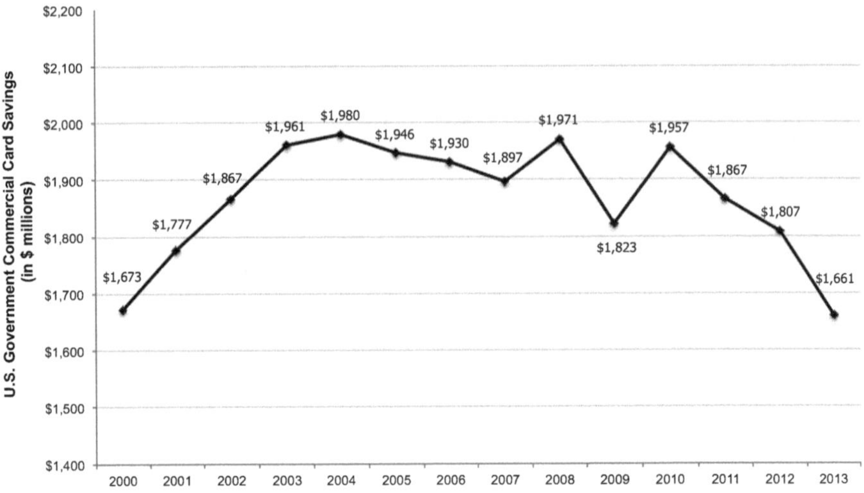

Fig. 3 Total cost savings from commercial card spending by the US Government, 2000–2013. Note: Administrative cost savings are calculated by multiplying $ 70 per purchasing card transaction (as per GSA estimate found at https://smartpay.gsa.gov/about-gsa-smartpay). Likewise, card issuer refund data ($ 272 million in FY 2013) may be found at https://smartpay.gsa.gov/program-refunds. *FY* fiscal year

ing by federal government agencies. Figure 2 shows that, excepting 2008 and 2010, the pattern of US Government commercial card spending as a percentage of the government budget has trended downward since the high water mark of 1.11 % in 2002, falling to 0.75 % in 2013.

Based on a combination of spending and transaction activity, Fig. 3 presents overall cost savings, including administrative cost savings and cash back incentives to the US Government generated from commercial card spending. As shown in Fig. 3, overall cost savings steadily increased from $ 1.7 billion in 2000 to $ 2.0 billion in 2004, remained relatively flat between 2004 and 2010, and has since fallen every year since to its current level of $ 1.7 billion.[1]

Benefits and Use of Different Card Platforms

As noted above, benefits derived by commercial card use vary by type of card used, manner of card use, and degree of integration with the procedural and technological fabric of the acquisition process. To understand the drop in overall commercial card spending more clearly, a breakdown of the spending by type of card is shown in Fig. 4, which indicates that:

[1] Card issuers bid for the business of providing commercial cards to the US Government agencies. Part of the contractual arrangement with a bid winner is a pre-negotiated "rebate" (cash back incentive) which is primarily based on the amount of spending conducted on the cards.

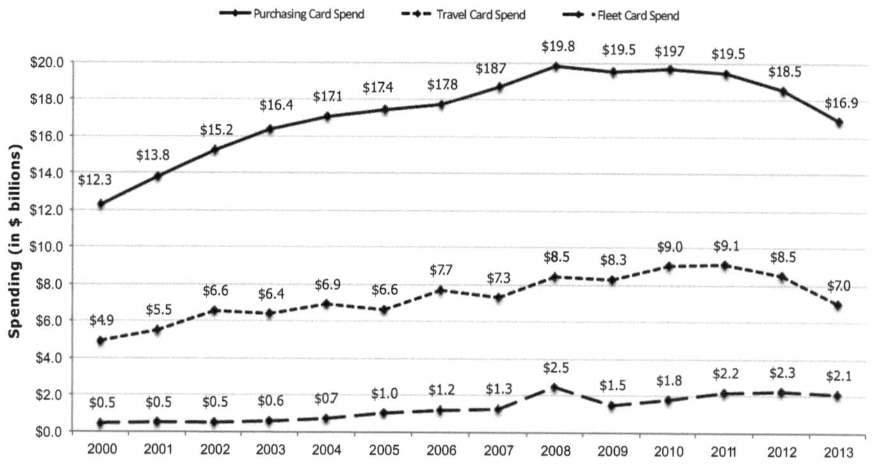

Fig. 4 The US Government spending on purchasing, travel, and fleet cards, 2000–2013. Note: Spending, transactions, and cardholders at the Department of Interior (a "one card" program where both travel and purchasing applications are paid with the same card) are prorated to match purchasing and travel card spending, transactions, and card distribution across the rest of the US Government

- Purchasing card spending rose steadily from $ 12.3 billion in 2000 to $ 19.8 billion in 2008, but has since fallen by $ 2.9 billion to its 2013 level of $ 16.9 billion.
- Travel card spending followed a generally upward trend, rising from $ 4.9 billion in 2000 to $ 9.1 in 2011, but has since fallen by $ 2.1 billion to $ 7.0 billion in FY 2013.
- Fleet card spending has risen from $ 500 million in 2002 to $ 2.3 billion in 2012. In FY 2013, fleet spending dropped modestly to $ 2.1 billion.
- While it has declined recently in its share of total spending, purchasing card spending continues to be the main component of total commercial card spending, accounting for 65 % of the $ 26 billion of commercial card spending in FY 2013.

Given the spending patterns in Fig. 4, it appears that the decline in purchasing card spending is the primary cause of the decline in overall commercial card spending by the US Government. Due to the higher percentage of total spending, changes in purchasing card spending have a greater effect on the benefits of card use that accrue to the US Government. Further, because of the impact on the administrative aspects of the purchasing process, purchasing cards drive all of the administrative cost savings reported by the government and (by virtue of the amount spent) the majority of cash back incentives. Therefore, the remainder of this chapter will focus on governmental use of purchasing cards.

A Closer Look at Purchasing Card Use

Figure 4 showed that purchasing card spending by the US Government steadily increased between FYs 2000 and 2008.[2] Purchasing card spending gyrated between $ 19.5 and 19.7 billion in the 2009–2011 timeframe, thereafter falling steadily to the FY 2013 level of $ 16.9 billion. Figure 5 shows that the number of transactions paid with the purchasing card actually began falling four years earlier. The highest number of annual purchasing card transactions was reported in 2004 (26.5 million). Since then annual purchasing card transactions have had headed in a generally downward direction to the FY 2013 level of 19.8 million, a 25 % decrease from the FY 2004 peak. Figure 5 also shows that total purchasing spending did not decline in the 2005–2008 timeframe because increases in the average transaction amount more than offset the reduction in the number of transactions. The average purchasing card transaction amount rose steadily from $ 446 in 1997 to $ 872 in 2009, but has since fallen to $ 851 in FY 2013.

Purchasing Card Distribution One potential contributor to the reduction in purchasing card spending and transactions by the US Government is change in employee access to purchasing cards. Figure 6 shows that the number of purchasing cards distributed to employees of the US Government peaked at 465,000 in 2001 and has since fallen to its current level of 301,926 (a 35 % drop). Though not shown in the figure, the percentage of the US Government employees has also slowly declined 12.2 % in FY 2001 to 7.6 % in FY 2013. The possible reasons for the drop

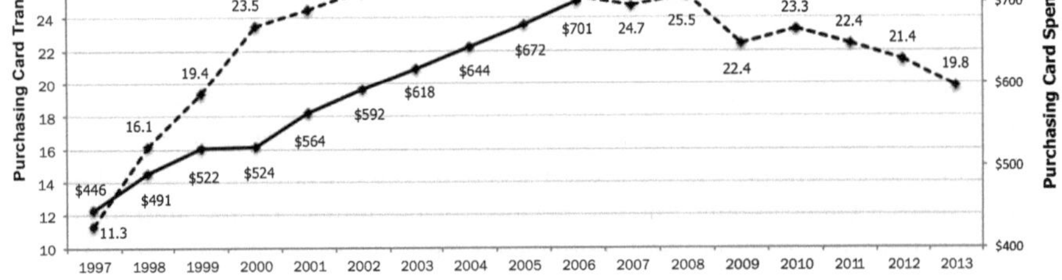

Fig. 5 Purchasing card transactions and spending per transaction by the US Government, 1997–2013. Note: Purchasing card data are available from the GSA from 1997 forward. Card issuer refunds and travel and fleet card data availability is available only from 2000 forward. Thus, this graph extends the timeframe to suit purchasing card data availability

[2] Actually, purchasing card spending increased consistently from 1990 to 2008. Exhibit 4 was constrained to the year 2000 and beyond because that is when data for all three card platforms was made available by the GSA.

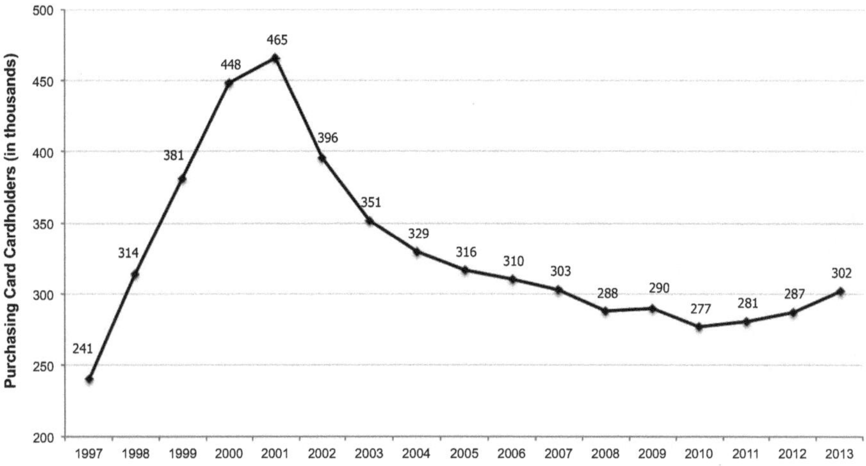

Fig. 6 Purchasing cards distributed to employees, by the US Government, 2000–2013

will be discussed below when we examine various audit outcomes and changes in federal guidelines over the past decade.

Cardholder Spending Behavior Changes in card distribution patterns may affect spending at the cardholder level. For example, Fig. 5 revealed that the average transaction amount of a purchasing card purchase had been trending upwards for most of the past 16 years. Thus, when purchasing cards are in the hands of fewer employees, those cardholding employees tend to make larger purchases (perhaps buying for themselves and others in their department who no longer have a purchasing card). Figure 6 showed that (with one exception in 2009) card distribution across the employee base steadily declined from 2001 to 2010. Likewise, Fig. 7 shows that the decline in card distribution that began in 2002 has meant that employees with

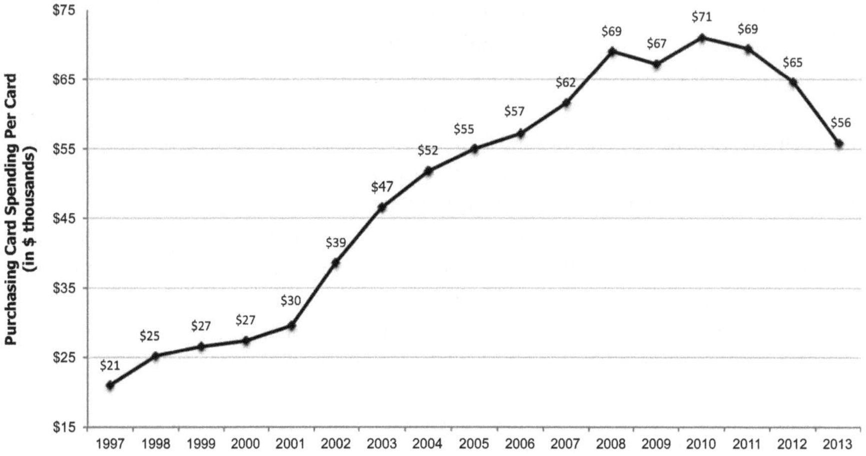

Fig. 7 Annual purchasing card spending per card, by the US Government, 2000–2013

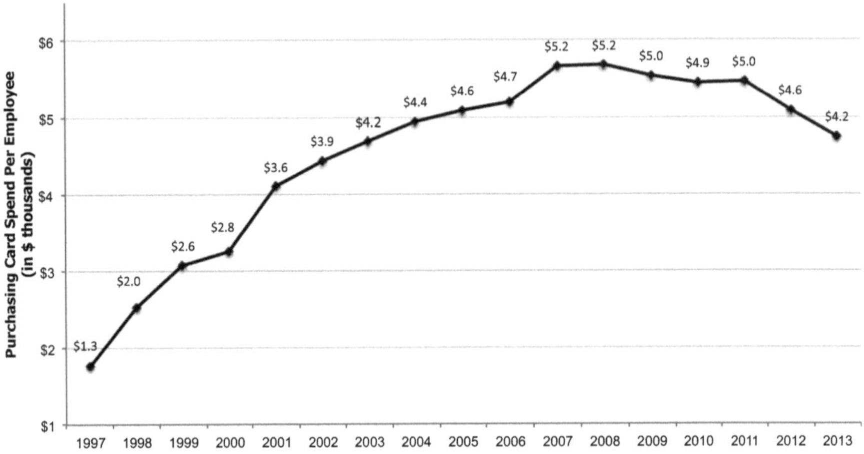

Fig. 8 Purchasing card spending per employee, by the US Government, 2000–2013

cards are conducting more purchases. In that timeframe, the annual purchasing card spending per card rose from $ 30,000 in 2001 to $ 71,000 in 2010. After 2010, the level of card distribution rose modestly (9 %) while the annual spending per card declined 21 % (from $ 71,000 to 56,000 per year).

Size-Adjusted Performance Metrics While "per card" metrics give an insight into cardholder behavior, size-adjusted metrics provide a more comprehensive view if the impact of the purchasing cards on the US Government spending habits. Purchasing card spending per employee is a program performance metric that reflects the extent of the transformation of governmental buying practices away from non-card payment methods to the purchasing card. Figure 8 shows that annual purchasing card spending per employee rose steadily from $ 1,300 in 1997 to $ 5,200 in 2007 where it plateaued for 1 year. Since 2008, purchasing card spending per employee has fallen to $ 4,200 in 2013.

Another size-adjusted performance metric which reflects the relative influence of purchasing cards on governmental buying practices is purchasing card spending as a percent of total budgeted spending. Figure 9 presents the US Government purchasing card spending as a percentage of the US Government budget (lagged on year) in relation to the purchasing card-to-employee ratio for the 1997–2013 time period.[3] The figure reveals that purchasing card spending as a percentage of budget was highest when card distribution was most liberal. Thus, the figure shows the high point of card distribution (in 2001 at 12.16 % of the employee base) is associated with the highest level of purchasing card spending as a percentage of the budget (in 2002 at 0.76 %). Since 2001, both card distribution and purchasing card spending as a percentage of budgeted spending have tracked downward.

[3] Purchasing card spending as a percentage of budget is lagged to allow for cardholder adaptation to card spending policies and procedures.

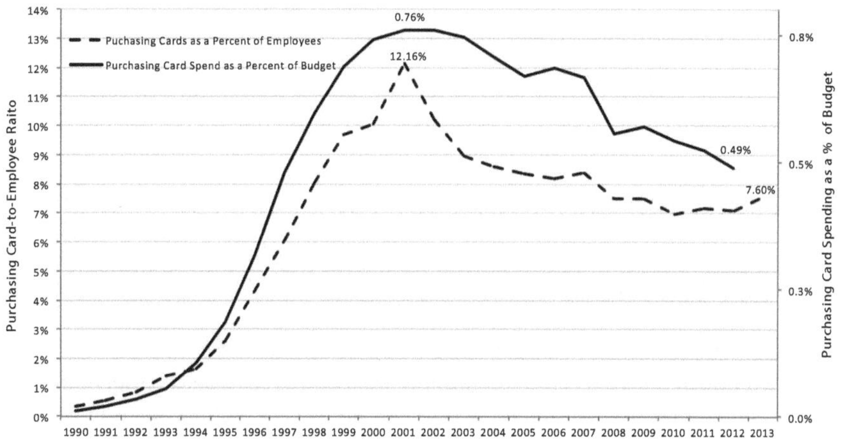

Fig. 9 Card to employee ratio with spend as a percent of budget (1 year lagged), 1990–2013. Note: Budgeted spending data from the Department of Treasury Financial Management Service Monthly Treasury Statements of Receipts and Outlays of the US Government. Government head-count data available at Federal Civilian Workforce Statistics: Employment and trends available at the Office of Personnel Management. Purchasing card spending data from 1990 to 1996 is taken from McHarg (2002)

Cost Savings The net effect of changes in purchasing card distribution and card-holder usage patterns associated is reflected in the savings experienced by the US Government. Figure 10 shows that the benefit derived from purchasing card use

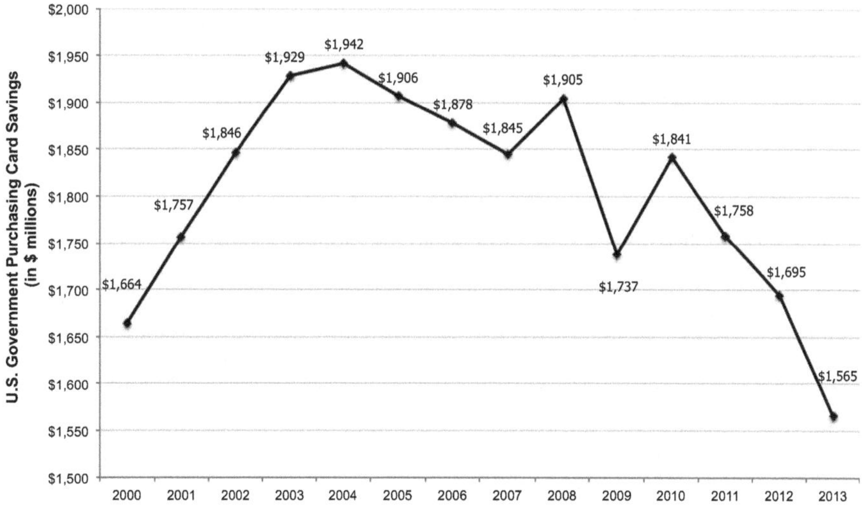

Fig. 10 Total administrative transaction cost savings and card issuer rebates from purchasing card spending by the US Government, 2000–2013Note: Administrative cost savings are calculated by multiplying purchasing card transactions by $ 70 as per GSA estimate found at https://smartpay.gsa.gov/about-gsa-smartpay). Card issuer rebate data is calculated by multiplying the percentage rate of the rebate experienced in each fiscal year times the purchasing card spending in that year. Presentation is limited to the years after 1999 due to availability of refund data

peaked in 2004 (at $ 1.9 billion in combined cash back incentives and transaction cost savings), primarily due to the record number of purchasing card transactions conducted in that year (26.5 million). With the exception of 2008 (where transaction activity spiked up to 25.5 million), total cost savings associated with purchasing card use drifted downward to $ 1.6 billion in FY 2013.

In sum, we find five key points associated with the US Government use of purchasing cards, as follows:

- Purchasing card spending peaked in 2008 at $ 19.8 billion, was flat between 2008 and 2011, and dropped significantly in both 2012 (to $ 18.5 billion) and 2013 (to $ 16.9 billion).
- Annual purchasing card transactions peaked in 2004 (at 26.5 million) and have declined (albeit unevenly) to 19.8 million in 2013. Purchasing card spending did not decline immediately upon reduction in transaction volume because the average card transaction amount was rising rapidly.
- The percentage of employees with purchasing cards fell from 12.2 % in 2001 to 7.0 % in 2010 (from 465,000 to 277,000 cards). Since 2010, the number of and percentage of employees holding purchasing cards has ticked upward modestly.
- Purchasing card spending as a percent of the budget was highest in 2002 and 2003, years in which card distribution was at high levels.
- The cost savings from purchasing card use peaked in 2004 (at $ 1.9 billion), the year of a record number of purchasing card transactions. While transactions were lower after 2004 the total cost savings were buoyed by rising card issuer rebates in the 2004 to 2010 timeframe. Notwithstanding, almost *all* of the decline in the benefits from the US Government commercial card use since 2010 is explained by changes in purchasing card use.

Military Versus Civilian Purchasing Card Activity

Palmer et al. (2010) observed that marked differences existed between military and civilian governmental agencies with respect to the use of purchasing cards.[4] Unlike civilian agencies, military agencies had begun a pattern of movement away from purchasing card use in 2002. The analysis of purchasing card spending in Fig. 11 breaks down civilian and military purchasing card spending and extends Palmer and Gupta's earlier analysis. The figure shows that while civilian purchasing card spending increased from $ 2.8 billion in 1997 to $ 12.1 billion in 2011, it has since dropped by 4 % ($ 0.5 billion) to $ 11.6 billion in 2013. By contrast, military purchasing card spending increased from $ 2.2 billion in 1997 to the high point of $ 8.4 billion in 2008, but has since decreased by 37 % ($ 3.1 billion) to $ 5.3 billion in 2013. In fact, the military reduction in purchasing card spending

[4] Military is defined as the Department of the Army, Navy, Air Force, and DOD-other. All other agencies are considered civilian in nature.

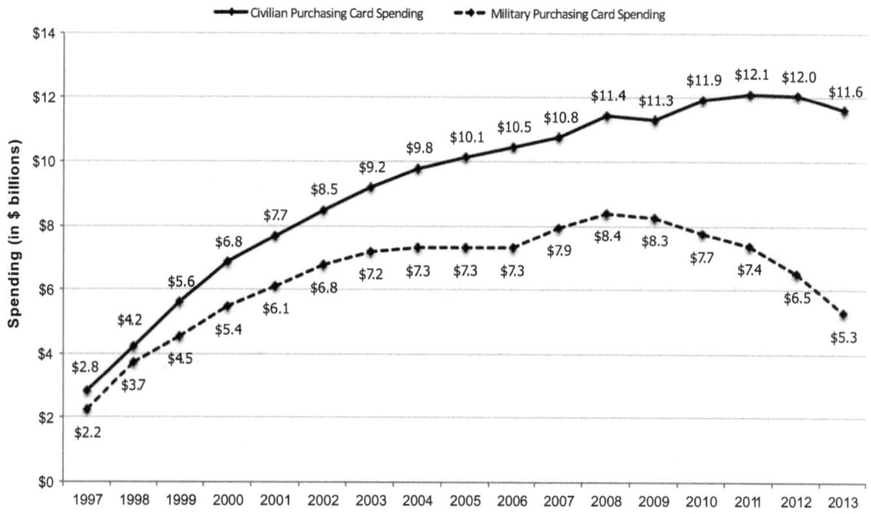

Fig. 11 Civilian versus military purchasing card spending, 2000–2013

between 2010 and 2013 ($ 2.4 billion) accounts for 86 % of the $ 2.8 billion drop in total US Government purchasing card spending (see Fig. 4) and 53 % of the $ 4.5 billion drop in total commercial card spending (see Fig. 1) in the 2010–2013 timeframe. Military spending as a percentage of total purchasing card spending has also slowly dropped from 47 % in 1998 to 42 % in 2009. Thereafter, annual military purchasing card spending as a percent of total purchasing card spending dropped more steeply, falling to 31 % in 2013.

Figure 12 presents purchasing card transaction activity in the 1997–2013 timeframe by military and civilian agencies. The figure shows that annual civilian purchasing card transactions increased from 6.3 million in 1997 to 16.1 million in 2004, remained relatively flat through 2008, dropped to 13.4 million in 2009, and

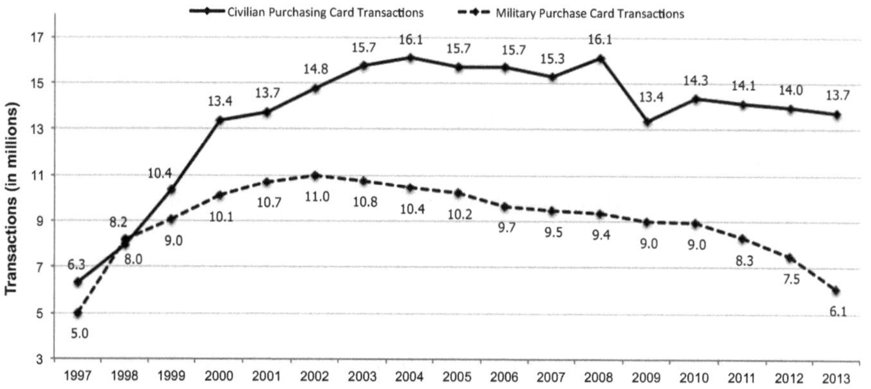

Fig. 12 Civilian versus military purchasing card transactions, 2000–2013

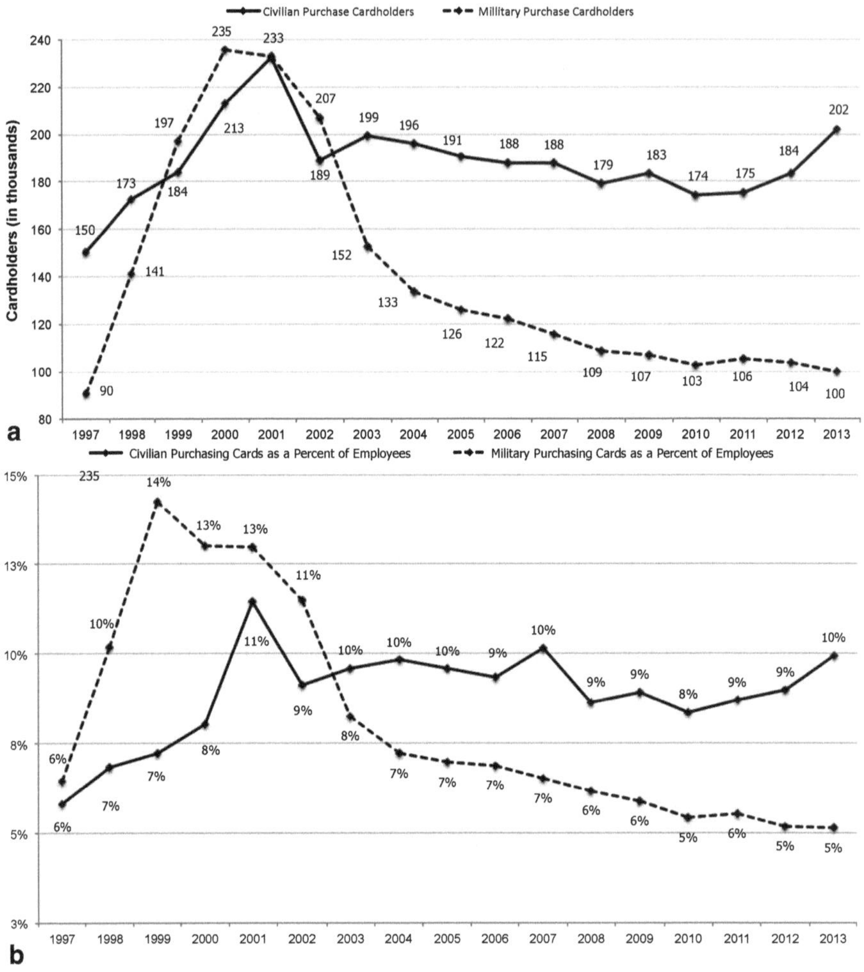

Fig. 13 **a** Civilian versus military number of purchasing cards, 2000–2013. **b** Civilian versus military purchasing cards as a percent of employees, 2000–2013

then rose again to 13.7 million by 2013. By contrast, annual military purchasing card transactions increased from 5.0 million in 1997 to 11.0 million in 2002, thereafter steadily decreasing to 6.1 million in 2013.

Purchasing Card Distribution Figure 13a presents the number of purchasing cardholders among civilian and military US Government agencies. The figure shows that the number of civilian purchasing cards rose from 150,000 to 233,000 in 2001, but fell sharply in 2002 to 189,000. After a brief uptick in 2003, the number of civilian purchasing cards generally fell between 2003 and 2010 (where it landed at 174,000). It has since risen back to 202,000 in 2013, 13.3 % off of its peak level in 2001. By contrast, the number of military purchasing cards rose dramatically from 90,000 in 1997 to 235,000 in 2000, followed thereafter by an equally dramatic decline to 133,000 cards 4 years later in 2004. From 2004 to 2013 the number of purchasing cards declined by another 33,000 cards to 100,000, 57% lower than its peak level in 2000.

Figure 13b shows the changes in the percentage of the civilian and military employees provided with purchasing cards between 1997 and 2013. Civilian cards started at 6% in 1997 and increased to the high point of 11% in 2001. Thereafter, the percentage of civilian employees given purchasing cards dropped to 9% by 2002 and has remained relatively constant since that time. The percentage of military personnel given purchasing cards, by contrast, started at 6% in 1997 and increased to the high point of 14% in 1999, and then dropped significantly to 7% by 2004. Since 2004, the percentage of military personnel given purchasing cards has gradually decreased to its 2013 level of 5%.

Purchasing Card Spending as a Percent of Budgeted Spending. Figure 14 presents civilian and military purchasing card spending as a percentage of their budget. The figure indicates that civilian purchasing card spending as a percent of their budget increased from 0.2% in 1997 to 0.5% in 2000 where it has remained relatively consistent, dropping to 0.4% in 2009 and staying at that level through 2013. By contrast, military purchasing card spending as a percentage of budget has changed dramatically, increasing from 0.9% in 1997 to the high point of 1.9% in 2001, thereafter falling every year (except 2007) to its 2013 level of 0.8%.

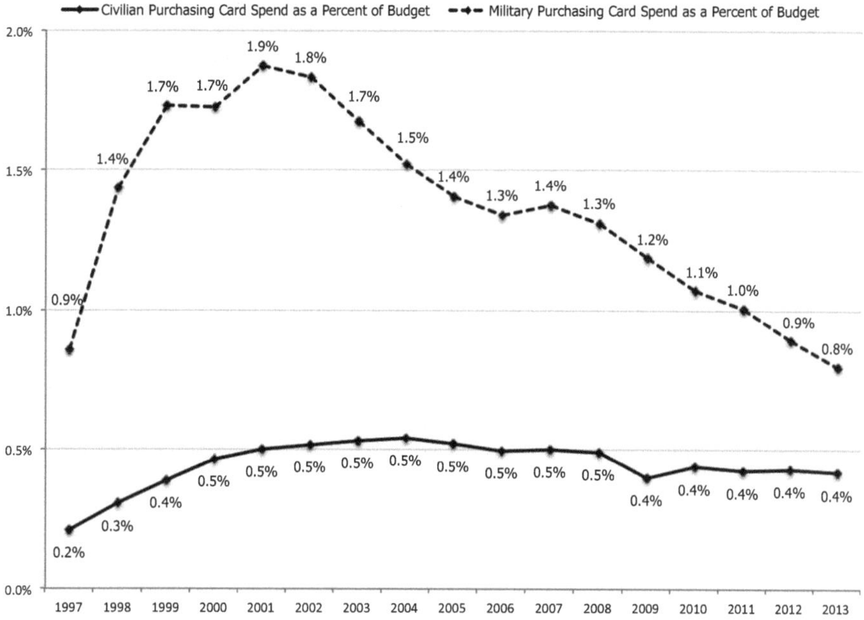

Fig. 14 Civilian versus military purchasing card spend as a percent of budget, 2000–2013

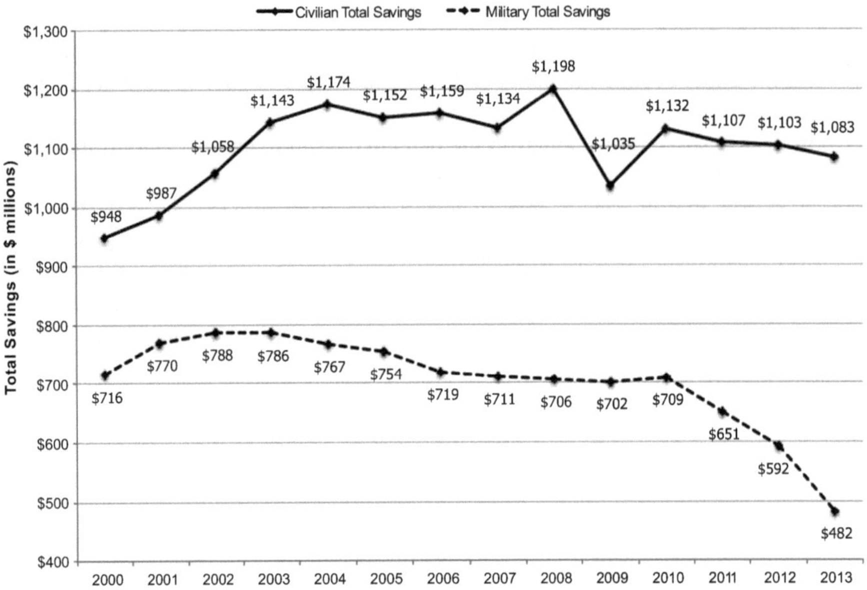

Fig. 15 Total military and civilian cost savings due to purchasing card use, 2000–2013

Cost Savings from Purchasing Card Use In a manner corresponding to spending, Fig. 15 shows the estimated total cost savings (including card issuer rebates and administrative cost savings) to the US Government by military and civilian agency use of the purchasing card.[5] The annual cost savings to civilian agencies increased from $ 948 million in 2000 to $ 1.2 billion in 2008, and has since dropped by 10 % (to $ 1.1 billion) in 2013. Annual cost savings attributable to military agency use of purchasing cards remained relatively flat between 2000 and 2010. Military cost savings attributable to purchasing card use peaked in 2002 (at $ 788 million), but have since dropped 39 % to its 2013 level of $ 482 million.

In Summary As shown in Table 1, the changes in purchasing card use by the military agencies has been declining steadily compared to trends experienced by civilian agencies over time, explaining how military purchasing card spending as a percentage of total US Government purchasing card spending has fallen from 47 % in 1998 to 31 % in 2013 (as shown in Fig. 11b). What would be more troubling to the US Government (in terms of cost savings) is if the pattern set by the military is now at the nascent stage of duplication among civilian agencies.

[5] Card issuer rebate data for analysis of cost savings over time is available only for 2000–2013.

Table 1 Summary of differences in military and civilian purchasing card statistics 1997–2013

	Military	Civilian
Annual purchasing card spending	Peaked in 2008 at $ 8.4 billion, *falling by 37 %* thereafter to $ 5.3 billion in 2013.	Peaked in 2011 at $ 12.1 billion, *falling by 4 %* thereafter to $ 11.6 billion in 2013.
Annual purchasing card transactions	Peaked in 2002 (at 11.0 million) and has since fallen steadily to 6.1 million in 2013 (*a 45 % decline* in transactions).	Peaked in 2008 (at 16.1 million) and has since fallen to 13.7 million in 2013 (*a 15 % decline* in transactions).
Number of cards	The number of purchasing cards given to Military employees has been *reduced by 57 %* since its high point in 2000, falling from 235,000 (14 % of employees) to 100,000 (5 % of employees) in 2013.	The number of purchasing cards given to Civilian agency employees has been *reduced by 13 %* since its high point in 2001, falling from 233,000 (11 % of employees) to 202,000 (10 % of employees) in 2013.
Purchasing card spending as a percent of budget	Rose to its high point in 2001 (1.9 %) and has since *dropped by more than half* to its 2013 level of 0.8 %.	Has *remained steady* between 0.4 % and 0.5 %.
Annual cost savings attributable to purchasing card use	Peaked in 2002 (at $ 788 million), but has since *dropped 39 %* to its 2013 level of $ 482 million.	Peaked in 2008 (at $ 1.2 billion), but has since *dropped 10 %* to its 2013 level of $ 1.1 billion

Understanding Changes in Military Purchasing Card Use: The Cost of Control and Program Transformation

This section seeks to explore potential explanatory factors for the changes in purchasing card spending, transactions, and cost savings by the military (and to a lesser extent, civilian) agencies of the US Government. To that end, we examine (a) alternative payment tools supplanting card use, (b) changes in military budgets, (c) the history of policy and legal changes that might affect card program structure or performance, and (d) the changes in card distribution patterns that might influence agency use of purchasing cards.

Alternative Payment Models

Differing methods of purchasing goods within the Military may explain the changing patterns of purchasing card use. For example, "Wide Area Workflow" (WAWF) is a secure web-based system for electronic submission and processing of receiving reports and invoices in order to support the Department of Defense's (DoD) goal of moving to paperless acquisition processes (Defense Logistics Agency 2013). WAWF provides the technology for government contractors and authorized DoD personnel to generate, capture, and process receipt and payment-related documentation. The 2009 Defense Authorization Act directed a plan to enable capture of acceptance data for items bought with a purchasing card by modifying the WAWF to enable receiving reports for card transactions (Public Law 110-417 2008). Because the system has not been previously compatible with purchasing cards, its ability to support purchasing card use could be or become a cause for a decrease in card use.

Another potential factor that could alter purchasing card is the Federal Strategic Sourcing Initiative (General Services Administration 2014). The GSA, through the FSSI, has been implementing strategic sourcing solutions for the government since 2005. The primary goals of FSSI are increase total cost savings, value, and socioeconomic participation by collaborating with agencies across the federal government to strategically source goods and services widely needed across federal agencies (office supplies, delivery services, print management, telecommunications services). Greater use of FSSI will result in more bulk purchases of items that were previously under the micro-purchase threshold and purchased with a purchasing card.

Changes in Military Activities and Funding

Military activities and readiness may have had an impact on purchasing card use in the timeframe under review. The war in Iraq began in March 2003 and ended in late 2011. The war in Afghanistan has been active since 2001 but is beginning a winding down process as of this writing.

In 2013, the Congress agreed to "sequester" discretionary spending levels. The sequester began in March 2013 and could have significantly influence the more recent decrease in purchasing card spending in the military (since defense is the largest component of discretionary spending by the US Government and is expected to absorb a 10% budget reduction). In 2014, the military is expected to absorb a $ 52 billion cut from its budget.

History of Policy Changes

A variety of audit findings, laws, and policy changes have influenced the growth of purchasing card spending since its initial use in 1982. We separate the chronology by military and civilian agencies into four time periods and discuss each time period below.

The Developmental Years

Palmer and Gupta (2007) summarized the developmental years of purchasing card use in the US Government. Briefly, the government's interest in purchase cards began in 1982 as a procurement reform initiative embodied in Executive Order 12,352

(Exec. Order No. 12,352 1982). The Executive Order called for federal government agencies to reduce administrative costs connected with procurement and that purchase cards be implemented to cut the cost of buying goods and services. Three years later, the Department of Commerce initiated a pilot program to test the use of a credit card program from the Office of Federal Procurement Policy (Poole and Welch 2002). The pilot program results indicated that purchasing cards were a more efficient way to buy goods and services that enabled end-users to acquire items directly from vendors instead of running the gauntlet of supporting procurement offices. The analysis of pilot program results indicated that instances of card abuse were negligible and, in some circumstances, purchase cards offered the potential to implement controls in areas where sufficient controls had not previously existed. As a consequence of the positive results of the pilot program, the GSA introduced a government-wide purchase card system in 1989.

Despite the potential for increased productivity, agencies resisted large scale use of purchasing cards in the early years (McHarg 2002). Purchasing card use got a boost in 1993 when the Clinton administration launched the National Partnership for Reinventing Government. As part of this initiative, Vice President Gore led a review which resulted in a report that recommended that all federal agencies increase the use of the purchase cards (Gore 1993).

Responding to the recommendation, the OD took the lead in advancing card use through a "pledge" program among members of the Procurement Executives Association (Poole and Welch 2002).[6] The Procurement Executives Association asked members to volunteer managers with the ability to authorize employees to buy small-dollar items directly and to double card spending over a one year period.[7] By September 1994, the Procurement Executives Association presented a report to the Director of the Office of Management and Budget (OMB), which read, in part: "by the end of the tenth month (after signing the pledge), [our agencies] had increased purchase card usage by 119 %, making 82,000 purchases per month worth almost $ 19,000,000 …. Since starting this project, the ten agencies have made 750,000 purchases faster, better and at less cost with the card. Plus, they report virtually no waste or abuse."[8]

1994–2000: Rapid Growth and Expansion

The pace of change in the use of purchase cards accelerated when Congress passed the Federal Acquisition Streamlining Act (FASA) of 1994 (FASA 1994). FASA encouraged the use of purchase cards by removing certain restrictions and shifting

[6] The Procurement Executives Association was a group of senior procurement executives from the US Departments of Commerce, Treasury, Interior, Health and Human Services, Transportation, Energy, State, and GSA.

[7] Later, other agencies, including the Office of Personnel Management (OPM), the Federal Emergency Management Agency (FEMA), the Drug Enforcement Agency (DEA), and the Federal Prison Industries, joined in the effort. An interagency work group, the Purchase Card Council, was chartered to lead the effort under the Treasury Department.

[8] Procurement Executives Association. 1994. *The Government Purchase Card.* Report to Alice Rivlin, Director, OMB. September, 2004.

micro-purchase (purchase transactions of less than $ 2,500 at that time) authority to personnel other than government procurement professionals. Specifically, FASA reduced restrictions that required purchases from small businesses when certain conditions and competition standards were met and raised the simplified acquisition threshold from $ 25,000 to $ 100,000. Thus, after FASA, micro-purchases could be awarded non-competitively (and acquired via purchase cards) if the item being purchased was a non-recurring purchase of a competitively priced off-the-shelf item.[9]As part of FASA implementation, an interim Federal Acquisition Regulation was issued in December 1994 (Federal Acquisition Circular 1994) that identified the purchase card as the *preferred* method for micro-purchases and enabled their use for payments above the $ 2,500 threshold.

An Executive Order (Executive Order 12,931 1994) issued late in 1994 further promoted the opportunities made available by FASA by instructing agencies to take maximum advantage of the new micro-purchase authority by delegating the authority, to the maximum extent practicable, to the offices that would be using the supplies or services to be purchased. The order focused partly on micro-purchases because these purchases account for the bulk of government transactions (but only a fraction of spending), do not require extensive procurement knowledge, and are often available for immediate delivery. The Executive Order also promoted spending by front-line employees, eliminating the need for contracting officials to be involved in purchases where their expertise was not required.

Military agencies were particularly supportive of purchasing card programs. In a 1997 memo to the military agencies, Under Secretary of Defense John Hamre stated that the Army Audit agency had found that, when compared to using purchase orders, the use of purchasing cards provided a savings of $ 92 per transaction (Hamre 1997). Further, Hamre stated that purchasing cards are "now considered by the Army organizations as the preferred method of obtaining goods and services valued at or less than $ 2,500." Within 2 years of the letter, military purchasing card spending doubled (going from $ 2.2 billion in 1997 to $ 4.5 billion in 1999. By the year 2000, Military agencies used 235,465 purchasing cards to pay for $ 5.4 billion of goods and services while civilian agencies used 212,705 purchasing cards to pay for $ 6.8 billion of goods and services.

2001–2002: Troubling Audit Findings Focus on Level of Card Distribution

A series of General Accounting Office (GAO) reports beginning in 2001 were to have a strong impact on the purchasing card program configuration and use for the next 12 years. In 2001, a GAO audit of the Navy card program (U.S. GAO 2001a) reported significant breakdowns of internal control over purchasing card use. These breakdowns included lack of:

[9] Notwithstanding the relaxation in procurement requirements, employees are required to "equitably distribute [purchases not greater than $ 2,500] among qualified suppliers (41 U.S.C. §428(d) (2004).

- Key policies regarding the issuance of purchase cards, establishing credit limits, and minimizing the federal government's financial exposure
- Employee training on card use policy
- Appropriate purchase documentation related to card purchases, and
- Internal review to ensure that internal controls were being effectively implemented

The weak control environment led to many cases of alleged fraud and abuse. The GAO connected many of these internal control issues to the high number of cards, recommending that the two Navy commands under review "establish specific policies and strategies governing *the number* of purchase cards to be issued with a focus on minimizing the number of cardholders" (p. 5, emphasis added) and that they "develop criteria for identifying employees eligible for the privilege of cardholder status" (p. 5).

Due to the concerns raised in the Navy audit, the scopes of a subsequent Army (U.S. GAO 2002a) and Air Force (U.S. GAO 2002b) audits in 2002 were expanded. The GAO audit of the Army found that the purchasing card program had significant benefits, but a weak overall control environment and breakdowns in key internal control activities left it vulnerable to fraud, improper use, and abuse. As with the earlier Navy audit, the GAO pointed to the level of card distribution as a causal factor, stating that the audit failures "…illustrate that the Army as a whole *may also need to reduce its active cards*" (p. 22, emphasis added) and that the Army "… can reduce the government's exposure to fraud, waste, and abuse by monitoring cardholder account activity and determining *whether issued cards continue to be required*" (p. 20, emphasis added).

The GAO audit of the Air Force held to the same pattern as the Navy and Army, with weaknesses in the control environment and breakdowns in key controls. Among its recommendations, the GAO also called on the Air Force to change its card distribution policy, specifically recommending that it:

- "establish specific policies and strategies governing *the number of purchase cards* to be issued with a focus on minimizing the number of cardholders" (p. 54, emphasis added)
- "direct all … agency program coordinators to review purchase card use with a view toward *eliminating unneeded purchase card accounts*" (p. 54, emphasis added)
- "eliminate purchase cards used to facilitate line item accounting" (p. 54)
- "deactivate purchase card accounts of alternate cardholders and approving officials when primary cardholders and approving officials are available" (p. 55), and
- "require cardholders and/or approving officials to reimburse the government for any unauthorized or erroneous purchase card transactions that were not disputed" (p. 55)

The GAO findings associated with military agencies engendered significant political criticism and drove the OMB to issue a memorandum in 2002 to executive branch agencies stating that card misuse identified by the GAO and inspectors general was unacceptable and required prompt remedial action if the purchase card programs were to continue (Office of Management and Budget 2002).[10] The memo requested that each agency review the adequacy of internal controls used to manage risk associated with purchase card programs, including an examination of the number of cards issued at each agency. The OMB recommended that agencies deactivate all purchase cards at that time and reactivate them selectively for a smaller number of cardholders.

Congress also responded legislatively to the unflattering audit outcomes of military agencies. The Bob Stump National Defense Authorization Act for FY 2003 (2002) required the DoD to take actions to improve the management of the purchase card program. Specifically, the Act required the DoD to limit the number of purchase cards, train purchase card officials, monitor purchase card activity, review purchase card activity to better aggregate purchases and obtain lower prices, establish guidelines and procedures to discipline cardholders who misused the purchase card, and assess the credit worthiness of cardholders. The 2003 DoD Appropriations Bill was more specific—requiring the DoD to limit the combined number of purchasing and travel cards to 1.5 million for FY 2003.

2003–2007: On-Going Evaluation of Purchasing Card Programs

The 2003–2007 timeframe was a period of on-going evaluation of purchasing cards. In this timeframe, the GAO engaged in two major initiatives. First, the GAO followed up on the military audits of 2001 and 2002. Second, they performed initial audits of purchasing card programs at the FAA (GAO 2003a), HUD (GAO 2003b), Forest Services (GAO 2003c), VHA (GAO 2004a), and the DHS (GAO 2006).

In December 2003, the GAO completed a review of the actions taken by the DoD to implement provisions included in the Bob Stump National Defense Authorization Act as well as evaluate the status of the response to recommendations and disciplinary actions taken against individuals identified in the prior GAO report (U.S. GAO 2003a). In this second audit review, the GAO reported that the DoD and the military services had taken strong actions to improve the controls over the purchase card program and had responded to nearly all of 109 recommendations made in its four reports on the purchase card program. The GAO noted that the DoD had issued

[10] The problems in military agencies were so acute that Senator Charles Grassley (R-Iowa) concluded that the Department of Defense's (DoD) purchase card program did little more than "create an army of spenders. With a DoD credit card in hand, they have almost unlimited authority to spend money. There are no controls, no responsibilities, and no accountability … Pentagon credit cards are being taken on a shopping spree, and taxpayers are footing the bill." Senator Grassley further asserted that charge cards had given the Pentagon a "short-cut to the cash pile" and that Pentagon leaders were "giving everyone a big scoop shovel and telling them to rip into the national money sack at both ends," found in *The Use and Abuse of Government Purchase Cards: Is Anyone Watching?: Hearing Before the H. Comm. on Gov't Reform, 107th Cong. 3 (2001) (statement of Sen. Grassley).*

key policy giving guidance to field activities to (a) perform periodic reviews of all purchase card accounts to reestablish a continuing bona fide need for each card account, (b) cancelled accounts that were no longer needed, and (c) devised additional controls over infrequently used accounts to protect the government from potential cardholder or outside fraudulent use. These policy, the GAO observed, resulted in a substantial reduction in the number of purchasing cards in military agencies—going from 233,000 in 2001 to 152,000 in 2003 (as shown in Fig. 13a).

Audits of civilian agencies by the GAO in the 2003–2007 timeframe resulted in many similar concerns over internal control but no recommendation to significantly change card distribution policies. As with military agencies, the GAO remarked on civilian agency purchases of a questionable nature, the proper accounting for asset acquisitions made with the purchasing card, split purchases, and lack of timely reconciliation by cardholders. Some GAO issues—non-closure of accounts, use of card by someone other than the authorized cardholder, inadequate segregation of duties, and disputed purchases not being tracked—occurred slightly more frequently in civilian agencies than in the military. Other issues—problems related to lack of training, excessive span of control, purchases made from "non-preferential" sources, allocation of inadequate resources to manage and monitor program, and improper purchases—were found slightly more frequently in military agencies. In spite of the similar results the between the civilian and military agencies, the GAO did not recommend that civilian agencies reduce the number of cards. Nevertheless, apparently taking their cue from earlier GAO recommendations to the military, the number of purchasing cards issued at civilian agencies did drop from 213,000 in 2000 to 196,000 in 2004, a decline far less precipitous than that undertaken by their military counterparts.

Going forward, the GAO declared its focus would turn to the establishment of procedures to enhance accountability for purchase card spending, including the monitoring the results of purchase card reviews conducted by the agencies, tracking whether agencies were consistently applying disciplinary guidelines to those who made and/or authorized improper or abusive acquisitions, and notifying the appropriate officials if disciplinary guidelines were not being consistently applied.

2008–2013: Tightening Control over Purchasing Cards

Given the range of findings over the preceding seven years, the GAO was asked to analyze government-wide purchasing card transactions in 2008 to determine whether internal control weaknesses existed in the government purchase card program and, if so, to identify examples of fraudulent, improper, and abusive activity (U.S GAO 2008). To examine these issues, the GAO extracted samples from two populations—one covering the population of purchasing card transactions over $ 50 from July 1, 2005 through June 30, 2006 (over 16 million transactions totaling almost $ 14 billion) and a second of about 600,000 purchase card acquisitions (totaling nearly $ 6 billion) over the micro-purchase threshold during the same time period.[11] From these two populations, two samples of 96 transactions each were extracted and examined for (a) proper authorization[12] and (2) independent receipt and acceptance.[13] Additionally, the GAO drew a non-representative sample of 550 transactions "data mined" from purchasing card activity from July 1, 2005 to September 30, 2006. The transactions were extracted because their profile matched that of a purchase of "highly pilferable" goods or services (e.g., the purchase was from a vendor or a vendor in a merchant category that offered goods or services found on restricted/prohibited lists, personal in nature, or of questionable government need).

In summarizing their analysis, the GAO recognized that purchasing cards could play a large part in adding to efficiency to government operations by reducing the amount administrative time required to process a purchase and increasing flexibility to meet a variety of government needs. If used properly purchasing cards can be a very effective tool to save time and money. However, since 2001 the GAO had found a number of agencies that demonstrated that when card programs are not properly controlled and managed, the use of purchasing cards results in fraud, waste, and abuse. Their 2008 analysis also showed that the government-wide purchasing card program overall internal control failure rate to be unacceptably high. An estimated 41 % of all transactions were not properly authorized, or had no evidence that the goods or services were received by an independent third party.[14] For purchases over the micro-purchase threshold ($ 2,500 at the time) an estimated 48 % of transactions did not have proper authorization or independent receipt and acceptance. It was also found that agencies could not provide evidence showing possession or otherwise account for a significant amount of pilferable items.[15]

---

[11] The second sample was selected because of additional requirements associated with purchases over the micro-purchase threshold and the higher dollar amount associated with these transactions. Specifically, while only 3 % of government-wide purchase card transactions from July 1, 2005 to June 30, 2006 were over the micro-purchase threshold, they accounted for 44 % of the dollars spent during that period.

[12] To determine if a transaction was properly authorized, the GAO review documentation to ascertain if an individual other than the cardholder was involved in the approval of the purchase. Such documentation might include (in the case of under $ 2,500 purchases) purchase requests from responsible officials, requisitions, e-mails, or other documents of government need. Transactions exceeding $ 2,500 required prior purchase authorization, such as a contract, a requisition, or other approval document. Additionally, the transaction had to comply with the Javits-Wagner-O'Day Act for sourcing.

[13] To determine whether goods were independently received and accepted, the GAO compared the quantity, price, and item descriptions on the vendor invoice and shipping receipt to the purchase requisition to verify that the items received and paid for were actually the items ordered. In addition, they sought evidence that a person other than the cardholder was involved in the receipt of the goods or services purchased. Independent receipt and acceptance existed if the vendor invoice, shipping documents, and receipt materially matched the transaction data, and if the signature or initial of someone other than the cardholder was on the sales invoice, packing slip, bill of lading, or any other shipping or receiving document indicating receipt.

[14] The GAO noted that the 41 % rate was actually a significant improvement of earlier audits from 2002 to 2006 (some of which had 85 % appropriate authorization failure rate and 60% independent receipt failure rate.

[15] Specifically, the results of the GAO analysis indicated that estimated 15 % of transactions did not have appropriate authorization and for 34 % of transaction independent receipt and acceptance

The GAO made thirteen recommendations to improve internal control over the government purchasing card program, and to strengthen monitoring and oversight of purchasing cards. Of these recommendations, three were clearly directed at purchasing card programs. First, the GAO recommended enhanced financial accountability from agency employees. Specifically, the GAO recommended that cardholders, approving officials, or both should reimburse the government for any unauthorized or erroneous purchase card transactions that were not disputed. Further, if and when an official directed a cardholder to purchase a person item for that official, and management later determines that the purchase was improper, the official who requested the item should reimburse the government for the cost of the improper item.

Second, to address the internal control failure rates, the GAO recommended that the GSA provide agencies guidance on how cardholders can document independent receipt and acceptance of items obtained with a purchase card. Specifically, the GAO called on the GSA to promulgate guidelines to encourage agencies to (a) identify a "de minimus" purchasing card purchase amount that would not be subject to internal control testing for independent receipt or acceptance and (b) indicate that the approving official or supervisor took the necessary steps to ensure that items purchased were actually received. In response to the recommendations, the GSA argued that it was not within the scope of its authority to issue guidance of this nature.

Third, the GAO recommended that the GSA provide agencies guidance regarding what should be considered sensitive and pilferable property. Pilferable property (i.e., iPods, digital cameras, computers) is easily converted to personal use and the GAO recommended that the GSA remind agencies that purchases of such nature should be subject to property accountability controls (e.g., tagging and logging equipment in the property records) and that property accountability officers promptly record sensitive and pilferable property that is obtained with a purchasing card.

The Military was an early adopter of GAO recommendations, attaching financial liability for purchasing card spending not only on to cardholder but also to departmental accountable officials and certifying officials. A memo from the department of the Under Secretary of Defense on November 7, 2008 stated that "a certifying officer is pecuniarily liable for illegal, improper, or incorrect payments resulting from improper certification" (Under Secretary of Defense 2008). The memo also stated that "accountable officials may be held pecuniarily liable for erroneous payments resulting from their fault or negligence…." Military agency implementation of enhanced accountability may have been a driving factor in the increased decline since 2009 of (a) purchasing card spending (Fig. 11a), (b) purchasing card spending as a

---

could not be verified. We believe that these failure rates to be misleading. Purchasing cards are generally used for low-dollar purchases where independent receipt is not feasible (an employee purchases a good at a hardware store while in the field) or economically irrational. We also disagree with the measurement of proper authorization. By its nature, when an agency provides an employee with a purchasing card it is "pre-approving" their purchases with that card. The technology of card will control much of their use of it (per transaction and monthly spending limits, restricted merchant category codes, etc.). If an employee must go through all the same steps to get approval from a supervisor it reduces the benefits to be derived and purpose of issuing the employee a card.

percentage of budgeted spending (Fig. 14), (c) the percentage of military personnel provided with purchasing cards (Fig. 13b), and (d) purchasing card cost savings as a percentage of budgeted spending (Fig. 15). Declines of this nature have not been experienced by civilian agencies.

In January 2009, the OMB drafted a memo in response to the recommendations made by the GAO. The OMB memo discussed four changes made to their Circular A-123 guidance, including (a) raising the micro-purchase threshold to $ 3000, (b) expanding descriptions for erroneous and improper purchases and the practices for minimizing such purchases, and (c) adding a requirement for charge cardholders, approving officials, or both to reimburse the government for any unauthorized transactions or erroneous purchase card transactions that were not disputed, and (d) guidance on disciplinary actions for fraud and other abuse of a government charge card.

GAO recommendations with respect to employee financial accountability (and the recovering costs for erroneous or improper purchases) on purchases cards found their way into Congressional discussions and became law in October 2012 when President Obama signed the Government Charge Card Abuse Prevention Act (Public Law 112-94 2011). The Act, which is consistent with the existing guidance in OMB Circular No. A-123 (OMB 2014), addresses the requirement of recovering costs for erroneous or improper purchases on purchasing cards.[16] Since the Act became law, Fig. 16 shows that purchasing card spending by civilian agencies has shrunk by similar increments as experienced by military agencies when they began implementing their enhanced accountability in 2009.

Despite the heightened sensitivity to control issues and the criticisms of overly liberal distribution of purchasing cards, some governmental reports have strongly

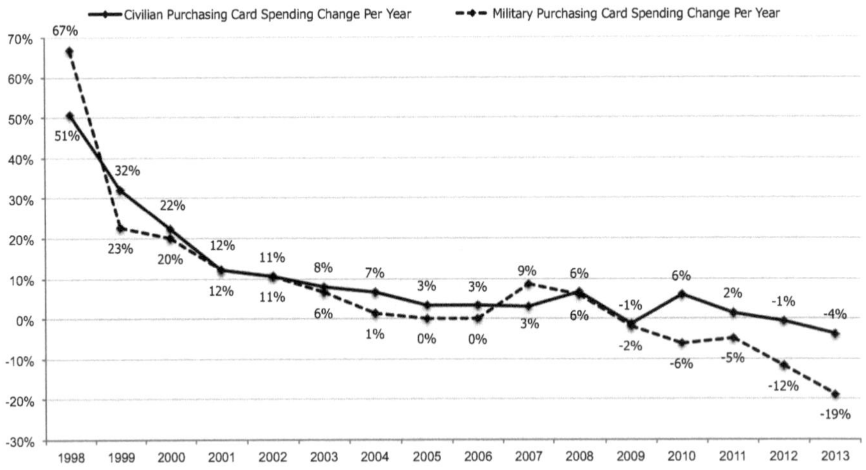

Fig. 16 Military and civilian annual increase in purchasing card spending, 2000–2013

---

[16] Such requirements relating to employee misuse of government travel cards have already been established.

supported expanded purchasing card use. In 2004, the GAO (U.S. GAO 2004b) remarked on how agencies generally did not take advantage of opportunities to obtain more favorable prices on purchase card buys with frequently used vendors and that "automating" the discounts through card technology could save hundreds of millions of dollars. In 2013, the VA Office of the Inspector General (2013) issued a report that chided the VHA for its failure to use maximize purchasing card use and "…miss[ing] opportunities to decrease procurement processing costs by about $ 20 million and obtain additional rebates of about $ 4 million" (p. 2).

Decentralized to Centralized "Transformation Failure"

As shown in Fig. 17, three key performance measures form the framework necessary to understand government purchasing card spending. They are the number of active cards, card transaction activity, and average transaction (or "ticket") size. The multiplication of these elements yields monthly purchasing card spending and provides insight into card program performance. The framework illustrates how agencies can make trade-offs to improve their purchasing card program. The key performance measures are derived from intermediate calculations which, in turn, are composed of basic organizational data. For example, the number of active cards

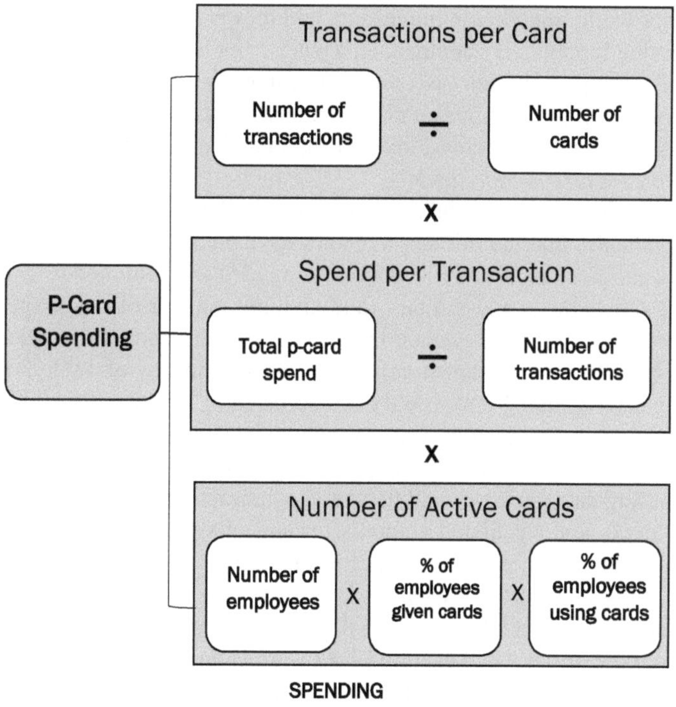

Fig. 17 A Framework for understanding purchasing card

in an organization is a function of the number of employees, the percent of employees given a purchasing card, and of those employees given a purchasing card, the percent that use the card to acquire goods or services. Thus, increases in the raw number of active cards can be accomplished by either giving a larger percentage of employees a purchasing card or by taking measures to insure that employees actually use the purchasing cards already in their possession. Similarly, the number of transactions per card and the average transaction amount can be influenced by restrictions on the types of goods and services that may be purchased, the vendor from whom goods and services may be purchased, and the transaction dollar amount of a purchase.

Spending

The framework provides insight into why successful agency purchasing card programs may differ in their approach to card program management. Because the key performance measures are multiplicative, agencies make trade-offs to achieve their purchasing card spending goals. For example, an organization can have a relatively large base of cardholders who individually engage in a modest number of transactions. Collectively, this can add up to a high dollar value of organizational spending. We call this the *decentralized card distribution* model. This model maximizes the potential for work reduction in purchasing and moves low dollar purchasing out of the purchasing function. By contrast, an agency can give cards to a relatively small number of employees. In this case, the agency may distribute fewer cards, but each card is associated with a high number of transactions and/or high average ticket amounts that ultimately increase overall organizational spending. We call this a *centralized card distribution* model.

Though in theory both models can generate similar card program spending, the evidence indicates that the military agencies have not made an effective transition from a decentralized to a centralized purchasing card program model. The first row of Table 2 shows the actual military (and civilian) number of cards, spending per card, transactions per card, average transaction amount, and total purchasing card spending in 2001. The rightmost column of the second row of Table 2 shows the purchasing card spending that would have occurred in 2013 had the military (civilian) agencies spent at the 2001 level of purchasing card spending as a percent of agency budget. The second row also presents the actual number of military (civilian) purchasing cards in 2013, a 2001 average transaction amount (CPI-adjusted to the 2013 level), and calculated amounts for annual spending per purchasing card and the annual number of purchasing card transactions per card.

Table 2 shows that military agencies have conceded cost savings by failing to direct the same level of spending to a shrinking number of purchasing cards. The table shows that if the military had captured 1.87 % of its budget on purchasing cards (as it had in 2001), then 2013 purchasing card spending would have been $ 11.5 billion instead of the $ 5.3 billion it actually spent on purchasing cards (a $ 6.2 billion trans-

Table 2 Projected versus actual military and civilian purchasing card spending based on 2001 purchasing card spending as a percent of budget and 2013 actual purchasing card distribution

	Number of cards	Spend per card ($)	Transaction per card	Average transaction ($)	Total spend (in $ millions)
Military Agencies					
2001 actual	232,928	26,230	46	570	6110
2013 projection based on 2001 P-card spending as a percent of budget, the 2013 actual number of P-cards, and a CPI-adjusted average transaction amount[a]	99,754	115,193	153	752	11,491
2013 actual	99,754	52,930	61	866	5280
Military transformation failure		(62,263)	(92)	113	(6211)
Civilian agencies					
2001 actual	232,505	33,023	59	559	7678
2013 projection based on 2001 P-card spending as a percent of budget, the 2013 actual number of P-cards, and a CPI-adjusted average transaction amount[b]	202,172	68,914	94	737	13,932
2013 actual	202,172	57,369	68	844	11,598
Civilian transformation failure		(11,545)	(26)	106	(2334)

[a] Projection is of military spending is calculated based on a 1.87 % of the budget as was the case in 2001. The number of cards is based on total actual cardholders in 2013. Average transaction is based on 2001 figure adjusted for changes in the Consumer Price Index (CPI)

[b] Projection is of civilian spending is calculated based on a 0.50 % of the budget as was the case in 2001. The number of cards is based on total actual cardholders in 2013. Average transaction is based on 2001 figure adjusted for changes in the CPI

formation failure). If the military had shrunk the number of cards but maintained its 2001 level of spending, it would have spent (on average) $ 115,193 per year on each card instead of the $ 52,930 per card it actually experienced in 2013. Further, if the military had shrunk the number of cards but maintained its 2001 level of spending, it would have conducted (on average) 153.1 transactions per year on each card instead of the 61.1 annual transactions per card actually experienced in 2013. These differences are offset by a modestly higher average transaction amount, to wit: a CPI-adjusted average transaction amount in 2013 would be $ 752.28, but military agencies actually report a higher average transaction amount in 2013 ($ 865.60), indicating that the reduction in cards is pushing up the amount of goods purchased when the cards are used.

Civilian agencies, by contrast, have maintained more of their cost savings despite changes in their level of purchasing card distribution. Table 2 shows that if the civilian agencies had captured 0.5 % of their budget on purchasing cards (as they had in 2001), then 2013 purchasing card spending would have been $ 13.9 billion instead of the $ 11.6 billion actually spent on purchasing cards (a $ 2.3 billion difference). If the civilian agencies had shrunk the number of cards but maintained their 2001 level of spending, it would have spent (on average) $ 68,914 per year on each card instead of the $ 57,369 per card it actually experienced in 2013. Further, if the civilian agencies had shrunk the number of cards but maintained their 2001 level of spending, it would have conducted (on average) 93.5 transactions per year on each card instead of the 68 annual transactions per card actually experienced in 2013. As with the military, civilian agencies report a 2013 average transaction amount ($ 844.02) that is higher than a CPI-adjusted average transaction amount of $ 737.32, indicating that the reduction in the number of cards is pushing up the amount of goods purchased when cards are used.

In sum, Table 2 indicates that military agencies have had less success at maintaining purchasing card spending in light of reductions in the number of cards than their civilian counterparts. For the military to generate the same purchasing card spending as a percent of their budget as in 2001, their 2013 cardholders would need to more than double their current annual spending (going from the current $ 52,930 to over $ 115,000). By contrast, for civilian agencies to generate the same purchasing card spending as a percent of budget as in 2001, their 2013 cardholders would only need to increase their current annual spending by only 20 % (going from $ 57,369 to 68,914).

Conclusion

The US Government and its agencies acknowledge significant administrative cost savings and cash rebates based on its spending on commercial cards. However, since 2008, commercial card spending (both in dollars and as a percentage of budgeted spending) has been lower than the 2008 level and dropped sharply in 2012 and 2013. An analysis of the US Government commercial card spending indicates that the changing patterns of purchasing card spending are primarily responsible for the overall decline in commercial card spending.

The US Government spending on purchasing cards reached its zenith in 2008 (at $ 19.8 billion) and has declined to $ 16.9 billion in 2013. The highest number of annual purchasing card transactions (26.5 million) harks back to 2004, 6.7 million more than the 19.8 million transactions paid with purchasing cards in 2013. The number of purchasing card distributed throughout the US Government agencies has fallen from 465,000 in 2001 to 302,000 in 2013.

An examination separating military and civilian agency purchasing card use provides some insight into the changing patterns of purchasing card use across the US Government agencies. Our analysis shows that civilian purchasing card spending increased from $ 2.8 billion in 1997 to $ 12.1 billion in 2011, but dropped by 4% ($ 0.5 billion) to $ 11.6 billion in 2013. By contrast, military purchasing card spending increased from $ 2.2 billion in 1997 to the high point of $ 8.4 billion in 2008, but has since decreased by 37% ($ 3.1 billion) to $ 5.3 billion in 2013. In fact, the military reduction in purchasing card spending between 2010 and 2013 ($ 2.4 billion) accounts for 86% of the $ 2.8 billion drop in total US Government purchasing card spending and 53% of the $ 4.5 billion drop in total commercial card spending in the 2010–2013 timeframe. Military agency transactions with purchasing cards have fallen steadily from a zenith of 11 million in 2002 to 6.1 million in 2013. Card distribution in the military has been cut by more than half since 2001.

A historical analysis of governmental card use indicates that several factors may have influenced the trends revealed in the record of military purchasing card spending. First, military purchasing card programs grew rapidly in the early years with the support of top leadership. By 2001, military agencies had distributed purchasing cards to 13% of their employee base and paid for 1.9% of their budgeted purchases with the purchasing card, figures that far outpaced their civilian counterparts (11%, 0.5%). GAO audit recommendations in 2001 to the Navy and in 2002 to the Army and Air Force to reduce the number of purchasing cards had a notably negative short and long-term impact on the military purchasing card program. Military spending as a percent of budget fell from 1.9% in 2001 to 1.4% in 2005 where it leveled off through 2008. In short, the military was not able to transform its successful decentralized purchasing card model to a more centralized edition—as the number of purchasing cards fell, the use of the remaining cards did not expand to support previous levels of spending

A second wave of decline occurred in 2009 when the military heightened financial accountability for purchasing card spending. Within the new control structure, officers may be held financially liable for illegal, improper or incorrect payments resulting from their improper certification of subordinate cardholder spending. One can argue that this control is not overly onerous. However, being held financially liable for a poor review of cardholder spending may not be viewed positively by certifying officers who may now discourage card use. What is certain is that purchasing card spending and transactions have dropped significantly between 2008 and 2013 (spending falling by $ 3.1 billion and transactions by 3.3 million).

Civilian agencies, which got off to a slower start with purchasing cards, have trod a less volatile path and were not subject to a GAO recommendation that they use fewer purchasing cards (though the GAO seemed to identify about the same degree of internal control issues within civilian agencies as found in their military counterparts). Civilian agency purchasing card spending has grown at a steady pace and its recent downturn (from $ 12.1 billion in 2011 to $ 11.6 billion in 2013) has been far less dramatic than that experience among military agency counterparts (which fell from $ 7.4 billion to $ 5.3 billion in the same time period). However, civilian agencies may be soon be affected by the enhanced financial accountability of certifying officers due to recent changes in legislation.

In conclusion, the analysis of the US Government purchasing card spending shows that the government needs to push its agencies to evaluate cost-benefit trade-offs and resolve control concerns to move forward. The GAO has identified the GSA as the appropriate promulgator of "purchasing card program management" directives, a role the GSA does not accept. Leadership is needed among the agencies to sort through and resolve the issues of accountability, control, and structure lest the taxpayer be asked to endure more unnecessary costs.

References

Bob Stump National Defense Authorization Act for Fiscal Year 2003, Pub. L. No. 107-314, § 1007, 116 Stat. 2623, 2633–34 (2002).

Cohen, W. H. (1998). *Annual Report to the President and Congress 1998*. Washington, DC: Secretary of Defense.

Defense Logistics Agency. (2013). Wide-Area Workflow. [Online]. www.dla.mil/wideareaworkflow/pages/default.aspx. Accessed 12 Jan 2014.

Exec. Order No. 12, 352. (1982). 47 Fed. Reg. 12,125 (Mar. 17), Section 1(a).

Executive Order No. 12, 931. (1994). 59 Fed. Reg. 52,387 (Oct. 17).

Federal Acquisition Streamlining Act of 1994. (1994). Pub. L. No 103-355, § 4301; 41 U.S.C. § 428.

Federal Acquisition Circular. (1994) 90-24, 59 Fed. Reg. 64,786 (Dec. 15, 1994).

Federal Reserve Bank of Philadelphia. (2011). Government use of payment card system: Issuance, acceptance, regulation. Payment Cards Center Conference Summary (July 11-12). [Online]. http://www.philadelphiafed.org/consumer-credit-and-payments/payment-cards-center/publications/conference-summaries/2012/C-2012-Government-Use-of-the-Payment-Card-System.pdf. Accessed 13 Feb 2015.

General Services Administration. (2013a). "Benefits." [Online]. https://smartpay.gsa.gov/program-coordinators/card-basics/benefits. Accessed 1 Sept 2013.

General Services Administration. (2013b). U.S. Government purchasing card spending statistics. [Online]. http://smartpay.gsa.gov/about-gsa-smartpay/program-statistics. Accessed 1 Sept 2013.

General Services Administration. (2014). Federal Strategic Sourcing Initiative. [Online]. http://www.gsa.gov/portal/content/112561. Accessed 1 Sept 2013.

Gore, A. (1993). *From red tape to results: Creating a government that works better and costs less* (Report of the National Performance Review). [Online]. http://govinfo.library.unt.edu/npr/library/review.html#system_reports. Accessed 1 Sept 2013.

Hamre, J. (1997). *Purchasing card reengineering implementation memorandum #4: Use of international merchant purchase authorization card for transactions with the defense automated printing service*. Washington, DC: Department of Defense.

McHarg, J. P. (2002). Note, doing more with less-continued expansion of the Government purchase card program by increasing the micro-purchase threshold: a response to recent articles criticizing the Government purchasing card program. *Public Contract Law Journal, 31*, 293–312.

McHugh, N. (2011). What is driving commercial purchasing card growth. *Journal of Corporate Treasury Management, 4*(3), 259–271.

Office of Management and Budget. (2002, April 18). Memorandum for the heads of departments and agencies: Use of Government purchase and travel cards (M-02-05). Washington, DC: Office of Management and Budget.

Office of Management and Budget. (2014). OMB Circular A-123-Management's responsibility for internal control. [Online]. www.whitehouse.gov/omb/circulars_a123_rev. Accessed 3 Jan 2014.

Palmer, R. & Gupta, M. (2007). A brief history and review of purchasing card use by the U.S. Government: 1990–2005. *Journal of Public Procurement, 8*(2), 174–199

Palmer, R., Gupta, M., & Dawson, R. (2010). U.S. Government use of commercial card technology and the case for change in Military card distribution policy. *Defense Acquisition Review Journal, 17*(3), 313–336.

Poole, C. & Welch, B. (2002, June). Purchase card: Best practices for a best in class program. Chantilly: Acquisitions Solutions, Inc. [Online]. www.wifcon.com/analwelch604.pdf.

Public Law 110-417. (2008, October 14). *Duncan Hunter National Defense Authorization Act for Fiscal Year 2009.*

Public Law 112-94. (2011, February 8). *Government charge card abuse prevention act.*

Under Secretary of Defense. (2008, November 7). Memorandum: Government Purchase Card Officer (GPC) certifying officer and departmental accountable official responsibilities. Washington, DC: Department of Defense.

U.S. General Accounting Office. (1996). *Report to congressional committees. Acquisition reform: Purchase card use cuts procurement costs, improves efficiency (GAO/NSIAD-96-138).* Washington, DC: U.S. General Accounting Office.

U.S. General Accounting Office. (30 Nov 2001a). *Purchase cards: Control weaknesses leave two navy units vulnerable to fraud and abuse (GAO-02-32).* Washington, DC: U.S. General Accounting Office.

U.S. General Accounting Office. (27 June 2002a). *Purchase cards: Control weaknesses leave army vulnerable to fraud, waste, and abuse (GAO-02-732).* Washington, DC: U.S. General Accounting Office.

U.S. General Accounting Office. (20 Dec 2002b). *Purchase cards: Control weaknesses leave the air force vulnerable to fraud, waste, and abuse (GAO-03-292).* Washington, DC: U.S. General Accounting Office.

U.S. General Accounting Office. (2 Dec 2003a). *Purchase cards: Steps taken to improve DoD program management, but actions needed to address misuse (GAO-04-156).* Washington, DC: Author.

U.S. General Accounting Office. (11 Aug 2003b). *Forest service purchase cards: Internal control weaknesses resulted in instances of improper, wasteful, and questionable purchases (GAO-03-786).* Washington, DC: U.S. General Accounting Office.

U.S. General Accounting Office. (11 April 2003c). *HUD Purchase cards: Poor internal controls resulted in improper and questionable purchases (GAO-03-489).* Washington, DC: U.S. General Accounting Office.

U.S. General Accounting Office. (7 June 2004a). *VHA Purchase cards: Internal controls over the purchase card program need improvement (GAO-04-737).* Washington, DC: U.S. General Accounting Office.

U.S. General Accounting Office. (28 April 2004b). *Purchasing card: Increased management oversight and controls could save hundreds of millions of dollars (GAO-04-717T).* Washington, DC: U.S. General Accounting Office.

U.S. General Accounting Office. (26 Sept 2006). *Purchase cards: Control weaknesses leave DHS highly vulnerable to fraudulent, improper, and abusive activity (GAO-06-1117).* Washington, DC: U.S. General Accounting Office.

U.S. General Accounting Office. (March 2008). *Governmentwide purchase cards: Actions needed to strengthen internal controls to reduce fraudulent, improper, and abusive purchases (GAO-08-333).* Washington, DC: U.S. General Accounting Office.

VA Office of the Inspector General. (9 Aug 2013). *Audit of non-purchase card micro-purchases (12-1860-237).* Washington, DC: VA Office of the Inspector General.

Richard Palmer PhD Copper Dome Faculty Research Fellow and professor of accounting, Harrison College of Business, Southeast Missouri State University. His research interests are e-procurement and commercial card applications in business as well as cost management systems.

Mahendra Gupta PhD is Geraldine J. and Robert L. Virgil professor of accounting and management, Olin School of Business, Washington University in St. Louis. His research interests are in strategic cost management, benchmarking, and performance measurement.

Nathan Palmer MAcc is a senior research associate at RPMG Research Corporation focused on card technology.

Defense Management Research Capacities and Topics: Blind Spots in Defense Acquisition Management?

Christian von Deimling, Andreas H. Glas and Michael Essig

Setting the Frame: An Introduction to European Defense

The financial crisis has put a strain on defense budgets worldwide and in particular across the 28 European Union (EU) member states. As public debts are likely to remain high, further cost-cutting measures are to be introduced in many EU member states to cope with the ongoing financial pressure (Mölling et al. 2014). Cost-cutting measures seem to be appropriate in peacetime because the military must be cost efficient, but modern forces should be prepared for an unexpected crisis and mobilization, in which cost performance and cost effectiveness are all that matters (Juntunen et al. 2012). The need to efficiently and effectively allocate resources implies the importance of economic considerations in the field of defense management.

There remain significant gaps in the literature's coverage of defense economics (Hartley 2007). Given the paucity of academic research into the general area of defense management, there obviously is considerable potential for focused research and application of ideas and concepts (Taylor and Tatham 2008). One focus could be defense acquisition, because costs to acquire new equipment or to maintain older systems have risen by up to 7.5–10% per annum in real terms, thus resulting in a doubling in unit costs between successive generations of equipment every decade (Hartley 2007). Even worse, a study in the UK reveals that the 25 largest defense equipment projects not only exceeded their forecast costs but also entered service an average of 3 years late, even then struggling to deliver their agreed-upon capabilities (Taylor 2003). Overall, it seems that the field of defense acquisition still has

C. von Deimling (✉) · A. H. Glas · M. Essig
Bundeswehr University Munich, Neubiberg (Munich), Bavaria, Germany
e-mail: c.von.deimling@unibw.de

A. H. Glas
e-mail: andreas.glas@unibw.de

M. Essig
e-mail: michael.essig@unibw.de

K. V. Thai (ed.), *International Public Procurement,* Public Administration, Governance and Globalization 14, DOI 10.1007/978-3-319-13434-5_5

economic potential, although there seem to be many open questions and areas in need of improvement.

The theoretical analysis of defense acquisition is very difficult because it is not a purely economic issue; instead, it is a mixture of economic, political, strategic, psychological, cultural, and moral issues (Dunne and Nikolaidou 2012). One aspect of this discussion is the initial purchase cost of a military system, which is only a fraction of the total cost of operating or maintaining it throughout its life. The figures can be particularly startling for defense equipment because such equipment typically has a long service life: 25 years is not uncommon (MoD 2001). Thus, politically influenced acquisition decisions might have severe cost impacts. Another aspect of the discussion centers on approaches that might improve the efficiency of defense acquisition, e.g., multinational programs and their prospects of generating economies of scale by pooling national demands and requirements. National acquisition officials fear the risk of high coordination costs and that program management complexity and problems will increase in a nonlinear fashion as the number of partner countries increases (James 2012).

The aspects mentioned above show that a managerial perspective on defense is necessary. Discussion about defense management is anything but new. In the German literature, "Militärökonomie" developed early in the nineteenth century (e.g., Hübler 1823). Today, numerous scientific journals and media conduct defense research, e.g., the journal "Defense and Peace Economics." Moreover, numerous research institutes and competence centers conduct defense research: examples include the "European Union Institute for Security Studies" in Belgium and the "Centre for Defence Studies" in the UK. Relatively contemporary developments have resulted in research that is more focused on defense acquisition issues in terms of specialized journals, such as the International Journal of Defense Acquisition Management (IJDAM, first issue in 2008), and focused research centers, such as the "Centre for Defence Acquisition" in the UK.

Together with the above mentioned developments, it appears that numerous research institutions focus on relatively diverse aspects of defense management, addressing key topics that include politics, security issues, military strategies, military analytics, industry lobbying, and defense acquisition. Therefore, this paper addresses the following research questions:

1. What is the institutional status quo of defense management research?
2. Which defense acquisition topics are addressed by that research?

The remainder of the paper follows the sequence proposed by Denyer and Tranfield (2009). The section on the analytical framework provides a brief overview on how the framework was developed and of the final framework, which is later on employed for the purpose of aggregation and explanation. The methodology section provides precise details about how the review was conducted, including its search and data extraction strategy, its selection criteria and its criteria for analysis and synthesis. The findings and discussion section contains a summary of all of the data extracted from the Web search and describes the nature of the data extracted from the sample. The section on the findings and discussion also specifies which topic the examined research organizations cover and which topics need further exploration. The limitations section elaborates on the study's restrictions and provides recommendations for further research needs and improvements. The conclusion section provides a summary of this review (Denyer and Tranfield 2009).

Analytical Framework

This research investigates research capacities and topics in the field of defense management and defense acquisition. To capture the variety of topics and to expose under- or unexplored issues in defense management and defense acquisition in contemporary research organizations, we developed the framework set forth below. To adhere to the design criteria suggested by Holsti (1969), the framework is configured in such a way that all major subject areas can be detected. It is derived from a theory-led perspective with brief insights into the corresponding literature. The topics are distinguished from each other to avoid an overlap of categories. The categories also must be evaluated independently of each other (Glock and Hochrein 2011). The analytical framework is used at a later point to aggregate and explain the collected data on research organizations.

A Brief Overview of the Theoretical Foundation in Public Management and Governance Theory

The starting point for the systematic analysis of "defense management" and "defense acquisition" is a brief overview of the theoretical framework proposed by Lynn et al. (2000) for the governance and management of public-sector entities. By considering the question of how public-sector regimes, agencies, programs, and activities can be organized and managed to achieve public purposes, they develop a unifying framework. In this unifying framework, public management is embedded into the context of governance theory. Whereas public management summarizes the discretionary actions, activities, and decisions of actors in managerial roles subject to formal authority, governance theory describes the formal and informal structures that predispose these actions, activities and decisions (Lynn et al. 2000). Both of the interacting elements—public management and governance—affect the outcome and performance of a public-sector entity (Lynn et al. 2000; Pilbeam et al. 2012). Lynn et al. (2000) summarize their findings in broad categories of a reduced-form model of governance and public management. According to that framework, a specific, targeted output (results and performance) is a function of the other categories, namely "environmental factors (contextual factors)," "client characteristics (stakeholder characteristics)," "treatments (processes, interventions and decisions)," "structures (formal and informal structures)," and "managerial roles and monitoring and controlling actions" (Lynn et al. 2000). For each of the general categories,

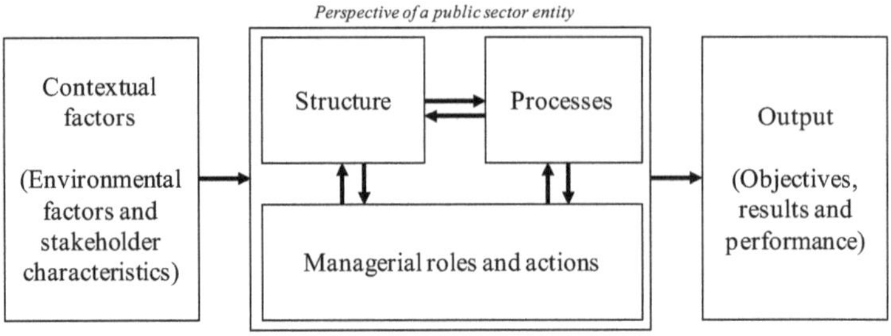

Fig. 1 Public management and governance framework (Sources: Lynn et al. 2000; Pilbeam et al. 2012)

they provide a list of subcategories and characteristics. These subcategories are not further elaborated here, but they are discussed below during the application of the framework to the fields of defense management and defense acquisition. The framework proposed by Lynn et al. (2000) is summarized in Fig. 1.

Seen from a general perspective, the identified broad categories in the reduced-form model are included a priori in any particular logic, model, or theory of governance or public management (Lynn et al. 2000). The value of this type of model lies in its strength in providing a broader context for empirical analyses when drawing conclusions from collected (and most often incomplete) data and information.

In the context of this contribution, the framework has been selected because it provides a "toolbox" for research in the field of public management and governance (Lynn et al. 2000). Its findings can be easily transferred to the defense sector and its management challenges. Another reason for selecting this framework is its compelling structure, in which researchers can locate particular theories and managerial themes and describe their dependencies. As a starting point, it helps to conceptualize the research, and additional categories might be introduced gradually into the initial model at a later point in the research process (Denyer and Tranfield 2009; Lynn et al. 2000).

Explaining Defense Management and Defense Acquisition

Building on the generic framework provided by Lynn et al. (2000), the topics "defense management" and in particular, "defense acquisition," are examined. The objective of this examination is to provide general insights into both themes from a managerial perspective. In a subsequent step, research organizations and corresponding areas of research are explored.

The term "defense management" is not uniformly discussed and defined in the literature (Barber 2013; Bucur-Marcu et al. 2009). From an institutional point of view, defense management is situated between defense policy formulation (politics) and actual command and control of operational military forces (Tagarev 2009). Thus, responsibility for defense management in the wider sense lies with the civilian and military managers in the defense department (Bucur-Marcu 2009). Typically, the defense department runs several different defense agencies. Defense agencies usually conduct business such as operations and processes to supply or service activities that are common to more than one military branch or department. Thus, in the narrow sense, defense management is performed by various defense agencies. Although most defense agencies operate on a national basis, there are also international defense agencies. The European Defense Agency (EDA) is just one example of a management entity tasked to manage common defense acquisition activities on a multinational scale. The underlying idea of modern defense management, however, is its ability to achieve desired goals and objectives in an efficient and effective manner (Ratchev 2009).

A more detailed view on defense management reveals that managers' overarching objective in defense management is to effectively and efficiently implement national and international security and defense policy goals (Barber 2013; Bucur-Marcu et al.2009). These policy goals and objectives are often generically described and contain goals such as contributing armed forces to national security during peacetime and achieving world peace and security, including securing allies and friends or participating in national defense (Tagarev 2009). To make defense objectives more tangible and measurable, a certain level of ambition is set or introduced (van Eekelen 2009). The description of the level of ambition provides a specific formulation of governmental expectations of the different roles to be fulfilled by the armed forces. These descriptions contain for example, an overview of operations that the armed forces should be able to carry out on its own (together with other militaries or security-sector organizations), its quality of personnel and its technological level (Tagarev 2009). Thus, defense managers are tasked with implementing those objectives at the set of level of ambition. Therefore, they configure, obtain, and maintain required civilian and military capabilities, structures, and processes.

In pursuing and implementing security and defense policy objectives, actors in the field of defense management are influenced and driven by exogenous and endogenous contextual factors (Georgiev 2010). Following Lynn et al.'s (2000) proposal in a general public management context, exogenous contextual factors contain influences from international binding agreements and policies, from national political structures and monitoring authorities, from the performance of the economy and corresponding funding constraints or dependencies, from market structure and the degree of competition, from readily available technology and from technological dynamism (Lynn et al. 2000; Tagarev 2009). In a defense management environment, additional external factors such as uncertainties, hazards and risks (Pilbeam et al. 2012) arising out of short- and long-term threat scenarios apply. Gansler and Lucyshyn (2005) summarized these threat scenarios into challenges originating from asymmetric warfare, terrorist attacks, acts of piracy, or threats from technologically advanced countries with unstable governments (Gansler and Lucyshyn 2005). Endogenous contextual factors include an organization's own resources situation, internal relationships and corporate culture (Ratchev 2009). Contextual factors are driven and led by various stakeholder groups, including government officials, political parties, nongovernmental and industrial lobby groups, and private company representatives and their corresponding history of relationships (Barber 2013; Bucur-Marcu et al. 2009).

Based on the aforementioned objectives and contextual factors, structures and processes are shaped and exercised through defense managers' actions and decisions (Lynn et al. 2000). The governance literature typically distinguishes between formal and informal structure. Whereas formal elements of structure comprise, e.g., organizational structure, written standards and contracts, informal elements of structure contain, e.g., norms, values, social behavior, and information-sharing practices (Pilbeam et al. 2012). As an example, due to budgetary constraints (exogenous contextual factor), a series of nations started a politically induced (exogenous contextual factor) force-transformation process (managerial action) and changed their organizational structures (formal structure) from a conscript-based to a professional military (output) (Snider 2008).

Considering the process perspective, Ratchev (2009) considers "defense management" as a decision-making procedure in which defense-management actors shape the implementation of defense policies together with stakeholders from the political practice and the operational military sector. Thus, defense management can be seen as the decision-making procedure that answers questions about the following issues: (1) planning and programming, (2) organization and staffing, (3) directing and leading, and (4) monitoring and controlling for each functional topic in the defense management sector (Ratchev 2009). The wide range of functional topics includes, inter alia, the strategic planning of the armed forces' capability profile; the structure and composition of civilian and military personnel bodies; financial budgeting and spending; the acquisition of technical equipment and services, training, infrastructure, logistics, and maintenance; and the response to crises or cooperation in a multinational context (Barber 2013; Bucur-Marcu et al. 2009).

The role of defense management actors is to direct and execute measures to achieve predetermined goals. Similar to decision-making situations in the private or other public sectors, management tools, and methods are used to prepare and conduct decisions. These instruments include, for example, project and risk management, data analysis, modeling and simulation, the derivation of action alternatives and scenarios, and performance measurement and improvement techniques (Ratchev 2009). In addition, the success of projects and large programs depends on leadership capacities, which include good leadership practices such as innovation and goal setting, employee motivation, recognition and support, problem solving, and delegation of authority or work tasks. It also includes the creation and implementation of performance standards, incentives, and sanctions (Lynn et al. 2000).

In summary, the characteristics of defense management are outlined in Fig. 2. In comparison to the framework provided by Lynn et al. (2000), the extra category of "functional themes and processes" has been added. The functional themes and processes are shaped by defense management actors through decisions, structure and overall, generic management processes.

As indicated below, the issue of "defense acquisition" can be understood as a functional theme in the field of defense management. In the literature, the terms "defense acquisition" and "defense procurement" are often used synonymously. Schmoll (1996) and Brown (2010) suggest that the term "defense acquisition" refers

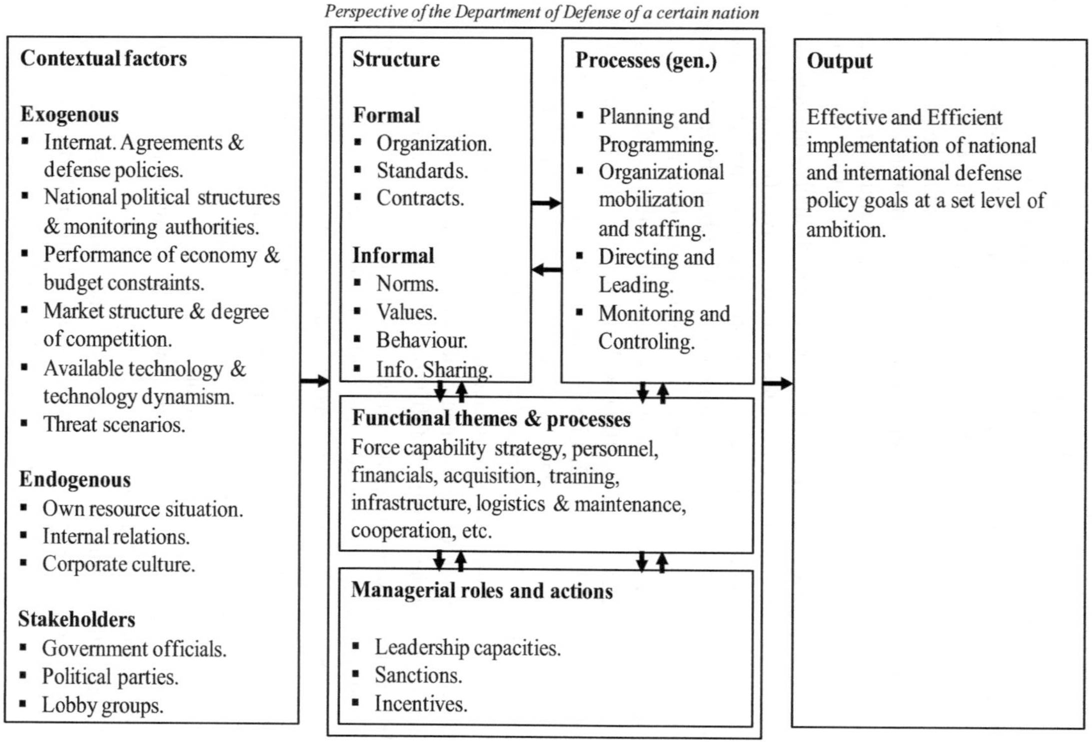

Fig. 2 Defense management and governance framework

to the entire process of acquiring (and disposing of) weapon systems, IT systems, and support services. Acquiring weaponry and IT typically includes requirements engineering and involves activities such as design and research and development. The entire acquisition cycle is usually subject to strict regulatory oversight. The term "procurement," however, focuses only on the pure act of buying or contracting goods and services. In contrast to "defense acquisition," "defense procurement" also encompasses purchasing goods and services such as passenger vehicles, office supplies, and waste removal. Thus, "defense procurement" is seen as only one of the many functions performed as part of the entire defense acquisition cycle. In the context of this contribution, we adopt a definition of defense acquisition that summarizes all of the activities and decisions required for the design, the procurement and the disposal of any type of military and nonmilitary equipment and services that contribute to the preservation and enhancement of the capabilities of the armed forces (Brown 2010; Georgiev 2010; Schmoll 1996; Wright 2010). The overarching aim of acquiring military goods and services is to provide high-quality military and operational capabilities in a timely manner against set objectives (level of ambition) and against the needs of the end user, according to economic principles (Lawrence 2009).

Similar to the defense management activities described above, the acquisition procedure encompasses a decision-making process composed of various elements. It is influenced by the same external and internal contextual factors as defense management (Georgiev 2010). Starting with the priorities set by security and defense policy (Dickow et al. 2012; Eliassen and Sitter 2002; Hartley 2003; Ojanen 2006) and taking other factors into consideration such as financial and budgetary constraints (Ballester 2013; Marrone 2012), strategic planning and programming examines what capabilities should be acquired at what time and with what (financial) resources. The aim of this strategic planning is the prioritization of acquisition programs (Georgiev 2010). To fulfill prioritized requirements as accurately as possible, the current structure of the armed forces and the current capability profile are assessed, together with an overview of the available capabilities on the market (Lawrence 2009). As a result, solutions from different vendors are carefully compared and selected according to predefined criteria, including economic decision criteria. After the selection of a provider and the conclusion of the contract, the other phases of the acquisition process begin, including design, engineering, test and evaluation, production, inspection, and operation, along with ongoing support for the system in use. The process usually ends with the disposal of the military system or the termination of a service contract (Brown 2010; Rendon 2008; Schmoll 1996). Usually, the defense acquisition management process itself is highly formalized and described in detail by various defense acquisition doctrines and directives from official defense administration authorities (e.g., US DoD 5000.01, German CPM 2010 in the updated version).

Due to their technical requirements, their enormous consumption of public resources, their large number of suppliers coordinated within a program and the influence of various interest groups, defense acquisition programs are considered very complex (Dillard 2005). Regularly, schedules are extended and budget overruns occur. Therefore, strict and transparent program and project management is required in defense acquisition management. Instruments such as project management, risk management, monitoring, controlling, and performance management are key to the success of acquisition programs (Brown 2010; Darnis et al. 2007; Dillard 2005; Kadish et al. 2005). Against a background of increasingly scarce resources for defense acquisition programs, the literature discusses different optimization initiatives, including, e.g., a consistent performance review of programs throughout their life cycles. However, detailed performance measurements due to a lack of standards or an integrated and consistent coverage of costs seem difficult to implement (Dillard 2005; Kadish et al. 2005; Rendon 2008). Moreover, there has been a discussion of assessing markets for existing solutions. That discussion encompasses the evaluation of existing commercial and civilian solutions (commercials off the shelf), existing solutions from other authorities (government off the shelf), or existing military components, products and services (military off the shelf) (Tagarev 2009; Lawrence 2009). In addition, particularly in Europe, stronger and improved cooperation between partners in current and future armament projects is required. Three different forms of cooperation are being examined (Fig. 3). They include a joint and coordinated procurement of required capabilities, the pooling of required maintenance or training capacities for similar systems and platforms, and a coordinated specialization of individual nations in predefined core skills, which are then further developed and provided to partners (Darnis et al. 2007; Marrone and Nones 2013; Mölling 2008, 2012; Reynolds 2013; Valasek 2011).

In summary, the characteristics of defense acquisition management can be similarly visualized as outlined in the explanations of defense management. In comparison to the framework provided in the defense management section, the category "functional themes and processes" has been modified to "functional processes and improvements" because this better reflects the defense acquisition perspective.

Applied Methodology

The methodology of this contribution has been selected and developed keeping the aforementioned considerations on "defense management" and "defense acquisition" in mind. The methodology follows the approach suggested by Pilbeam et al. (2012), Denyer and Tranfield (2009), and Armitage and Keeble-Allen (2008). Thus, the study has been conducted in five phases: (1) searching, (2) screening, (3) extraction, (4) synthesis, and (5) reporting.

In the first phase, a set of German and English keywords clustered in three groups was created. The three groups contained terms and synonyms for (A) research organizations, (B) defense, and (C) acquisition/procurement. These keywords were later used to build search strings, which were applied to a Web-based search using the Google search engine. The search strings were built by connecting single keywords from at least two groups using Boolean AND/OR connectors. To retrieve results for research organizations with a focus on defense management in general groups,

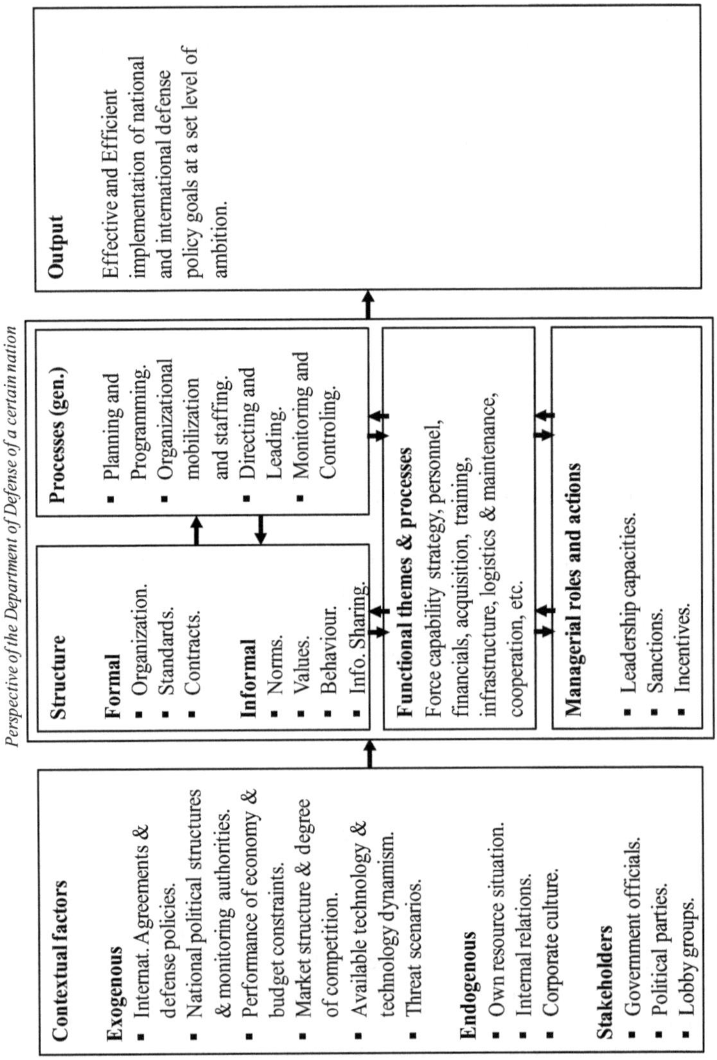

Fig. 3 Functional view on defense acquisition management

(A) and (B) were combined. To specify the search for research organizations with a special focus on defense acquisition, the groups (A), (B), and (C) were combined. The search was conducted in English because most research organizations provide their Web-based content in English. Research organizations not providing English-language content were excluded from the review. Appendix A lists the keywords used in the Web-based search.

In the second phase, screening for relevant results was conducted. Due to the overwhelming number of search results, the screening was limited to the first five result pages. The search results were assessed by titles and the short descriptions provided by Google. Relevant entries were transferred to an MS Excel datasheet, considering the title of the research organization, the link to the research organization, and the date that the Web page was accessed. Defense procurement agencies and private consultancy companies were excluded from the review because the research focused on entities providing research in the applied sciences. The final sample, which can be considered a preliminary dataset, contained 56 defense research organizations. Appendix B lists the organizations included in the sample.

In the third phase, content-relevant data were collected. The relevant data contained the (self-) description of each research organization in the sample. The data were directly retrieved from each research organization's Web page, typically from a navigation section titled "About us", "Who we are," or "Our profile." These data were extracted and added to the aforementioned MS Excel database. The extracted descriptions were assessed in two steps. The first step contained a fully automatic search for relevant keywords concerning organizational setup and the two research themes of defense management and acquisition in the extracted descriptions. The aim was to filter only for those research organizations with a dedicated focus on defense management or acquisition topics in general. The second step involved a manual re-assessment to assure the quality of semantic meanings. This resulted in a reduction of the sample from 56 entries in total to 41 entries involving defense management and 17 entries involving defense acquisition. In a subsequent step, detailed data on defense management research topics were gathered from publication lists or sections of Web pages about past or current research projects of the corresponding research organization. The identification of those topics was conducted by applying a (co-) word analysis proposed by Callon et al. (1983). It uses the most important words and conceptual keywords to study the structure and dynamics of a research field. The aim is to map the structure of the defense science research, along with the development of research fields and subfields (Van Den Besselaar and Heimeriks 2006). The different topics were collected in a summative approach (Hsieh and Shannon 2005). The value of this approach is that only relevant topics can be gathered. The disadvantage is the increasing number of topics and their growing complexities for evaluation, because some topics have different names but cover the same thematic core. An in-depth analysis of publications, such as briefs, alerts, reports, Chaillot papers, and journal publications has not been conducted, which is indicated as a limitation below.

In the fourth phase, an aggregative and explanatory synthesis was conducted (Denyer and Tranfield 2009; Rousseau and Manning 2008). Although research topics where collected in a summative approach, and complexity was rising, the topics were structured and examined with the help of the analytical framework introduced at the beginning of this paper. The value of that approach lies in its ability to cluster and aggregate collected research topics according to predefined and generalized categories and to uncover blind spots in defense management and defense acquisition. The synthesis of this paper focused exclusively on research institutions that concentrate on European security and defense management matters. This selection was made due to shared circumstances within the EU. The authors are well aware that this selection eliminated the possibility of showing differences in research topics among different geographical locations. Thus, the final sample contained 41 research organizations with a focus on defense management and procurement topics. Of those 41 research organizations, 29 were identified with a clear focus on European security and defense matters. The other 12 organizations had a purely national focus or could not be classified. Of the 29 organizations with a focus on European security and defense matters, 13 research organizations were identified as having a focus on defense acquisition.

In the fifth and final phase, the results were translated into this contribution. The aim is to report the intermediate results and to reveal and test the methodology and results with a broader audience.

Descriptive Analysis of the Sample

In this section, the retrieved data are presented to generate initial insights into the defense research organizations under investigation. By examining the sample dis-

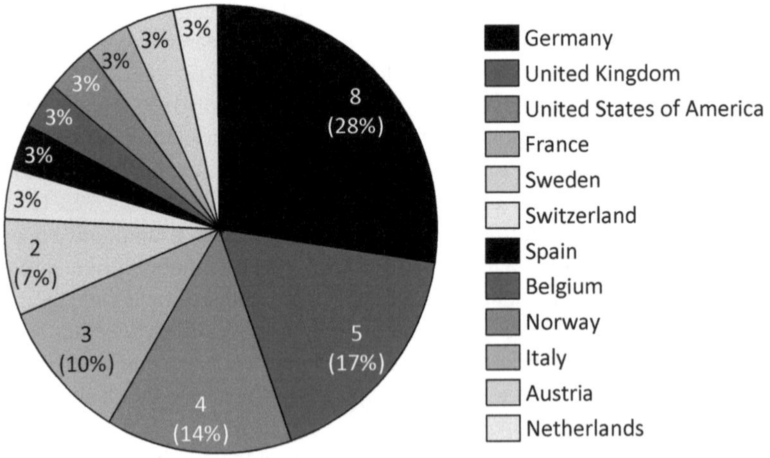

Fig. 4 Distribution of research organizations across country of origin

Table 1 Distribution of research organizations according to funding

	Funding			
Type of research organization	Public	Private	Hybrid	SUM
Institute	4	1	3	8
University	7	0	1	8
Think-tank	1	3	3	7
Association	1	1	0	2
Foundation	1	1	0	2
Center	0	2	0	2
SUM	14	8	7	29

tribution, the authors focused on five specific descriptive parameters: (1) country of origin, (2) funding, (3) type of organization, and (4) thematic focus.

With respect to country of origin, the sample data shows that the 29 research organizations with a focus on European security and defense are located in 12 different countries. The top 5 countries represented in the sample are Germany (8 organizations/28 % of sample data), the UK (5 organizations/17 % of sample data), the USA (4 organizations/14 % of sample data), France (3 organizations/10 % of sample data), and Sweden (2 organizations/7 % of sample data). In total, these countries represent more than 75 % of the selected population (Fig. 4). A reason for the high number of Germany- and UK-based research organizations in the sample was the use of German and English keywords. During the data collection process, it became apparent, that the majority of Web pages were provided in several languages, although this was not true for some research organizations located in Spain and France. Consequently, those research organizations were excluded from the sample. When comparing these results to the European countries with the highest defense budgets, namely the UK, France, Germany, Italy, and Spain (Berteau et al. 2011), one can state that research institutions from most important countries are included. Moreover, it is not surprising that research organizations in the UK and the USA examine European security and defense topics. This is most probably due to close relations and cooperation within NATO and the USA and UK's natural interest in European developments, particularly in terms of higher demand for operational responsibility in robust missions and operations.

In terms of funding and type of organization, one can observe that 14 research organizations were predominantly funded by public authorities, eight were funded through private initiatives and seven were funded through a hybrid approach, combining public and private financial resources Table 1). Most of the publicly funded research organizations are universities or institutes, sometimes founded by a combined university effort. It can also be observed that security and defense research is not conducted only by public entities. More than 50 % of the organizations are funded by private initiatives or through a combined, hybrid approach. Most of these research organizations name themselves think tanks or centers and are organized as foundations or associations that have different lobby groups acting in the back-

Table 2 Distribution of research organizations according to their funding with a specific focus on defense procurement research entities

	Funding			
Type of research organization	Public	Private	Hybrid	SUM
University	5	0	0	5
Think tank	1	2	0	3
Institute	2	1	0	3
Center	0	1	0	1
Foundation	0	1	0	1
SUM	8	5	0	13

ground. It must be acknowledged that a plethora of organizational names were used in the self-provided descriptions of the corresponding research entities. It has not always been clear how to classify certain research entities because they sometimes used a combination of different terms to describe their type of organization.

In terms of examining the thematic focus of the research organizations, the selected sample contained only those research entities with a clear focus on defense management. Of those 29 entries focusing specifically on defense management, only 13 focused on its subtheme, defense procurement. When examining the research entities with a specific focus on defense procurement according to funding and organizational type, one can recognize that there appears to be a split in the research landscape (Table 2). On the one hand, the public authorities seem to have a clear interest in further investigating defense procurement challenges. On the other hand, the privately organized side seems to be of almost equal importance. Interestingly, there is little to no combined effort in defense procurement research.

When considering the entire sample ($n=29$), one must clearly state that subsequent conclusions must be treated as indicative statements. The size of the sample is a clear limitation and must later be expanded. In addition, there is a notable bias toward research organizations based in Germany, the UK, and the USA based. A detailed overview of research organizations and descriptive data can be found in Appendix B.

Findings and Discussion According to the Research Questions and the Framework

The subsequent section is divided into two parts. The first part describes the results and findings from the summative collection of key research areas. The value of this analysis lies in its mapping of the themes covered by the examined research organizations. The second part addresses a generalization and aggregation of the findings by employing the analytical framework described above. The value of this approach lies in the condensed perspective, which should help to quickly identify thematic areas covered or areas in which future research can be conducted.

The summative approach led to the collection of 29 different themes within the research field of defense management. These themes were identified using an iterative approach that applied manual and fully automatic checks (a formula based on text search was developed and utilized). This approach included the manual and summative collection of keywords extracted from the (self-) descriptions of the first five research organizations in the MS Excel database. In a second iteration, a fully automatic check for these initial keywords was applied to the remaining research organizations in the database. In the final step, a manual quality check was applied to correct semantic errors. This three-step iteration cycle was repeated because through reading and analysis, additional themes were identified and extracted to the list. The value of this approach lies in its ability to detect keywords in texts that have not yet been coded. This is especially helpful when conducting a summative approach in which keywords can be added to the analysis that therefore requires the recoding of already-read passages. In addition to utilizing the (self-)descriptions, a brief assessment of research themes, research projects in progress and closed projects was conducted. For this assessment, project lists and Web page sections titled "research," "research themes," or "our focus" were checked for relevant key topics.

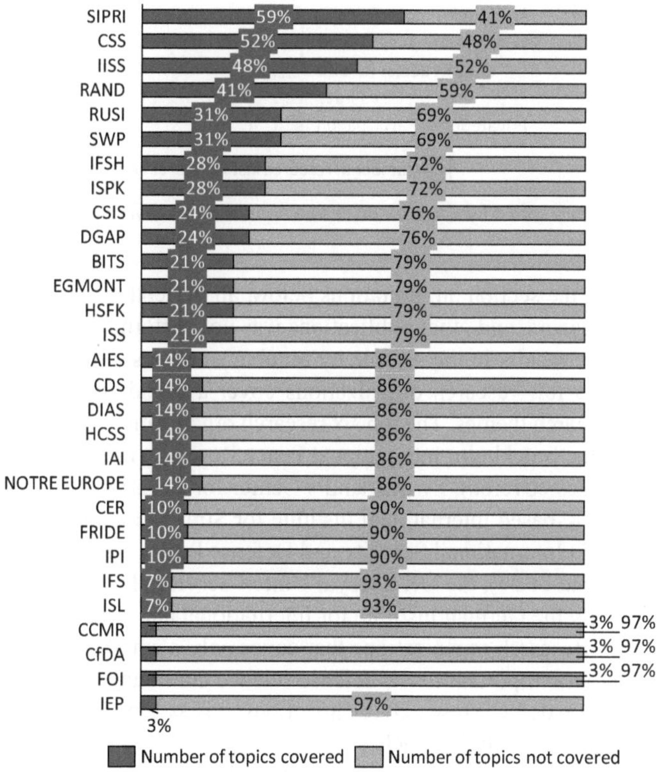

Fig. 5 Number of topics covered by each research organization

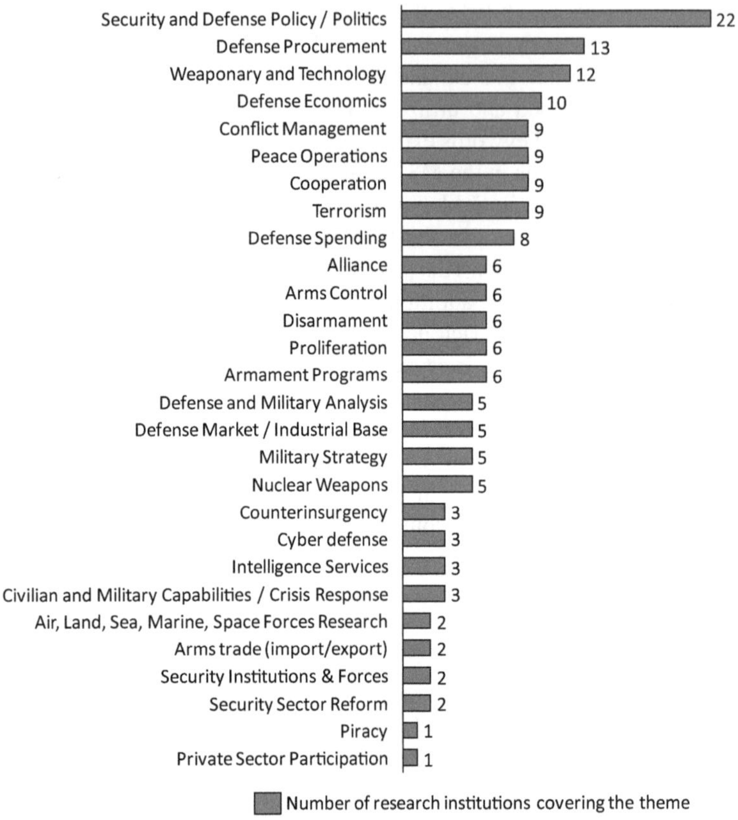

Fig. 6 Research topics sorted by number of research organizations covering the theme

As mentioned in the section on limitations below, an in-depth assessment of alerts, briefs, Chaillot papers, and other publications was not performed.

By sorting the results in the sample by number of topics covered, one can observe that only a few research organizations cover a broad spectrum of defense management research themes. The top six research organizations by number of covered topics are the Stockholm International Peace Research Institute (SIPRI) (with 17 out of 29 topics covered), Switzerland's Center for Security Studies (CSS) (15 out of 29), the UK-based International Institute for Strategic Studies (IISS) (14 out of 29), the RAND International Security and Defense Policy Center (ISDP) located in the USA (12 out of 29), the UK's Royal United Services Institute (RUSI) (9 out of 29), and finally the German Institute for International and Security (SWP) (9 out of 29) (Fig. 5). Research organizations that cover only a small range of topics are not necessarily less important to the defense science community. In the absence of an impact factor on defense research organizations, it is assumed that such organizations are specialized research branches.

The 29 different topics in the sample covered a broad spectrum of defense management themes (Fig. 6). Topics range from security and defense policy challenges to defense spending, cyber defense, terrorism, piracy, etc. By sorting the collected topics according to the number of research organizations covering a theme, it becomes apparent that the majority of the examined research entities focus on similar key topics. By far the most-treated topic is that of security and defense policy challenges. Twenty-two out of the 29 research organizations cover this research field. As already hinted in the aforementioned analytical framework, this is one contextual factor that is key to an effective, efficient defense-management system. It is unsurprising that defense procurement seems to be a topic that is also covered widely by the applied science research. Thirteen out of 29 research organizations are covering this research field. This topic, especially in austere times, is closely connected to the discussion of security and defense policy challenges. The exact focus of the underlying research must be examined in the analytical portion of this paper on defense procurement themes. Other topics widely covered are elaborations on weaponry and technology, primarily covered from either a capabilities perspective and/or a technical lens; defense economics, which mostly embrace the study of wars and conflicts (both conventional and nonconventional), including the economic study of civil wars, revolutions, and terrorism, which is, according to Hartely (2007), a relatively new scientific field; conflict management and peace operations; cooperation; and many more. Equally interesting are topics that have received little coverage. These include the arms trade, security sector reform, piracy and many more. A detailed list of defense research organizations and corresponding defense-management themes can be found in Appendix C.

For defense acquisition, 13 themes were collected. The collection process followed the exact same procedure described in the section on defense management findings.

By sorting the results in the sample by number of topics covered, one can observe that four research organizations cover almost the entire spectrum of identified defense acquisition research themes. The top four research organizations with respect to number of covered topics are the following: (1) the RAND International Security and Defense Policy Center (ISDP) located in the USA, which covers 13 out of 13 topics; (2) the Center for Civil-Military Relations at the Naval Postgraduate School in the USA, with its IDARM branch that focuses on activities designed to strengthen

Fig. 7 Number of topics covered by research organizations that consider defense acquisition topics

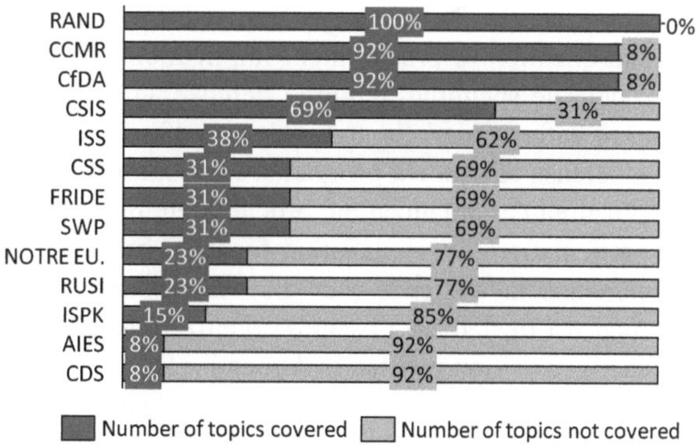

Fig. 8 Research topics sorted by number of research organizations covering the theme "defense acquisition"

defense acquisition processes and decision making and on helping nations to understand and adopt business practices; (3) the Center for Defense Acquisition (CfDA) located in the UK, which focuses on research and education across the range of specialist subjects in acquisition; and (4) the Center for Strategic and International Studies (CSIS) located in the USA, which focuses on understanding, from an acquisition perspective, challenges to the global defense industrial base and challenges related to defense reform. It is interesting that among the top four research organizations examined in the sample, only one is located in Europe. The center of gravity for research on defense acquisition is located in the USA. This seems logical because the USA is the number-one country in the consumption of defense-related products and services. Although these institutes examine European defense acquisition challenges, they often bring in a transatlantic perspective. This is interesting because it makes room for comparison and corresponding potential improvements (Fig. 7 and Fig. 8).

The 13 different topics contained in the sample cover a variety of defense acquisition themes. Topics range from security and defense policy challenges with special attention to procurement implications, to armaments acquisition cooperation, defense spending, required defense, and mission-critical capabilities, to the setup of defense markets, to the degree of competition and regulations, to steering huge defense equipment programs. Less-studied fields include procurement strategy, procurement organization, procurement processes and surprisingly, private sector participation. An explanation for this observation could be that public–private partnerships have already been discussed in detail and thus are not a "hot topic." A detailed list of defense research organizations and their corresponding themes on defense acquisition is listed in Appendix D.

By applying the proposed analytical framework for defense acquisition to the results mentioned above, we intend to depict thematic priorities in current defense acquisition research and to reveal less-covered topics. The result is a condensed map that can be used as a starting point for further research. To generalize the findings, the topics identified through the search process were mapped to the general framework. The mapping process was conducted in several steps. First, the themes in defense acquisition management were matched with the broader categories of the proposed framework. For example, the topic "defense capabilities" was matched to the framework category "output" and the topic "defense and security policy" was mapped to the framework category "exogenous contextual factors." Second, as mentioned above, "defense management" and "defense acquisition management" share the same contextual factors; shared themes from "defense management" were also included in the defense acquisition management map. The first two steps lead to a preliminary map that answered the question of whether parts of the framework are covered through the work of the research organizations in the sample or whether some areas were not covered. This mapping followed a binary approach. The results are pictured in Fig. 10. A detailed list of the mapping can be found in Appendix F.

When examining the map provided above, one can observe that the research organizations seem to cover a series of topics. Covered topics seem to include the description of exogenous contextual factors, formalized structures, overall processes, functional processes, and how to effectively and efficiently procure defense equipment against a set of ambition levels. Topics that were not identified in the conducted research contain a more detailed description of endogenous contextual factors, the influence of different stakeholder groups, informal structures and managerial roles and actions (Fig. 9).

In the third and final step, the number of research organizations was added to the chart. A representation of this examination can be seen in Fig. 10. This step was intended to indicate areas of research focus. It must be mentioned that the indicated numbers of research organizations contain duplicates because defense acquisition management is a subtopic of defense management. In certain areas, however, they share some research findings, as seen in the area of exogenous contextual factors that influence managerial activities in defense acquisition. Although one can observe that some topics are less covered, the general findings mentioned above do not substantially change. The only "difference" can be observed when examining the endogenous contextual factors. Although there was no observation in the defense acquisition research of the topics "available technology" and "threat scenarios," both topics were well covered in defense management research. When focusing on the number of research organizations in the field "defense acquisition," three relatively better-treated areas can be identified. These areas are "exogenous contextual factors," "functional processes and improvements," and "output" of acquisition management. Less-covered areas considering that perspective included "stakeholder influence," "managerial roles and actions," and "informal structures" (similar to the findings in the binary approach indicated above).

All of these preliminary conclusions shown above must be treated with the utmost caution. As mentioned in the limitations section, results need to be safeguarded and enriched with further information pieces.

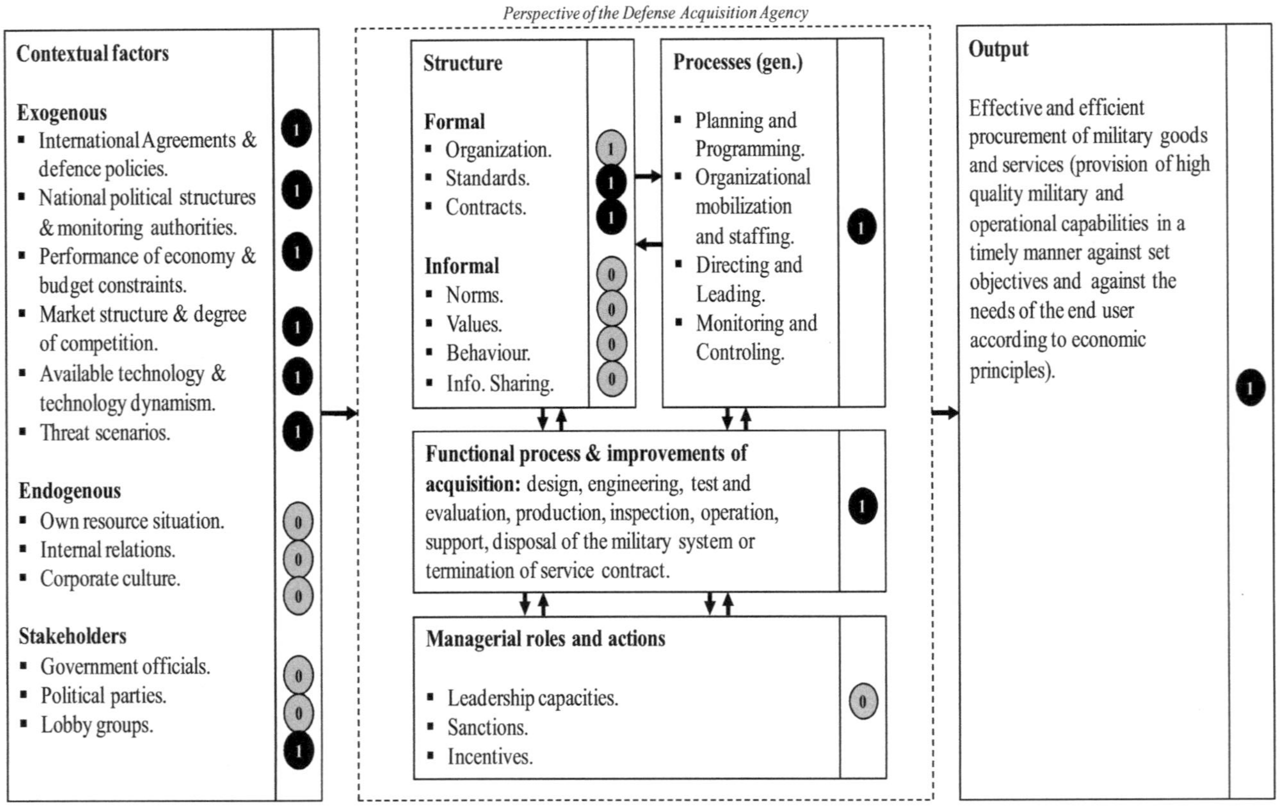

Fig. 9 Mapping findings from search on research organizations to generalized framework (preliminary results)

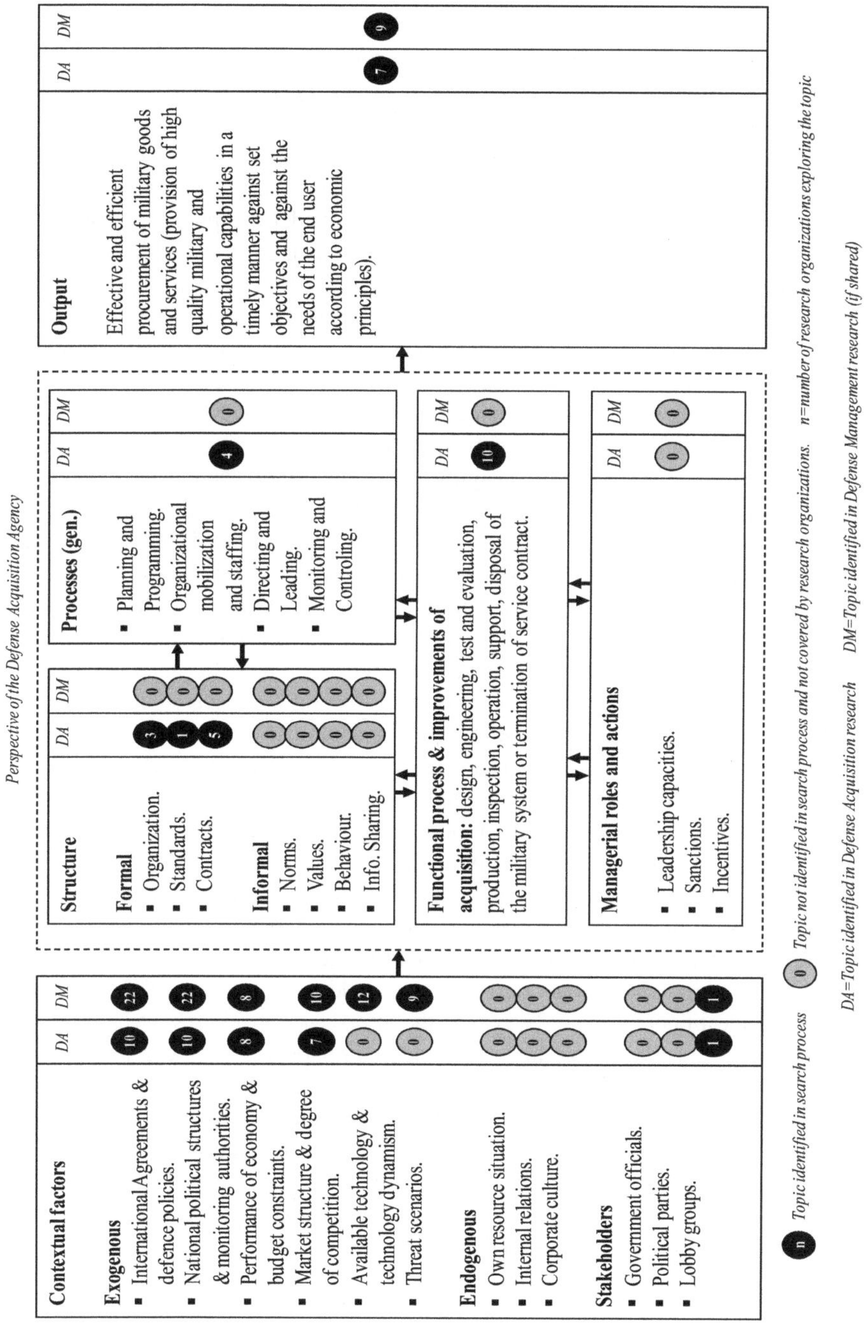

Fig. 10 Mapping findings from defense management and defense acquisition (preliminary results)

Limitations

The authors are well aware of the limitations of this paper, which is a work in progress. Elaborations on the paper's limitations can be structured into four primary topics that essentially follow its storyline: (1) framework, (2) methodology, (3) sample, and (4) findings.

In terms of framework, the reduced model proposed by Lynn et al. (2000) is used and gradually complemented with insights from defense management and defense procurement practice. It is based on principles derived from public management and governance theory. Although these insights from theory provide some guidance, other theories must be assessed and evaluated to further expand and detail the framework. Valuable insights can be drawn from classical economic theories that are closely connected to governance theory discussions. Examples include transaction cost economics (Williamson 1999, 2002), the dynamic capabilities view (Ambrosini and Bowman 2009), and strategic choice theory (Child 1972, 1997). They can assist in understand the relationships between and impacts of the single elements of the framework provided. Thus, a more insightful analysis could be conducted on matters already under investigation or on matters neglected by research organizations.

In terms of methodology, the authors selected a structured and logical approach following good practice as suggested by several other sources (Armitage and Keeble-allen 2008; Denyer and Tranfield 2009; Glock and Broens 2013; Pilbeam et al. 2012). As with any qualitative review and content analysis, the selected method contains room for bias because it allows the authors to make subjective judgments. Subjective bias can be observed in selecting the research organizations for the sample. Due to the overwhelming number of search results, the screening was limited to the first five result pages. An expanded view could help to broaden the sample. The limitations of the method continue with the interpretation of the studied areas of defense management and defense procurement. This is because there is no common standard or description for similar fields of study. In a way, each research organization and project attempts to distinguish itself to claim a unique research proposition in defense management and procurement science. One possible improvement would be to conduct an empirical investigation using a structured questionnaire with closed questions that would assist in categorizing research fields. The questionnaire could be sent to the already-identified research organizations. Thus, as a result, it would be possible to compare the initial classification to an external perspective.

In terms of content data collection, the authors chose a Web-based analysis. It is important to address that even though the data collection process was made transparent, the repeatability of the search cannot be guaranteed. This is because Web-based content is subject to continuous changes and updates. Following the recommendations on evidence-based research (Rousseau and Manning 2008) the authors collected content data in an MS Excel spreadsheet to render the analytical steps transparent. Moreover, the geographical distribution of the data examined is limited to research organizations with a focus on European security and defense matters. The scope might be improved by widening the sample to other regional areas, such as the Americas, Africa, and Asia. The value of such a sample would lie in the possibility of uncovering differences in research agendas and topics in defense and procurement management. Another vital improvement would involve examining the impact of research organizations on the development of defense science and public policy authorities.

In terms of findings, because this is a work in progress, an in-depth analysis of publications such as briefs, alerts, reports, and Chaillot papers typically provided on the various research organizations' homepages has not been conducted. Without a doubt, such an analysis would enhance findings on research organizations and their fields of study. Second, the analysis considers only content that is shared by the studied research organizations on their homepages. Most sources are comparable in their structures and degree of provided information, but there are some information gaps. Therefore, this work-in-progress research could bolster its findings by using additional sources, such as the journal publications of research organizations' staff members. Moreover, it is also vital to compare this paper's findings on thematic priorities to publications in respected and ranked journals. This would assist in making a more thorough judgment of research priorities.

Conclusion

This contribution provides two key contributions. First, to the authors' knowledge, this paper represents one of the first overviews of applied science research on defense management and defense procurement. The objective was to uncover research organizations in the field of defense science and to map them according to the topics covered. In summary, a sample of $n=29$ research organizations was examined. Defense management is a very broad and (sometimes) not-very-well-structured field of research. It encompasses a wide variety of research topics, among them "defense procurement." It seems that defense procurement is deeply rooted in applied science research. However, preliminary findings indicate that certain topics are handled less frequently, such as a more detailed description of endogenous contextual factors, a description of the influence of different stakeholder groups, informal structures and managerial roles and the actions and the interactions among them. Furthermore, empirical research, as suggested in the limitations section, is required to safeguard these findings.

Aware of these limitations, suggested improvements such as the proposed empirical research are expected to improve the quality of this paper's findings and conclusions. The preliminary results outlined above can help researchers and practitioners to gain a quick and condensed overview of the research landscape of defense management and defense procurement. This paper further provides details on covered topics and can thus be utilized to identify experts for discussions, group panels or Delphi studies. As research and publications in ranked defense management journals, and defense procurement journals in particular, are limited, this research also provides information about how to obtain research content and materials despite the gap in ranked journals. A targeted assessment of alerts, briefs, reports, and Chaillot papers can be conducted based on the information provided in this paper.

The second contribution of this paper is its examination of the variety of researched themes through the provision of an analytical framework based on insights from public management and governance theory. The framework helps to reduce the complexity that arises out of the great variety of collected research topics and helps to generalize this paper's findings. This framework can be used as a starting point and can be expanded through additional research.

Appendix A

Search Strings Used to Identify Defense Research Organizations

Group A—Organization (AND/OR)	Group B—Defense (AND/OR)	Group C—Procurement (AND/OR)
English language (German expression)		
Agency (Agentur)	Conflict (Konflikt)	Acquisition (Rüstung)
Center (Zentrum)	Crisis (Krise)	Procurement (Beschaffung)
Center (Zentrum)	Defense (Verteidigung)	Purchasing (Einkauf)
Foundation (Stiftung)	Defense (Verteidigung)	Supply (Versorgung)
Institute (Insitut)	Military (Militär)	–
Think tank (Think tank)	Peace (Frieden)	–
University (Universität)	Security (Sicherheit)	–
(Working) Group (Arbeitsgruppe)	Strategic (Strategie/strategisch)	–

Appendix B

List of Identified and Reviewed Organizations in Defense Management Research

NR	Name	Abbreviation	Links to web site
01	Arbeitsgemeinschaft für Friedens- und Konfliktforschung e.V.	AFK	http://www.afk-web.de/
02	Austria Institut für Europa- und Sicherheitspolitik	AIES	http://www.aies.at/
03	Australian Strategic Policy Institute	ASPI	https://www.aspi.org.au/about-aspi

NR	Name	Abbreviation	Links to web site
04	Brandenburgisches Institut für Gesellschaft und Sicherheit	BIGS	http://www.bigs-potsdam.org/
05	Berlin Information Center for Transatlantic Security	BITS	http://www.bits.de/
06	Center for Defense Studies	CDC	http://www.kcl.ac.uk/sspp/departments/warstudies/research/groups/cds/index.aspx
07	Center for European Reform	CER	http://www.cer.org.uk/topics/eu-foreign-policy-and-defense
08	Centro Superior de Estudios de la Defensa Nacional	CESEDEN	http://www.defensa.gob.es/ceseden/
09	Center for Defense Acquisition	CfDA	https://www.cranfield.ac.uk/about/people-and-resources/schools-and-departments/cranfield-defense-and-security/groups-insititutes-and-centers/center-for-defense-acquisition.html
10	CIPS Aerospace and Defense Procurement Group (ADPG)	CIPS	http://www.cips.org/en/Community/Groups-listing/Aero-space-Defense-Procure-ment-Group-ADPG-/
11	Center for International Security & Resilience	CISR	http://www.cranfield.ac.uk/cds/cisr/
12	Center for Security and Defense Studies	CSDS	http://www3.carleton.ca/csds/publications.html
13	Center for Strategic and International Studies	CSIS	http://csis.org/category/topics/defense-and-security
14	Center for Security Studies Georgetown	CSS	http://css.georgetown.edu/research/
15	ETH Zürich—Center for Security Studies	CSS	http://www.css.ethz.ch/
16	Defense Acquisition University	DAU	http://www.dau.mil/default.aspx
17	Deutsche Gesellschaft für Auswärtige Politik	DGAP	https://dgap.org/de/think-tank/schwerpunkte/sicherheitspolitik
18	Düsseldorfer Institut für Aussen- und Sicherheitspolitik	DIAS	http://www.dias-online.org/
19	Defense Science and Technology Laboratory	DSTL	http://www.dstl.gov.uk/

NR	Name	Abbreviation	Links to web site
20	Egmont—Royal Institute for International Relations	EGMONT	http://www.egmontinstitute.be/papers_other.html#ep
21	Swedish National Defense College	FHS	http://www.fhs.se
22	Swedish Defense Research Agency	FOI	http://www.foi.se
23	A European Think Tank for Global Action	FRIDE	http://www.fride.org/homepage_english
24	The Hague Center for Strategic Studies	HCSS	http://www.hcss.nl/
25	Heidelberger Institut für Internationale Konfliktforschung	HIIK	http://www.hiik.de/
26	Hessische Stiftung für Friedens- und Konfliktforschung	HSFK	http://www.hsfk.de/
27	Istituto Affari Intenazionali	IAI	http://www.iai.it/index_it.asp
28	Center for Civil-Military Relations (Naval Postgraduate School)	IDARM (CCMR)	http://www.ccmr.org/international-defense-acquisition-resource-management-idarm
29	Institute for Defense Studies and Analyses	IDSA	http://www.idsa.in/
30	Institute for Strategic and International Studies (IEEI), Lisbon	IEEI	http://www.euromesco.net/index.php?option=com_content&task=category&sectionid=5&id=1390&Itemid=39&lang=en
31	Institut für Europäische Politik	IEP	http://www.iep-berlin.de/index.php
32	Norwegian Institute for Defense Studies	IFS	http://ifs.forsvaret.no/en/Pages/default.aspx
33	Institut für Friedensforschung und Sicherheitspolitik an der Universität Hamburg	IFSH	http://www.ifsh.de/
34	Institut für Krisenprävention	IFTUS	http://www.iftus.de/index.php
35	Jane's Defense Procurement Intelligence Center	IHS	http://www.ihs.com/products/janes/defense-business/procurement-intelligence-center.aspx
36	International Institute for Strategic Studies	IISS	http://www.iiss.org/en/topics/defense
37	Institute for National Strategic Studies	INSS	http://inss.dodlive.mil/about/
38	International Peace Institute	IPI	http://www.ipinst.org/
39	Institute for the Protection and Security of the Citizen	IPSC	http://ipsc.jrc.ec.europa.eu/home.php

NR	Name	Abbreviation	Links to web site
40	Institut de Relations internationales et strategique	IRIS	http://www.iris-france.org/
41	Deutsch-Französisches Forschungsinstitut Saint-Louis	ISL	http://www.isl.eu/
42	International Relations and Security Network	ISN	http://www.isn.ethz.ch/About-Us/Who-we-are
43	Institut für Sicherheitspolitik Universität Kiel	ISPK	http://www.ispk.uni-kiel.de/
44	Europäische Union—Institut für Sicherheitsstudien	ISS	http://www.iss.europa.eu/de/willkommen/
45	Konrad Adenauer Stiftung	KAS	http://www.kas.de/wf/de/71.3573/
46	The National Institute for Defense Studies	NIDS	http://www.nids.go.jp/english/research/index.html
47	Notre Europe—Institute Jacques Delors	NOTRE EUROPE	http://www.notre-europe.eu/
48	Forschungsforum Öffentliche Sicherheit	Not available (FÖS)	http://www.sicherheit-forschung.de/forschungsforum/index.html
49	Arbeitsstelle Transnationale Beziehungen, Außen- und Sicherheitspolitik	POLSOZ	http://www.polsoz.fu-berlin.de/polwiss/forschung/international/atasp/index.html
50	RAND Corporation	RAND	http://www.rand.org/nsrd/ndri/centers/isdp.html
51	Royal United Services Institute	RUSI	http://www.rusi.org/
52	Security Research in Italy	SERIT	http://www.inspire-inco.eu/presentations/SERIT-conferenza%20v2.pdf
53	Stockholm International Peace Research Institute	SIPRI	http://www.sipri.org/
54	Bundeswehr Institute of Social Sciences	SOWI	www.sowi.bundeswehr.de
55	Deutsches Institut für Internationale Politik und Sicherheit – Stiftung Wissenschaft und Politik	SWP	http://www.swp-berlin.org/
56	Zentrum für Militärgeschichte und Sozialwissenschaften der Bundeswehr	ZMSBw	http://www.zmsbw.de/html/zms_wissenschaft_sipo_streitk.php?PHPSESSID=0477e7ef68d121ce01d0d201326277d8

Note: All websites were accessed on January 30, 2014

Appendix C

Sample (n = 29) and Descriptive Data/Classification

No.	Institute	Country of Origin	Funding	Type	Focus on defense management (EU)	Focus on defense procurement (EU)
SUM					29	13
01	AIES	Austria	Private	Institute	1	1
02	BITS	Germany	Private	Association	1	0
03	CCMR	USA	Public	University	1	1
04	CDS	UK	Public	University	1	1
05	CER	UK	Private	Center/think tank	1	0
06	CfDA	UK	Public	University	1	1
07	CSIS	USA	Public	Institute	1	1
08	CSS	Switzerland	Public	University	1	1
09	DGAP	Germany	Private	Think tank	1	0
10	DIAS	Germany	Hybrid	University	1	0
11	EGMONT	Belgium	Hybrid	Think tank	1	0
12	FOI	Sweden	Public	Institute	1	0
13	FRIDE	Spain	Private	Think tank	1	1
14	HCSS	Netherlands	Hybrid	Think tank	1	0
15	HSFK	Germany	Public	Foundation	1	0
16	IAI	Italy	Hybrid	Institute	1	0
17	IEP	Germany	Public	Association	1	0
18	IFS	Norway	Public	University	1	0
19	IFSH	Germany	Public	University	1	0
20	IISS	UK	Hybrid	Institute	1	0
21	IPI	USA	Hybrid	Think tank	1	0
22	ISL	France	Public	Institute	1	0
23	ISPK	Germany	Public	University	1	1
24	ISS	France	Public	Institute	1	1
25	NOTRE EUROPE	France	Private	Think tank	1	1
26	RAND	USA	Private	Center	1	1
27	RUSI	UK	Public	Think tank	1	1
28	SIPRI	Sweden	Hybrid	Institute	1	0
29	SWP	Germany	Private	Foundation	1	1

Appendix D

Research Organizations and Defense Management Topics

Number	Institute	Air, land, sea, marine, space forces research	Alliance	Arms control	Arms trade (import/export)	Counter insurgency
Sum		2	6	6	2	3
01	AIES	0	0	0	0	0
02	BITS	0	0	1	0	0
03	CCMR	0	0	0	0	0
04	CDS	0	0	0	0	0
05	CER	0	0	0	0	0
06	CfDA	0	0	0	0	0
07	CSIS	0	0	0	0	0
08	CSS	0	0	1	0	0
09	DGAP	0	1	0	0	0
10	DIAS	0	0	0	0	0
11	EGMONT	0	1	0	0	0
12	FOI	0	0	0	0	0
13	FRIDE	0	0	0	0	0
14	HCSS	0	0	0	0	0
15	HSFK	0	0	1	0	0
16	IAI	0	1	0	0	0
17	IEP	0	0	0	0	0
18	IFS	0	0	0	0	0
19	IFSH	0	0	1	0	0
20	IISS	1	1	0	0	1
21	IPI	0	0	0	0	0
22	ISL	0	0	0	0	0
23	ISPK	1	0	0	0	1
24	ISS	0	0	0	0	0
25	NOTRE EU	0	0	0	0	0
26	RAND	0	0	0	0	1
27	RUSI	0	0	0	0	0
28	SIPRI	0	1	1	1	0
29	SWP	0	1	1	1	0

(continued)

Conflict management	Cyber defense	Defense and military analysis	Defense market /industrial base	Defense spending	Defense economics
9	3	5	5	8	10
0	0	1	0	0	0
0	0	0	0	0	0
0	0	0	0	0	0
0	0	0	1	0	1
0	0	0	0	0	1
0	0	0	0	0	0
0	0	0	0	0	0
1	1	1	1	0	0
1	0	0	0	0	1
0	0	0	0	0	1
1	0	0	0	1	0
0	0	0	0	0	0
0	0	0	0	0	0
0	0	0	0	1	1
0	0	0	0	0	0
0	0	0	0	1	1
0	0	0	0	0	0
0	0	0	0	0	0
1	0	0	0	0	0
1	0	0	0	0	1
0	0	0	0	0	0
0	0	0	0	0	0
0	0	1	0	0	0
1	0	0	1	0	0
0	0	0	0	1	0
1	1	0	1	1	1
1	1	1	0	1	1
1	0	1	1	1	1
0	0	0	0	1	0

(continued)

Security and defense policy/politics	Defense procurement	Disarmament	Military strategy	Nuclear weapons	Peace operations
22	13	6	5	5	9
1	1	0	0	0	1
0	0	1	0	1	0
0	1	0	0	0	0
1	1	0	0	0	0
1	0	0	0	0	1
0	1	0	0	0	0
1	1	0	1	1	0
1	1	1	1	0	1
1	0	0	0	0	0
0	0	0	0	0	0
1	0	0	1	0	0
0	0	0	0	0	0
1	1	0	0	0	0
1	0	0	0	0	0
1	0	1	0	0	1
1	0	0	0	0	0
1	0	0	0	0	0
1	0	0	0	0	0
1	0	1	1	0	1
1	0	0	1	0	1
0	0	0	0	1	1
0	1	0	0	0	0
1	1	1	0	0	0
1	1	0	0	0	1
1	1	0	0	0	0
1	1	0	0	0	0
1	1	0	0	1	0
1	0	1	0	1	1
1	1	0	0	0	0

(continued)

Intelligence services	Piracy	Proliferation	Private security companies	Security institutions and forces	Security sector reform
3	1	6	0	2	2
0	0	0	0	0	0
0	0	1	0	0	0
0	0	0	0	0	0
0	0	0	0	0	0
0	0	0	0	0	0
0	0	0	0	0	0
1	0	1	0	0	0
0	0	0	0	1	0
1	0	0	0	0	0
0	0	0	0	1	0
0	0	0	0	0	0
0	0	0	0	0	0
0	0	0	0	0	0
0	0	0	0	0	0
0	0	1	0	0	0
0	0	0	0	0	0
0	0	0	0	0	0
0	0	0	0	0	0
0	0	1	0	0	0
0	1	0	0	0	0
0	0	0	0	0	0
0	0	0	0	0	0
0	0	0	0	0	1
0	0	0	0	0	1
0	0	0	0	0	0
1	0	0	0	0	0
0	0	0	0	0	0
0	0	1	0	0	0
0	0	1	0	0	0

(continued)

Civilian and military capabilities /crisis response	Cooperation	Armament programs	Private sector participation	Terrorism	Weaponry and technology
3	9	6	1	9	12
0	0	0	0	0	0
0	0	0	0	1	1
0	0	0	0	0	0
0	0	0	0	0	0
0	0	0	0	0	0
0	0	0	0	0	0
0	0	0	0	1	0
0	1	1	0	1	1
0	0	1	0	0	1
0	0	0	0	1	1
0	1	0	0	0	0
0	0	0	0	0	1
0	1	0	0	0	0
0	0	0	0	0	1
0	0	1	0	0	0
0	0	0	0	0	0
0	0	0	0	0	0
0	1	0	0	0	0
0	0	0	0	0	1
0	1	1	1	1	1
0	1	0	0	0	0
0	0	0	0	0	1
0	0	0	0	1	0
0	0	0	0	0	0
0	1	0	0	0	0
0	0	1	0	1	1
0	0	0	0	1	0
0	1	1	0	1	1
0	1	0	0	0	1

Appendix E

Research Organizations and Defense Procurement Topics

Number	Institute	Focus on defense procurement (EU)	Defense and security policy (proc.)	Defense capabilities	Defense equipment market	Defense equipment programs	Armaments acquisition coop.	Defense spending/ investment	Defense acquisition management	Defense contracting	Procurement rules/ directives	Private sector participation	Organization	Process	Strategy
Sum			10	7	7	6	10	8	4	5	4	1	3	3	4
01	AIES	1	1	0	0	0	0	0	0	0	0	0	0	0	0
02	CCMR	1	1	1	1	1	1	1	1	1	1	0	1	1	1
03	CDS	1	0	0	0	0	0	0	0	0	0	0	0	0	0
04	CfDA	1	1	1	1	1	1	1	1	1	1	0	1	1	1
05	CSIS	1	1	1	1	1	1	1	1	1	1	0	0	0	0
06	CSS	1	1	1	1	0	1	0	0	0	0	0	0	0	0
07	FRIDE	1	1	0	1	0	1	0	0	0	0	0	0	0	1
08	ISPK	1	1	0	0	0	1	0	0	0	0	0	0	0	0
09	ISS	1	1	0	1	1	1	1	0	0	0	0	0	0	0
10	NOTRE EU.	1	0	0	0	1	1	1	0	0	0	0	0	0	0
11	RAND	1	1	1	1	1	1	1	1	1	1	1	1	1	1
12	RUSI	1	0	1	0	0	0	1	0	1	0	0	0	0	0
13	SWP	1	1	1	0	0	1	1	0	0	0	0	0	0	0

Appendix F

Mapping of Research Topics and Framework Categories (For Defense Acquisition Research Map)

Research topic	Framework category	# of research organizations
Defense acquisition		
Defense and security policy (proc.)	Contextual factors—exogenous	10
Armaments acquisition coop.	Functional process and improvements of acquisition	10
Defense spending/investment	Contextual factors—exogenous	8
Defense capabilities	Output	7
Defense equipment market	Contextual factors—exogenous	7
Defense equipment programs	Output	6
Defense contracting	Structure—formal	5
Defense acquisition management	Functional process and improvements of acquisition	4
Procurement rules/directives	Functional process and improvements of acquisition	4
Strategy	Processes	4
Organization	Structure—formal	3
Process	Functional process and improvements of acquisition	3
Private sector participation	Stakeholders	1
Defense management (if shared with defense acquisition framework)		
Security and defense policy/ politics	Contextual factors—exogenous	22
Defense procurement	Functional process and improvements of acquisition	13
Weaponry and technology	Contextual factors—exogenous	12
Defense economics	Contextual factors—exogenous	10
Conflict management	Not shared	9
Peace operations	Output	9
Cooperation	Not shared	9
Terrorism	Contextual factors—exogenous	9
Defense spending	Contextual factors—exogenous	8
Alliance	Contextual factors—exogenous	6
Arms control	Contextual factors—exogenous	6
Disarmament	Contextual factors—exogenous	6
Proliferation	Contextual factors—exogenous	6
Armament programs	Not shared	6

Research topic	Framework category	# of research organizations
Defense and military analysis	Not shared	5
Defense market/industrial base	Contextual factors—exogenous	5
Military strategy	Not shared	5
Nuclear weapons	Contextual factors—exogenous	5
Counterinsurgency	Contextual factors—exogenous	3
Cyber defense	Contextual factors—exogenous	3
Intelligence services	Not shared	3
Civilian and military capabilities/ crisis response	Output	3
Air, land, sea, marine, space forces research	Not shared	2
Arms trade (import/export)	Contextual factors—exogenous	2
Security institutions and forces	Not shared	2
Security sector reform	Not shared	2
Piracy	Contextual factors—exogenous	1
Private sector participation	Stakeholders	1

References

Ambrosini, V., & Bowman, C. (2009). What are dynamic capabilities and are they a useful construct in strategic management? *International Journal of Management Reviews, 11*(1), 29–49.

Armitage, A., & Keeble-allen, D. (2008). Undertaking a structured literature review or structuring a literature review: Tales from the field. *Electronic Journal of Business Research Methods, 6*(2), 103–114.

Ballester, B. (2013). Cost of non-Europe report. In European Added Value Unit (Ed.), *European common security and defence policy* (pp. 1–91). Brussels: European Union.

Barber, E. (2013). Theoretical foundations of defense management: In particular militarization of humanitarian aid. *Journal of Defense Management, 2*(4), e117.

Berteau, D., Ben-ari, G., Sanders, G., & Lombardo, N. (2011). *Defense contract trends—US department of defense contract spending and the supporting industrial base*. Washington, DC: Center for Strategic & International Studies.

Brown, B. (2010). *Introduction to defense acquisition management* (10th ed.). Fort Belvoir: United States Government Defense Acquisition University.

Bucur-Marcu, H. (2009) Introduction, In H. Bucur-Marcu, P. Fluri, & T. Tagarev (Eds.), *Defence management: An introduction* (Security and defence management series no. 1). Geneva: Geneva Centre for the Democratic Control of Armed Forces

Bucur-Marcu, H., Fluri, P., & Tagarev, T. (2009). *Defence management: An introduction* (1st ed). Geneva: Geneva Centre for the Democratic Control of Armed Forces.

Callon, M., Courtial, J.-P., Turner, W. A., & Bauin, S. (1983). From translations to problematic networks: An introduction to co-word analysis. *Social Science Information, 22,* 191–235.

Child, J. (1972). Organizational structure, environment and performance: The role of strategic choice. *Sociology, 6*(1), 1–22.

Child, J. (1997). Strategic choice in the analysis of action, structure, organizations and environment: Retrospect and prospect. *Organization Studies, 18*(1), 43–76.

Darnis, J., Gasparini, G., Grams, C., Keohane, D., Liberti, F., & Maulny, J. (2007). *Lessons learned from european defence equipment programs*. (Occasional paper no. 69). Paris: European Institute for Security Studies.

Denyer, D., & Tranfield, D. (2009). Producing a systematic review. In D. A. Buchanan & A. Bryman (Eds.), *The sage handbook of organizational research methods* (pp. 671–689). Thousand Oaks: Sage Publications Inc.Dickow, M., Linnenkamp, H., & Mölling, C. (2012). *The case for a European defence review: Why national-level armed forces planning is not enough.* Berlin: Stiftung Wissenschaft und Politik.

Dillard, J. T. (2005). Controlling risk in defense acquisition programs: The evolving decision review framework. *International Public Management Review*, *6*(2), 72–86.

Dunne, J.P., & Nikolaidou, E. (2012). Defence spending and economic growth in the EU15. *Defence and Peace Economics*, *23*(6), 537–548.

Eliassen, K. A., & Sitter, N. (2002). *Defence procurement in the European Union*. (Report 8/2002). Sandvika: Centre for European and Asian Studies.

Gansler, J. S., & Lucyshyn, W. (2005). *A strategy for defense acquisition research*. College Park: Center for Public Policy and Private Enterprise, School of Public Policy, University of Maryland.

Georgiev, V. (2010). Modeling defense acquisition strategy. *The Quarterly Journal, IX*(4), 53–68.

Glock, C.H., & Hochrein, S. (2011). Purchasing Organization and Design: A literature review. *German Academic Association for Business Research,* 1–43.

Glock, C. H., & Broens, M. G. (2013). Size and structure in the purchasing function: evidence from german municipalities. *Journal of Public Procurement, 13*(1), 1–38.

Hartley, K. (2003). The future of European defence policy: An economic perspective. *Defence and Peace Economics, 14*(2), 107–115.

Hartley, K. (2007). Defence economics: Achievements and challenges. In *Proceedings of the 10th Annual International Conference on Economics and Security* (pp. 1–14). 22nd–24th of June, Thessaloniki, Greece.

Holsti, O.R. (1969). Content analysis for the social Sciences and humanities. Addison-Wesely: Reading.

Hübler, F. (1823). Militär-Ökonomie-System der Kaiserlich Königlichen Österreichischen Armee. Vienna, Austria [Online]. http://books.google.de/books?hl=de&lr=&id=r5ZTAAAAcAAJ&oi=fnd&pg=PA1&dq=milit%C3%A4r%C3%B6konomie&ots=Wx5viaezNU&sig=x_YoHGqs-bV8hxrHYfzYZ-faVRW4#v=onepage&q&f=false. Accessed 10 Aug 2014

Hsieh, H.-F., & Shannon, S. E. (2005). Three approaches to qualitative content analysis. *Qualitative Health Research, 15*(9), 1277–1288.

James, A. D. (2012). Smart business models. Industry's role in efficient multinational development and procurement. In L. Aronsson & J. Louth (Eds.), *Reflections on industry's contributions to SMART defence* (pp. 22–25). London: Royal United Services Institute.

Juntunen, J. T., Juntunen, M., & Autere, V. (2012). Outsourcing strategies of the security sector through acquisition procedures. *International Journal of Physical Distribution and Logistics Management, 42*(10), 931–947.

Kadish, R., Abbott, G., Cappuccio, F., Hawley, R., Kern, P., & Kozlowski, D. (2005). *Defense acquisition: Performance assessment—Executive summary*. (A report by the assessment panel of the defense acquisition performance assessment project). Washington, DC: Deputy Secretary of Defense.

Lawrence, A. (2009). Acquisition management. In H. Bucur-Marcu, P. Fluri & T. Tagarev (Eds.), *Defence management: An introduction* (Security and defence management series no. 1, (1st ed.). Geneva: Geneva Centre for the Democratic Control of Armed Forces.

Lynn, L. E. Jr, Heinrich, C. J., & Hill, C. J. (2000). Studying governance and public management: Challenges and prospects. *Journal of Public Administration Research and Theory, 10*(2), 233–261.

Marrone, A. (2012). Defence spending in Europe in light of the economic crisis. In Istituto Affari Internazionali (Ed.). *IAI Working Papers, 12*(27), 1–15. Istituto Affari Internazionali, Rome.

Marrone, A., & Nones, M. (2013). More Europe on defence or no Europe. In Istituto Affari Internazionali. *Documentati IAI, 13*(3E), 1–30. Istituto Affari Internazionali, Rome.
Mölling, C. (2008). The European armaments sector: The need for the state to adapt. *CSS Analyses in Security Policy, 3*(31), 1–3.
Mölling, C. (2012, June). Pooling and sharing in the EU and NATO. *SWP Comments*: pp. 1–4.
Mölling, C., Chagnaud, M., Schütz, T., & Von Voss, A. (2014). European Defence Monitoring (EDM) Research Division International Security European Atlantic Security, German Institute International Security Affairs, Working Paper: pp. 1–46.
Ojanen, H. (2006). The EU and Nato: Two competing models for a common defence policy. *JCMS: Journal of Common Market Studies, 44*(1), 57–76.
Pilbeam, C., Alvarez, G., & Wilson, H. (2012). The governance of supply networks: A systematic literature review. *Supply Chain Management: An International Journal, 17*(4), 358–376.
Ratchev, V. (2009). Governance, management, command, leadership: Setting the context for studies of defence management. In H. Bucur-Marcu, P. Fluri, & T. Tagarev (Eds.), *Defence management: An introduction* (Security and defence management series no.1.). Geneva: Geneva Centre for the Democratic Control of Armed Forces.
Rendon, R. G. (2008). Procurment process maturity: Key to performance measurement. *Journal of Public Procurement, 8*(2), 200–214.
Reynolds, R. H. (2013). Systems acquisition and international armarments cooperation. In Grafton, J. S. (Ed.), *The management of security cooperation (Green Book)* (Chap. 13). Wright-Patterson Air Force Base,Ohio, United States of America: Defense Institute of Security Assistance Management.
Rousseau, D. M., & Manning, J. (2008). Evidence in management and organizational science: Assembling the field's full weight of scientific knowledge through syntheses. In J. P. Walsh & A. P. Brief (Eds.), *Annals of the academy of management* (2nd ed., Vol. 2). London: Routledge.
Schmoll, J. H. (1996). *Introduction to defense acquisition management*. Fort Belvoir: Defense Systems Management College Press.
Snider, K.F., & Rendon, R.G. (2008). Public procurement policy: Implications for theory and practice. *Journal of Public Procurement, 8*(3), 310–333.
Tagarev, T. (2009). Defence planning—Core processes in defence management. In H. Bucur-Marcu, P. Fluri & T. Tagarev (Eds.), *Defence management: An introduction* (Security and defence management series no. 1). Geneva: Geneva Centre for the Democratic Control of Armed Forces.
Taylor, C. (2003). *UK Defence Procurement Policy*. [Online]. http://www.parliament.uk/documents/commons/lib/research/rp2003/rp03-078.pdf. Accessed 4 Aug 2010.
Taylor, T. & Tatham, P. (2008). Five key challenges for the management of UK defence: An agenda for research? *International Journal of Defense Acquisition Management, 1*(2), 22–38.
Valasek, T. (2011). *Governments Need Incentives to Pool and Share Militaries*. Centre for European Reform. [Online]. http://centreforeuropeanreform.blogspot.de/2011/11/governments-need-incentives-to-pool-and.html. Accessed 6 June 2014.
van Eekelen, W.F. (2009). Transparency in defence management. In H. Bucur-Marcu, P. Fluri, & T. Tagarev (Eds.), *Defence management: An introduction* (Security and defence management series no. 1). Geneva: Geneva Centre for the Democratic Control of Armed Forces.
Van Den Besselaar, P. , & Heimeriks, G. (2006). Mapping research topics using word-reference co-occurrences: A method and an exploratory case study. *Scientometrics, 68* (3), 377–393.
Williamson, O. E. (1999). Strategy research: Governance and competence perspectives. *Strategic Management Journal, 20,* 1087–1108.
Williamson, O. E. (2002). The theory of the firm as governance structure: From choice to contract. *The Journal of Economic Association, 16*(3), 171–195.
Wright, E. (2010). *Comparative assessment project—Defense acquisition-resource management systems*. Monterey: International Defense Acquisition and Resource Management Program U.S. Naval Postgraduate School.

Christian von Deimling is a doctoral student and research fellow in the Bundeswehr University Munich. His research focuses on cooperative buying of complex services in the defense sector and on defense supply chain management in general.

Andreas H. Glas is a senior research fellow and postdoctoral student in the Bundeswehr University Munich. His research focuses on performance-based contracting, service supply management, and complex product-service systems, with a focus on the aerospace, automotive, manufacturing, and defense industry.

Michael Essig is a full professor, is a professor, chair of Materials Management and Distribution, and co-director of the Research Center for Law and Management of Public Procurement as well as the Transfer Center for Defense Supply Chain Management, at the Bundeswehr University Munich. He is specializing in industrial procurement, in strategic public procurement, and in defense procurement.

Customers' Preferences in Municipal Waste Services Procurement

Alessandro Ancarani, Carmela Di Mauro, Francesco Mascali and Liborio La Marca

Introduction

The government sector is, to a large degree, a service sector. In the past decade government services have become more externally sourced than they used to be in the past. In Europe, it is estimated that around 50% of the total external sourcing in local governments is made up of contracts for services, such as construction work, maintenance work, public transport, municipal waste collection, social services and consultants, network services, etc.

The growth of public service outsourcing implies that public buyers increasingly operate in service triads, whereby the provider directly delivers services to the citizen. Therefore, public buyers are highly dependent on providers for their business performance, since private providers control service delivery, and measures must be taken to ensure appropriate behaviour, through contracts and service-level agreements (van der Valk and van Iwaarden 2011). With respect to equivalent service triads in the private sector, the relationships involved in public sector triads are much more complex (Ancarani 2009). On the one hand, many public services are offered under monopolistic market conditions, leading to lower power of control and "voice" of citizens. On the other, public buyers' decisions are under scrutiny through administrative controls and internal audits (Pettijohn and Qiao 2000), leading buyers in public organisations to focus on the public's perception of procedural appropriateness (Schiele 2005), more often than on value creation (Murray 2001).

Municipal waste services (MWS) provision is one of the services shifting from public in-house management to outsourcing to private firms. Typically, MWS contracting-out involves a single commissioner placing contracts with a single provider and is based on an explicit specification of the service and performance criteria. These criteria are predetermined taking into account environmental and technical constraints, while user requirements and needs are taken into account, if at all, only

A. Ancarani (✉) · C. Di Mauro · F. Mascali · L. La Marca
University of Catania, Catania, Italy
e-mail: aancaran@dica.unict.it

K. V. Thai (ed.), *International Public Procurement,* Public Administration, Governance and Globalization 14, DOI 10.1007/978-3-319-13434-5_6

indirectly. However, in recent years due to the processes of rationalisation of public expenses and to increasing customer demand for improvements in service quality (Sweeney and Soutar 2001), the evaluation of the performance of suppliers of public services is gaining more importance (Bovaird 2006). In particular, the rising emphasis on customer orientation and customer value (Brady and Cronin 2001) also in public services (Osborne et al. 2013; Thomas 2013) makes it essential for public organisations to understand how to assess value from the customer's perspective (Woodruff 1997; Leroi-Werelds et al. 2014). This implies that the attributes of the service should be carefully planned considering customer needs and expectations, in order to maximise benefits provided with the service (Lai and Chen 2011).

Further, not only in MSW, but also in other public services, providing customer value is crucial also to avoid a lack of customer collaboration, which may undermine the effectiveness of the service provision itself (Ancarani and Mascali 2012). In MWS the collaboration of users is paramount and a proactive role of the users is asked for, as the capacity of the provider to meet the targets strongly depends on the willingness of the users to differentiate waste before passing it to the collector for waste recycling. In this perspective, effective service provision and value cocreation is grounded in a commitment to collaborative processes among users, public buyers, and providers (Lusch et al. 2007; 2008). According to this approach, the customer's value-creating processes receive input also from the customer's own activities (Vargo and Lusch 2011).

A corollary to the above line of reasoning is that the assessment of users' preferences is crucial for service design in order to motivate and promote collaboration and maximise customer value. Therefore, prior to proceeding to entrusting a provider with service delivery, public procurers should incorporate these preferences in the definition of service-level agreements.

Various qualitative and quantitative approaches have been proposed in the literature to measure users' preferences for service attributes. In this chapter we propose the use of discrete choice experiments (DCE), a quantitative methodology in the tradition of environmental economics and management, in alternative to other qualitative methodologies proposed in the marketing literature (Sánchez-Fernández and Iniesta-Bonillo 2007). The DCE is built on random utility theory, which assumes that the decision-maker, when choosing among available alternatives, prefers the alternative providing the highest utility (McFadden 1980; Louviere et al. 2000).

DCE has already been used to analyse MWS (among others Jin et al. 2006) but the relevance for public procurement has never been underlined. This chapter presents and contrasts the results of two DCE studies conducted in two municipalities in a southern region in Italy, with the aim to illustrate the insights that public buyers can derive from such an analysis, and to show implications for public procurement. The DCE studies investigate the relevance for customers of significant service attributes (waste tariff, frequency of door-to-door waste collection, percentage of recycling).

The rest of the chapter is organised as follows: First, an overview of the concept of customer value is provided. Next, the main features of the choice experiment methodology adopted, and the case study descriptions and analysis are presented. The chapter concludes with a discussion and implications of results.

Value for Customer

The concept of value for customer has become predominant in the marketing literature recently. It has been applied also to public service provision assuming that it implies a customer focus replacing the product focus and a service dominant logic replacing a process focus (Osborne et al. 2013).

A review of the literature on customer value provides some key insights into the nature of the concept. First, a well-accepted definition is that proposed by Zeithaml (1988, p. 14), in which customer value is "the consumer's overall assessment of the utility of a product based on perceptions of what is received and what is given". Second, customer value is perceived by the customer, i.e. it is the customer who defines the value of a product/service and not the supplier (Vargo and Lusch 2008; Woodruff 1997). Third, customer value is personal. Each customer perceives value based upon personal characteristics such as his/her own needs and desires, knowledge, previous experience, and financial resources (Grönroos 2011; Holbrook 1999; Woodall 2003). Fourth, the value perceived by the customer depends on circumstances, time frame, and location (Woodruff 1997; Woodruff and Gardial 1996). Fifth, customer value implies an interaction between the customer and the product/service and is experiential, which means that it resides in the consumption experiences derived there from. According to the notion of value-in use, which implies that real value only emerges during use, "value is not created and delivered by the supplier but emerges during usage in the customer's process of value creation" (Grönroos and Ravald 2011, p. 8). When the supplier produces and delivers resources that the customer perceives as potential value, this contributes to the value creation process.

Research in service markets suggests that measuring value requires the consideration of personal interactions, in line with the notion of value cocreation mentioned by Grönroos (2011). Customers' self-generated activities (e.g. using personal knowledge and skill sets) may integrate resources provided by the supplier and other sources contributing to the cocreation (Vargo and Lusch 2011). These activities are relevant for customers who may derive pleasure and reward from self-tailoring and gaining control of the service (Bateson 1985; Dabholkar 1996). However, customers' likelihood to be involved into these co-production activities depends not only on the evaluation of the efforts involved, but also on the willingness to engage in this evaluation (Etgar 2008). In the MWS setting, value cocreated by the actors involved in MWS may include simple and complex activities ranging from compliance with the service provider operating rules for collection, to co-learning, to actively searching for information about waste separation and recycling, to providing feedback to providers.

All these activities take place within social systems in which individuals can learn, adapt, and make choices based on their perceptions of the reality through their "sense-making" activities (Edvardsson et al. 2011). Individuals may prefer to engage in certain activities rather than in others, and may (or may not) like a role as resource integrator according to the given context (Schau et al. 2009).

The view that value cocreation is essentially personal and experiential is in line with Woodall's classification (2003), which identifies five main concepts of value

Table 1 Time and experience phases along the public service provision

Time phases	Experience phases
1) *Ex ante* (prepurchase)	Collecting information
2) *Transaction* (at the point of contract and during experience)	Purchase
3) *Routine* operations (normal operations)	Learning
3 bis) *Failure/Recovery* from failures (during use/experience)	Emergency
4) *Re-agreement* or disposition	Purchase/disposition

for the customer, namely net VC (in terms of balance of benefits and sacrifices), derived VC (in terms of use/experience outcomes), marketing VC (in terms of perceived product attributes), sale VC (in terms of reduction in sacrifice or cost), and rational VC (in terms of assessment of fairness in the benefit–sacrifice relative comparison). In the context of MWS, we can apply this theoretical conceptualisation considering the customer value provided by the service as an aggregate including all the customer perceptions across the different time phases of interaction, experience cycle with the service, and experience cycle with the supplier. The relevant time phases for a generic public service are reported in Table 1.

Combining the concepts of value and the phases along the service experience, the model of value can be sketched as a Rubik cube in which each small face represents one of the components of the value perceived (Fig. 1).

In particular, the model takes into account both the longitudinal perspective (temporal dimension of value for the customer) and the transversal perspective (value perceptions change during the transition from an experience phase to another). The model of value for customer can be applied by considering aggregated value cube projections on planes corresponding to the time phases.

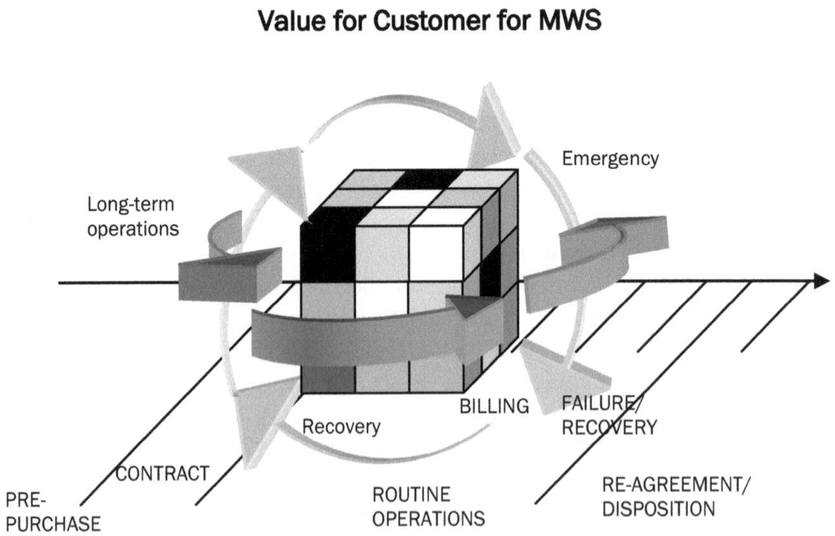

Fig. 1 Model of aggregated value for customer for MWS

Value for Customer in Public Procurement

The concept of customer value can be applied to the public sector, where the object of public procurement is to provide the users of public services with increased value (Jackson 2001). The concept of public value can be defined as the means to deliver the goals of public policy (Kelly and Muers 2002), and several authors have argued that this concept involves finding out what the public thinks, and requires techniques effective at investigating public preferences. Further, Erridge (2007) reinforces the link between public value and procurement, stressing that consultation is crucial to guarantee the match between service delivered to citizens and public preferences. In the same vein, other authors have argued that the operative definition of public value calls for a deliberation involving the key stakeholders. As a consequence, public procurement for services must incorporate consultative and participative processes in order to mediate between the particular values pursued by potentially competing publics (Stoker 2006).

According to the stakeholder theory (Parent and Deephouse 2007), the need for participative procedures and consultations have increased in the past few years, as the direct customers of public services have acquired salience by exhibiting attributes (power and urgency) they did not own before. This has turned end users into key stakeholders whose preferences need to be measured in order to assure their participation in value creation.

Direct consultation procedures may become an essential element of public service codesign, especially for local public services. This participative approach differs in important ways both from the traditional focus on formal consultations with interested parties, and with the method of eliciting users' satisfaction ex post through customer satisfaction, which is then fed into the future service programming efforts.

The direct codesign avoids the risk that users perceive the service are designed in a top–down fashion, and emphasises procedural fairness, thus fostering acceptance, even among those who disagree with the final decision, and increasing participation in service production (Bryson et al. 2013). Moreover, the codesign of the public services may produce better outcomes, above all in delivering services that require knowledge sharing and training in executing complex activities, as in the case of MWS. In this case, the effort required may be better balanced in the customers' perception by the reduction of uncertainty and clear goal setting.

Though the difficulties of going beyond formal participation cannot be denied, several authors have identified ways of dealing with the issue of substantive participation and of measuring perceived customer value. Studies have focused, among others, on motivations for participating (Lowndes et al. 2001), on ways of building participation chains (Simmonds and Birchall 2005), and on newer ways of assessing customer value that keep public preferences into account (Leroi-Werelds et al. 2014). These approaches offer grounds for basing public procurement not only on value-for-money concepts but also on the wider concept of value for customer.

Analysis of Users' Preferences

In this chapter customers' preferences for the appropriate design of MWS provision have been investigated through two case studies in which the current attributes of the service were considered unsatisfactory by the buyer (municipal government), and in which the buyers were in the process of entrusting a private supplier with the service provision through a public tender, and of defining the new attributes of the service itself.

In both cases, buyers implemented a consultation with the residents in order to measure user preferences for various attributes of MWS by means of the DCEs methodology. In what follows, the results of such studies are reported, with the aim to show the kind of information that can be retrieved from choice-based methods, as opposed to more traditional methods based on intention to participate or on the rating of the desirability of single attributes of the MWS. From a managerial point of view, the two cases show how even a small municipality can implement public preference measurement as an effective tool to evaluate the most appropriate attributes of the service and to foster customer participation.

Method: Discrete Choice Experiments

The DCE method relies on the identification of the relative weights of a set of attributes among which the decision-maker trades off when asked to choose among a set of possible alternatives. The method is grounded in the theory of random utility and has been widely adopted in environmental management, marketing, and the social sciences to analyse user preferences and to evaluate nonmarket goods and services (Adamowicz et al. 1994, 1998). Hence, the DCE method is suitable when the service to be evaluated is multidimensional, and importance is attributed to trade-offs between them. DCE allows modelling complex trade-offs between attributes by treating the price of the service as just one component attribute of the valued good. Typically, a DCE builds and contrasts a set of hypothetical multi-attribute scenarios with respect to the status quo scenario.

DCE has been previously used to measure the various economic values of the urban waste disposal system (Birol et al. 2008; Ezebilo 2013; Karousakis and Birol 2008; Ku et al. 2009 among others). In the case of waste disposal, relevant attributes of the service are tariff, frequency, mode of collection, percentage of recycling, etc. After the identification of the appropriate attributes and of their values, the set of scenarios are generated through experimental design techniques. In our experiment, we follow the design used by Verma and Pullman (1998) based on fractional factorial design.

Organisation of Service

In the first municipality (population 10,859 as of 2012), the service had been run by a private entity since 2010 and had been implemented through door-to-door collection of the organic fraction of waste for about 25 % of the population residing in the town centre. For the rest of the town population, the service collected waste and/or recyclables and/or organics on a scheduled basis from waste bins distributed across town, and dedicated to plastic, paper, glass, and to nonrecyclable matter. About 20 % of waste was recycled at the time of the analysis.

In the second municipality (population 10,391) service was run in-house at the time of the study. The mode of waste collection included waste being dumped in street dustbins, emptied by collectors, to be then taken to a landfill. Recycling of paper, plastic, glass, clothing, and tin was further undertaken with the same method. Only 5 % of waste was recycled. At the time of the study, the municipality was contemplating the possibility of introducing door-to-door collection to improve the service and increase the percentage of recycling.

Study Deployment

In both municipalities data collection was carried out in the period May–July 2013. Scenarios based on the DCE methodology were built and administered to a randomly extracted sample of the population. A second section of the study (not reported in this chapter) collected information about the degree of satisfaction with the current service in terms of tariff, percentage of recycling, customer care of the service provider, kindness, and competence of personnel. In this second section, each attribute of the service was evaluated individually, without consideration of the trade-offs with respect to other attributes.

In the first municipality, only residents that received the door-to-door service were included in the study. Three attributes of service provision were considered (waste tariff, schedule of collection, and percentage of recycling). Three levels were considered for each attribute. The resulting factor structure (Table 2) was used to build eight scenarios (plus the status quo configuration), which were then combined into four choice sets, each made up of two scenarios and the status quo.

In the second municipality, the mode of collection was further added to the attributes, distinguishing among the standard collection system through dustbins, door-to-door collection, and a municipal collection centre (MCC) (Table 3).

Respondents in the second municipality were further split into two groups (Groups A and B) in order to allow for the evaluation of different schedules of door-to-door collection. This practice is common among researchers undertaking DCE studies (Verma and Pullman 1998).

Table 4 summarises the characteristics of the two samples in terms of gender, age, and level of education.

Table 2 Attributes and levels of attributes—first municipality

Attribute	Level 1	Level 2	Status quo
Schedule of collection	Twice a week for organics and nonrecyclables, once a week recyclables	Once a week irrespective of type of solid waste	Three times a week for organics and nonrecyclables, once a week recyclables
Tariff reduction	10 %	40 %	None
% recycling	30 %	60 %	20 %

Table 3 Attributes and levels of attributes—second municipality

Attribute	Level 1	Level 2	Status quo
Mode of collection	MCC	Group A—door-to-door (three times a week for organics, once a week for other types of waste) Group B—door-to-door (twice a week for organics, once a week for other types of waste)	Waste bins
Tariff reduction	10%	40%	None
% recycling	30%	60%	5%

Table 4 Sample characteristics

		Municipality 2 (*n*=211)		Municipality 1 (*n*=86)	
		Group A (*n*=104) (%)	Group B (*n*=107) (%)	Standard (%)	Door-to-door (%)
Gender	Male	58	57	44	42
	Female	42	43	56	58
Age	<40	40	43	50	47
	40–60	39	39	40	38
	>60	21	18	10	15
Education	Primary	17	13	12	19
	Secondary-low	44	37	36	27
	Secondary-high	34	42	45	39
	University degree	5	8	7	15

Results

First Municipality

Data obtained from the scenarios were analysed through logit and alternative specific conditional logit (ASCL) models. Data analysis shows some distinct patterns of choice: first, respondents prefer scenarios offering a high frequency of waste collection, and/or a marked reduction in the waste service tariff. Marginal attention is paid to the fraction of recycled waste. In particular, the condition leading users to opt for a service configuration alternative to the status quo is the joint presence of a marked reduction in the tariff (−40%) vis-a-vis only a moderate decrease in the frequency of waste collection.

This pattern suggests that the frequency of collection is a key attribute for the citizen, who is on average willing to trade off a reduction in frequency only in exchange for a significant reduction in the payment. This conclusion is further strengthened by the finding that the majority of respondents opted for the maintenance of the status quo configuration (in which the frequency of service collection

Table 5 Logit model on service attributes—first municipality

	Coefficient	St. error	*p*-value
Tariff reduction	1.688	0.543	0.002
Frequency of collection	0.270	0.097	0.005
% recycling	−4.238	0.473	0.000
Constant	−0.313	0.263	0.232

was highest). Table 5 shows the estimated coefficients for the three attributes as obtained from a logit regression.

The size of the coefficients shows that the tariff reduction is the most important attribute in determining the choice of a waste collection scenario, followed by the frequency of collection. Conversely, the percentage of recycling attribute is negatively related to the probability of choosing a scenario. This can be attributed to the fact that many households perceived a higher percentage of recycling as involving extra effort in separating waste for collection on different days, disposing it in separate street bins, etc. Interestingly enough, in the questionnaire that accompanied the DCE and aimed at investigating the most relevant and valuable aspects of a waste collection service, recycling emerged as one of the most valued attributes. The fact that this statement is at odds with the results of the DCE is a testament to the fact that when faced with trade-off choices, single attributes may not turn out to be as important as they may appear to be at first.

The application of the ASCL model allows disaggregating results based on selected control variables. In the first municipality, this model was applied to the valuation of different percentages of waste recycling. In Table 6, choice was disaggregated according to the binary variable gender (males = 0, women = 1). The interest in the gender variable rests with the fact that women are often, especially in the south of Italy where data were gathered, the "waste managers" of the household. Therefore, their preferences are important because they may be more sensitive to noneconomic attributes of the service which require active participation or which have effects on the life of the family. Quite interestingly, women seem to be the least interested in the attribute "percentage of recycling", and the ones most in favour of the current configuration of the service.

Table 6 Condition-specific logit model (by gender)—first municipality

	Coefficient	St. error	*p*-value
Tariff reduction	6.413	0.9113	0.000
Frequency of collection	0.1260	0.0996	0.206
30 % recycling	−0.7835	0.3286	0.017
gender	−3.0501	0.4120	0.000
constant			
60 % recycling	−0.6036	0.2870	0.035
gender	−2.5821	0.3710	0.000
constant			

Second Municipality

Results from the second study basically confirm the same choice patterns found in the first municipality. In particular, frequency of collection for the door-to-door mode and tariff reduction are viewed as the two most important attributes of the service, while recycling is only marginally related to the probability that a scenario is chosen. Again, this is at odds with the results obtained from the questionnaires measuring the perceived importance of each attribute and the willingness to engage in recycling.

For the A group, the most frequently selected scenarios involve the high-frequency door-to-door collection (three times a week) with MCC selected only by 8% of respondents. For group B, in which the frequency of the door-to-door collection is lower, MCC is selected by 19% of respondents. Further, while the variable "frequency of door to door collection" is statistically significant for Group A it is not for Group B. This suggests that door-to-door collection is considered a valuable attribute of the service only if it is matched by a high frequency. Tables 7 and 8 summarise the estimates from a logit model for the two groups.

Conclusions

Public service procurement needs to be grounded in a greater participation of the stakeholders involved in service attribute design. Direct users are clearly crucial among these stakeholders and this entails that consumer preferences must be explicitly held into account through various forms of consultations. MWS has a special role among services provided by the public sector, since the match between consumer needs and service specification is crucial to guarantee the collaboration of users and thus service effectiveness.

Table 7 Logit with covariates (Group A)—second municipality

LR $chi^2(8)=180.01$, prob > $chi^2=0.0000$
Log likelihood = −698.70452
Pseudo $R^2=0.1141$

	Coefficients	St. error	*p*-value
Tariff	4.85	0.51	0.000
Door-to-door (2)	−0.31	0.30	0.301
MCC	−0.19	0.30	0.532
% recycling	0.56	0.50	0.260
Age	0.04	0.11	0.704
Gender	−0.04	0.14	0.746
# Household members	0.02	0.08	0.757
Education	0.02	0.09	0.856
Constant	−1.73	0.49	0.000

Table 8 Logit with covariates (Group B)—second municipality

LR $chi^2(9)=497.83$, prob > $chi^2=0.0000$
Pseudo $R^2=0.3046$
Log likelihood = −568.36705

	Coefficients	St. error	*p*-value
Tariff	7.30	0.55	0.000
Door-to-door (3)	0.85	0.34	0.013
MCC	−0.30	0.36	0.412
% recycling	1.06	0.53	0.047
Age	$1.70e^{-16}$	0.13	1.000
Gender	$7.23e^{-17}$	0.16	1.000
# household members	$7.27e^{-17}$	0.08	1.000
Education	$1.12e^{-16}$	0.12	1.000
Constant	−2.75	0.57	0.000

Although customer participation to MWS design cannot be given for granted, various qualitative forms of customer participation (focus groups or general consultations to elicit customer motivations and expectations) have been experienced. In this chapter we suggest that these qualitative approaches may be inferior to choice-based methods, which are no more difficult to administer than standard questionnaires but offer the advantage of presenting customers with trade-offs between alternative specifications of the same service. Our two cases clearly show that while waste recycling emerged as an important feature of the MWS in questionnaires measuring desirability of each individual attribute, they rate quite poorly in the choice-based study, where waste tariff and frequency of collection appear to be far more important.

References

Adamowicz, W., Louviere, J., & Williams, M. (1994). Combining revealed and stated preference methods for valuing environmental amenities. *Journal of Environmental Economics and Management, 26*(3), 271–292.

Adamowicz, W., Boxall, P., Williams, M., & Louviere, J. (1998). Stated preference approaches for measuring passive use values: Choice experiments and contingent valuation. *American Journal of Agricultural Economics, 80*(1), 64–75.

Ancarani, A. (2009). Supplier evaluation in local public services: Application of a model of value for customer. *Journal of Purchasing and Supply Management, 15*(1), 33–42.

Ancarani, A., & Mascali, F. (2012). What does it mean value for customer in public services? In Proceedings of 5th IPPC, August 16–18, Seattle, Washington (pp. 2211–2232). www.ippa.org.

Bateson, J. E. (1985). Self-service consumer: An exploratory study. *Journal of Retailing, 61*(3), 49–76.

Birol, E., Koundouri, P., & Kountouris, Y. (2008). Applications of the choice experiment method in Europe: A review. In E. Birol & P. Koundouri (Eds.), *Choice experiments informing environmental policy: A European perspective* (pp. 12–57). Cheltenham: Edward Elgar.

Bovaird, T. (2006). Developing new forms of partnership with the 'market' in the procurement of public services. *Public Administration, 84*(1), 81–102.

Brady, M. K., & Cronin, J. J. (2001). Customer orientation effects on customer service perceptions and outcome behaviors. *Journal of Service Research, 3*(3), 241–251.
Bryson, J. M., Quick, K. S., Slotterback, C. S., & Crosby, B. C. (2013). Designing public participation processes. *Public Administration Review, 73*(1), 23–34.
Dabholkar, P. A. (1996). Consumer evaluations of new technology-based self-service options: An investigation of alternative models of service quality. *International Journal of Research in Marketing, 13*(1), 29–51.
Edvardsson, B., Tronvoll, B., & Gruber, T. (2011). Expanding understanding of service exchange and value co-creation: A social construction approach. *Journal of the Academy of Marketing Science, 39*(2), 327–339.
Erridge, A. (2007). Public procurement, public value and the Northern Ireland unemployment pilot project. *Public Administration, 85*(4), 1023–1043.
Etgar, M. (2008). A descriptive model of the consumer co-production process. *Journal of the Academy of Marketing Science, 36*(1), 97–108.
Ezebilo, E. E. (2013). Willingness to pay for improved residential waste management in a developing country. *International Journal of Environmental Science and Technology, 10*(3), 413–422.
Grönroos, C. (2011). Value co-creation in service logic: A critical analysis. *Marketing Theory, 11*(3), 279–301.
Grönroos, C., & Ravald, A. (2011). Service as business logic: Implications for value creation and marketing. *Journal of Service Management, 22*(1), 5–22.
Holbrook, M. B. (1999). Introduction to consumer value. In M. B. Holbrook (Ed.), *Consumer value: A framework for analysis and research* (pp. 1–28). New York: Routledge.
Jackson, P. M. (2001). Public sector added value: Can bureaucracy deliver? *Public Administration, 79*(1), 5–28.
Jin, J., Wang, Z., & Ran, S. (2006). Comparison of contingent valuation and choice experiment in solid waste management programs in Macao. *Ecological Economics, 57*(3), 430–441.
Karousakis, K., & Birol, E. (2008). Investigating household preferences for kerbside recycling services in London: A choice experiment approach. *Journal of Environmental Management, 88*(4), 1099–1108.
Kelly, G., & Muers, S. (2002). *Creating public value*. London: Cabinet Office, Strategy Unit.
Ku, S. J., Yoo, S. H., & Kwak, S. J. (2009). Willingness to pay for improving the residential waste disposal system in Korea: A choice experiment study. *Environmental management, 44*(2), 278–287.
Lai, W. T., & Chen, C. F. (2011). Behavioral intentions of public transit passengers—the roles of service quality, perceived value, satisfaction and involvement. *Transport Policy, 18*(2), 318–325.
Leroi-Werelds, S., Streukens, S., Brady, M. K., & Swinnen, G. (2014). Assessing the value of commonly used methods for measuring customer value: A multi-setting empirical study. *Journal of the Academy of Marketing Science, 42*(4), 430–451.
Louviere, J. J., Hensher, D. A., & Swait, J. D. (2000). *Stated choice methods: Analysis and applications*. New York: Cambridge University Press.
Lowndes, V., Pratchett, L., & Stoker, G. (2001). Trends in public participation: Part 1–local government perspectives. *Public Administration, 79*(1), 205–222.
Lusch, R. F., Vargo, S. L., & O'Brien, M. (2007). Competing through service: Insights from service-dominant logic. *Journal of Retailing, 83*(1), 5–18.
Lusch, R. F., Vargo, S. L., & Wessels, G. (2008). Toward a conceptual foundation for service science: Contributions from service-dominant logic. *IBM Systems Journal, 47*(1), 5–14.
McFadden, D. (1980). Econometric models for probabilistic choice among products. *Journal of Business, 53*(3), S13–S29.
Murray, J. G. (2001). Improving purchasing's contribution: The purchasing strategy of buying council. *International Journal of Public Sector Management, 14*(5), 391–410.
Osborne, S. P., Radnor, Z., & Nasi, G. (2013). A new theory for public service management? Toward a (public) service-dominant approach. *The American Review of Public Administration, 43*(2), 135–158.

Parent, M. M., & Deephouse, D. L. (2007). A case study of stakeholder identification and prioritization by managers. *Journal of Business Ethics, 75*(1), 1–23.
Pettijohn, C., & Qiao, Y. (2000). Procuring technology: Issues faced by public organizations. *Journal of Public Budgeting, Accounting & Financial Management, 12*(4), 441–461.
Sánchez-Fernández, R., & Iniesta-Bonillo, M. Á. (2007). The concept of perceived value: A systematic review of the research. *Marketing Theory, 7*(4), 427–451.
Schau, H. J., Muniz, A. M., & Arnould, E. J. (2009). How brand community practices create value. *Journal of Marketing, 73,* 30–51.
Schiele, J. J. (2005). Meaningful involvement of municipal purchasing departments in the procurement of consulting services: Case studies from Ontario, Canada. *Journal of Purchasing and Supply Management, 11*(1), 14–27.
Simmonds, R., & Birchall, J. (2005). A joined-up approach to user participation in public services: Strengthening the 'participation chain'. *Social Policy and Administration, 39*(3), 260–283.
Stoker, G. (2006). Public value management a new narrative for networked governance? *The American Review of Public Administration, 36*(1), 41–57.
Sweeney, J. C., & Soutar, G. N. (2001). Consumer perceived value: The development of a multiple item scale. *Journal of Retailing, 77*(2), 203–220.
Thomas, J. C. (2013). Citizen, customer, partner: Rethinking the place of the public in public management. *Public Administration Review, 73*(6), 786–796.
van der Valk, W., & van Iwaarden, J. (2011). Monitoring in service triads consisting of buyers, subcontractors and end customers. *Journal of Purchasing and Supply Management, 17*(3), 198–206.
Vargo, S. L., & Lusch, R. F. (2008). Why "service"? *Journal of the Academy of Marketing Science, 36*(1), 25–38.
Vargo, S. L., & Lusch, R. F. (2011). It's all B2B… and beyond: Toward a systems perspective of the market. *Industrial Marketing Management, 40*(2), 181–187.
Verma, R., & Pullman, M. E. (1998). An analysis of the supplier selection process. *Omega, 26*(6), 739–750.
Woodall, T. (2003). Conceptualising 'value for the customer': An attributional, structural and dispositional analysis. *Academy of Marketing Science Review, 12*(1), 1–42.
Woodruff, R. B. (1997). Customer value: The next source for competitive advantage. *Journal of the Academy of Marketing Science, 25*(2), 139–153.
Woodruff, R. B., & Gardial, S. (1996). *Know your customer: New approaches to customer value and satisfaction.* Chichester: Wiley.
Zeithaml, V. A. (1988). Consumer perceptions of price, quality, and value: A means-end model and synthesis of evidence. *Journal of Marketing, 5*(3), 2–22.

Alessandro Ancarani PhD is an associate professor in managerial engineering, University of Catania (Italy). He is the co-editor-in-chief of the Journal of Purchasing and Supply Management. His research interests are in customer satisfaction in service provision, public procurement, suppliers' performances evaluation, behavioural operations, analysis of intangibles in public service organisations, evaluation of hospital efficiency and performances.

Carmela Di Mauro DPhil is an associate professor in managerial engineering, University of Catania, Italy. Her research focuses on health care organisation and management, organisational behaviour and behavioural operations, public procurement.

Francesco Mascali PhD is a postdoctoral researcher, University of Catania, Italy. His research interests include public procurement and local public services.

Liborio La Marca MSc University of Catania, Italy. His research interests include discrete choice experiments and waste management.

Part II
Public Procurement Transparency

Rationalising Public Procurement of Complex Construction Projects by the Price Component Selection

Pertti Lahdenperä

Introduction

It has long been the custom in construction to select service providers, especially contractors, solely on the basis of the lowest bid. The practice has led to risk taking and adversarial relations and created problems in the sector, thereby, impeding its development. Pressures to renew the implementer selection come also from a broader cultural change: a value-added strategy is now being pursued also in construction and more collaborative, relational project practices are increasingly applied in various forms (see, e.g. Lahdenperä 2012b). A collaborative approach often also means early involvement of the key parties to the process since traditional, sequential involvement of the parties does not allow mutual exchange of information and collaboration for the benefit of the project. Therefore, early involvement of the construction team is increasingly utilised especially in demanding projects to incorporate versatile expertise in their planning. Early involvement has also become part of governments' strategies (Valkenburg et al. 2008; Edwards 2009; Alliancing Association of Australasia 2010; Procurement/Lean Client Task Group 2012; HM Treasury 2013).

At an early stage, the project is fraught with too much uncertainty which makes it impossible to estimate (all) costs reliably. Due to the resulting risk premiums, it is not sensible to fix the price in the early stages of project development. On the other hand, procurement methods involving competitors in early proposal design (for complete design and full price) forego the opportunity of collaboration with the client (owner) and stakeholders. Even if competitive ideas are presented, the owner's decision making can be conservative and ignore possible improvements since evaluation of alternative solution and ensuring the absence of gimmicks is often impossible in the middle of a hectic process where the public owner is required to treat all competitors equally and non-discriminatorily. If nothing else, those project

P. Lahdenperä (✉)
VTT Technical Research Centre of Finland Ltd, Tampere, Finland
e-mail: pertti.lahdenpera@vtt.fi

K. V. Thai (ed.), *International Public Procurement,* Public Administration, Governance and Globalization 14, DOI 10.1007/978-3-319-13434-5_7

constraints that require laborious administrative procedures to remove usually constitute an obstacle. Thus, collaboration is seldom genuine and profitable and much potential may be wasted in cases like this.

Thus, the current solution is to strive for an open process (incl. independent cost estimators, etc.) where the price (target cost) of the project is set later after a joint development phase by the owner and the selected team. However, it is not reasonable to ignore the cost and price elements totally even then and give the service provider disproportionate power to price the service/project subsequently which might happen as a result of the contractors' higher cost consciousness (or information asymmetry; e.g. Xiang et al. 2012). Actually, it is necessary especially for public owners to set constraints and/or a mechanism for price formulation in order to ensure price competitiveness also in the case of early involvement in order to comply with public sector accountability concerns. This leads to a complicated set-up and it is uncertain how such an approach works in practice. Accordingly, the essential goal of the study is to determine whether it is possible to find procurement procedures that integrate broad-based competition with good, creative collaboration. That is of critical importance especially since "public sector accountability concerns" have been considered the number one factor hindering the use of relational contracting in public construction (Ke et al. 2012).

More precisely, this chapter aims to increase the understanding of the possibilities and appropriateness of using partial price factors in case of early involvement in public procurement by delving into the practices and experiences of four different infrastructure projects. In those Australian and Finnish public projects team selection was based only on price tenders for some cost items or parts in addition to capability assessment. These items do not cover the total project price. The price components used in those four projects were, for instance, fee, project overhead, risk and opportunity provision, preliminaries and defect correction cost. In the case of assigned components tenders are binding. That which was not covered by the components was left to be priced during subsequent collaboration.

In other words, the proponents themselves do not seek/present a total price for a project: just an estimate of the unpriced part is prepared on the basis of the owner's own cost-estimate items and/or offered component prices to determine the comparative price. In the end, the selection criterion is the "most economically advantageous tender" which means that capability/quality is always taken into account in selection in addition to (comparative) price although it is not delved into here. The descriptions focus mainly on price components, and other aspects are described only to the extent that they are linked to the use and use criteria of components. Correspondingly, for the purposes of this study, the listed approaches are jointly called "price component selection" despite the term's possibly limited interpretation.

The chapter starts with a closer look at the need for targeted practice due to the on-going tendency towards relational contracting and better integration of the construction team. That is followed by an analysis of cost uncertainty and the ability to impact costs, which vary during the advancing process. The analysis produces two imprecise critical points to serve as a frame of reference for an examination of the practical examples thereafter. There, the focus is on the price components used as selection criteria in four different case projects which are also examined in relation to the said frame of reference for a better understanding of the wide range of possibilities in existence. Appropriateness of the different approaches is then discussed based on interviews of parties to the projects while some remarks are also made from the viewpoint of public procurement regulations. The European perspective is emphasised in the study; the different constraints possibly existing in other parts of the world are not examined.

Need for a Change

From Adversarialism to Collaboration

Fragmentation of the construction process and the resulting adversarial relationships between the involved parties have led to a lot of criticism towards prevailing procurement practices. The initial reason seems to be the separated design and construction, or disintegration of the construction project process in general (e.g. Latham 1994), where the low bid syndrome can be recognised as a major determinant behind the customary adversarial behaviour (Weston and Gibson 1993; Scott 2001; Stehbens et al. 1999; Nicholson 1991; Loraine 1994).

"Relational contracting" has been offered as a solution to these challenges. This is due to the fact that a contract based upon a relationship of trust between the parties, where responsibilities and benefits are apportioned fairly and transparently, is called "relational" as opposed to "transactional". This kind of duality can be traced back to "the relational theory of contract" (e.g. Macneil and Campbell 2001). In practice, relational and contractual mechanisms are complementary parts of the governance continuum of a project (Hartmann et al. 2010; Roehrich and Lewis 2010). While explicit contracts are needed to reduce uncertainty and minimise opportunism, they can only cover foreseeable contingencies—specifying everything would increase planning costs and prevent a flexible and quick response to unforeseen events. This is where the relational aspect, with its socially complex routines, comes into play in inter-organisational relationships.

Critical consideration of contract law also provides a basis for the theory of "transaction cost economics" when examined jointly with economics and organisation theory (see Williamson 1979). In reference to the theory, Sweeney (2009), for instance, writes that due to "bounded rationality", the actors in any contract have limited foresight and are unable to foretell the future, nor can they fully, precisely and unambiguously specify the known aspects due to the limitations of language and the cost of calculating and communicating plans and solutions (cf. Williamson 1985). While "asset specificity" (or "process specificity"; Chang and Ive 2007) ties the contracting parties together due to the losses caused by termination and changing service providers, "opportunism" in the form of pricing of extras may occur. Bearing this in mind, the initial tender may have been manipulated already considering the existing loopholes referred to above. Moreover, it is stressed that in traditional delivery methods an increase in reimbursable costs generates also costs that are not allocated to the project meaning that part of the cost effects often go unrecognised. For these reasons, traditional contracting would lead to an uneconomical result especially in complex projects from the viewpoint of the owner (see e.g. Sweeney 2009; Bajari and Tadelis 2001; Bajari et al. 2014), which explains the contents of "the low bid syndrome" referred to above.

Relational contracting is also called for by the change that has taken place within the modus operandi of the industry and its clients. The owners of built assets have increasingly regarded them as strategic means to improve the performance of their core operations (e.g. Krumm 2001). Correspondingly, they have in many cases started buying business solutions, not just construction capacity, which, moreover, requires employing relational contracting practices (Roehrich and Lewis 2010). In general, there are various forces driving towards further servitisation of construction (Leiringer and Bröchner 2010). Servitisation, which means integration of additional services, knowledge and support to the supplier's core product offerings, also puts the firm face-to-face with its customer (Vandermerwe and Rada 1988) increasing thereby the importance of the relational mechanisms that supplement the contract (Hartmann et al. 2010). Moreover, performance in demanding, risky projects could obviously be improved by joint risk management (Rahman and Kumaraswamy 2002; Pishdad and Beliveau 2010).

From Sequential Process to Joint Development

Studies aimed at fostering innovation in construction also stress the need for closer integration and improved collaboration (Blayse and Manley 2004; Holmen et al. 2005; Rutten et al. 2009). Systemic innovations, especially, require comprehensive or multidisciplinary expertise. It is also clear that co-operation that begins early enough with respect to design creates the best possibilities for utilising the partners' expertise in seeking better and more cost efficient solutions than the conventional ones. This is based on the fact that the ability to impact the cost weakens, and the cost of design changes increases, when the process proceeds as illustrated at the top of Fig. 1 imitating literature (e.g. Connaughton and Green 1996; American Institute of Architects 2007; Russell et al. 1992). Yet, conceptualisation of the project prior to the mobilisation of the entire team is needed to direct the work.

Although innovation-orientation may be considered the main driver for renewal, studies on the negative influence of project changes in the current practice provide some understanding of the existing potential. Hsieh et al. (2004), for instance, conclude that the fragmentation of the design and construction process increases the likelihood of change orders with conventional project procurement methods causing significant cost and time overruns. Most change orders arise from problems in planning and design (Hsieh et al. 2004; Arain and Pheng 2005; Cox et al. 1999; Hanna et al. 1999), which early team integration is believed to alleviate. Ibbs (2005), again, shows how late change is more disruptive of project productivity than early change as shown in the figure.

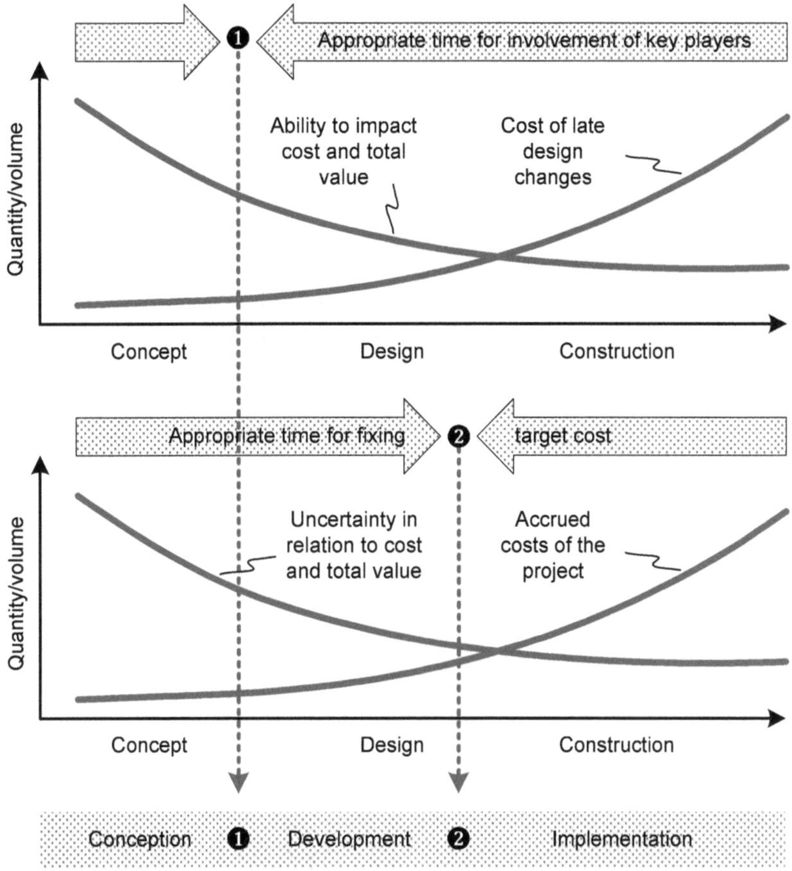

Fig. 1 Illustrations of the two conceptual fulcrums of the involvement process

On the other hand, as illustrated for instance by Bredehoeft (2012) and Lundman (2011), a project budget evolves towards an increasing level of accuracy: the spread of uncertainty becomes narrower, as would be expected due to the intensive work undertaken by the team to develop the plans. Since risk premiums alternate in parallel with risks (e.g. de Neufville and King 1991), the owner should aim to fix the pricing of the project relatively late in the process as outlined in the middle of Fig. 1. In other words, early pricing with inadequate planning lead contractors to add arbitrary premiums to their quoted prices potentially resulting in money being wasted by the client (Mosey 2009). Yet, the pricing should normally be agreed prior to launching the costly construction phase to avoid the situation where the owner carries all the risks.

Practical application of both of the above viewpoints means early involvement of the construction team (Step 1 in Fig. 1) combined with late fixing of the price level (Step 2). In other words, early involvement of the construction team, which leads to the signing of a final contract (although conditional) is of primary importance for the project's success providing that an arrangement ensuring a reasonable price later in the process can be developed. Such arrangements, for the most part, are examined later in the chapter, and the two-node process reintroduced at the bottom of Fig. 1 forms a tentative frame of reference for that.

The importance and potential of this "development stage" (between Steps 1 and 2) is obvious also on the basis of earlier research. The reported experiences from early involvement are mostly positive (National Audit Office 2005; Valkenburg et al. 2008; Ballard 2008; Song et al. 2009; Edwards 2009; Mosey 2009) especially when the team is involved with the intention of implementing the project to completion—consultative involvement is not likely to work as efficiently due to the inadequateness of incentives or, more precisely, the existence of disincentives (Lahdenperä 2010). All in all, it is clear that the trustful relationship of "relational contracting" should not be understood only as a collaborative component of a contract after all its price-inclusive conditions have been fixed.

Case Examples

Common Project Characteristics

This chapter presents four projects adhering to the practice of "price component selection" to introduce the change of the previous section (partially) to traditional practice while yet remaining cost conscious and observing public sector accountability requirements—not putting the owner at the service providers' mercy.

More precisely, these projects are alliancing projects for major infrastructure procured by public bodies. Project alliance is a project delivery method based on a joint contract between the key actors to a project (owner, designer, and constructor) whereby the parties assume joint responsibility for the design and construction of the project to be implemented through a joint organisation, and where the actors share both positive and negative risks related to the project and observe the principles of transparency of information in pursuing collaboration (Lahdenperä 2009; Department of Infrastructure and Transport 2011). The alliancing practice also typically leans on the early involvement of the team for joint development. Thus, it truly is a form of relational contracting.

The project alliance system evolved from the need to improve the implementation of demanding and risky investment projects—due to, for instance, new technology and project conditions or interfaces—and it has broken through especially in Australia (Department of Treasury and Finance 2006, 2009).

Overall Selection Process

The overall selection method naturally varies per project but is generally based on both qualitative and price components. Typically the competition entrants, who have been selected as tenderers, receive a request for proposals. After the first round proposals have been submitted, the number of tenderers is reduced based on an assessment including interviews. Thereafter, two competing teams usually continue to the stage involving workshop tasks that are evaluated as a part of qualitative criteria. Then, the competitors give their quotes for the requested price components. Sometimes pricing is openly discussed already during the preceding workshops (e.g. in case of a risk analysis which is of no real value if cost consequences are not dealt with), but most often they are finally tendered in a sealed envelope that is opened only after other evaluation measures have been completed. As a rule, the tendered price components have been binding. Selection is then made based on joint assessment of the team's capability and a comparative price constructed from the quotes.

Overall, that was the process primarily followed in the presented cases with a few exceptions. In Case 4, the final evaluation of capability was done already in an earlier stage and the three competitors continuing to the last stage focused just on project design and pricing. Case 4 was also different from the others in that cost escalation provision was not needed due to later index-linking whereas in the other cases the tenders also had to cover cost escalation. In Case 3, again, some of the presented price components were not binding.

Subsequently, selected service providers develop the project and its design in co-operation with the owner before the actual target cost (or target outturn cost, TOC) is set and the parties are ready to finally commit to the implementation of the project in question. Thus, TOC is agreed prior to launching construction and termination is possible if the parties are not able to agree on, for instance, the TOC. The TOC is to be based on quoted price components and, the remaining part, on project/risk- and market-adjusted (or tested), audited direct costs of earlier projects. After the completion of the project, the owner and service providers share the difference between the target and outturn costs.

One characteristic of the selection process needs to be emphasised in particular since the following presentations skip examination of the quality/capability assessment: evaluation of capability—with its manifold meanings—is a very in-depth, stage-wise process especially if the price components are rare (cf. Department of Treasury and Finance 2006; Lahdenperä 2012a). It includes interviews and collaborative development workshops often with a psychologist involved in the evaluation—in addition to the more usual criteria of past performance, know-how and experience of section managers, and project specific narratives on strategies, approaches and management plans.

Case 1: Road Tunnel with Junctions

The project involves relocating an arterial road that is a major entry road to a city as well as a through road for long distance traffic. The aim is to bury part of the road, that currently divides the city and becomes regularly congested, in two 2.3 km tunnels with three lanes in each direction, to widen the rest of it (along 3 km), and to connect it to the surrounding traffic network by graded interchanges. Besides the city infrastructure, the tunnels will also pass under the rapids traversing the city at 20 m below the river bed. The price components used in the selection were the following (Finnish Transport Agency 2012):

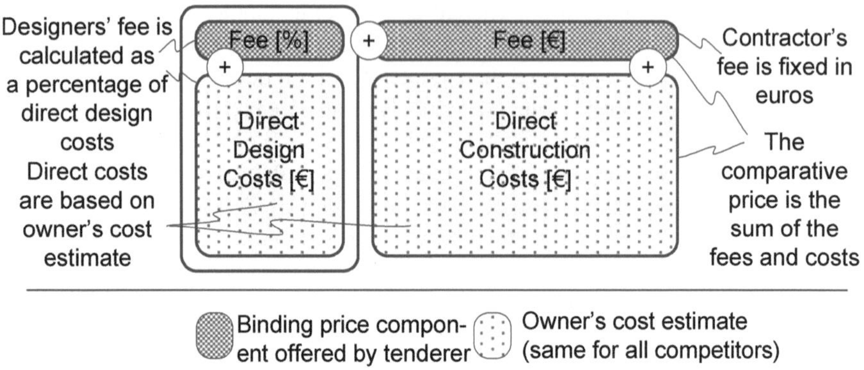

Fig. 2 Formation of comparative price in the road tunnel project

- Fee percentage of design companies which consists of company-level overheads and expected profit when the fees of designers to the main contract are combined according to their work shares.
- Fixed-fee of contractors which consists of company-level overheads and expected profit when the fees of contractors to the main contract are combined according to their work shares.

The owner used the same—his own—direct cost estimate in comparing competitors, which thus became the basis of the assumed size of the direct costs of both last stage proponents. Based on data from earlier projects, the owner divided the total cost estimate into likely design and construction costs for the calculation of a comparative cost. Designers' fee was calculated from the design share (based on the percentages) after which all items were added up to arrive at a total comparative cost (Fig. 2). Selection was then made based on joint assessment of the team's capability and the comparative price where the former carries greater weight than the latter. Due to the small number and limited coverage of concrete price components, the cost viewpoint is reflected in the selection primarily as a component of capability through the proposed method for control of the economy, presented budget critique and suggested development possibilities. Thus, it is not question of track records and formal qualification, but a solution-oriented view is required.

Case 2: Water Treatment Plant

The project involves renovation of a water treatment plant that processes the sewage of about 1.5 million people. Before the renovation, the treatment system consisted of two main stages that

were not modified. Instead, the renovation added a third stage to the process, which improved the treatment result considerably. The project was a new type of combination of technologies, which means that the implementation also involved technologically demanding development. Besides, the intermediary storage of water between the second and third stages and its reorganisation/location posed a big challenge to the project. The price components used in the selection were as follows (Melbourne Water Company 2010):

- Preliminaries costs that cover costs related to the erection of temporary structures for launching the site (such as fences, site roads, warehouses and site offices).
- Project overheads, which here cover the project-level management costs (e.g. safety officers, supervisors, accountants and financial systems) of the entire project until completion.
- Risk and opportunity contingency based on the risk analysis made by proponents, that is, the pricing and summary of risks and opportunities constituting a risk allowance to be included in the TOC.
- Fee percentage which consists of company-level overheads and expected profit when the fees of designers and contractors are combined according to their work shares.

The owner used the same—his own—direct material and labour cost estimate in comparing competitors, which thus became the basis of the assumed size of the direct costs of both proponents. The cost items priced by the proponents were added to the cost level of the owner's estimate: management costs, site establishment costs and risk contingency (Fig. 3). This total cost was then increased by the share of the fee derived from this sum based on the fee percentage submitted by the competitors. The result of this calculation provided a comparative price for the competitors. Selection was then made based on joint assessment of the team's capability and the comparative price.

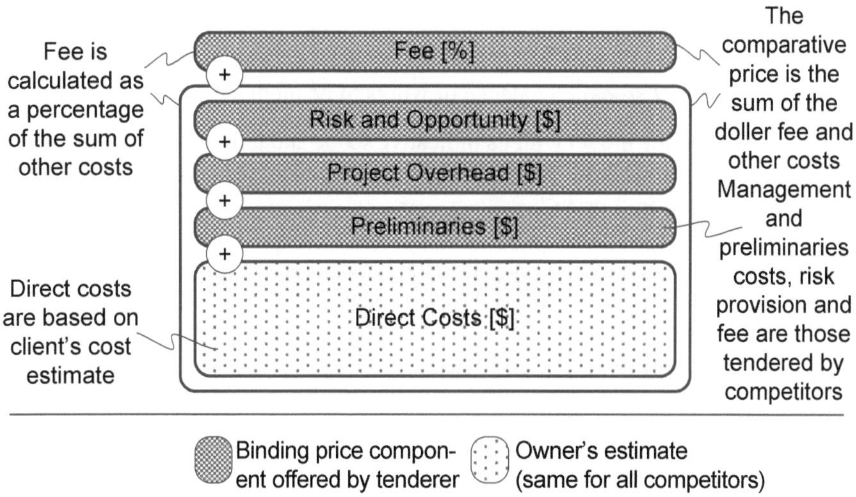

Fig. 3 Formation of comparative price in the water treatment plant project

Case 3: Road Bridge and Surroundings

The project involves replacing an existing road bridge across a river with a new one next to a rural community. The new approx. 150 m long two-lane bridge with a separate lane for light traffic will be built in the immediate vicinity of the old bridge that is to be dismantled later. The work includes the implementation of walls subjected to loading from earth and erosion reinforcements as well as road connections and nearby access and intersection arrangements. The special challenges of the project derive from the fact that the bridge is connected to the adjacent square of special cultural-historical importance.

In the competition, most of the components needed to determine the full price were tendered for. Only some relatively insignificant parts, such as the relocations of utilities/services networks, were not priced. Yet, some price components were indicative only while others were binding. The price components to be tendered for at binding prices were (Roads and Maritime Services 2012):

- Bridge TOC, which is the total of the labour and material costs needed to build the bridge (without a specific risk provision).
- Risk contingency for bridge, a risk premium produced by risk analysis of bridge building to be included in total TOC.
- Project overheads TOC, which cover the overheads of both the bridge and the so-called balance of works of the project.
- Risk contingency for project overheads, a risk premium produced by risk analysis of overheads to be included in total TOC.
- Fee percentage consisting of company-level overheads and profit margin. A corresponding share of the sum of all other cost items is included in the tender/TOC.
- In addition to the above binding components, the following price components were offered as tentative prices:
- Budget TOC for the balance of works, that is, a preliminary estimate of the total cost of inputs other than those required for building the bridge.
- Risk contingency for balance of works, a preliminary risk premium produced by risk analysis of a so-called balance of works to be included in total TOC.

At the same time, the model with its indicative scope and unit price data determined the way of calculating how later changes in components tendered for at tentative prices affect the overall price.

The owner calculated the total prices of the alternatives on the basis of the price components submitted by the proponents as illustrated in Fig. 4, i.e. including the contribution and influence of the owner's estimator. The final selection of the contractor was based on both capability and price. In principle, the intention was to assign equal weights to quality and price.

Case 4: Arterial Road with Junctions

The project involves a massive road investment for improving a main road network and increasing its capacity. The works centre around an about 10 km section of a

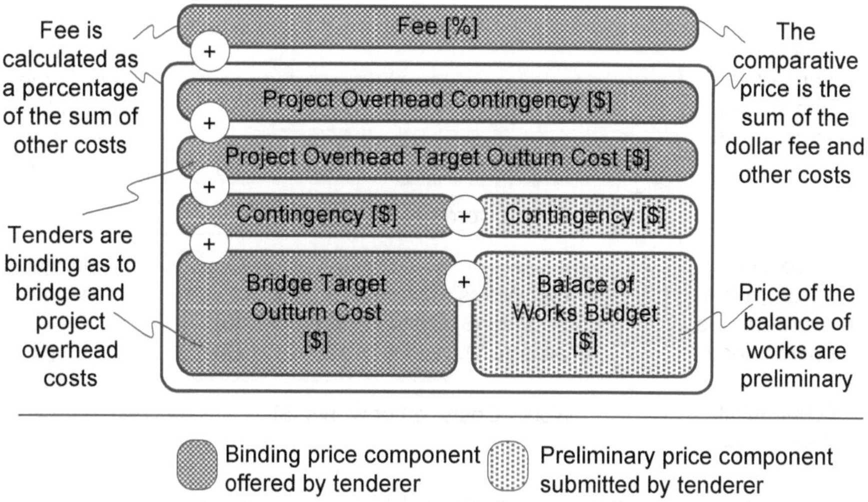

Fig. 4 Formation of comparative price in the road bridge project

highway bypassing a major airport. Additional lanes are being built for this section and many junctions are being rebuilt, a few are being expanded into complete interchanges. The project also includes the improvement of many kilometres of roads intersecting the main road and some other roads in the area. The works are mainly restricted by existing urban structure and the airport area.

The selection model can be considered a partial price competition model due to the extensive scope of the project, although the pricing concerned a considerable part of the road network practically in its entirety, covering all costs at binding prices. The price data to be specified in the tender consisted of the following parts (Main Roads Western Australia 2012):

- Total price of construction works covering the specified part of the project (road network; utilities/services networks, etc. excluded) based on a unit cost calculation to be submitted as part of the tender.
- Defect correction percentage, which is a cost item reserved for warranty works, calculated from and added on top of actual construction costs.
- Project overheads (site overheads and other staff costs) which are supplemented in the case of design and supervision with the related staffing plan and corresponding breakdown of costs.
- Risk provision percentage that describes the risk provision to be added on top of direct costs and calculated on their basis, which in the light of the risk analysis is sufficient to cover expected variation in costs.
- Fee percentage that consists of company-level overheads and expected profit when the fees of designers and contractors are combined according to their work shares.

The owner used the unit costs submitted by the proponents in determining the comparative cost while calculating the estimated magnitudes of the costs of actual construction works for parts of the project to be designed later. These parts were not

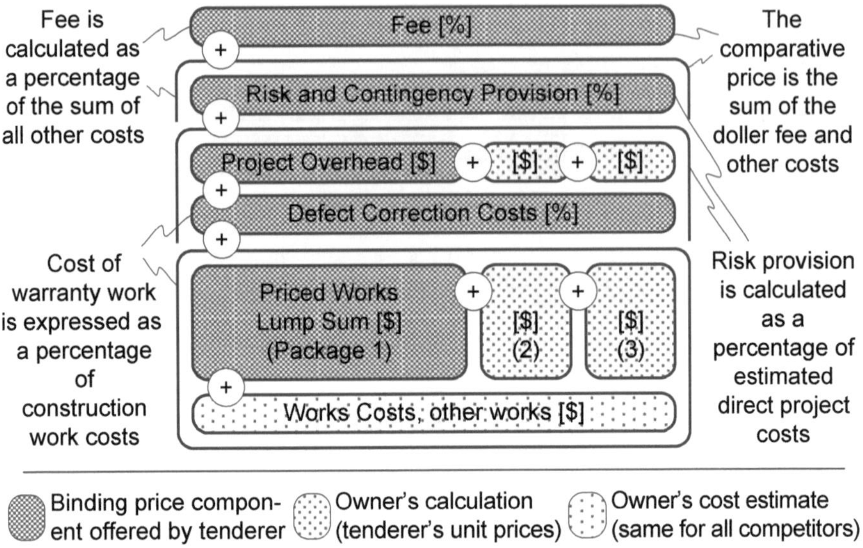

Fig. 5 Formulation of comparative price in the arterial road project

subject to design in the competition, although they were also meant to be included in the works under the very same contract together with the road section priced in the tender. Thus, we are dealing with areas 2 and 3 of Fig. 5 illustrating the calculation of the comparative price (whereas only part 1 was included in proposal planning and pricing). Besides, the owner used his own cost estimate for some works excluded from tender pricing, which was the same for all competitors.

The total comparative price was arrived at by adding to the construction costs determined phase by phase first the cost of warranty works calculated as a percentage of them, and then the sum of project overheads also compiled phase by phase, as well as the risk provision and fee of the service providers to be calculated later on the basis of the percentages submitted by the proponents. The risk provision was calculated from the mentioned item covering direct costs and project overheads, and it was added to the cost estimate before calculating the fee from the resulting sum of costs that included the risk provision. However, the setting of the comparative price was not just mechanical calculation, but the evaluation team also had to do a lot of work in making the tenders comparable. The selection, yet again, was made on the basis of both capability and comparative price while the latter carried more weight this time due to the relatively complete design of a critical section of the project.

Discussion and Conclusions

General Assessment

The case projects shed interesting light on both the possible applications of price component selection and the reasons behind its use. Both the reasons and applications were different in all mapped cases:

- In Case 1 the model was used in the most minimalist way where the fee was the only price component quoted by the proponents. It was considered that the most important determinant of efficient project solution was early integration of the team and genuine, collaborative joint development due to the uniqueness and uncertainty related to the project. Competitive tendering on sub-contracts and price transparency were also of importance, in addition to the fact that the owner's budget had already initially been considered stringent.
- In Case 2 the model was used mainly to determine project and company overheads and joint costs. Direct costs were determined largely on the basis of later competitive tendering on sub-contracts, so there was no need to price them during the selection of the alliance team. Thus, the use of indirect costs as competition components locked in the price determination criteria reliably enough, and use of the owner's own cost estimate for direct costs made it possible to calculate a reliable comparative price.
- In Case 3 the model was used due the genuine uncertainty related to implementation. The whole was clearly composed of different types of largely independent sections: the main part of the project could be priced and there was significant uncertainty only about the other part of the project, which justified the use of this model. The former project part was priced in the competition, while an estimate was adequate for the latter part of the comparative price, as project overheads were included in the tenders comprehensively.
- In Case 4 the challenge was the extensive scope of the project, which is why a large portion of the project had not yet been defined by the competition phase. A key part of the project was developed and priced during the competition. On that basis the owner could calculate a comparative price for each proponent using the tender prices submitted and the default project size and contents. Thus, the unit prices specified in the tender also acted as guidelines for the price level of the project part that had not yet been designed.

A summary of price components used in the case projects is presented in Table 1. A characteristic feature of most components is that they are contingency provisions or joint costs and overheads added on top of direct costs. Direct material and labour costs are also priced partially sometimes in search of innovative project solutions. Their use can also be the solution when the owner considers it inadequate to base the selection on contingency provisions and overheads only (in addition to capability, etc.). In the case of a large project it may be reasonable, for instance, to request proposals for a certain part of the project area-wise while selection is based on the

Table 1 Bases for definition of price components of case projects

	Case 1: Road tunnel with junctions	Case 2: Water treatment plant	Case 3: Road bridge and surroundings	Case 4: Arterial road with junctions
Fee	✓	✓	✓	✓
Cost escalation		✓[a]	✓[b]	
Risk contingency		✓	✓	✓
Project overhead		✓	✓	✓
Preliminaries costs		✓		
Direct costs, structure-specific[c]			✓	✓
Direct costs, section-specific[d]				✓
Defect correction				✓

[a] Part of risk contingency
[b] Part of direct costs
[c] Tendered in the case of certain structures of a diverse project
[d] Tendered in the case of a certain section/area of a wider project

comparative cost of the entire project (cf. Case 4). In determining the comparative cost, the owner can use the unit costs submitted by the proponents as a part of their proposals to calculate the estimated magnitudes of the costs of actual construction works for parts of the project to be designed later in the joint development phase. An alternative is to break down the project structure-wise so that the proposals cover only critical structures throughout the project (Case 3) or within a section (Case 4). (More information on Cases 2–4 is available in Lahdenperä, 2014, and on Case 1 in Alliance Executive Team, 2013; Alliance Leadership Team, 2014).

As to Case 4, the owner had already used a very similar price component selection procedure to select the team for an earlier road project. Its components corresponded to those used in this project with the exception that in terms of direct costs only part of the pavement had to be priced, although the contract covered the design and construction of the entire road structure so that the total costs were many times larger than the priced part. Both the owner and the service provider seemed to be highly satisfied with this previously used lighter model, but the huge size of the current project together with public accountability concerns forced extending the set of components to cover a bigger share of the project. To illustrate other possibilities deviating from Case 1 (where the owner used the same direct cost estimate for both proponents), only a fee quote can be requested while a proponent-specific estimate is prepared by the owner's estimator for the comparison adhering to a model used in another Finnish project where a proposal included a partial concept design for the project (University of Helsinki, 2011; the comparison was structured differently in the actual case, however). And other possibilities not captured by the study surely exist.

All in all, there are numerous ways of applying price component selection as shown just by the case examples. The used price components were different, and

Table 2 Relative efforts needed for the two stages of the development phase in case projects (indicative only)

	Case 1: Road tunnel with junctions	Case 2: Water treatment plant	Case 3: Road bridge and surroundings	Case 4: Arterial road with junctions
Competition	✓	✓✓	✓✓✓✓	✓✓✓
Joint development	✓✓✓✓	✓✓✓	✓	✓✓

the organisation of the selection processes also differs, for example, in the timing of the workshops. The amount and nature of proposal planning also vary. Perhaps the most important factor is the weights the owner assigns to competitive pressure and genuine joint development for the benefit of the project, i.e. how the "development phase" of Fig. 1 breaks down into the "competition" and "joint development" stages of Table 2. Some procedures are not very far from traditional auction while some really are. Accordingly, the more design is needed for a proposal, the more weight is assigned generally to comparative price in the selection. In fact, the extreme models apply very different strategies to the development of the project and its value for money which allows drawing only general conclusions.

Experiences

Experiences from the use of price component selection in the presented cases vary correspondingly with the fact that the mode used in the four case projects differ from each other in many ways. In the case of partial price selection models that aim at a relatively unambiguous and comprehensive comparative price, the same doubts often arise that have been found problematic in pure price competition. Besides, the use of price components may make procurement more challenging, unless the contents of the components have been clearly defined. At worst, the proponents get frustrated interpreting the contents. The formation of the costs of projects is a complex equation including many interdependencies and even overlaps where the interpretation of the content of an individual component may depend on the performer of the calculation. On the other hand, there is the risk that the design solution is manipulated to lower the comparative price without really improving the efficiency of the project.

This also makes the comparison of tenders more challenging. Practice has shown that the owner often has to work to make the tenders commensurate before deriving genuinely comparable reference prices from the tenders (Cases; Chipman and Woodman 2010). For these reasons, the price components of the partial price selection model should naturally be as independent cost items as possible. This is also required by the fact that the low prices of components included in the competition cannot be compensated for later by other cost items priced only at the development phase. Moreover, price components should be defined so that they play a central role in the formation of the overall costs and that they allow the competitors to stand out from each other.

To make comparisons easier in the case of an alliance project with a joint organisation, proponents should also assume at the competition phase that all tasks are performed solely by the staff of the service providers. Risk contingency is a more conceptual factor that also poses a challenge. It is worthwhile incorporating the risk view of all proponents in the owner's register at first, and later to let them price the revised version. Risk contingency may not, however, be a reasonable factor in price component selection unless the related uncertainties can be expected to be largely minimised during the joint development stage before fixing the TOC. Fees and even project overheads, again, are appropriate in most cases due to their insensitivity to variations in direct costs. The breakdown of costs into direct and indirect ones must, however, always be clarified, since companies seem to have different practices in that respect. Direct costs, on the other hand, can be eliminated from the competition the more likely, the larger the share of the project purchased from the market or based on standardised solutions is.

Thus, in some cases, the use of the price component method may be even more demanding than full-price selection. Experiences from the projects have, however, been for the most part very encouraging and support the validity of price component selection due to the reasons given in the "need for a change" section above although possible caveats were listed as an advisory for future applicants. Especially in the case of more demanding projects it is evident that the other advantages gained by early involvement and collaborative project development weigh more than the challenges of competitive tendering. This was also underlined by the participants of the studied projects. In the case of the simplified applications of the studied projects, no express criticism was levelled at the selection method either.

It must be emphasised that the presented view is based on interviews of the owner's and service provider's representatives in all presented cases. At the time of the interviews, some of the projects (Cases 3 and 4) had just completed the selection phase and, naturally, there is no certainty about what the definitive experiences will be. Yet, the overall assessment was highly positive and optimistic. The projects that had progressed to implementation/construction (Case 1) or completion (Case 2) were even more so: the parties were absolutely satisfied with the cost efficiency and believed that better results could not have been achieved by any other methods.

Public Procurement View

Although all the presented cases represent public construction projects, Case 1 is obviously the most interesting one from the public procurement perspective for two reasons. First, it is a procurement that was carried out in Europe, in Finland, while Cases 2–4 describe Australian activities. (Based on anecdotal evidence, a model similar to that of Case 1 has also been occasionally used in Australia although it is not dealt with in this study.) The author's view is based on the fact that in Europe public procurements are controlled by basically clear regulations (whereas in Australia there are no similar, universally applicable regulations, and the decisions on procurement practices are mostly made by public servants and politicians under the guidance of various policies). Second, in Case 1, the price components were the least comprehensive leaving most of the pricing to take place only after the selection which may be presumed to provide the most potential for violating the regulations. This view is based on the fact that although the European directive on public procurement allows the application of "the most economically advantageous tender" criterion, it implicitly also includes the price viewpoint.

Yet, a project that applies the price component method in selection can rely on numerous means for managing its costs. Naturally, the actual method depends on the project and used price components. In general, however, at least the following means were used in the studied projects:

- The owner reserves the right to subject final stage competitors to financial audits where the level of costs of realised projects can be assessed to serve as a benchmark in evaluation.
- Besides the specified price components, the proponents are expected to include their pricing bases in their tenders for additional auditing and to serve as benchmarks for the parts to be estimated later on.
- Major purchases of the project are to be jointly subjected to competitive bidding later and, at the minimum, the prices are to be market-tested (the contractor may do the work if competitive enough).
- An independent third-party estimator is involved to assess the appropriateness of the TOC and the cost items it consists of (evaluation of costs and justification material).
- A financial auditor is involved to verify costs incurred and financial management in general (auditions of financial systems, breakdown/limitation of direct and indirect costs, audition of reporting and invoicing).
- The owner's budget guiding the joint development and pricing of the project is based on two expert estimates completed independently and is made strict compared to the general cost level in the market.
- The owner has the right to terminate the project for convenience, without default, for instance, but the owner has to pay a fair compensation for all work and services carried out by then.

These features of the practice led the owners of the presented case projects to regard it the most appropriate method to provide good value for money in the targeted projects considering their properties, constraints and objectives. The requirements of owners included flexibility in scope definition and fast completion as well as the ability to introduce novel technologies for improved performance. Another reoccurring challenge was created by the fact that the work disturbed on-going operations and that numerous stakeholder issues had to be solved in the course of the project. The uncertainty due the project constraints and conditions was part of the challenge as were the multi-dimensional value systems of projects. That is to say, that although the study speaks for the use of price component selection it is not suggested as an all-round solution for all projects.

On the above basis, also the owner of Case 1, the Finnish Transport Agency, made a decision to use the described selection model. Due to the cost management measures itemised above, it was considered that the price view was incorporated into the decision making process to a reasonable degree except for part of company overheads and profit. Therefore, it was seen necessary in the completion phase to request a fee which was also seen as the minimum condition for procurement to meet the requirements of the regulations on public procurements (i.e. Directive 2004/18/EC; Act on Public Contracts 348/2007). In terms of the current public procurement legislation, the described procurement practice is based on the stage-wise "negotiated procedure" where "the most economically advantageous tender" is the selection criterion (Finnish Transport Agency 2012). According to the directive, this procedure could be used "in exceptional cases, when the nature of the works, supplies, or services or the risks attaching thereto do not permit prior overall pricing". Yet, 13 % of all public construction by value is procured by the negotiated procedure in Europe (Strand et al. 2011). All of the above suggest that there is room for the presented models despite the restriction.

What is more important, however, is that the directive has recently been updated (Directive 2014/24/EU), and within 2 years it (the relevant parts) should be guiding the practice after having been transposed into national laws within the European Union (EU). Although the author refrains from legal interpretations, it is clear that the new directive broadens the possibilities for negotiation. Thus, it provides a long awaited opportunity to consider new approaches and, consequently, use of price component selection also in the procurement of major, largely public, infrastructure projects. Yet, it should be noted that when EU directives are implemented through national laws, they may set stricter terms for various alternatives. Therefore, it is not necessarily certain that the practice is applicable as such to all countries within the EU.

Closing Remarks

Along with the change in procurement and project delivery practices, and the corresponding increase in the use of relational contracting, project alliance has proved its applicability as a project delivery method of demanding projects. At the same time, it has established itself in the realisation of complex infrastructure projects in Australasia and is also spreading to other continents. Early involvement of implementers in collaborative design is a central part of the solution, and it cannot be combined effectively with full-price competition. This has caused price components to be used in parallel with qualitative criteria since that is often considered necessary to maintain competitive pressure and gain acceptance in the eyes of politicians, auditing authorities and the general public. In selection based on price components, the tender covers only part of the items that finally make up the total price of the project.

The study has examined experiences gained from projects applying various forms of competition that include price components as selection criteria. In their totality, the experiences from case projects have been highly positive and definitely also encourage considering the possibilities of using the partial price selection model also in challenging future projects of the public sector. Especially, since the performance of full-price selection is often questionable in projects requiring innovative approaches and flexibility and ones that involve many constraints and uncertainty. Yet, the practice should be combined with the principles of transparency of information (incl. external auditors and estimators) and emphasis given to the creation of collaborative, trustful relationships among the team members.

It must, however, be remembered that different projects call for different selection methods derived from project properties and boundary conditions of implementation. Price component selection is not expected to be the answer to all situations and projects: more straightforward and standard projects may still be best procured by more conventional methods than the one discussed in this chapter. Yet, since projects are becoming more complex and more constraints and requirements are set by society and stakeholders, the number of projects that would most likely benefit from price component selection is growing. It seems to be a model, which at best, efficiently integrates competitive pressure and genuine joint development for the benefit of the project.

References

Act on Public Contracts 348/2007. (2007). *Statutes of Finland*. (Unofficial English Translation). Helsinki: Ministry of Justice.

Alliancing Association of Australasia. (2010). *Early contractor involvement*. Sydney: Alliancing Association of Australasia.

Alliance Executive Team. (2013). *Rantatunneli alliance project. Project plan*. Tampere, Finland: Tampere City, Finnish Transport Agency, Lemminkäinen Infra, Saanio & Riekkola and A-Insinöörit Suunnittelu.

Alliance Leadership Team. (2014). *Rantatunneli alliance. Value for money report. Project development phase*. Tampere, Finland: Tampere City, Finnish Transport Agency, Lemminkäinen Infra, Saanio & Riekkola and A-Insinöörit Suunnittelu.

American Institute of Architects. (2007). *Integrated project delivery: A guide*. Washington, DC: American Institute of Architects.

Arain, F., & Pheng, L. (2005). The potential effects of variation orders on institutional building projects. *Facilities, 23*(11/12), 496–510.

Bajari, P., & Tadelis, S. (2001). Incentives versus transaction costs: a theory of procurement contracts. *RAND Journal of Economics, 32*(3), 387–407.

Bajari, P., Houghton, S., & Tadelis, S. (2014). Bidding for incomplete contracts: an empirical analysis of adaptation costs. *The American Economic Review, 104*(4), 1288–1319.

Ballard, G. (2008). The lean project delivery system: an update. *Lean Construction Journal, 4*, 1–19.

Blayse, A., & Manley, K. (2004). Key influences on construction innovation. *Construction Innovation, 4*, 143–154.

Bredehoeft, P. (2012). *Cost estimate classification system—as applied for the building and general construction industries* (AACE International Recommended Practice No. 56R-08). Morgantown, WV: AACE International.

Chang, C.-Y., & Ive, G. (2007). Reversal of bargaining power in construction projects: meaning, existence and implications. *Construction Management and Economics, 25*(8), 845–855.

Chipman, P., & Woodman, T. (2010). Value for money in the wyaralong program: an owner's perspective. In: AIPM conference 2010, 10–13 October, 2010. Darwin, NT: Australian Institute of Project Management (AIPM).

Connaughton, J., & Green, S. (1996). *Value management in construction: a client's guide*. (Special Publication 129). London: Construction Industry Research and Information Association.

Cox, I., Morris, J., Rogerson, J., & Jared, G. (1999). A quantitative study of post contract award design changes in construction. *Construction Management and Economics, 17*(4), 427–439.

de Neufville, R. & King, D. (1991). Risk and need-for-work premiums in contractor bidding. *Journal of Construction Engineering and Management, 117*(4), 659–673.

Department of Infrastructure and Transport. (2011). *National alliance contracting guidelines. Guide to alliance contracting*. Canberra: Department of Infrastructure and Transport.

Department of Treasury and Finance. (2006). *Project alliancing: Practitioners' guide*. Melbourne: Department of Treasury and Finance.

Department of Treasury and Finance. (2009). *In pursuit of additional value. a benchmarking study into alliancing in the Australian public sector*. Melbourne: Department of Treasury and Finance.

Directive 2004/18/EC of the European parliament and of the council of 31 March 2004 on the coordination of procedures for the award of public works contracts, public supply contracts and public service contracts. (2004). *Official Journal of the European Union* L 134, *47*: 114–240.

Directive 2014/24/EU of the European parliament and of the council of 26 February 2014 on public procurement and repealing directive 2004/18/EC. (2014). *Official Journal of the European Union* L 94, *57*: 65–242.

Edwards, R. (2009). *Early contractor involvement (ECI) contracts in the South Australian transport infrastructure construction industry*. Adelaide: Department for Transport Energy and Infrastructure (DTEI).

Finnish Transport Agency. (2012). *Vt12 Tampereen tunneli, Allianssiurakka. Tarkennettu tarjouspyyntö* (in Finnish) [Vt12 Tampere tunnel, an Alliance Contract. Revised Request for proposal]. Helsinki: Finnish Transport Agency.

Hanna, A., Russell, J., & Vandenberg, P. (1999). The impact of change orders on mechanical construction labour efficiency. *Construction Management and Economics, 17*(6), 721–730.

Hartmann, A., Davies, A., & Frederiksen, L. (2010). Learning to deliver service-enhanced public infrastructure: balancing contractual and relational capabilities. *Construction Management and Economics, 28*(11), 1165–1175.

HM Treasury (2013). *Infrastructure procurement routemap: A guide to improving delivery capability*. London: HM Treasury.

Holmen, E., Pedersen, A.-C., & Torvatn, T. (2005). Building relationships for technological innovation. *Journal of Business Research, 58*(9), 1240–1250.

Hsieh, T., Lu, S., & Wu, C. (2004). Statistical analysis of causes for change orders in metropolitan public works. *International Journal of Project Management, 22*(8): 679–686.

Ibbs, W. (2005). Impact of change's timing on labor productivity. *Journal of Construction Engineering and Management, 131*(11), 1219–1223.

Ke, Y., Ling, F., Zou, P., Wang, S., & Kumaraswamy, M. (2012). Positive and negative factors influencing the implementation of relational contracting in public construction projects in Australia. *Joint CIB international symposium on construction management research* (Vol. 2, pp. 754–765), June 26–29, 2012, Montreal, Canada.

Krumm, J. (2001). History of real estate management from a corporate perspective. *Facilities, 19*(7/8), 276–286.

Lahdenperä, P. (2009). *Project alliance: The competitive single target-cost approach*. (Research Notes 2472). Espoo: VTT Technical Research Centre of Finland.

Lahdenperä, P. (2010). Conceptualizing a two-stage target-cost arrangement for competitive cooperation. *Construction Management and Economics, 28*(7), 783–796.

Lahdenperä, P. (2012a). *Allianssitiimin Valinta. Ensimmäisen Hankkeen Menettelyt ja Niitä Koskevan Palautekyselyn Tulokset.* [Alliance Team Selection. Procedures of the First Finnish Project and Related Feedback]. (VTT Technology 34). Espoo: VTT Technical Research Centre of Finland. (in Finnish)

Lahdenperä, P. (2012b). Making sense of the multi-party contractual arrangements of project partnering, project alliancing and integrated project delivery. *Construction Management and Economics, 30*(1), 57–79.

Lahdenperä, P. (2014). *In search of a happy medium: price components as part of alliance team selection.* (VTT Technology 174). Espoo: VTT Technical Research Centre of Finland.

Latham, M. (1994). Constructing the team. *Final report of the government/industry review of procurement and contractual arrangements in the UK construction industry.* London: Her Majesty's Stationery Office.

Leiringer, R. & Bröchner, J. (2010). Editorial: Service-led construction projects. *Construction Management and Economics, 28*(11), 1123–1129.

Loraine, R. (1994). Project specific partnering. *Engineering, Construction and Architectural Management, 1*(1), 5–16.

Lundman, P. (2011). *Cost management for underground infrastructure projects: A case study on cost increase and its causes.* Doctoral Thesis. Luleå, Sweden: Luleå University of Technology, Department of Civil, Environmental and Natural Resources Engineering.

Macneil, I. & Campbell, D. (2001). *The relational theory of contract: Selected works of Ian Macneil.* London: Sweet & Maxwell.

Main Roads Western Australia. (2012). *Request for proposals. Gateway WA, Perth airport and freight access project.* [Parts A, B and C]. East Perth: Main Roads Western Australia.

Melbourne Water Company. (2010). *ETP tertiary upgrade project. alliance implementation strategy, rev 11(b)—as executed.* Melbourne: Melbourne Water Company.

Mosey, D. (2009). *Early contractor involvement in building procurement: contracts, partnering and project management.* Chichester: Wiley-Blackwell.

National Audit Office. (2005). *Improving public services through better construction.* London: National Audit Office.

Nicholson, J. (1991). "Rethinking the competitive bid." *Civil Engineering, 61*(1), 66–68.

Pishdad, P., & Beliveau, Y. (2010). Integrating multi-party contracting risk management (MP-CRM) model with building information modeling (BIM). Paper presented at the CIB W78 27th international conference on applications of IT in the AEC industry, November 16–19, Cairo, Egypt.

Procurement/Lean Client Task Group. (2012). *Government construction strategy: final report to government.* London: Cabinet Office.

Rahman, M., & Kumaraswamy, M. (2002). Joint risk management through transactionally efficient relational contracting. *Construction Management and Economics, 20*(1), 45–54.

Roads and Maritime Services (2012). *Windsor bridge alliance. Request for proposals.* North Sydney: Roads and Maritime Services.

Roehrich, J., & Lewis, M. (2010). Towards a model of governance in complex (product–service) inter-organizational systems. *Construction Management and Economics, 28*(11), 1155–1164.

Russell, J., Gugel, J., & Radtke, M. (1992). Documented constructability savings for petrochemical-facility expansion. *Journal of Performance of Constructed Facilities, 7*(1), 27–45.

Rutten, M., Dorée, A., & Halman, J. (2009). Innovation and interorganizational cooperation: A synthesis of literature. *Construction Innovation, 9*(3), 285–297.

Scott, B. (2001). *Partnering in Europe. Incentive based alliancing for projects.* London: Thomas Telford.

Song, L., Mohamed, Y., & AbouRizk, S. (2009). Early contractor involvement in design and its impact on construction schedule performance. *Journal of Management in Engineering, 25*(1), 12–20.

Stehbens, K., Wilson, O., & Skitmore, M. (1999). Partnering in the Australian construction industry: Breaking the vicious circle. In P. Bowen & R. Hindle (Eds.), *CIB W55 and W65 joint triennial symposium customer satisfaction: a focus for research and practice* (pp. 195–201), September 5–10, 1999, Cape Town, South Africa.

Strand, I., Ramada, P., & Canton, E. (2011). *Public procurement in Europe. Cost and effectiveness. A study on procurement regulation.* Brussels: European Commission (Prepared for the European commission).

Sweeney, S. (2009). *Addressing market failure: using transaction cost economics to improve the construction industry's performance*. Ph. D. Thesis. Melbourne, Australia: Department of Civil and Environmental Engineering, the University of Melbourne.

University of Helsinki. (2011). *Tarjouspyyntö. Allianssihanke Vuolukiventie 1b*. [Request for Proposals, an Alliance Project Vuolukiventie 1b]. Helsinki: University of Helsinki. (in Finnish)

Valkenburg, M., Lenferink, S., Nijsten, R., & Arts, J. (2008). Early contractor involvement: a new strategy for 'buying the best' in infrastructure development in the Netherlands. Paper presented at the 3rd international public procurement conference, 28–30 August, 2008, Amsterdam, The Netherlands. www.ippa.org.

Vandermerwe, S., & Rada, J. (1988). Servitization of business: Adding value by adding services. *European Management Journal, 6*(4), 314–324.

Weston, D., & Gibson, G. (1993). Partnering-project performance in US army corps of engineers. *Journal of Management in Engineering, 9*(4), 410–425.

Williamson, O. (1979). Transaction-cost economics: The governance of contractual relations. *Journal of Law and Economics, 22*(2), 233–261.

Williamson, O. (1985). *The economic institutions of capitalism: firms, markets, relational contracting*. New York: The Free Press.

Xiang, P., Zhou, J., Zhou, X., & Ye, K. (2012). Construction project risk management based on the view of asymmetric information. *Journal of Construction Engineering and Management, 138*(11), 1303–1311.

Pertti Lahdenperä DSc (Tech) is a principal scientist in the VTT Technical Research Centre of Finland. His research interests are in the built environment and its project procurement and delivery systems.

Pricing for Public Purchase: A Qualitative-Empirical Analysis of Public Procurement and Price Setting Practices

Michael Georgi and Sascha Kemmeter

Introduction

Public purchase has an essential impact on the economy. In Germany, goods and services for about 360 billion € are ordered by public institutions such as federal or state departments, town councils, or other public institutions (e.g., fire or police departments) (Öko-Institut 2008). This includes about 17% of the German gross domestic product. The Consolidated Federal Funds Report mentions a number of over US$ 500 billion that were spent by federal institutions in the USA (US Department of Commerce 2009). For getting the goods and services in the most economical way, basically two key questions come up:

1. How do we find the contract partner who is able to satisfy public needs for goods or services as cheaply as possible with sufficient quality?
2. Is the price appropriate?

These questions might be easy to answer for products and services that are part of everyday life for which the adequacy of offers and prices can be researched with low effort. But especially for complex and individualized products (e.g., military equipment, IT, or research and development (R&D) services) there might not exist an obvious market with several suppliers and customers. When market mechanisms fail, the above mentioned questions are highly relevant to make sure that tax payers' money is not wasted inefficiently. To meet these requirements, governments implemented regulation systems to find the appropriate contract partner and price

M. Georgi (✉)
Department of Management Accounting and Control,
TU Dortmund University, Dortmund, Germany
e-mail: michael.georgi@tu-dortmund.de

S. Kemmeter
Department of Management Accounting,
University of Duisburg-Essen, Essen, Germany
e-mail: sascha.kemmeter@uni-due.de

K. V. Thai (ed.), *International Public Procurement,* Public Administration, Governance and Globalization 14, DOI 10.1007/978-3-319-13434-5_8

for public orders under cost-effective and money-saving aspects. Despite a highly globalized world where companies specialize, their products and services to have advantages in a worldwide competition, public purchase systems still remain very national. While there is a tendency toward a harmonization of public procurement in Europe, pricing regulation still remains exclusively in the hands of individual states. International comparative studies on the price finding process for public purchase contracts are missing.

In Germany, public procurement and pricing regulation are basically individual but connected to give answers to the above mentioned questions. To answer question 1, public procurement regulation was implemented to the process of public purchase. Public procurement regulation helps federal institutions to generate and decide about the most economical offer of potential contract partners for public needs. Fiscal aspects create the motivation for this instrument.

When the best fitting offer is filtered out, question 2 comes up. To ensure that the price for a public contract is appropriate, price regulation was implemented to the process of public purchase. Price regulation for public purchase displays a discrete framework to find the adequate price based on market mechanisms (Hoffjan et al. 2013). In monopolistic settings market mechanisms might fail. In these settings, price regulation provides norms to calculate prices based on a "costs-plus-profit" approach.

As in Germany (VO PR 30/53 with LSP) the public institutions in the USA use a public procurement and "cost-plus" pricing regulation system to protect themselves from excessively high prices, but also to guarantee companies to get the full costs they had for compensating their effort (e.g., Federal Acquisition Regulations). Pricing regulation in Germany was implemented in 1953 mainly with a focus on military goods and public constructions. It is still enforced without any crucial changes. Current circumstances as, e.g., a significantly higher relevance of the services sector compared to the industrial sector as well as changing (cost) accounting practices (e.g., HGB after BilmoG and IFRS, USGAAP) have not been adequately considered yet. Problems with the price-building processes especially for IT or research services are the consequence. Hence, in Germany a reform of the existing framework is discussed.

Despite its relevance for public purchases, price regulation is not widely looked at in science and practice. The objective of this chapter is to empirically analyze (1) the common practice of how the current system for public purchase in Germany is composed and (2) to assess if and at which point of the purchasing process problems occur. Finally we give (3) recommendations for how the existing system or the habits of involved parties will have to change. Therefore, we use a qualitative grounded-theory based approach with 20 interviews among price auditors and managers with experience in the public purchase process. Developing hypotheses about their relationship, we attempt to create an in-depth understanding of the current regulatory framework and its problems. Through an investigation into public procurement and price regulation processes in Germany, a special focus of our chapter is on situations in which market mechanisms fail so that cost-based pricing regulation comes up.

In a further step of this research project, a comparison of German practices with the regulatory system in the USA is planned (1) to assess problem-solving approaches and (2) to give advice about an international harmonization of public procurement and pricing systems. Economic similarities between Germany and the USA as well as the advanced history of the USA in regulation can provide conclusive information for a best-practice regulatory design of price regulation for public acquisitions.

This chapter proceeds as follows: In Section "Public Purchase System in Germany" we review the existing literature regarding the design and implementation practices of public procurement and cost-based pricing regulation in Germany. The methodological approach of our study is described in Section "Methodology." In Section "Empirical Results," we present the empirical results on the procurement and pricing process for public purchase. Section "Conclusion" concludes the chapter with a discussion of our results with regard to controversies between theory and practice and with suggestions to smooth-out existing problems. Furthermore, opportunities for future research are worked out. In Section "Completed and Further Steps of This Research Project," this chapter is classified into the overall research project.

Public Purchase System in Germany

The system designed for public purchase in Germany basically consists of two parts. While the first part includes the procurement process for public utilities (basically through the decree of VOL), the second part includes the regulations of the price setting process (VO PR 30/53 and LSP). Both rules are individual but connected. In this section, first the theoretical framework for public procurement and second the pricing for public purchases are shortly illustrated.

Public Procurement System

Basically, the system of public procurement in Germany is divided into three parts. VOB deals with the procurement of construction work. VOF focuses freelancer activities. In VOL the process of procurements of goods and services is organized. Pricing regulation for public construction works is made differently from the one of goods and services. That is why in this chapter we focus on public procurement and pricing regulation for goods and services except constructions.

While the procurement process above the threshold level of 207 t €[1] is harmonized at a European level to equalize the chances for European companies to get contracts with public institutions in entire Europe, procurement under this threshold

[1] Exceptional amounts exist for defense and sectoral contractors as well as for higher federal authorities.

level falls "only" under national rules. Anyway, both processes resemble each other with only a few differences.

Under the threshold level, basically two forms of procurement are provided: First, open or closed competitive bidding where the public need is announced by the purchaser so that companies can decide whether they want to give an offer or not. Open competitive bidding means that the public need is published without any constraint so that every company is potentially informed about it. Here, the number of participants is potentially unlimited. Closed competitive bidding means that companies have to be invited to give an offer to the purchaser. Therefore, they normally have to prove their ability first. In cases when competitive bidding processes are initialized, the most economical offer out of a number of offers is taken by the purchaser. The criteria for what is seen as "economical" can be defined by the purchaser. Price and quality aspects or experience are examples for relevant criteria. Closed processes are preferred when potentially too many bids are handed in to the purchaser or when it is essential to get further information about the ability of companies to work off orders in the sense of the purchaser. Second, the public order can be given directly to a contract partner without a competitive bidding process. Here, an invitation for tenders with discretionary award of contract is given by a public purchaser. In this case, the company also sometimes has to give proof of their ability to work off the public order based on, e.g., the above mentioned criteria. Discrete procurement processes are used especially when competitive bidding processes do not lead to an adequate result or when highly specialized requirements for goods or services need to be discussed and developed in detail.

Above the threshold level, also open and closed competitive bidding are provided. Moreover, two additional procedures of public procurement exist: First, in a negotiation with or without an ability-check purchaser and supplier discuss conditions of a contract. Second, potential contract partners start a competitive dialogue about goods and services that should be produced. Both additional forms of procurement include the possibility of negotiations after the contract partner has already been chosen. These modes are adequate if complex projects (as, e.g., a transportation system in rough environments) need to be realized.

No matter what procedure of procurement is chosen, it results in the public purchasers' decision for a proposed offer, which includes an amount of money that quid pro quo has to be paid by the purchaser. Especially in cases in which complex and specialized products or services need to be bought, there is an information asymmetry between public purchaser and supplier concerning the size of the price. Sometimes the public purchaser has only little experience if the envisaged price is reasonable. Therefore, public procurement ordinance refers to pricing law in which a system is provided that should verify an appropriate price for a certain public order.

Pricing Regulation

The main intention of the pricing regulation law for public purchase is to keep a justified price level. That means an adequate price based on market mechanisms should be paid for a public purchase. According to that, public institutions should be protected from unfairly high prices and also the supplier should be protected from inadequately low prices (Ebisch et al. 2010, p. 24). Compared to the cost-saving intention of the public procurement system, the intention of pricing regulation for public purchase is neutral. It only aims at prices that are as market-conform as possible.

Generally, every public purchase in Germany falls under pricing law. In detail, this includes contracts of public purchase for federal, state, or municipal institutions as well as public undertakings (e.g., state-owned research institutes or municipal companies that are founded to satisfy local services such as waste disposal or street cleaning).

The German pricing law is organized in two steps: First, depending on the company and product-specific marketability, a price type has to be identified. Basically, five price types are provided by pricing law. These price types are hierarchically organized. If requirements for a higher ranked price type fail, the next lower price type has to be checked.

The highest ranked price type is the "by the state defined price." It is used, e.g., for medicine. That is not a further part of our analysis because there is no price-finding process for this price type. Anyway it has to be mentioned for the sake of completeness.

The "market-price" is on the next step of the hierarchy (§ 4 VO PR 30/53). For having this price type, an active market has to exist. Therefore, pricing law provides the following requirements (Ebisch et al. 2010, p. 90): An objective market-price exists if products are traded so that every customer of a certain product by a certain company has to pay the same price at a fixed point in time. For a company-subjective market-price, prices for equal products or services have to be realized constantly with nonpublic contract partners. Contracts with other public institutions cannot be used to prove an active market.

If the requirements of a "market-price" cannot be fulfilled for a public order, cost-based pricing comes up. Based on a hierarchical organization, three cost-based price types are provided by pricing regulation for public purchase. The lower the hierarchical level, the more distant are active market mechanisms. To be as close to the market as possible, cost-based pricing calculation can comprise market-prices for parts of the final product or service.

For a "fixed-price" planned costs of products or services have to be clearly calculable. This is the case if there already exists enough experience about the production process because of other similar orders (e.g., for other public institutions) (Ebisch et al. 2010, p. 137).

A "conversion-price" is designated for orders when there is not enough experience to be able to calculate transparently at the beginning of the production process, but it is expected that it will be possible at a certain point of the production. In this case, a conversion date is negotiated before the production starts. Costs that occur before that point of time are reimbursed. After that point of time, the "reimbursement-price" is replaced by a "fixed-price" (Ebisch et al. 2010, p. 141).

The lowest price type on the hierarchy is the "reimbursement-price." This price type comes up if costs for a public purchase cannot at all be planned in advance. In these cases, costs are reimbursed if they can be documented based on calculation norms that are provided by pricing law (Ebisch et al. 2010, p. 147).

Second, when the criteria of a market-price cannot be proved, cost-based price calculation comes up. Pricing law provides a "cost-plus" approach in which overhead costs are allocated to the cost-by-cause principle (LSP). Besides direct costs, pricing law provides the possibility to add calculatory costs to the cost-based prices (e.g., calculatory interests on operating assets). While there are exact norms for which costs can be included in the calculation, the benefit margin is generally negotiable between the contract partners. Previous studies mention margins between 1 and 6 %, in exceptional cases more (Hövelborn 2014, p. 51).

Methodology

In this study, we use a qualitative-empirical approach based on grounded theory methodology. Grounded theory methodology implies the process of building theory inductively by means of the qualitative analysis of data (Lueger 2009, p. 192). It therefore provides the researcher with greater freedom to explore the research area. As a consequence, grounded theory is useful in providing rigorous insight into highly complex areas that are relatively unknown by the researcher (Corbin and Strauss 2008, p. 8). As already mentioned, prior research in the fields of procurement and price-setting practices for public purchases is relatively little. This process involves using the data collection via interviewing experts in the fields of public purchase and pricing.

Aim of the interview sessions was to gain deep understanding about procurement and price-setting practices for public purchases. Because not a probabilistic representativity is in the focus of this study, theoretical sampling was used (Charmaz and Belgrave 2012, p. 358). In that way, structures and interrelations between key aspects and determinants can be seen. Generalizable hypotheses and theoretical models are worked out as a basis for further (quantitative or theoretical) studies.

The study was announced via email, interview appointments were acquired through the following direct calls. Further interview opportunities were generated by personal references. Every dialog partner had an academic or professional background. The discipline was not necessarily restricted to experts with a strong focus on finance and accounting. The discussions were strategically and operationally expanded and covered financial as well as legal aspects. Data triangulation aspects were the reason for the dualistic approach of this study which includes the interviews of price auditors as well as of organizational interview partners. In summary, it was possible to personally interview 26 experts in 20 interviews. Ten of them were generated within companies of defense industry, R&D, public-private-partnerships, IT industry, as well as research institutes. In that way, company-subjective perspectives were considered. For getting a neutral and overall view of interrelations, the other ten interviews were generated with price auditors.

The interviews were conducted from March 2012 till May 2013 and were all guided by a semistructured guideline consisting of a pool of 30 open questions. These questions were mainly deducted from literature and impressions of prior experiences (Parker and Roffey 1997, p. 221). In order to assure the validity of the study, the complete interview guideline was pretested and discussed with two practitioners and three persons with research background in the field of pricing and public services (Bortz and Döring 2006, p. 355). As proposed by grounded theory, the interview guideline was constantly adapted to recent insights gained from prior interviews.

The interviews' duration ranged between 65 and 170 min with an average of around 115 min per interview. Seventeen interviews were tape recorded and transcribed, only in three cases the researchers had to take notes during the interview process and to directly paraphrase the interviews afterwards. No names of interview partners are mentioned throughout this study, as privacy was assured to the participants.

The data was analyzed using an iterative approach following the grounded theory methodology. According to this approach, the processes of collecting and analyzing the data ran simultaneously (Glaser 1992, p. 16). For data analysis, the researchers built over 2000 codes from the data collected. Following the grounded theory methodology, the data analyzing process included open, axial, and selective coding for being able to isolate key-categories at an abstract level (Kuckartz 2012, p. 66). Therefore, the use of software MAXQDA was helpful. During the process of data collection and analysis, memos helped to identify key-aspects and their interrelations.

Empirical Results

In this section, results of this qualitative-empirical investigation among price auditors as well as organizational interview-partners are presented and analyzed for describing the structure of concerned companies and their problems during the process of public purchase. Therefore, the first part is about the business environment in which the price finding process for public purchase plays a dominant role. In the second part, organizational requirements that are necessary for the pricing process are analyzed. In the third and fourth part of this section, results concerning the pricing process are focused.

Business Environment of Price Regulation for Public Purchase

Especially price auditors as interview partners could help to create an idea of what the business environment that falls under price regulation for public purchase looks like. Analyzing the interviews concerning this topic, it becomes clear that the structure of companies that follow price regulation continuously to find prices for public orders especially consist of the defense industry as well as R&D institutes. In some cases also local publically owned undertakings use price regulation norms, too. In other branches, price regulation norms are not an important instrument to generate prices for public orders.

The interview partners reported that the structure of public orders for which price audits come up is basically of a wide variety of goods and services. Price auditors distinguish between audits for industrial products and services. They underline the growing importance of service contracts in the past decade. In general, it becomes obvious that price audits occur more frequently for military equipment, IT products and services, as well as R&D services. In these cases, market mechanisms seem to fail more often because of a high level of specialization.

Following the asked price auditors, organizations that work for the public sector give a heterogeneous image concerning their size and the revenue they generate with a public contract partner in relation to the total revenue. Small companies with below a dozen employees as well as international enterprises work for public institutions. A high dependence on public contracts can be seen especially in R&D institutes as well as in local publicly owned undertakings. Also some highly specialized companies for military goods and services generate relatively high revenue with public orders compared to orders from private contract partners.

Dependent on the relevance of the public orders as well as on the size of the organizations cooperating with public purchasers, pricing for public orders as well as price audits are either organized as a part of management accounting with a few experts on these topics or as an own section that runs parallel to management accounting. The first can be mainly found in SME's and companies where the revenue from public contract-partners has a small volume no matter if they are big or small, whereas independent sections occur in companies that are highly dependent on orders of public institutions. In any case, a close relation of pricing and price audits for public purchase with management accounting is obvious.

Operating Requirements for Public Purchase

In general, through the qualitative-empirical investigation of this study, three major requirements that are needed by companies to deal with the public procurement and pricing process adequately were identified: First, there has to be expertise about public procurement and pricing rules within the companies. Both, the asked price auditors and organizational interview partners underline the importance of knowledge already before the public procurement process starts. This is necessary to be able to work formally to meet the requirements that come up later in the procurement and pricing process. Exact formal requirements are analyzed in Sections "A Closer Look at Purchasing Card Use" and "Military Versus Civilian Purchasing Card Activity" of chapter "The Impact of Changing Patterns of Commercial Card Use by the U.S. Government on Governmental Efficiency and Cost Savings", this volume. Both groups report that problems especially occur when companies are audited the first time, because the majority has not anticipated the requirements during the procurement process because of missing expertise. By analyzing the interviews, it becomes obvious that while the majority of companies have a certain expertise about public procurement, knowledge about pricing regulation is missing when companies do not work off public orders constantly. Certainly pricing regulation leads to difficulties especially when market mechanisms fail.

Second, a permanent documentation of costs and revenues is needed to manage the process of public pricing without deeper problems. Because the exact size of the price for a public order gets finally verified by a price audit, until then there exists uncertainty in the companies. That is the reason why it is not enough just to document the revenue and costs of an exact public order that is worked off. In fact, it is absolutely necessary to exactly document every revenue and costs that occur during the production of goods and services. Price auditors as well as organizational interview partners report that especially when there is no expertise about price regulation rules or when contract partners assume conditions that are not conform with price regulation rules, the demanded documents will have to be presented to price auditors that the seller does not to come into the situation to give a part of the revenue back to the public purchaser. Because price audits mostly happen after the order is fully worked off, companies are surprised and unprepared for them. Surely the prerequisite of a permanent documentation is necessary in order to proceed with price audits. What exactly has to be documented will be shown in the following sections.

Third, pricing for public purchase requires a structured accounting system. Especially in case of cost-based pricing to meet the regulation norms (LSP) this has to be based on financial accounting, but also on management accounting. While for example direct costs are valued based on the financial accounting standards, overhead cost calculations are part of management accounting. In practice, companies with a high percentage of public orders tend to organize their accounting system based on the calculation norms designated in the regulatory norms of cost-based pricing (LSP). Especially R&D institutions, local publically owned undertakings, and some companies of the defense industry prefer this structure for being optimally prepared for price audits. On the other hand, in most cases companies that generate only a smaller percentage of their revenues with public orders work with "bridge-calculations" to transfer the numbers of their accounting system into conformity with the cost-based pricing norms.

Identification of the Adequate Price Type

Especially price auditors who have a good overview of pricing practices for public orders report that every price type can be found in practice. In practice, the "market-price" is the most common type, because it is the usual result of a procurement process in which many companies bid for a public purchase. By bringing different offers together, a "synthetic" market is created that meets the requirements for a norm conform "market-price." If there is only one bid or if there is no procurement in form of competitive bidding, companies can prove that the price for an order is a "market-price" by presenting documents that show that an equal product or service was already sold to another private contractual partner for the same amount of money.

By analyzing the interviews it turned out that difficulties for proving a "market price" especially occur in (1) publically owned undertakings, (2) companies that split from their mother only to work off public purchase and (3) service companies. While local publically owned undertakings usually provide services like waste disposal or R&D institutes for which only public institutions give the order, companies that separated from their mother only to work off public purchase report that they had met the requirements for "market prices" before they were separated. Because they only work off public orders, they do not have revenue from other private contract-partners so they do not meet the legal requirements for the price type "market-price" any more even if they have obviously merchantable products or services. Interview partners of service companies especially of the IT-branch report that price auditors refuse them to get a "market price" because of the individuality of their products that are adapted especially for the (public) customer. There is a discontent between price auditors and service companies in this case because while service companies see themselves in efficient markets, price auditors do not.

If contract partners agree to have cost-based pricing, or if price auditors refuse "market prices" as the adequate price type, price regulation rules provide three price types on a cost-plus basis. First, a "fixed price" is certain before the public purchase is worked off by a company. Therefore, costs have to be calculable in advance of the execution of the order. The interview partners report that this is only the case if an equal product or service has already been produced several times. The asked price auditors confirm that mostly industrial products fall under this category. Following them, "fixed prices" are preferred for large orders because politics can communicate a price that should not be exceeded later on. Nevertheless, price auditors report that for large contracts it is difficult to foresee planned costs transparently, so the prices are sometimes adapted by using add-on contracts.

Second, a "conversion-price" is the price type that is used when a company cannot oversee the costs at the beginning of a project but it is expected that at a certain time of the production process they can oversee the costs of the whole project because they generated enough experience. So before the production process starts, a date is fixed when the company has to have enough data about upcoming costs till the project is finished. The interview partners report that this price type is used for large projects where there is not enough data to present a transparent plan of the expected costs at the beginning of the project. As a result of the interviews, this price type is least preferred by price auditors as well as by companies. The reason for that is a high-administrative effort and a certain arbitrariness concerning the date when the planned costs for the rest of the project have to be presented. Both groups of interview partners assume that this price type is politically motivated. Large defense projects that include the development and production of military equipment are mentioned here.

Third, a "reimbursement-price" is not certain before the production process starts. Here, public institutions order products or services for which the entrusted company cannot make any resilient cost plans. In these situations, the final price for the product or service is calculated when the production process has finished. During the production process, costs have to be documented in detail so that they can be charged. Organizational interview partners as well as price auditors report that the "reimbursement-price" is mostly used for individualized services like IT-services but also repairs, etc. Concerning this point, there exists a controversy between the two interviewed groups. While organizational interview partners see a well-doing and fast-emerging market in services, price auditors do not. Because of their individual adaptation to the customer's needs, the interviewed price auditors report that these services are not comparable most of the time, so the requirements of a norm-conform "market-price" are not fulfilled.

By analyzing the interviews of this study concerning "price types," mainly two problems occur: The first problem concerns the definition especially of the "market-price" which is based on company subjective facts and which does not consider other forms of verification for existing markets for certain products or services.

The second problem is based on the price audit process. The correct "price type" for public orders has to be ascertained by a price auditor. He is the one who irrevocably declares it. The consequence of this is that organizations are in uncertainty concerning the "price type" until a price auditor decides on it. Because of undercapacities, price auditors report that it is common practice that the ascertainment of the adequate price type lies sometimes after the order is worked off so that companies documented under a wrong assumption of a price type during their production process. As it is described in former sections, the different "price types" require different documentation. For a "market-price" revenues of equal products are essential. For "fixed-prices" planned costs have to be transparently presented, so former production processes with equal products or services create the basis of calculation for this "price type." On the other hand, "reimbursement-prices" require a documentation of the actual costs for the public order. Documentations of former orders do not play any role for this "price type." Especially organizational interview partners report that problems occur when the price type is (1) not ascertained before the production process starts or (2) when an assumed price type is changed during price audits. In these cases, companies might not document the information that is needed for the finally ascertained price type but for a different one. The interview partners of this study report that acting under the assumption of a different price type might have the consequence of not being able to charge a part of the costs to the public purchaser. In practice, this problem occurs especially for orders for which first a "market-price" was assumed, then the production process started under this assumption and finally a "reimbursement-price" was ascertained.

Cost-Based Pricing Practices

In this section, calculation practices are evaluated and critical aspects are worked out. By analyzing the 20 semistructured interviews of our study, several inconsistencies within the actual calculation norms were identified. In this chapter, we focus on two essential structural discrepancies between the actual calculation norms and the requirements of today's economy. First, actual calculation norms were basically introduced in 1953. Since then no adaptations to accounting standards have been made. Our interview partners report that therefore there are discrepancies because the financial accounting system is the main source of data for a cost-based calculation. Systems used to be harmonized in that case, but since there have been adaptations between financial accounting and taxation standards, generated numbers are not in accordance with calculation norms of pricing law (e.g., expected salary increases are now part of pension devices). Also price auditors suggest a reform even if a harmonization will have higher prices as a consequence.

Second, present calculation norms do not consider the changing of the economic structure. During the last 60 years, there has been a shift in the economic structure from the mainly industrial to a service oriented one. Calculation norms are still focused only on industrial production processes. Moreover, (knowledge based) service companies with highly specialized products do not use classical overhead cost-accounting approaches to calculate their costs and prices. Activity-based approaches are state of the art in modern research and practice, but are hardly adaptable to cost-based calculation norms of pricing law. Furthermore, we identified for calculating calculative interest for production relevant capital or benefit margins that are still recommended by commentary and used by price auditors.

Conclusion

In this chapter, we analyze the pricing process for public purchase. By using a grounded theoretical approach we investigate empirically *who* is concerned about this topic, *how* principles of pricing law are transferred into practice, and *which* problems occur. Because of a close interrelation, it was necessary also to include public procurement in our study. To get a holistic overview of this poorly investigated field of research, we provided 20 semistructured interviews equally representing price auditors and organizational interview partners. By our analysis, we were able to develop an integrative model considering public procurement as well as pricing practices. However, our study also reveals many areas of research that need to be extended. In this section, we summarize our findings, give recommendations, and comment on a few of the most promising streams for further research.

By considering previous studies and analyzing our data, we identified defense and IT industry, research institutes, as well as public-private-partnerships as especially concerned branches. Further, descriptive studies are absolutely necessary to get detailed knowledge about the concerned branches, products, services, and order volumes.

Based on our study, we identified three aspects that lead to problems in the present system of pricing for public orders. First, the connection between public procurement and pricing law is not clearly defined. Both rules are independent but anyway in this study we identified a close interrelation. While public procurement is an instrument to find the most economical offer, pricing law is an instrument to verify if the price for the offer is appropriate. Public procurement is the first rule that has be followed by public purchaser and supplier. In fact, it refers to pricing law, but it is not clear at which point the connection starts. There has to be defined a concrete point of time in the process of public procurement, when a price type finally has to be defined. In the present system, only price auditors have the competence to verify the final price type even after the production process has finished. In our opinion, this point of time needs to be before the company has started the production process for being able to document based on the price-type-specific requirements. Further, normative studies are necessary to give advice how to solve this structural ambiguity.

Second, there is a serious lack of information about pricing law concerning public purchaser and also supplier. With the fact of good public procurement rules, pricing law has to be considered for every public order, but only few public purchasers respect it. Our study provides evidence that many public institutions disregard pricing law and/or do not inform suppliers about the duty to consider it for public orders. However, suppliers also do not inform themselves adequately about the requirements of pricing law. As a consequence, this can lead to inadequate or missing documentation so that a "market-price" cannot be proved even if there exists an active market. Also, costs can only be reimbursed if their existence is documented based on the calculation norms. If companies are not informed about the documentation requirements, they might not be able to add costs to the reimbursed cost-plus price. Because of a lack of (management) accounting expertise, especially SMEs seem to face differences here. By analyzing the qualitative data of our study, there is a clear understanding that as the owner of the highest competence in pricing law, the ministry of economics with their price auditors is seen as in charge to distribute information about the duty to execute public orders under requirements of pricing law. As an instrument to guarantee appropriate prices for public purchase, this should also be on the tax payers' behalf.

Third, the cost-plus calculation norms for cases in which active markets cannot be proven are not up-to-date considering the status quo of the German economy. The present outdated but still relevant pricing law with its cost-plus price calculation approach does not consider modern accounting standards and seems to be still focused on industrial production processes. Especially for complex and highly specialized knowledge based services (e.g., of IT or R&D) these norms are hardly transferable. For them, classic cost accounting systems as provided by pricing law are mostly replaced by activity based approaches. Also the appreciation of idle-time costs mainly determined by the degree of capacity utilization is totally different in services than in the industrial production processes. Furthermore, the formula to calculate the benefit margin in defense contracts as well as the one in the calculative interest for production relevant capital provided in accompanying commentary indicate that here revisions are necessary, too. Further empirical investigations as well as normative studies will be helpful and necessary to give further recommendations for a reform of the pricing law in Germany. International comparative studies are seen as valuable for integrating international best practices.

Practicable rules and procedures have to be implemented to enhance commitment to the regulatory system of public purchase and to support processes in the regulatory context.

Completed and Further Steps of This Research Project

So far, completed project steps of the research project include a qualitative status quo investigation concerning public procurement practices and cost-based pricing rules in Germany (VO PR 30/53) and their effects on company-internal processes; analysis of existing constraints of public procurement and cost-based pricing rules in Germany and the assessment of hypotheses as a basis for further (quantitative) investigations.

Anticipated further project steps are the identification and evaluation of the regulation system for public purchase in the USA (e.g., Public Procurement, Federal Acquisition Regulation (FAR), Defence Acquisition Regulation System (DARS)), the analysis of key aspects, organization and effects of the pricing rules for public acquisitions in the USA, and the evaluation of the regulatory commitment and the practical relevance of the public procurement and cost-based price regulation system in the USA compared to the German system.

The examination of the public procurement process and the reflection of cost-oriented regulation systems in Germany and the USA are regarded as an essential part of the overall research project. The close relation and economic similarities between Germany and the USA as well as an advanced history of the USA in regulation can provide conclusive information for a best practice regulatory design of price regulation for public acquisitions in Germany. The existing regulatory systems across sectors and borders should be the subject of a constant process of evaluation and development.

References

Bortz, J., & Döring, N. (2006). *Forschungsmethoden und Evaluation: Für Human- und Sozialwissenschaftler* (4th ed.). Heidelberg: Springer Medizin Verlag.

Charmaz, K., & Belgrave, L. (2012). Qualitative interviewing and grounded theory analysis. In J. F. Gubrium, J. A. Holstein, A. B. Marvasti, & K. D. McKinney (Eds.), *The SAGE handbook of interview research: the complexity of the craft* (2nd ed., pp. 347–367). Thousand Oaks: SAGE Publications.

Corbin, J., & Strauss, A. (2008). *Basics of qualitative research: techniques and procedures for developing grounded theory* (3rd ed.). Thousand Oaks: Sage Publications.

Ebisch, H., Gottschalk, J., Hoffjan, A., Mueller, H., & Waldmann, B. (2010). *Preise und Preisprüfungen bei öffentlichen Aufträgen* (8th ed.). München: Verlag Franz Vahlen.

Glaser, B. (1992). *Emergence vs. forcing: basics of grounded theory analysis*. Mill Valley: Sociology Press.

Hoffjan, A., Hövelborn, T., & Strickmann, C. (2013). Das Preisrecht bei öffentlichen Aufträgen: Status Quo und empirische Befunde vor dem Hintergrund aktueller Reformbemühungen. *Zeitschrift für öffentliche und Gemeinwirtschaftliche Unternehmen, 36*(1), 3–16.

Hövelborn, T. (2014). *Angemessener Gewinnaufschlag von Entsorgungsunternehmen bei öffentlichen Aufträgen zu Selbstkosten* (1st ed.). München: Springer Fachmedien.

Kuckartz, U. (2012). *Qualitative Inhaltsanalyse: Methoden, Praxis, Computerunterstützung* (1st ed.). Weinheim: Beltz Juventa.

Lueger, M. (2009). Grounded theory. In R. Buber, H. Holzmüller (Eds.), *Qualitative Marktforschung: Konzepte – Methoden – Analyse* (1st ed., pp. 189–205). Wiesbaden: Betriebswirtschaftlicher Verlag Dr. Th. Gabler.

Öko-Institut e.V. (2008). *Nationale Umsetzung der neuen EU-Beschaffungsrichtlinien, Forschungsbericht.* http://www.umweltdaten.de/publikationen/fpdf-l/3666.pdf. Accessed 9 January 2014.

Parker, L., & Roffrey, B. (1997). Back to the drawing board: revisiting grounded theory and the everyday accountant's and manager's reality. *Accounting, Auditing and Accountability Journal, 10*(2), 212–247.

US Department of Commerce. (2009). *Consolidated federal funds report for fiscal year 2008.* Washington, DC: U.S. Census Bureau.

Michael Georgi is a PhD student and a research assistant in the Department of Management Accounting and Control, TU Dortmund University, Germany. His teaching and research interests are in pricing regulation, incentive systems, and market mechanisms.

Sascha Kemmeter is a PhD student in the Department of Management Accounting, University of Duisburg-Essen, Germany. His research and consulting interests are strategic management for large-scale projects, cost estimation, and pricing.

Procurement Conspiracies and Procurement Governance: Some Lessons from Thailand

Sirilaksana Khoman

Introduction

Network relationships are nothing new. Worldwide social networking has indeed exploded within the past decade. Network relationships facilitate efficient interaction by reducing the three components of transactions costs: information and search costs, negotiating and contracting costs, and policing and enforcement costs. Whether in business or politics, or any other area of interaction, network relationships play an important role and help to create efficiency. Indeed, investment into creating trust, brand loyalty, recognition and reputation, whether in personal or business relationships, are part of the process of networking. Trust implies confidence that some person or institution will behave in an expected way. But there are also built-in dangers when networking turns into conspiracy aimed at siphoning public funds into private coffers, particularly through connected dealings in public procurement. Often the status quo is preserved and situations of monopoly are created to facilitate transactions with corrupt intent.

This chapter focuses on a public project as fertile ground for both petty corruption and "grand state capture," and examines the role of network relationships in facilitating corrupt activity. The characteristics of network relationships are examined to ascertain the aspects of group or network relationships that are conducive to corrupt activity. The case of Klong Darn wastewater treatment is used to illustrate the pattern of patron-client networks that can affect a government project. The institutional and legal framework in Thailand is also briefly explored, and possible measures to alleviate current problems are considered. The chapter argues that although procurement regulations are clear and seemingly strict, loopholes can be found that allow patron–client networks to engage in wrongdoing with impunity, to the detriment of Thailand's development. Blatant violations also occurred as network members believed that they were "protected" by their network relationships.

S. Khoman (✉)
National Anti-Corruption Commission, Nonthaburi, Thailand
e-mail: siri.nacc@gmail.com

K. V. Thai (ed.), *International Public Procurement,* Public Administration, Governance and Globalization 14, DOI 10.1007/978-3-319-13434-5_9

The Nature of Network Relationships

A network may be regarded as a set of contracts, which can be loose or tight, formal or informal, that establishes internal rules of exchange and cooperation. In some cases, the set of contracts gives the group a collective identity vis a vis others and replaces individual identity in transactions. An organization, or clan, is thus a set of contracts and rules defining roles and establishing their relationships within the network. Individuals play defined roles, perhaps negotiate mobility within the network, or leave them. Investment in identity takes place in the selection for roles, and in the process by which individuals select the organization/clan that they join. This network may start out from being an innocuous social network where members assist each other with some kind of reciprocity established as the norm. However, it can be transformed into a patron–client relationship, paving the way to formation of more pernicious networks, whereby the patron provides resources and protection to the clients who, in return, provide services, rent collection, and other forms of support to the patron, including facilitating corrupt acts.

Since there are many competing networks of patrons and clients, each patron needs to accumulate resources to feed the needs of the clan. Corruption then becomes a method to accomplish this task and allows the network to accumulate funds and attract numbers to compete successfully against other clans. Members recruited into the corruption ring may actually not be aware of the ring in the beginning. But the cost of leaving the network becomes prohibitive and the option of moving to another network may not be available due to the mutual distrust and possible hostility between clans/networks. Trust may imply confidence, but not certainty (Rose-Ackermann 2001, p. 1), and therefore network members also need to constantly "prove themselves" to remain a member as well.

In the broadest sense, a transaction consists of activities or transfers of property rights by or between at least two individuals or groups. All individuals engage in two kinds of transactions: personal (where identity dominates) and impersonal (where identity is subsumed). In petty corruption, such as extortion of motorists by traffic police, or bribery for queue-skipping, identity is not important, and suppression of identity may even be desirable. But in certain forms of illegal transactions, especially corrupt transactions that take on the nature of conspiracies, the identity of the people engaged in a transaction is vital. Some transactions can take place only between mutually or unilaterally identified parties, and many corrupt practices of significance fall under this category. Parties in an identified relationship invest resources that are specific to that relationship in order to save transactions costs. And there are economies of scale related to these "set-up" costs. This facilitates activity between them and leads to a concentration of exchange between the same parties. Ben-Porath (1980) calls this "specialization by identity," and patron–client relationships are repeated relationships of exchange between specific patrons and their clients (Khan 1998).

Where do network members come from? In order to set up a successful corruption ring, several dimensions in terms of member characteristics are important.

There is a built-in bias in favor of homogeneity in terms of some dimensions but heterogeneity in terms of others. Family and close friends may be the first choice for recruitment due to existing ties. This first ring of relationships will then recruit others. Routine actions that do not require a great deal of expertise, such as hiding documents or engaging in protest rallies, favors homogeneity—working with the same people. However, when purchasing sophisticated equipment, trust in friends or relatives cannot compete with the technical know-how of a specialist. Thus, it becomes necessary to recruit technical expertise and business associates as well.

With differences in the importance of identity in various transactions and in the specificity of investment in identity to certain activities, people will be organized in small clusters for some purposes and large ones for others, and these groupings may intersect for different purposes (Ben-Porath 1980). Parties who have already invested specifically in each other are in a short-run position of bilateral monopoly. If the self-enforcement mechanism is imperfect, trust, or fear, or violence and intimidation, or the threat thereof, becomes more important. In Thailand, there is a common saying that defines six different groups of people that comprise a network (especially a corrupt network): family members, school friends or disciples, financial contributors, obsequious followers, marriage ties, and competent specialists. These clan or group members therefore cut across the usual socioeconomic dimensions such as income class or occupation. Understanding group membership allows us to see that not all conflict situations are "class struggles." References to "Arab Spring" and inequalities (that exist and persist in most societies) completely miss the mark in analyzing Thailand's current political situation.

In present-day Thailand, it can be seen that political networks are defined by their head. The head of the network serves as director for communication, trust, and redistribution, and reduces the transaction costs within the network by reducing the need for bilateral relationships. The pairwise investment of each member with the center links him to all the others. In his theory of social interaction, Becker (1974) shows why a central figure who cares, or appears to care, can generate optimal behavior for the group from the others, even if the head is an egoist. When the head is absent, miscommunication often occurs, or miscommunication can be blamed for unpopular deeds by the network. The difficulty is to distinguish between the truly benevolent head and the self-serving one (Khoman 2012). A corruption ring can be represented in Fig. 1, where layers of patrons and clients direct the flow of resources.

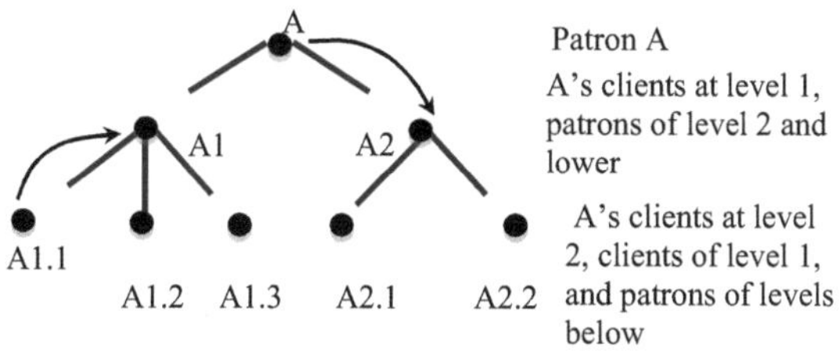

Fig. 1 Typical patron–client structure. (Source: Khoman et al. (2010))

From Fig. 1, Patron A is the ultimate power of the clan. Below Patron A are the clients shown by nodes connected to Patron A with dashed lines. For simplicity, this patron is shown to have two clients at level 1, labeled A1 and A2. Below each level-1 client, there may be many layers of clients that propagate downward. The patron in this clan could also serve as a client of yet another larger patron–client structure located higher up.

Members in the same clan relate to each other in two ways, vertically and horizontally, the former in cooperative exchange and the latter sometimes in the form of rivalry. The patron is expected to provide vital resources that the client needs. In Thailand, the patron may provide land to the client for cultivation, give loans for emergency use, settle conflicts with other clients within the clan, provide protection against threats from other clans, promote the client to a higher position in the clan, and/or ensure that clients receive government procurement contracts. The solid arrow in Fig. 1 represents the flow of resources or protection provided by the patron.

In return for the patron's support, the client has the duty to serve the immediate patron, and those located in higher positions, in whatever tasks the patron may assign. If procurement contracts are obtained, usually at inflated prices, then kickbacks are paid up the hierarchy. The dashed arrow in Fig. 1 shows the flow of returns from the client to the patron. The returns could take the form of simple labor (such as pouring drinks, carrying suitcases), or bodyguards. Or it could be a supporting role against other clans, beating up the patron's enemies, rallying people to support the patron's political ambitions, protesting against unfavorable court decisions, and extracting economic rent from awarded contracts for the patron. The resources could consist of monetary support or member count. Thai political parties always consist of many factions, or subclans, in which the leader of that faction acts as the patron. If the leader of the faction manages to bring in sufficiently large numbers of elected MPs under his wing, he is entitled to become a minister in a grade A ministry, such as the Ministry of Transportation, which commands a large government budget. He would also have the right to nominate members under his wing to be appointed as ministers in grade B or C ministries, or as deputy ministers in grade A ministries.

Due to this quid pro quo, members of the group evaluate actions or policies as being beneficial or detrimental to the group or subgroup's interests, and to a large extent, political loyalties are based on the identity of the leader. Therefore, for the most part, it is not ideological persuasion, but the identity of individual politicians that determine political structures.

Although members of a clan tend to work cooperatively in the vertical hierarchy, there is often rivalry when they deal with members at the same client level. Many examples can be found in Thai political parties where leaders of factions try to outperform each other in terms of getting more members of parliament under his or her wing. The leader of that faction is then entitled to a cabinet position. And there is of course rivalry between clans, which accounts for why some long-running projects do not get implemented. The plans for a new international airport, for example, were laid down 30 years before construction finally commenced. And a large number of procurement cases connected with the new international airport are currently being investigated.

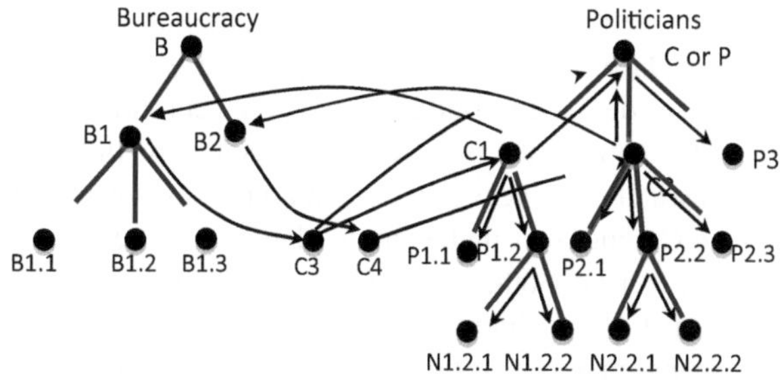

Fig. 2 Flows within patron–client networks in Thailand notes. *B* bureaucracy, *C* capitalists, *P* politicians, *N* nonpoliticians. (Source: Khoman et al. 2010)

The patron-client network in Thailand can be represented by Fig. 2. The bureaucracy (B) is represented on the left, while the network of politicians (P) is depicted on the right. The capitalists (C) refer to big businesses, while the nonpoliticians (N) include small businesses as well as nongovernmental organizations (NGOs), and other social or lobbying groups. Solid arrows show the flows of the benefits from C1 to B1 and C2 to B2. The capitalists who act as the patrons of the subclans, kick back some of their corrupt benefits to the bureaucracy who originally facilitated the special licenses, concessions, and procurement projects. The patrons of the subclan and the nonpolitician capitalists also need to provide the political and financial support to the highest patron who is either a politician or a capitalist turned politician. Thus, government procurement is a vehicle for corrupt enrichment.

A large number of businessmen made fortunes by receiving favored subsidies, licenses, and concessions from the patron–client network three-way interaction among politicians, the bureaucracy and business, shown by the solid arrows pointing from B1 and B2 to C3 and C4.

One somewhat unique point about the patron–client network in Thailand is that capitalists often place themselves high up or at the top of the network, rather than merely content themselves with influencing policy. In fact, the share of businessmen in Thailand's parliament is the highest in the region (Sidel 1996). A recent trend was the movement of many capitalists, formerly located at high client levels, to become the highest patron of the political party or the faction leader. Many leaders of Thai political parties are businessmen and tycoons.

The Case: The Klong Darn Wastewater Treatment Project

The Klong Darn wastewater treatment project illustrates how strategically placed parties can allow wrongdoing to occur with impunity. In November 1995, the Asian Development Bank (ADB) approved a US$ 150 million loan to support the Thai government's Pollution Control Department (PCD) in establishing systems to manage wastewater discharged by factories and residents in the Bangkok metropolitan area, including the adjacent Samut Prakarn Province. The initial plan was to build two separate treatment plants close to the main pollution sources, consisting of about 5000 factories. However, by the time the ADB approved an additional loan of US$ 80 million, the project site had been relocated some 20 km away to Klong Darn, situated toward the eastern edge of Samut Prakarn province. A new plan was devised to build a single very centralized plant, one of the largest wastewater treatment plants in Southeast Asia at the time, to process 525,000 cm^3 a day of wastewater with heavy metals and hazardous waste. The rationale that was offered to the Cabinet was that a single plant would be more economical than two separate plants. It turned out, however, that even though the rationale for re-location was to save cost, the Cabinet approved an increase in the budget for the project. Japan's International Cooperation Agency (JICA) cofinanced the project with an additional US$ 50 million loan. After the site change, the total cost of the project more than doubled to US$ 687 million.

Klong Darn villagers came to know about the project after the construction had started. In late 1998, they saw a sign put up by a joint venture (JV) construction company, in front of the wastewater management facility. They were surprised to learn that a huge wastewater treatment plant was already under construction in their neighborhood. Apart from the total lack of information disclosure to and meaningful participation of the local community, stakeholders were able to point out the following major flaws with the project:

- The plant was not equipped to properly treat heavy metals and hazardous waste. They would be discharged into the sea and would destroy local fishing activities.
- The plant was built on soft soil along the coast and would be impacted by flooding and erosion.
- An environmental impact assessment (EIA) was not conducted in Klong Darn.
- The project site included public land, such as canals, which could not be for sale. The land for the plant, approximately 1900 "rai" (1 "rai" is equal to 1600 m^2), was sold at a price much higher than the official price.

The land for this new site belonged to a local politician, and suspicions were raised about whether this could account for the sudden change in the project site. In addition, the transport of waste from the source or pollution, through a long and winding pipeline for some 20 km, was not technically sound.

On January 13, 2004, PCD filed charges against 19 private firms and individuals in the Thai criminal court, including Vatana Asavahame, a former Deputy Minister of Interior for having illegally obtained title deeds to the project site land and sold it to PCD at an inflated price. In March 2004, the land department revoked the deeds to the land of 1358 "rais." This invalidated the government's contract with the JV. On 14 June 2007, the NACC concluded that nine government officials, including Vatana, had been involved in illegal land deed acquisition and forwarded the case to the Supreme Court's Criminal Division for holders of political positions. By that time Vatana had fled Thailand, but the court ruled that he was guilty of bribing and/or coercing officials in the land grab connected with the project and sentenced him in absentia to 10 years in prison.[1]This part of the case shows the connection between

[1] See http://www.mekongwatch.org/english/country/thailand/MW_SMBrief(2010.02.27).pdf. Another case involving land is that of Somchai Khunpleum, a Chon Buri godfather with powerful political connections, wanted in a local land-conflict case. He has since been arrested.

the minister and collaborators in the land department who were involved in issuing the illegal land deeds.

But the case is far from over. The laws in place at the time of project include:

- OPM Regulations B.E.2535 (1992) (for procurement)
- Environmental Protection Law B.E. 2537 (1994)
- Public land designations

Other laws that were enacted include the Act on Offences Relating to the Submission of Bids to State Agencies B.E. 2542 (1999). In addition, there are various cabinet resolutions that authorize certain actions. An interesting question is whether these laws, regulations, and resolutions were violated, or whether there are loopholes that need to be examined. The issues involved in this case are illustrated in Fig. 3.1. The case can be broken down into the following main issues:

- Project approval
- Cabinet decision
- Award of contract
- Land purchase and acquisition

Each of these issues involves connected individuals playing a key role in defrauding government agencies, with complicity from government agents. First, the project approval issue. Other similar projects were being launched, such as the wastewater treatment system proposed by the Department of Industrial Factories in 1991 and the wastewater and garbage treatment project by the Department of Public Works and City Planning (1992–1994). In addition, there is the question of why it was necessary to submit the project as a "turnkey" project. Turnkey projects are supposed to be those that are technologically sophisticated beyond the ability of the technicians in the proposing department to design, and thus the design phase is incorporated into the project, in the form of "design-build" projects. Questions have arisen regarding the relative simplicity and standardized technology that could have been handled by the government department, rather than left in the hands of the contractor, who was then responsible not only for construction but also design and land acquisition.

Then the cabinet resolution was distorted to allow the relocation of the project. Irregularities were also found in the bidding process. Once the project was changed to a single wastewater treatment plant, the second bidder withdrew because of inability to acquire the necessary land. According to regulations, the tender process should have been restarted, but this was not done. In addition, when the main partner in the winning consortium withdrew, this was not reported, leading to annulment of the contract.

In the case of the land purchase, land department officials who courageously refused to issue falsified land deeds were transferred to the southernmost volatile provinces. The minister who ordered the transfer, Vattana Asawahame, was convicted of administrative misconduct, and the officials transferred back to Bangkok. Thus integrity played a key role in convicting the minister.

Brief Chronology

1986 Asian Development Bank (ADB) provides funds to the Office of National Environment Board[2] to survey options to manage industrial waste water (treatment and control) in Samut Prakarn province.

1991 Department of Industrial Works started to implement the project to build waste water treatment plants, as authorized by the cabinet resolution on July 2, 1991 in Pra Pradaeng district and Pra Samut district on the west bank of the Chao Phraya River. The budget was approved for purchase of land in 1994.

1993 ADB approves another US$ 350,000 to develop a waste water treatment system in Samut Prakarn province and undertake a feasibility study under the Environment Rehabilitation Project (ERP).

1993 ADB approves another grant of US$ 600,000 to the Pollution Control Department (PCD), Ministry of Natural Resources and Environment, to conduct a feasibility study and preliminary design for waste water treatment under the project "Wastewater Management and Pollution Control in Samut Prakarn" to manage wastewater in the pollution control zone of Samut Prakarn. ADB also assisted the PCD in preparing bidding documents and selection of contractor in the design of wastewater treatment.

1993 The National Environment Board (NEB), at a meeting on December 15 (#6/2536), designated Samut Prakarn province as a "pollution control" province, directing the provincial authority of Samut Prakarn (under the Ministry of Internal Affairs) to coordinate with the PCD in drawing up an action plan to manage environmental quality at the provincial level (including an action plan to reduce and eliminate pollution in the pollution control area), designating the PCD as the agency to carry out the action plan. Later NEB announcement No. 9 B.E. 2537 (1994) officially declared Samut Prakarn as a pollution control province, with effect from December 15, 1993. This declaration is significant in that regulations regarding pollution control and pollution-control projects would now apply.

1994 ADB hired Montgomery-Watson Asia together with a local engineering consulting company, Southeast Asia Technology Company (SEATEC) to conduct the feasibility and design. A seminar was convened on December 16 involving the Ministry of Science and Technology and Environment, the PCD, the ADB, and representatives from provincial agencies in Samut Prakarn.

---

[2] The National Environment Board is a high-level body set up under the Enhancement and Conservation of National Environmental Quality Act B.E. 2535 (1992), consisting of the Prime Minister as the Chair, a designated Deputy Prime Minister as the First Vice Chair, the Minister of Natural Resources and Environment as the Second Vice Chair, and 8 committee members consisting of Ministers in related Ministries including qualified specialists, with the Permanent Secretary of the Ministry of Natural Resources and Environment as Secretary. The duties are to consider policies, plans, and measures regarding the management of the nation's natural resources and the environment.

February 28 Toward the final stages of the feasibility study, a seminar was convened to discuss the findings.

March Montgomery-Watson Asia et al. submitted their final report detailing 13 options for wastewater treatment, proposing two plants (aerated lagoon) as the best long-run option in terms of cost-saving and minimal risks: one on the east bank emitting treated water into the sea, and one on the west bank, emitting into a canal. The proposed plants were at Bangpu-mai on 1550 rai of land on the east bank, and at Klong Bangplakod on 35 rai on the west bank (1 rai = 0.40 acres or 0.16 ha or 1600 m^2).

The report also found that the soft soil conditions in Klong Darn would be an obstacle to engineering and construction. In addition, the lowland nature at Klong Darn was subject to flooding of seawater, and therefore the site was not appropriate.

It was also recommended that one of the causes of delay in construction projects in Thailand, was the problem related to land acquisition. Thus during the feasibility study, it was recommended that a committee should be set up to deal with land acquisition, and that the consulting company should assist this committee in acquiring the land, studying its suitability, negotiating its price, and purchasing the land for the project.

Eight contracts were to be executed, complying with the procurement guidelines of the ADB: four construction contracts and four materials and equipment contracts. The cost estimates for construction were 9.14 billion Baht and 2.185 billion Baht for the east and west banks respectively, totaling 11.325 billion Baht.

1995 June 14 the PCD submitted the report to the NEB meeting (#6/2538). The Board concluded that there was an urgent need to address the wastewater problem in Samut Prakarn, but there needs to be control on land use so that the wastewater problem does not spread beyond the project site. The Board also made the following observations: (1) the running cost of 580 million Baht should be checked; (2) the project needs to be discussed with the public through community leaders, to promote understanding regarding the benefits of the project, and to ensure willingness to pay, since this is the first project that involves fees for wastewater treatment; (3) before submitting to the cabinet, a projected cash flow should be undertaken, with input from the Budget Bureau and the Ministry of Finance, as loans from OECF (Overseas Economic Cooperation Fund, the implementing agency for loan aid furnished by the Japanese government) will have to be considered.

At this meeting, Suwat Liptapanlop (Minister of Science, Technology and Environment) as second Vice-Chair of the Board, Pakit Kiravanich (director-general of PCD) and Sirithan Pairojboribul (deputy director-general of PCD) were in attendance.

1992–1994	The Department of Public Works (DPW) under the Ministry of Interior studies the wastewater treatment system in Samut Prakarn. Cabinet resolution on June 28, 1994 authorizes the DPW to tackle the wastewater problem, and is allocated 3.8 million Baht for the study. In 1994 the DPW's study recommends construction of 3 wastewater treatment plants at Samrong, Poojaosamingprai, and Klong Plakod.
1994 November 8	a Cabinet resolution approves DPW's project to deal with wastewater and garbage in Samut Prakarn.
1995 June 19	Suwat Liptapanlop (Minister of Science, Technology and Environment: MOSTE) sends a letter (WW0302/9228) proposing the project to the cabinet with 5 contracts, namely: (1) A turnkey contract to design and build a wastewater treatment plant on the east bank, with a budget of 10.148 billion Baht through international competitive bidding. It was advanced that the turnkey nature would reduce the implementation time by 1.5–2 years as the need for re-bidding to construct would be avoided. This turnkey contract would include land acquisition as well (2) A turnkey contract to design and build a wastewater treatment plant on the east bank, with a budget of 2.724 billion Baht under the same conditions as the east bank; (3) A project monitoring contract for both systems with a budget of 269 million Baht, with selection of engineering firm through international competitive bidding; (4) Contract for procurement of equipment to monitor the quality of treated water, both permanent and mobile systems, with a budget of 148 million Baht; (5) Knowledge transfer contract regarding prevention of industrial waste and environmentally friendly technology, with a budget of 323 million Baht, to be awarded to skilled architectural or engineering consultants. Total budget: 13.612 billion Baht. The cabinet wanted greater coordination among the agencies, and asked the Public Works Department, Ministry of Industry, and the Department of Pollution Control to coordinate, and the Budget Bureau for an opinion.
1995	Change of government on July 13. Banharn Silpa-archa becomes Prime Minister. Yingphan Manasikarn becomes Minster of MOSTE, Pakit Kirawanit is director-general of DPC and resubmits the project for cabinet consideration on October 17, 1995. Opinions sought from five agencies (National Economic and Social Planning Board (NESDB), Ministry of Industry, Ministry of Interior, Ministry of Finance, and Budget Bureau) caused the cabinet to issue instructions to the PCD on October 17 to take into account of these considerations and approve the project in principle.

1995	PCD hires Sinthu-Montgomery-Watson to prepare an implementation plan, taking into account the Cabinet's instructions, and prepare prequalification documents and short listing criteria, bid documents, and terms of reference.
1996 January	Tender committee appointed, tender period announced, closing date being January 15. Submissions were received from 13 companies, including NVPSKG group consisting of Northwest Water International (NWWI), Vichiphan Construction (V), Prayoonwit Engineering (P), Sisang Construction (S), Krungthon Engineering (K), and Gateway Development (D). The tender document of NVPSKG submitted financial data of the UK company, North West Water Group (NWWG), together with qualifications and experience record of NWWG of over 100 years.
May 15	4 submissions selected out of 13.
June 7	sale of bidding documents
August 30	Pakit (director-general of PCD) informs bidders that the treatment plants can be collapsed into one plant.
October 7	only two bidders remain: NVPSKG and Marubeni.
December 6	AMS consulting company proposed one combined plant. Pakit informers bidders to collapse the plants into one and submits request to increase the budget.
December 9	Contract to hire AMS signed.
1997 January 20	NVPSKG alone submits bid.
February 17	NEB approves increase in budget and one site.
March 25	submitted to cabinet for acknowledgement. Cabinet acknowledged the proposal to change the location from the six areas on the east and west banks, and have wastewater pumped by tunnel to Kong Darn, and an increase in the budget. With only one bidder remaining, the DPC was to negotiate the cost down from 26.52 to 22.955 billion Baht.
July 28	NWWI informs NVPSKG of unwillingness to sign the contract, and cancels power of attorney to NVPSKG.
August 20	PCD signs contract with NVPSKG (including NWWI), and 1.9566 billion Baht paid to NVPSKG. NEB informs PCD that documents from the local administration allowing use of land for 50 years and public hearing are missing. False documents are then submitted to NEB.
September 1	NWWI cancels contract with NVPSKG.
1998 May 25	Sirithan approves replacement of NWWI with OPCO, a company set up by NVPSKG, without cabinet approval.
2002	Government inquiry into the project.
2003 February 24	Government orders cessation of construction due to invalidity of contract.

September 5	NPVSKG appeals to Arbitration Tribunal, claiming 6.2 million Baht plus interest, in damages.
2008 August 18	Court orders the invalidation of land deeds to five plots of land due to falsification, and sentences Wattana Asawahame to prison according to Article 148 of the criminal code. 2009 Case 254/2547 Department of Pollution Control against NPVSKG, Dusit Court rules against 18 defendants (including Wattana Asawahame) and sentences them to 3 years imprisonment according to Article 341 and fine of 6000 Baht for each company involved.
2011 December 6	National Anti-Corruption Commission finds 19 accused persons (including Wattana Asawahame and Yingphan Manasikan) culpable.

Chronology of the Klong Darn Land Purchase

1960	Contract for land SK.1 Number180/98 sale of 37.3 rai for 200 Baht per rai.
1974	Sale contract for 6578 Baht per rai.
1988	Lanthong Mining Company with Wattana Asawahame as the major shareholder buys land at Moo 11, Klong Darn at 20,000 Baht per rai, and sold it to Palm Beach development (owned by Wattana Asawahame, Somsak Thepsuthin, and Preecha Laohapongchana) at 100,000 Baht per rai. In addition SK.1 and NS.3 land was acquired, totaling 20,000 rai was acquired, including a public waterway.
1994	Palm Beach development sells the land to Klong Darn marine and fishery (connected company).
1998	PCD buys 1,900 rai of land from Klong Darn marine and fishery for 1.9566 billion Baht (or more than 1 million Baht per rai).

Lessons Learned

It can be seen from the above case that some corrupt acts were in direct violation of rules and regulations, but others take advantage of legal and administrative loopholes, and also the judicial process. What can be done to reduce connected dealings and improve procurement in Thailand?

To counter corruption networks, it is important to note that certain types of social action, even if effective, change the types of connections created, but do not necessarily reduce their number or importance. The threat of punitive social action on certain transactions induces connections of mutual dependence within the network at different stages. High penalties on crimes in general increase the mutual dependence of the criminals, but not necessarily their number, if the network is strong.

The difficulty with network relationships and social capital is that it can benefit or harm society. Close-knit, trusting criminal groups may create networks based on a mixture of empathy, threats, and shared goals that negate law enforcement efforts. And trust among law enforcers facilitates processing of cases. But trust motivated by moral values, such as respect, even when extended altruistically, can mitigate against effective law enforcement. Both kinds of organizations can exhibit interpersonal solidarity, reinforced as in repeated a prisoners dilemma game, can create benefit or harm, and a critical mass of desirable networks needs to be created because people are affected by their perception of what others are doing (Fehr and Gächter 2000).

What is perhaps alarming in Thailand is that harmful networks are being created and perpetuated. Massive proceeds of corruption can be used to mobilize supporters to protest court verdicts, indictments, and anticorruption efforts. Network members show solidarity with the group or network leader, whatever the issue, by their readiness to protest, block roads, put up barricades, and even openly threaten the lives of judges and their families. The creation of networks is grafted on the "democratic" machinery, and right and wrong becomes a popularity context.

What complicates the situation further is that sometimes assistance given to particular persons or failing to act against certain persons does not have any corrupt intent or even expectation of reciprocity. A person's good reputation, or affiliation, or being sons or daughters of a respected person can cause people to act in their favor without any personal gain. Deference to an "institution" can assume priority. For example, Thais often advise children to respect "the monk's cloth" and ignore the individual monk's behavior.

Accusations of "double standards" float around everyday. The question on many people's minds though is whether "good" people should allow themselves to be punished, knowing that the "bad" people would get off scot-free because of their connections? There are a few examples of "good people" resigning when faced with corruption charges; the really corrupt however cling on to their positions tenaciously. Both good and bad people have connections. "Everybody knows everybody" and are related to everybody, and this is the key to Thailand's political turmoil. Even among uncorrupt academics, when suspicions arise concerning "someone known for a long time" they would refuse cooperation even when they know the facts. Both the Thai word "khon gun eng" and Chinese word "kaki nung" are often evoked. It can be seen that interpersonal relationships play an important role in every aspect of life, including securing procurement contracts.

The returns to corrupt acts depend on how diffused corruption is in society, that is, how much corruption is inherited from the past. The larger the share of corrupt agents, the higher the returns to corruption, because of several reasons. First, with widespread corruption in society, the task of auditing corrupt officials is not easy. Second the expected profitability of corruption from an individual point of view is a positive function of the degree to which a society as a whole is corrupt (Andvig and Moene 1990). Third, corrupt officials have an incentive to establish communication or networking among themselves and will fuel the corruption ring (Sah 1988). In addition, in societies where rent-seeking and bribery abound, the return to rent-seeking relative to entrepreneurship is high (Murphy et al. 1991, 1993; Acemoglu 1995). Last, when corruption is widespread, individuals may be discouraged from trying to fight it, even if everybody would be better off if corruption were eliminated.

To tackle corruption in procurement, reform or measures are needed in the following areas: (i) legal infrastructure, (ii) corrupt-friendly economic policies, (iii) upgrading of the database, and (iv) social mobilization for enhanced transparency. This chapter also argues that membership in international conventions, such as the World Trade Organization's Government Procurement Agreement (WTO-GPA) could serve as a tool to help alleviate current problems.

Improving the Legal Infrastructure

The legal infrastructure needs to be reformed in many ways, and only a few key points are made here. First, even though Thai procurement regulations emphasize openness and transparency as the main principles, many improvements can be made. In terms of openness and transparency, announcements and dissemination of information through the Public Relations Department, Mass Communication Organization of Thailand, the G-Procurement website, etc., are required. Procurement committees have to be formed, often with citizen participation. Contracts worth more than 1 million baht have to be sent to the office of the Auditor-General and Revenue Department within 30 days of signing. Regulations for e-procurement also include additional criteria: value for money, transparency, efficiency and effectiveness, and accountability and responsibility for completion. At least three tenderers (in the case of standards license or meeting quality control systems) are required. However, cabinet decisions are only placed on the OPM website in very brief form. Many cases that have led to corruption cases were approved by cabinet decisions, and more detailed disclosure should be required.

Second, the technical specifications allow what is called "locking of specifications," in order to favor certain suppliers. The dilemma is how to specify enough detail so as to verify suitability and at the same time avoid such specificity that includes/excludes suppliers, particularly for complex, sophisticated procurement that needs customized designs. Often the suppliers themselves are consulted for the expert knowledge. Under the WTO-GPA Article X Technical Specifications and Tender Documentation, it is required that:

> A procuring entity shall not seek or accept, in a manner that would have the effect of precluding competition, advice that may be used in the preparation or adoption of any technical specification for a specific procurement from a person that may have a commercial interest in the procurement.

There are similar provisions in Thailand, but enforcement is a problem, especially with projects involving very advanced technology, where the suppliers themselves are often informally invited to write the specifications.

> GPA's Article X is particularly interesting in stating that:
> In prescribing the technical specifications for the goods or services being procured, a procuring entity shall, where appropriate:
>
> a. Specify the technical specification in terms of performance and functional requirements, rather than design or descriptive characteristics.

The *functional requirements* are not specified in Thai regulations, and technical specifications are invariably related to physical characteristics. This is an area that could be the focus of reform in Thailand, and would require nationwide training of procurement officers.

In terms of the legal infrastructure, it is also necessary to coordinate various law-proposing channels. The "Cleansing Act" of 2007, for example, allowed criminal proceedings against defendants indicted for procurement corruption to be dropped.

The NACC recently amended the Anti-Corruption Law that allows it to closely monitor large procurement projects, and requires procuring agencies to publish and explain how the reference prices are calculated. Whistle-blowing protection has also been introduced. In addition, a new integrity index has been constructed to evaluate all government agencies at the departmental level. The index features a procurement component that gives marks for proper procedure and transparency in procurement.

Targeting Corruption-Friendly Economic Policies

At the present time, the National Anti-Corruption Commission is playing an increasingly proactive role in scrutinizing economic policies and measures that open up opportunities for corruption. Several preemptive interventions have been made, such as in the case of the scheme to procure 4000 natural-gas operated city buses, and the auction of 3-G telecommunications licenses, that have had the effect of subjecting the projects to greater scrutiny. The Cabinet, for example, asked the proposers of the bus scheme to withdraw the project in order to conduct further studies in the areas indicated by the NACC technical committee, when the project was submitted for cabinet approval in 2009 and 2010.

Reform is also needed in areas such as the intervention schemes in the agricultural sector. At the behest of the NACC, reform in this area had been beginning. But the new government in 2011 seems to be bringing back some of the old risky policies.

Upgrading of the Database

Proactive approaches to countering corrupt networks require knowing the identity of the network members. Efforts are currently underway to improve the anticorruption database, with linkages to information from financial institutions, the land department, vehicle registry, business ownership, and tax returns.

Nongovernment groups are also collecting information and analyzing the behavior of elected officials. For the election in 2011, a civil society group collected information on members of parliament who were absent from parliamentary meetings, and distributed copies of each member's "report card." However, in spite of the dismal scores given to the MPs that failed to attend any parliamentary sessions or were absent for more than 50 % of the time, they were all reelected.

Increased Social Mobilization for Enhanced Transparency

Transparency of procurement information is vital to prevent wrongdoing. The Thai OPM regulations actually do require publication of information. For complaint and appeal procedures, the OPM regulations state that aggrieved suppliers or contractors may lodge complaints directly with the procuring agency, the PMO's Committee in Charge of Procurement, or the Petition Council. In the case of the Petition Council, the petitioner must lodge the complaint within 90 days of knowledge of wrongdoing. The council will then consider the petition "without delay," and remedial measure(s) (if any) will be recommended within 7 days to the prime minister. Remedy might include overturning the act that is inconsistent with the law, or that cannot be supported by "justifiable reason." It is also possible for an interim remedy to be issued by the council itself when appropriate.

However, transparency remains a problem, and efforts are needed to mobilize stakeholders in society. This sounds like a broken record, but the means of mobilization itself has to be overhauled, so that some benefits can be obtained from citizen involvement that would make it worth their while. The Klong Dan case of citizen involvement is a rare "success story." With network connections and the possibility of retaliation, Thailand is still grappling with the means to mobilize and incentivize citizens in the fight against procurement corruption.

Sirilaksana Khoman et al. (2009) and Somkiat Tangkitvanich et al. (2009) propose that the GPA could be a tool to increase transparency in Thailand's government procurement. Membership could possibly lead to greater transparency, more efficient use of government budget as it would stimulate fair competition, help honest and efficient suppliers, and may foster industrial growth and development. Greater foreign involvement and competition can thus help to uncover wrongdoing. However, there is some apprehension about becoming a member of the GPA. First opportunities for Thai suppliers to access GPA member procurement markets remain limited, while domestic suppliers will face stiffer competition. On the other hand, foreign competition may result in difficulties for domestic suppliers in certain sectors. This is the familiar "infant industry" argument that has both pros and cons. If long-run efficiency is the goal, then gradual expansion of competition may help to attain that objective. Second, there is some concern that opening up may or may not lead to greater competition and efficiency, if it leads to international collusion. Finally, if foreign governments subsidize their service sectors, particularly construction, the GPA does not have any provision for countervailing action or remedy, unlike the case of subsidies under World Trade Organization's General Agreement on Tariffs and Trade (Khoman et al. 2009).

Conclusion

In a society dominated by interpersonal relationships, for social, business, as well as other activity, understanding these relationships is the key to understanding corrupt activity. Networks cut across the usual socioeconomic characteristics because members of different skills and characteristics are required for a corrupt network to be effective. There are also the various difficulties involved in designing a procurement system. First, government procurement usually involves multiple objectives, with efficiency being just one of them. Often procurement is used as a means to effect a geographical redistribution of income, or to favor underprivileged groups such as the disabled. It is also difficult to design a system that aligns with personal incentives with public benefit, as the same observed behavior could be motivated by opposite motives. Strict conformity to rules sometimes results in less efficiency; the "special method" could reflect a sinister motive or a desire to be efficient; the lowest price may involve sacrifice of quality, and detailed specifications could limit competition.

At the societal level, social enforcement of private contracts, ready access to adjudication, morality, and religious pressure for generalized honesty (in contrast to "contextual morality") cannot be overlooked. These elements all tend to reduce the importance of identity, to facilitate transactions between strangers, and to reduce the need for specific mutual investment by connected parties. But procurement also needs to be accompanied by effective monitoring systems (e.g., corruption report, witness protection, etc.) and sufficiently stringent penalties for the wrongdoers and conspirators. The larger the network of corruption rings, the larger the returns to corrupt acts. The creation of networks of clean officials up to a certain critical mass is absolutely vital to counter the corrupt networks. The fight against corruption is most effective when preventive, punitive, and educational measures are combined, and public involvement encouraged, as the case of Klong Darn shows. Most will agree that education is central to preventing corruption. And one way is to illustrate through cases and engagement of external stakeholders, so that value-driven reforms will be based on actual vulnerabilities.

References

Act on Offences Relating to the Submission of Bids to State Agencies. (1999). www.moj.go.th/Law/MojLaw/EngLaw/Act%20Con. Accessed 10 Sept 2011.

Andvig, J. C., & Moene, K. O. (1990). How corruption may corrupt. *Journal of Economic Behaviour and Organization, 13(1),* 63–76.

Becker, G. S. (1974). A theory of social interactions. *Journal of Political Economy, 82,* 1063–1093.

Ben-Porath, Y. (1980). The F-connection: families, friends, and firms and the organization of exchange. *Population and Development Review, 6*(1), 1–30.

Fehr, E., & Simon, G. (2000). Cooperation and punishment in public goods experiments. *The American Economic Review, 90(4),* 980–994.

Khan, M. H. (1998). Patron-client networks and the economic effects of corruption in Asia. *The European Journal of Development Research, 10(1),* 15–39.

Khoman, S., Wanrak, M., Vatchareeya T., Chayun, T., Chatchai, C., Sutthi, S., Sittikorn, N., & Napon, S. (2009). The World Trade Organisation's government procurement agreement: A study of Thailand's preparation for accession. Research report submitted to the Comptroller-General's Department, Ministry of Finance. Bangkok, Thailand. (in Thai).

Khoman, S., Chayun, T., Phongthorn, W., & Sayamon, S. (2010). Comparative study of anti-corruption measures and procedures in selected APEC economies. Research Report submitted to APEC-ACT (Asia-Pacific Economic Co-operation- Anti-Corruption Task Force). Bangkok, Thailand.

Khoman, S. (2012). "Corruption and network relationships: theory and evidence from Thailand." Paper presented at the first OBEGEF conference, "Interdisciplinary insights on fraud and corruption" at the Faculdade de Economia da Universidade do Porto, Portugal, September 14–15.

Khoman, S., Tantivasadakarn, C., Wrasai, P., & Prasertsri, L. (2008). Corruption and cultural factors. *NACC Journal, 1*(1), 66–82 (in Thai).

Khoman, S., Mingmaneenakin, W., Thosanguan, V., Tantivasada-karn, C., Chetsumon, C., Suntaranurak, S., Nipaya, S., & Sooksai, N. (2009). The world trade organisation's government procurement agreement: a study of Thailand's preparation for accession. research report submitted to the Comptroller-General's Department, Ministry of Finance. (in Thai). Bangkok, Thailand: Comptroller-General's Department.

Khoman, S., Tantivasadakarn, C., Wrasai, P., & Saksmerprome, S. (2011). *Comparative study of anti-corruption measures and procedures in selected APEC economies* (Research report submitted to the Asia-Pacific Economic co-operation anti-corruption task force). www.apec.org.

Mekong Watch. (2010). Samut Prakarn (Klong Darn) wastewater management project in Thailand. www.mekongwatch.org/english/country/thailand/MW_SMBrief(2010.02.27).pdf. Accessed 20 Sept 2011.

Murphy, K. M., Shleifer, A., & Vishny, R. W. (1991). The allocation of talent: Implications for growth. *Quarterly Journal of Economics,* 106, 503–530.

Murphy, K. M., Shleifer, A., & Vishny, R. W. (1993). Why is rent seeking so costly to growth? *American Economic Review Paper and Proceedings,* 83, 409–414.

National Anti-Corruption Commission. (continuous database, not dated). Decisions on cases. http://www.nacc.go.th/cul_search.php. Accessed 5 March 2013 (in Thai).

Office of the Auditor-General. (continuous database, not dated). http://procurement-oag.in.th. (Password Required). Accessed 10 June 2012.

Office of the Prime Minister. (1992). *Regulation of the office of the Prime Minister on procurement* (Amendment No. 6, 2002). Bangkok, Thailand.

Rose-Ackerman, S. (2001). Trust, Honesty, and Corruption: Reflection on the State-Building Process. http://digitalcommons.law.yale.edu/lepp_papers/255. Accessed 23 Nov 2011.

Sah, R. K. (1988). *Persistence and pervasiveness of corruption: new perspectives.* New Haven: Yale Economic Papers.

Security and Exchange Commission. (2010). SEC charges two global tobacco companies with bribery. www.sec.gov/news/press/2010/2010-144.htm. Accessed 10 Sept 2011.

Sidel, J. T. (1996). Siam and its twin? Democratization and Bossism in Contemporary Thailand and the Philippines. *IDS BULLETIN, 27(2),* 56–63.
Tangkitvanich, S., Chetta, I., & Saowarat, R. (2009). Evaluating costs and benefits of joining the Government Procurement Agreement (GPA). Research report submitted to the Comptroller-General's Department, Ministry of Finance. Bangkok, Thailand. (in Thai).
World Economic Forum. (2012). Global competitiveness report. www.weforum.org/en/initiatives/gcp/Global%20Competitiveness%20Report/index.htm. Accessed 10 Sept 2011.
World Trade Organisation. (2006). Government procurement agreement. www.wto.org/english/tratop_e/gproc_e/gp_gpa_e.htm. Accessed 20 Sept 2011.

Sirilaksana Khoman PhD is the Chair in the Economic Sector Corruption Prevention, National Anti-Corruption Commission, Thailand. She was formerly Dean of the Faculty of Economics, Thammasat University. Her research interests include public policy and the economics of corruption.

Collaborative Public Procurement: A Comparative Review of the Indian Position with International Practices on Pooled Procurement from Competition Law Perspectives

Sandeep Verma

Introduction

Collaborative public procurement in its various forms, including pooling of procurement volumes by distinct procuring entities and by way of common framework agreements, is expressly permitted under procurement regulations in India; for instance, her rules on public procurement envisage the creation of a *Central Purchasing Organisation* to bring in rate contracts for common user items frequently needed in bulk by various ministries/departments (Government of India 2006).

Pooled procurement has indeed been encouraged by the government in a variety of cases for reasons of public interest; and recent instances include an attempt by public sector banks to jointly procure ATM services (Yahoo 2012) and the ongoing joint industry tenders for ethanol procurement by oil marketing companies (OMCs) for blending with retail petrol marketed by them (Government of India 2012). Current proposals in India also include creation of a *Special Purpose Vehicle* for direct aviation fuel imports where the *Airports Authority of India*, OMCs and airlines will have equity participation (Business Standard 2013) as well as a proposed joint venture company promoted by public sector oil companies for streamlining crude oil imports into India ("Panel Moots Joint Venture of PSUs" 2013).

In fact, under certain situations, collaborative public procurement may perhaps be the only significant strategic tool available to developing countries, as producers from industrialised countries are known to operate as international cartels in markets of interest, with potential for considerable harm to consumers and producers in developing countries (Levenstein and Suslow 2004). However, all possible forms of collaborative procurement may not be necessarily compliant with Indian competition laws ("Ethanol Bid Process" 2013); and it is in this context that a quick study of international best practices and a comparative review of the Indian situation may be of value to various stakeholders such as public policy makers, procurement entities,

S. Verma (✉)
www.BuyLawsIndia.com
e-mail: sverma.ias@gmail.com

K. V. Thai (ed.), *International Public Procurement,* Public Administration, Governance and Globalization 14, DOI 10.1007/978-3-319-13434-5_10

antitrust regulators, end-consumers of public services, and of course, the affected suppliers as well. The analysis of the Indian situation in this chapter has been undertaken from a competition law and case law perspective, and specifically excludes analysis from a competition policy perspective, as the *National Competition Policy 2011* is still in a draft form (Ministry of Corporate Affairs 2011) and has yet to be formally adopted by the government of India.

Collaboration in public procurement implies the coming together of various purchasing entities, which may or may not be competitors in their respective markets of interest. For instance, government hospitals could combine their procurement volumes in order to obtain best price discounts for drugs or medical equipment (Barbosa and Fiuza 2011), and electricity utilities could combine their strengths to drive hard bargains with other wholesale players in electricity markets (Florida Municipal Power Agency 2013). In a different context, as in India, OMCs competing with each other in the retail petroleum market could pursue joint buying of transportation services in order to encourage overall allocative efficiencies in transportation assets management (Lok Sabha Secretariat 2012).

Such contract collaboration can take both "hard" and "soft" forms: the former *hard* category being cases where procurement qualities are clubbed together ("demand aggregation") usually for the purposes of obtaining efficiency and better value for money, although requisite economies may not necessarily arise particularly in cases where inefficient purchasers (high credit risk purchasers) combine their procurement with relatively inefficient purchasers (Barbosa and Fiuza 2011). Another variant of the former *hard* approach is framework agreements (rate contracts, as they are known in India) for use by various procuring entities, where both technical specifications and prices could be negotiated and/or finalised by a contract-setting authority, but individual subcontracts or supply orders may be placed separately by each procuring entity, as in the USA, where a commonly used framework agreements is an *Indefinite Delivery Indefinite Quantity* (IDIQ) contract (in this context, refer to Federal Acquisition Regulation, FAR ¶16.504 for an exact definition of IDIQ contracts). The latter *soft* category includes cases such as mandatory common technical specifications or interoperability standards for equipment/supplies as in India, where the *Ministry of Home Affairs* routinely issues standard technical specifications/qualitative requirements for technical equipment procured by central armed forces under its jurisdiction (Ministry of Home Affairs 2014). However, standardisation *per se* can have a *de facto* adverse effect in terms of limiting suppliers or innovation under certain circumstances (Pappalardo and Suzor 2011). For reasons of focus and brevity, only the former category of *hard* collaborations is examined in this chapter.

Institutional Arrangements for Collaborative Procurement

In terms of the possible institutional arrangements for joint purchasing, the available literature classifies them into two broad categories (European Commission 2008): (i) *Permanent* Collaborative/Joint Procurement Organisations where a central purchase organisation (CPO) is established by various procuring entities to provide a centralised procurement function, whose services could be financed through a small commission charged on all procurement actions; and (ii) *Collaborative agreements* between contracting authorities, without separate legal status, that come together on a one-time basis or permanently through an agreed model of participation, with a lead entity normally taking responsibility for contract-setting on behalf of all members.

Examples of the first category in the form of permanent organisations are the *Eastern Shires Purchasing Organisation*, UK, owned by member local authorities, and the *Eco-Procurement Service of Vorarlberg*, Austria, providing a centralised procurement service for 80 local authorities in the Region of Vorarlberg (European Commission 2008); and examples in the USA of such permanent organisations include the *STARS Alliance LLC*—an association of seven nuclear utility operators that procures certain supplies/services jointly on behalf of association members (STARS 2014). In Tanzania, the *Petroleum Importation Coordinator* (PIC) collects procurement requirements from OMCs and concludes and administers contracts with suppliers and the PIC and OMCs (Petroleum Importation Coordinator 2014).

As instances of the second category, permanent collaborative arrangements in the UK include the *London Contracts and Supplies Group* providing for coordinated procurement actions on behalf of the *Greater London Council*, the *Inner London Education Authority* and *London Boroughs* (LCSG 2013). Such collaborative arrangements can also be *one-off*, such as the joint procurement of ATM services recently attempted by public sector banks in India, or the ongoing cases of joint industry tenders for ethanol procurement by OMCs in India, for blending with retail petrol marketed by them (Government of India 2012).

Effects of Collaborative Purchasing

Under certain circumstances, collaborative public procurement can have beneficial impacts in terms of lower prices (Burnett 2003), administrative cost savings and pooling of skills and expertise amongst various procuring entities (European Commission 2008), although as stated earlier, combining high credit risk purchasers with relatively inefficient purchasers may lead to higher procurement costs for those purchasers who were already more efficient than the rest of the group (Barbosa and Fiuza 2011). In addition, particularly in the European Union, collaborative public procurement is also being increasingly used as a convenient entry door for introducing sustainable procurement and standardising environmental demand (European Commission 2008), although frequent use may also result in creation of artificial entry barriers for nondomestic suppliers of competing products (Brenton et al. 2000).

Perhaps a matter of greater concern with joint purchasing agreements is their potential to result in *buyers' cartels*, especially when large competitors come together with an illegitimate aim of using their high degree of buyer power to cause competitive harm to suppliers or for retaining excess profits without any pass-through to their end-consumers (Koponen 2011). In addition, large buyers may also collaborate to abuse their monopsony (or *near*-monopsony) power to depress the purchase of a product below competitive levels, or, at another end, buying group formation can become a convenient instrument/front to facilitate collusion through downstream coordination amongst suppliers (for a more detailed analysis of theories of harm relating to joint buying, including monopsonies and bilateral monopolies, refer to Fiandeiro et al. 2011).

International Perspectives on Collaborative Public Procurement

Collaborative public procurement, either through joint buying by distinct procuring entities, or through *piggybacking* mechanisms such as framework agreements, falls within an interesting intersection of public procurement law and competition law. However, to the extent that public procurement marketplaces in advanced jurisdictions such as the USA have comparatively fewer public procurement entities that are expected to compete in commercial marketplaces, a cursory review of available literature seems to suggest that anticompetitive effects of collaborative public procurement have not received due attention in academic or regulatory documentation on the subject. A recent OECD/EU publication (SIGMA 2011), however, clearly recognises *market concentration*, *uniformity & standardisation*, and *reduction in SME opportunities* as potential adverse effects of collaborative (centralised) procurement.

The United States' acquisition guidance for federal contracts does not specifically require a competition/antitrust law analysis, and even the European Commission's toolkits on joint public procurement do not *contain* any specific references to the otherwise rather extensive EC guidelines on horizontal cooperation agreements. Public procurement laws in these jurisdictions allow for collaborative procurement amongst procuring entities; and separately, specific government/regulatory guidance is available that addresses joint purchasing agreements in general *amongst competitors*, without focusing on joint purchasing agreements *amongst government entities* as such. The following section discusses certain best practices in both procurement law and competition law guidance on collaborative procurement in some of these national jurisdictions.

Collaborative Public Procurement in the USA

The US Federal Acquisition Regulation (FAR) contains extensive guidance on a number of ways in which federal public procurement authorities may collaborate in respect of their procurement actions. As an important example, the FAR permits "interagency acquisition" as a permissible procedure by which an agency needing supplies or services (*requesting* agency) can obtain them through another federal government agency (*servicing* agency), either through: (i) *direct acquisitions*, where the requesting agency places an order *directly* against a servicing agency's contract; or (ii) *assisted acquisitions*, where a servicing agency and a requesting agency enter into an interagency agreement *pursuant to which* the servicing agency performs acquisition activities on behalf of the requesting agency, such as awarding a contract or issuing a task or delivery order (JAGLCS 2012). Contractual arrangements that are most frequently used for interagency acquisitions are *IDIQ contracts*, using vehicles such as *GSA Schedules* (*Multiple Award Schedules/ Federal Supply Schedules*), *GWACS* (Government-Wide Acquisition Contracts) and *Multi-Agency Contracts*. As mentioned earlier, the FAR does not appear to contain any specific requirements for addressing potential antitrust implications of such contracting arrangements; although as a separate, unrelated matter, the FAR requires contract *unbundling* to be examined at the acquisition planning stage from a small business set-aside perspective (Federal Acquisition Regulation, FAR ¶2.101 read with FAR ¶7.107; see, also, § 413, Public Law No. 105-135 and FAR ¶7.104(d) read with 15 United States Code (USC) § 644(a) & (e).

Insofar as antitrust issues are concerned, the Federal Trade Commission (FTC) and the Department of Justice (DoJ) issued extensive guidelines (FTCDOJ 2000) in 2000 for collaboration amongst competitors. Under these guidelines, joint purchasing agreements, to the extent that they do not, or tend not, to raise prices or reduce output are required to be addressed under the "Rule of Reason" and may not be *per se* illegal. Under these guidelines, the analytical framework for horizontal cooperation requires a close assessment of the following: (i) the nature of the relevant agreement, especially if it facilitates collusion; (ii) relevant markets affected by the collaboration, including goods markets, technology markets and innovation markets; (iii) market shares and market concentration; (iv) factors relevant to the ability and incentive of the participants and the collaboration to compete (for instance, exclusivity, control over assets, financial interests, control of the collaboration's competitively significant decision making, likelihood of anticompetitive information-sharing, and duration of the collaboration); (v) entry requirements; (vi) identification of any pro-competitive benefits; and (vi) overall competitive effect. These guidelines also establish safety zones for competitor collaborations in general at not more than 20 % in relevant output market and 35 % in the relevant input market in which competition may be affected (Bigart et al. 2013).

In terms of executive/regulatory guidance, the DoJ in a joint purchasing alliance case recently issued a business review letter (Department of Justice 2013), indicating that, *inter alia*, the following aspects could be important in determining whether:

- Such horizontal cooperation agreements would be in violation of antitrust law monitoring the buying group's market shares in the input and output markets for compliance within permissible safety zones
- The purchasing program imposes minimum purchasing requirements on association members
- Participation of members is equally available to all and is not limited by size, type or location of member

- Joint purchasing results in control/stabilisation of prices, or is used to boycott suppliers
- Competitively important information is shared between association members
- Joint buying activity is independently handled and negotiated with suppliers (Bigart et al. 2013; Fales and Bigart 2013).

Collaborative Public Procurement in the European Union

As in the USA, framework agreements are a favoured contractual vehicle for collaborative procurement in the EU. More specifically, EU directives on public procurement allow the use of one agency's framework agreements by another (European Commission 2004a), including collaborative procurement by utilities (European Commission 2004b). In addition, procurement agencies are also allowed pooling through the process of national governments designating one or more central procurement body(ies) (CPBs) that could be exclusively mandated to procure certain goods and services for user departments. One such CPB in the UK is the Government Procurement Service (GPS), setup as a *trading fund* under its Government Trading Funds Act of 1973, and working on a *supplier commission* model. The GPS provides essentially three models of procurement services' delivery: (i) self-service by buying organisations through frameworks and other contracting arrangements; (ii) assisted delivery such as spot buying and eAuctions; and (iii) end-to-end managed procurement services (SIGMA 2011).

The EU does not appear to have specific procurement guidance addressing collaborative public purchasing from a competition law/antitrust law perspective. Collaborative public procurement in the EU may therefore need to satisfy the *normal* competition requirements placed by EC laws and guidance on cooperation agreements. In particular, joint purchasing agreements, if carried out as a full-function joint venture, need to comply with the *EU Merger Regulation* (EUMR) (Koponen 2011); and other forms of horizontal cooperation need to comply with Article 101 of the *Treaty on the Functioning of the European Union* (TFEU) (European Commission 2005). There is, however, one view (Sanchez-Graellis 2013) that "the Court of Justice of the European Union (CJEU) has excluded the applicability of Art 101 to public contracting authorities in a clear line of case law"; but this contrarian view assuming a complete exemption to procurement actions of public entities in the EU may not be entirely correct or complete, in that the cited judgments essentially related to appeals on abuse of dominant position in relation to Article 82/86 of the EC Treaty generally,[1] and not specifically in relation to Article 101 of the TFEU.

[1] Article 82 of the EC Treaty states that any abuse by one or more undertakings of a dominant position within the common market or in a substantial part of it shall be prohibited as incompatible with the common market insofar as it may affect trade between member states. Such abuse may, in particular, consist in (a) directly or indirectly imposing unfair purchase or selling prices or other unfair trading conditions; (b) limiting production, markets or technical development to the prejudice of consumers; (c) applying dissimilar conditions to equivalent transactions with other

Further, the two cited judgments in this contrarian view may need to be viewed in the specific context of the appeals where purchasing/regulatory authority exercised by the public entities was not treated as "economic activity" inviting the application of competition law provisions of the EC Treaty on the following grounds: (i) purchasing activities of public procurement authorities were not disassociated with subsequent use of the subject of procurement (in the 2006 judgment); and (ii) the subsequent use happened to be of a purely social nature (in the 2006 judgment) or related to technical standardisation in exercise of pan-European regulatory powers (in the 2009 judgment). Since procurement actions of a large number of public entities in the EU may extend well beyond the specific scenarios in the two judgments of the CJEU, for instant in the case of State-owned Enterprises (SoEs), it may not be entirely correct to presume that all procurement actions of public entities are exempted from operation of competition provisions of the EU Treaty. In any case, and at the very least, EU guidance on collaborative procurement under TFEU provides useful frameworks for conducting an anticompetition effects analysis that could guide meaningful policy and legal formulations internationally.

Inter alia, Article 101 of TFEU declares as prohibited any agreements that directly or indirectly fix purchase prices between covered undertakings, but allows qualified derogation in respect of any agreement or category(ies) of agreements. In pursuance of this authority, the European Commission (2011) has issued *Guidelines on the Applicability of Article 101 of the Treaty on the Functioning of the European Union to Horizontal Co-operation Agreements* (EUHC Guidelines); and part 5 of these guidelines deals specifically with cooperative purchasing agreements.

The EUHC Guidelines recognise that joint purchasing could be pro-competitive in cases where they allow smaller rivals to achieve similar purchasing economies to larger competitors in the form of lower prices, but also caution about the complexities involved when dominant market operators enter into joint purchasing agreements (Ashurst 2011). These guidelines, therefore, require joint purchasing agreements to be analysed in terms of both horizontal and vertical elements: the horizontal arrangements between competitors purchasing jointly, and the vertical arrangements between the suppliers and the joint purchasing group, including, in some cases, downstream arrangements between the purchasing group and its members. In addition, the EUHC Guidelines also require an examination of the purchasing

trading parties, thereby placing them at a competitive disadvantage; or (d) making the conclusion of contracts subject to acceptance by the other parties of supplementary obligations which, by their nature or according to commercial usage, have no connection with the subject of such contracts. Article 86 of the EC Treaty states that: (i) in the case of public undertakings and undertakings to which member states grant special or exclusive rights, member states shall neither enact nor maintain in force any measure contrary to the rules contained in the EC Treaty, in particular to those rules provided for in Article 12 and Articles 81 to 89; and (ii) Undertakings entrusted with the operation of services of general economic interest or having the character of a revenue-producing monopoly shall be subject to the rules contained in the EC Treaty, in particular to the rules on competition, insofar as the application of such rules does not obstruct the performance, in law or in fact, of the particular tasks assigned to them. The development of trade must not be affected to such an extent as would be contrary to the interests of the Community.

markets (input markets) and the selling markets (output markets) in terms of geographical distribution and the collaborating parties' market positions.

In general, the guidelines indicate that competition harm would be less likely if the collaborating parties have a combined market share of not more than 15 % on both the purchasing market(s) and the selling market(s). If these "safe" harbours are breached, the guidelines then require a detailed examination of a number of issues under a "Rule of Reason" approach as follows: (i) whether the cooperating purchasers are active in different selling markets; (ii) whether commercial sensitive data is being collated by a joint purchasing agency that does not pass on information to its members (Ashurst 2011). Separately, the UK Office of Fair Trading has adopted a more benign approach to joint purchasing in a short-form opinion in 2010 on joint purchasing agreements, indicating that competitive harm would be unlikely where the collaborating parties have no downstream market power (Office of Fair Trade 2010).

Collaborative Public Procurement in China

Centralised procurement is permitted under China's Government Procurement Law for items decided by Central/Provincial governments (People's Republic of China 2002), although the law by itself does not cover SoEs, implying thereby that various forms of collaborative procurement could, in fact, be practiced by SoEs in China, although detailed/specific reports on the same are not available. A separate antimonopoly law came into effect in China in 2008, and regulates monopolistic behavior and unfair competition possibly including government procurement in China, although, in practice, no intervention seems to have been noticed by administrative departments entrusted with competition compliance (UNCTAD 2012). Article 13 of its antimonopoly law prohibits five types of horizontal monopoly agreements: (i) price-fixing; (ii) production/sales quantity restrictions; (iii) dividing sales/procurement markets for raw materials; (iv) restrictive practices relating to procurement of new technologies/equipment; and (v) restrictive practices on development of new technologies/equipment. Price-fixing includes (i) fixing or changing price levels of products; (ii) fixing or changing magnitude of price changes; (iii) fixing or changing fees or discounts that influence prices; (iv) applying an appointed price as the basis for transacting with a third party; (v) agreeing to apply a standard formula as the basis to calculate prices; and (vi) agreeing to a price that cannot be changed without the consent of competitors. Based on this limited guidance, it may be fair to presume that China prohibits most forms of joint purchasing under a *per se* rule, and in particular, in the case of separate public entities arriving at identical procurement prices through collaborative procurement efforts.

Lessons from International Best Practices

A number of useful pointers can be safely drawn from a review of US and EU guidance on collaborative public procurement. Firstly, insofar as joint purchasing arrangements between competitors is concerned, the general inclination seems to be to adopt a "Rule of Reason" approach rather than a "per se" approach for analysing the competition effects, although certain countries such as South Africa, for instance, appear to treat joint purchasing as per se illegal (Fiandeiro et al. 2011). The primary intention in these two major antitrust jurisdictions to allow the survival of collaborative procurement seems to be to permit joint purchasing amongst *smaller* economic operators to enjoin the benefits of joint purchasing in terms of lower prices, and both US and EU therefore draw tolerance limits through *safe harbours* in input (buying) markets and output (selling) markets beyond which an analysis of competition effects is necessarily warranted.

An important and common area of concern in these two jurisdictions is the potential for sharing of commercially sensitive information between collaborating entities, where antitrust guidance seems to suggest that maintaining an arms-length between collaborators may be necessary by routing collaborative purchases through a *separate/ independent* purchasing agency. Other important lessons, arising out of the US experience, relate essentially to (i) whether participation in the joint purchasing arrangements by association members is voluntary—the anticompetitive effects being presumed to be much less if participation is voluntary rather than mandatory; and (ii) whether joint purchasing arrangements are used by collaborators for price stabilisation and/or price control, without passing on economic benefits to their consumers—the anticompetitive effects being higher if the economic advantages of joint buying are retained by collaborators rather than being passed-through to end-consumers.

In regard to joint purchasing by public procurement entities that are not competing amongst themselves in commercial marketplaces, a common tendency under public procurement laws both in the US and the EU, is to permit or encourage such collaboration, although as stated earlier, the procurement guidance seems to avoid a specific discussion on potential competitive harm issues, rather than addressing them upfront from an antitrust perspective. To that extent, while highlighting competition concerns with agglomerated buying, the procurement guidance in the two jurisdictions does not really attempt to distinguish collaborations between *hardcore government* purchases vis-à-vis collaborations between *public entities operating as dominant economic operators in commercial marketplaces.*

Collaborative Purchasing in India

The government of India has allowed joint tenders by *Central Public Sector Enterprises* (CPSEs, internationally known as SoEs) in a few cases in the recent past, although no cases of different government departments bundling their requirements are evident. This appears to have been done sometimes through *plain administrative orders* by the concerned administrative department (as in the case of joint tendering for ATMs by public sector banks), and sometimes through *policy decisions* of the government (as in the case of ethanol procurement by OMCs), without citing any specific provision of *General Financial Rules 2005* (GFR-2005) or any other relevant/applicable procurement rules of concerned entities or statutory authority of the government (Government of India 2005). In order to appreciate the legal position better, it may therefore be worthwhile to examine the procurement rule position, as well as the competition law position, relating to joint purchasing agreements in India.

The Procurement Rule Position in India

While both *GFR-2005* as well as the *Manual for Policies and Procedures for Purchase of Goods* ("Manual") issued thereunder are silent on collaborative purchases through one single contract issued by one procuring entity on behalf of a group, the *Manual* does contain an enabling provision for rate contracts (framework agreements), whereby a designated CPO[2] can bring in rate contracts for common user items frequently needed in bulk by various ministries/departments (Government of India 2006). Two important features of the provision are (i) placement of supply orders by a user organisation against a rate contract established by a CPO is at the *option* of the user organisation; and (ii) the provision does not appear to allow for one user organisation to place supply orders against rate contracts established by *other* user organisations, but *only* against a rate contract established by a CPO. Separately, certain recent CVC instructions (Central Vigilance Commission 2012) that apply uniformly to government departmental purchases as well as to purchases by CPSEs, to the extent that they cast aspersions that only purchase orders placed by one government organisation/PSE on another and followed up by single source procurement without any "value-addition" in the process, could be interpreted to imply that *interagency contracting*—a key feature of some joint purchasing agreements—is perhaps also not really prohibited under the CVC guidance.

Read together, these two instructions issued independently by the Ministry of Finance and by the CVC appear to have a small area of divergence: as per CVC instructions, one government department/CPSE can nominate another government department/CPSE for taking over its procurement activities so long as the order receiving government department/PSE conducts its procurement in an open and competitive manner, presumably also through open and competitive framework agreements; while the Ministry of Finance guidance only allows a designated CPO to undertake procurement actions on behalf of a government department, without clarifying what rules are to be followed in respect of collaborative purchases between CPSEs.

The Competition Law Position in India

Under Indian law, insofar as horizontal cooperation is concerned, any agreement entered into between enterprises/associations or any other enterprises, which, *in-*

[2] The *Directorate General of Supplies and Disposal* (DGS&D) under the Ministry of Commerce is one such CPO in India; *see* www.dgsnd.gov.in.

ter alia: (i) directly or indirectly determines purchase prices; (ii) limits of controls the production, supply, markets or technical development of services; (iii) shares markets by way of allocation of geographical area or number of customers; or (iv) directly or indirectly results in bid rigging or collusive bidding, shall be *presumed* to have an appreciable adverse effect on competition and shall be void, with the exception of agreements by way of joint ventures if such agreements increase efficiencies in acquisition of goods or services-§ 3(3) and its *Proviso*, Competition Act 2002 (Act No. 12 of 2003).

Under this rule, it would appear that collaborative procurement amongst competitors by way of joint purchasing agreements through a joint tender—an exercise that *inherently* involves the fixation of a common price of procurement of supplies by participating members—would be presumed to have an appreciable adverse effect on competition and shall be void under a *per se* approach (this legal position under Indian law is not different from the legal position for joint tenders in South Africa (Fiandeiro et al. 2011). On the other hand, collaborative procurement through joint ventures, if such arrangements increase efficiency in acquisition of goods or services, shall not be presumed to have an appreciable adverse effect on competition, and would therefore need to be analysed for potential anticompetitive effects under a "Rule of Reason" approach (Competition Commission of India 2012a). Also, joint purchasing agreements that contain elements of exclusive supply agreements and "refusal to deal" agreements are void under Indian law if they can be shown, under a "Rule of Reason" approach, to result in appreciable adverse effect on competition in India.

In respect of vertical cooperation, the competition law in India prohibits, inter alia: (i) imposition of unfair or discriminatory conditions in purchase or sale of goods or services, or imposition of unfair or discriminatory price in purchase of goods or services; (ii) arrangements that result in denial of market access in any manner; and (iii) use of the dominant position of one enterprise or group to enter into another relevant market [Competition Commission of India 2012a, 2012b). Joint purchasing agreements that incorporate these elements would therefore be anticompetitive under a "Rule of Reason" approach; and to the extent that the competition law in India does not exclude public entities from its coverage, collaborative public procurement in India would also be subject to the aforesaid analysis on both horizontal and vertical cooperation aspects.

The Competition Case Law Position in India

There appears to be no case law in India dealing with collaborative public procurement across government departments *inter-se* from a competition law perspective. However, in the context of joint purchasing agreements between CPSEs that can be competitors in the commercial marketplace, majority opinion in the two cases [India Glycols Ltd. vs. Indian Oil Corporation & Others 2012; Royal Energy Ltd. 2012) that have been settled by the competition regulator in India—*Competition*

Commission of India—on the subject thus far create a very different legal position, as compared to the strict position in law described in the preceding section. For instance, majority opinions in both these cases did not adopt a *per se* approach in analysing the anticompetitive effects of joint purchasing, and therefore closed both cases *without* specifically analysing the competition law aspects of either the joint tenders issued by the OMCs or the underlying government instructions regulating prices, purchases and supplies.

A review of these two cases of interest reveals the following case law conclusions for future guidance: (i) that joint purchasing by government departments/CPSEs may not be reviewed by the competition regulator in India under the *per se* rule mandated by the competition law, but under a "Rule of Reason" analysis; (ii) that joint purchasing by government departments/CPSEs may not be put to the prescribed mandatory tests by the competition regulator in India for abuse of dominance or for agreements-in-concert with potential appreciable adverse effects on competition, even though the competition law in India, by itself, does not allow any special or deferential treatment of cooperation agreements between public entities or government-owned commercial entities.

Interestingly, case law evolution on the subject seems to have suffered from a lack of timely action by competition regulators in India: the typical scenario has been a delay on the part of the Competition Commission of India to intervene in joint tenders through timely investigations, or a general hesitance to grant injunctive relief to affected parties even though joint purchasing amongst economic operators appears to be illegal in India under the *per se* rule. This has invariably resulted in conclusion of contracts by the time a case is ripe for decision by the forum of first or the second appeal, by which time injunctive relief or final decisions of competition authorities are rendered redundant or infructuous (India Glycols Ltd. vs. Competition Commission of India & Ors 2013).

The Comparative Situation in India, So Far

The strict legal situation in India on collaborative public procurement is more akin to the South African position, where joint tenders resulting in fixation of a common purchase price for supplies procured by competing entities would be deemed to be *per se* illegal. Other elements of competition law in India are more similar to the US and the EU guidance, in that aspects such as geographical distribution of buyer and seller markets, dominant positions of the buyers in the relevant markets, and arbitrary restrictions on supplier behavior, are all required to be analysed for an overall *anticompetitive effects* determination.

But the regulatory orders in the two cases dealt with so far, as stated earlier, have created an interesting situation because of the divergence between the competition law and the case law in India. The *India Glycols* case, for instance, probably contained a significant number of important tender design issues with potentially anticompetitive effects as commonly understood in academic literature on the subject, for instance: (i) dominance of buyers in both input markets as well as in output markets; (ii) consumer expectation of competition between the dominant buyers in the commercial market place (the downstream market); (iii) mandatory (involuntary) participation of dominant buyers in the scheme with pre-fixed purchasing commitments; (iv) sharing of commercially sensitive information amongst the members of the buying group; (v) artificial geographical market segregation and similar unilateral restrictions imposed on suppliers during the contract finalisation process; (vi) denial of responses to tender queries by the purchasing entities unless such queries were *jointly* raised by suppliers; (vii) invitation of expressions of interest from suppliers without intimating in advance intended purchase prices or specific quantities to be allocated to each participant, and subsequent restrictions on future participation of any respondents who choose not to sign final contracts if the purchase prices unilaterally mandated or quantities unilaterally allocated by the OMCs were unacceptable to ethanol suppliers; and (viii) arbitrary and nonmonitorable restrictions on use of transport assets by suppliers during return trips.[3]

Recommendations and Conclusions

A comparative review of the Indian legal position and case law on collaborative procurement suggests that the time may perhaps be ripe for regulators to issue explicit guidance on joint purchasing agreements, on the same pattern as in the US

[3] These possibilities have been extrapolated by the author from a joint reading of the underlying purchasing framework on ethanol purchase by OMCs (http://www.pib.nic.in/newsite/erelease.aspx?relid=89270) and a subsequent joint EOI issued by OMCs, specifically, EOI No. Ethanol/Industry/2012–2013 (copy available with author), presuming that similar tender design defects would have existed in the relevant joint EOI invitation as well. The identified potential competition design defects in the joint EOI listed earlier are *in addition to* other procurement design defects noticed in the EOI, for instance, the EOI under reference contained the following elements that could be problematic from a purely procurement rule perspective: (i) invitation of expressions of interest from suppliers without intimating in advance intended purchase prices or specific quantities to be allocated to each participant; (ii) non-specification of the pricing formula that would govern ethanol supplies upon changed specifications; (ii) non-specification of specific delivery schedules other than mentioning the total annual requirement per annum at various depots; (iii) restrictions on offerors to make any individual queries, presumably even genuine ones; (iv) seemingly contradictory clauses on supplier responsibility in the event of non-issue of movement permits by state excise authorities; (v) prohibitions on subletting of the contract eventually awarded but permission to execute an irrevocable power of attorney to be executed by suppliers allowing *de facto* subletting of the supplier's performance obligations under contract; and (vi) permitting individual OMCs to recover pending dues/penalties of other, unrelated contracts executed by a supplier with the same or any other OMC while receiving payments for supplies against the ethanol contract(s). In addition, the majority order in the *India Glycols* case notes that the *Cabinet Committee on Economic Affairs* is the *apex body for deciding the prices of commodities for procurement and supply by the government of India*—a statement that is different from the procurement rule stipulation in India assigning this role specifically to designated *CPOs*—a problem that could get further compounded in view of the fact that procurement in the *India Glycols* case was not being undertaken by departments or offices of the government of India, but by *government-owned enterprises* as distinct legal entities operating in commercial markets.

and in the EU that have issued detailed, explicit guidance on joint purchasing agreements. This task could perhaps be undertaken jointly by the Ministry of Corporate Affairs and the Competition Commission of India, and may perhaps involve altering the legal position by allowing the application of a "Rule of Reason" approach rather than a *per se* approach for *anticompetitive effects* determination. In addition, insofar as collaborative procurement between government agencies or government-owned entities, there appears to be an emerging, definite need for clearer and more coherent instructions on the subject, as the existing guidance under procurement rules issued by the Ministry of Finance is far too limited to effectively address the important emerging issues in joint purchases by government departments/CPSEs, and as stated earlier, may not always tally with the advisories independently issued by the CVC.

Joint purchasing by public entities can have beneficial effects in terms of lower procurement costs and other efficiencies that can be passed on directly to consumers of public services, or indirectly to citizens in the form of reduced public expenditure. At the same time, the design of underlying public policies and procurement processes for collaborative procurement would need to be undertaken with due diligence, as it is imperative for the cumulative scheme to stay clear of any adverse competition law concerns. A proper study and understanding of joint purchasing agreements is therefore important from strictly legal perspectives, as quite apart from liabilities of joint collaborators under the competition laws arising out of the collaborations being held to be anticompetitive, the collaborating entities could face additional legal consequences, since if the objective of a joint purchasing contract violates the relevant competition law, then the underlying agreement itself may be *void ab initio* in terms of the contracts law as applied in that particular jurisdiction; for instance, under Indian contract law, an agreement is *void ab initio* if it is made with an unlawful object-§ 2(g) *read with* § 10 and § 24, Indian Contract Act, 1872 (Act No. 9 of 1872).

Additional research into anticompetitive effects of joint purchasing in other BRICS countries, such as Brazil and South Africa, could also inform our understanding of *State-run* or *State-sponsored cartels*, similar to standardisation cartels in the EU that operate by getting the EC to impose health and environmental restrictions that discriminate against foreign bidders and foreign technologies (Wikipedia 2013), or *Military-Industrial cartels* in the US that survive because of, *inter alia*, extreme "Buy American" requirements and subjective methods of public procurement such as competitive negotiations (Verma 2013). In addition, a full and proper understanding of joint purchasing arrangements could also inform public policy formulation particularly in developing countries, with relatively poorer policy making, accountability and oversight mechanisms, where joint purchasing could be a completely artificial cover for artificial government intervention, using its control over government entities and SOEs to cause undue benefits to private monopolistic/oligopolistic suppliers.

In the near future, an important constructive outcome of intensive research in this area could be useful in the context of international cooperation in cartel-prevention, as the present national or regional frameworks, for instance in the EU, appear to permit joint purchasing arrangements as long they cause competitive harm only to foreign economic entities (Ashurst 2011). The OECD has already taken initial steps for establishing international cooperation in cartel investigations (OECD 2012); and legal studies on collaborative public procurement, both from a procurement law as well as from a competition law perspective, could significantly inform this important emerging engagement. Of course, the biggest gainers in this process of alignment of public procurement rules with competition law issues could be developing countries themselves, as collaborative procurement is beginning to emerge as an important strategic tool of public policy in the efforts to contain domestic as well as international cartels that are active both in raw materials markets and in production markets, for the end-purposes of obtaining proper economic gains for consumers of public services and for their citizens.

References

AAI to Create Common Infra For Direct Aviation Fuel Imports. (7 June 2013). *Business Standard.*

Ashurst. (2011). Quick Guides: Co-operation Agreements between Competitors. http://www.business-standard.com/article/companies/aai-to-create-common-infra-for-direct-aviation-fuel-imports-113060600692_1.html. Accessed 14 Sept 2013 (5, pp. 4–5).

Barbosa, K., & Fiuza, E. (2011). Demand aggregation and credit risk effects in pooled procurement: Evidence from the Brazilian public purchases of pharmaceuticals and medical supplies. http://bibliotecadigital.fgv.br/dspace/bitstream/handle/10438/10009/TD%20299%20-%20C-Micro%2014%20%20Klenio%20Barbosa%20e%20EduardoFiuza.pdf?sequence=1. Accessed 3 Dec 2013, pp. 8–9.

Bigart, A., Fales, L.J., & Tenenbaum, J.S. (2013). Managing association joint purchasing programs without violating the anti-trust laws: Lessons from a DOJ business review letter. http://www.venable.com/managing-association-joint-purchasing-programs-without-violating-the-antitrust-laws-lessons-from-a-doj-business-review-letter-02-08-2013. Accessed 22 Dec 2013.

Brenton, P., Sheehy, J., & Vanvcauteren, M. (2000). Technical barriers to trade in the European Union: Importance for accession countries. www.ceps.eu/files/book/54.pdf. Accessed 11 Dec 2013.

Burnett, F. (2003). Reducing costs through regional pooled procurement. http://apps.who.int/medicinedocs/en/d/Js4940e/4.html. Accessed 12 Jan 2014.

Central Vigilance Commission (2012). Transparency in works/purchase/consultancy contracts awarded on nomination basis—Reg. http://cvc.nic.in/181212_12122012.pdf. Accessed 24 Aug 2013.

Competition Commission of India (2012a). Cartels. http://www.cci.gov.in/images/media/Advocacy/Cartels2012.pdf. Accessed 24 Sept 2013.

Competition Commission of India (2012b). Abuse of dominance. http://www.cci.gov.in/images/media/Advocacy/AOD2012.pdf. Accessed 24 Sept 2013.

Department of Justice (2013). STARS Alliance LLC second business review request. http://www.justice.gov/atr/public/busreview/290492.htm. Accessed 4 Jan 2014.

Ethanol Bid Process under CCI Scanner (3 June 2013). *Financial Express.*

European Commission (2004a). Directive 2004/18/EC. Brussels. Belgium: Author.

European Commission (2004b). Directive 2004/17/CE. Brussels. Belgium: Author.

European Commission (2005). Treaty on the Functioning of the European Union. http://eur-lex.europa.eu/legal-content/EN/TXT/PDF/?uri=CELEX:12012E/TXT&from=EN.

European Commission (2008). Joint Procurement-Fact Sheet. http://ec.europa.eu/environment/gpp/pdf/toolkit/module1_factsheet_joint_procurement.pdf. Accessed 5 Jan 2014, pp. 4–5.

European Commission (2011). Guidelines on the applicability of Article 101 of the Treaty on the Functioning of the European Union to Horizontal Co-operation Agreements. http://eur-lex.europa.eu/LexUriServ/LexUriServ.do?uri=OJ:C:2011:011:0001:0072:EN:PDF. Accessed 23 Nov 2013.

Fales, L. J., & Bigart, A. E. (2013). United States: Ten practical tips for joint purchasing without violating the antitrust laws. http://www.venable.com/ten-practical-counseling-tips-for-joint-purchasing-without-violating-the-antitrust-laws-01-09-2013/. Accessed 22 Nov 2013.

Fiandeiro, F., Choudhary, K., & Anderson, P. (2011). The Assessment of Joint Purchasing: Can Too Much "Buying Power" Ever Be A Problem. http://reference.sabinet.co.za/webx/access/electronic_journals/jefs/jefs_v4_si1_a2.pdf. Accessed 11 Nov 2013.

Florida Municipal Power Agency (2013). Fact Sheet. http://www.fmpa.com/index.php/about-us/fact-sheet. Accessed 16 Nov 2013.

FTCDOJ-Federal Trade Commission & Department of Justice (2000). Antitrust guidelines for collaborations amongst competitors. http://www.ftc.gov/os/2000/04/ftcdojguidelines.pdf. Accessed 25 Sept 2013.

Government of India (2005). General Financial Rules. http://finmin.nic.in/the_ministry/dept_expenditure/gfrs/GFR2005.pdf. Accessed 12 Jan 2014.

Government of India (2006). Manual of policies and procedures for purchase of goods. http://finmin.nic.in/the_ministry/dept_expenditure/acts_codes/MPProc4ProGod.pdf. Accessed 2 Jan 2014. 1.1.3(iii), p. 4.

Government of India (2012). PIB Press Release, November 22 2012. http://www.pib.nic.in/newsite/erelease.aspx?relid=89270. Accessed 11 Dec 2013.

India Glycols Ltd. vs. Indian Oil Corporation & Others, Competition Commission of India Case No. 14/2012, Orders dated July 26, 2012. http://www.cci.gov.in/May2011/OrderOfCommission/142012.pdf. Accessed 24 Dec 2013.

India Glycols Ltd. vs. Competition Commission of India & Ors., Competition Appellate Tribunal, IA 45/2013 in Appeal No. 25/2013, Orders dated November 12, 2013. http://compat.nic.in/upload/PDFs/novordersApp2013/12_11_13.pdf. Accessed 25 Jan 2014.

JAGLCS-The Judge Advocate General's Legal Center and School (2012). 165th Contract Attorneys Handbook. www.jacnet.army.mil. Accessed 15 Aug 2013. Chapter XI.

Koponen, J. (2011). Joint Purchasing Agreements-The EC's 2011 Horizontal Co-operation Guidelines. https://www.coleurope.eu/content/gclc/documents/J.%20Koponen%20-%20Joint%20purchasing%20agreements%20(2).pdf. Accessed 11 Nov 2013.

LCSG (2013). About LCSG. http://www.lcsg.org/site/about.htm. Accessed 3 Dec 2013.

Levenstein, M., & Suslow, V. Y. (2004). Contemporary International Cartels and Developing Countries: Economic Effects and Implications for Competition Policy. *Antitrust Law Journal, 71*(3), 801–852.

Lok Sabha Secretariat (2012). Chapter II-marketing organisation structure: Report of the Standing Committee on Petroleum & Chemicals. http://164.100.24.208/ls/committeeR/Petro&Chem/23/2-4.html. Accessed 25 Nov 2013. 4.5.

Ministry of Corporate Affairs (2011). Draft National Competition Policy 2011. http://www.mca.gov.in/Ministry/pdf/Draft_National_Competition_Policy.pdf. Accessed Jan 15, 2014.

Ministry of Home Affairs (2014). Police modernisation division-qualitative requirements. http://mha.nic.in/uniquepage.asp?Id_Pk=240. Accessed 21 Jan 2014.

OECD (2012). Policy Roundtables: Improving International Co-operation in Cartel Investigations. www.oecd.org/daf/competition/ImprovingInternationalCooperationInCartelInvestigations2012.pdf. Accessed 23 Sept 2013.

Office of Fair Trade (2010). P & H/MAKRO Joint Purchasing Agreement. http://www.oft.gov.uk/shared_oft/SFOs/SFO_on_Joint_Purchasing.pdf. Accessed 19 Sept 2013.

"Panel Moots Joint Venture of PSUs for Smooth Crude Oil Imports." (8 May 2013). Hindu Business Line.

Pappalardo, K., & Suzor, N. (2011). Standardisation and Patent Ambush: Potential liability under Australian competition law. *Competition & Consumer Law Journal, 18*, 267.

People's Republic of China (2002). The Government Procurement Law of the People's Republic of China: Order of the President No. 68. http://english.gov.cn/laws/2005-10/08/content_75023.htm. Accessed 26 Aug 2013. (Article 7).

Petroleum Importation Coordinator (2014). Functions of PICL. www.picltz.com. Accessed 22 Jan 2014.

Royal Energy Ltd. vs. Indian Oil Corporation & Others, Competition Commission of India MRTP Case No. 1/28(C-97/2009/DGIR), Orders dated May 09, 2012. http://www.cci.gov.in/May2011/OrderOfCommission/MRTP1-28main.pdf. Accessed 24 Dec 2013.

Sanchez-Graellis, A. (2013). *Email to Sandeep Verma dated October 11, 2013.* Copy available with author, citing: (i) FENIN vs. Commission of the European Committees & Ors. CJEU Grand Chamber Judgment dated July 11, 2006. http://curia.europa.eu/juris/document/document.jsf?text=&docid=56460&pageIndex=0&doclang=En-US&mode=lst&dir=&occ=first&part=1&cid=24590. Accessed 2 Nov 2013; and (ii) SELEX Sistemi Integrati SpA vs. Commission of the European Communities & Eurocontrol, CJEU Second Chamber Judgment dated March 26, 2009. http://curia.europa.eu/juris/document/document.jsf?text=&docid=73630&pageIndex=0&doclang=En-US&mode=lst&dir=&occ=first&part=1&cid=24610. Accessed 2 Nov 2013.

SIGMA (2011). Central Purchasing Bodies. http://www.oecd.org/site/sigma/publicationsdocuments/48630136.pdf. Accessed 11 Dec 2014.

STARS (2014). STARS Alliance LLC. http://www.starsalliance.com/about_us.asp. Accessed 3 Jan 2014.

UNCTAD (2012). Written Contribution by China for Roundtable on Competition Policy and Public Procurement. http://unctad.org/meetings/en/Contribution/ciclp2012_RT_PP_China_en.pdf. Accessed 11 Nov 2013.

Verma, S. (2013). Too Big for the Recycle Bin: A Procurement Insight into the Latest USTR Report. http://papers.ssrn.com/sol3/papers.cfm?abstract_id=2251199. Accessed 24 Nov 2013.

Wikipedia (2013). State Cartel Theory. http://en.wikipedia.org/wiki/State_cartel_theory. Accessed 6 Nov 2013.

Yahoo (2012). State Bank of India Led State-run Bank's Consortium to Install 40,000 ATMs by March 14. http://in.finance.yahoo.com/news/state-bank-india-led-state-120603813.html. Accessed 13 Dec 2013.

Sandeep Verma L.L.M. in Government Procurement Law, is a senior civil servant in India and a member of the Indian Administrative Service. His professional and research interests include government contracts, procurement integrity and defence acquisition. In 2009, he established www.BuyLawsIndia.com as a free-to-use resource dedicated to the advancement of public procurement research in India

Regulating the Pre-procurement Phase: Context and Perspectives

Willem A. Janssen

Introduction

This contribution considers the legal context and perspectives of regulating the pre-procurement phase in relation to public service delivery.[1] The pre-procurement phase encompasses the democratic decision-making phase, in which a public authority decides to favor either internal or external performance of a public service (Manunza 2010, p. 111). At this point in time, these authorities can choose freely between different modes of service performance. This discretion allows them to either internalize public service delivery by carrying it out themselves, possibly in collaboration with other public authorities, or to externalize the delivery of a public service (or to use the common EU terminology; service of general interest (SGI)) by approaching a third party. In the Netherlands, recent developments have revived the discussion surrounding the extent of this freedom. Internal performance of public services has become increasingly popular. This can, amongst other reasons, be explained by the Dutch government's policy combined with a diminished belief in competition. However, and perhaps more importantly, it is currently permitted by the possibilities created in European public procurement law and the jurisprudence from the Court of Justice of the European Union (ECJ; the Court). The law, by facilitating this freedom, appears to leave open undesired possibilities of inefficient and ineffective public service delivery.

[1] This contribution is part of an ongoing PhD research and concerns a revised and updated version of Janssen, W.A. (2014). "Public Procurement Law and In-house Delivery of Public Services: Improving a Paradox". In A. McCann, A. E. van Rooij, A. Hallo de Wolf & A. R. Neerhof (Eds.), When Private Actors Contribute to Public Interests: A Law and Governance Perspective (Vol. 1, pp. 7–26). The Hague, the Netherlands: Eleven Publishing. For comments please contact: w.a.janssen@uu.nl.

W. A. Janssen (✉)
Public Procurement Research Center and Utrecht Center for Regulation and Enforcement in Europe, University of Utrecht, Utrecht, Netherlands
e-mail: w.a.janssen@uu.nl

K. V. Thai (ed.), *International Public Procurement,* Public Administration, Governance and Globalization 14, DOI 10.1007/978-3-319-13434-5_11

This contribution takes a twofold approach. The first part discusses the context of the freedom to decide upon public service delivery within European Union (EU) public procurement law. The role of competition law, state aid law and free movement law are not assessed, but can also be relevant. The newly adopted public procurement directives further emphasize this freedom, justifying a focus on such field of law. In light of this discretionary power, it describes four Dutch sectors in which, despite the initial introduction of competition by ways of public procurement procedures, the performance of an SGI is internalized by a public authority, or is excluded by the legislature from competition. First, waste collection and supportive services such as IT illustrate the state's discretionary power in relation to SGI performance and the consistent application of these exemptions by Dutch courts. Second, public transport and social support suggest a situation in which the legislature (partially) reversed its obligatory tendering policy.

The second part of this contribution concludes by discussing two perspectives that can improve decision making in relation to public service delivery. For this purpose, the Dutch Public Procurement Act 2012 ("Wet van 1 november 2012, houdende nieuwe regels omtrent aanbestedingen, St. 2012, 542," 2012; PPA, 2012) and the US Federal Activities Inventory Reform Act of 1998 (US FAIR Act) are briefly discussed to aid shaping the legal contours of the pre-procurement phase. The introduction of a legal framework, which governs this pre-procurement decision-making phase, should identify internal and external service delivery modalities as equal alternatives with their own advantages and disadvantages.

Context: The Freedom to Provide and Define SGIs

It is important to initially discuss the freedom that European member states have to define SGIs. In recent years, the academic debate in Europe has focused on what SGIs are, and to what kind of services the internal market rules should apply. Despite this extensive debate, the member states have thus far kept their discretionary power in defining their public interests and SGIs. This freedom also allows member states to decide how these interests should be safeguarded and organized, and if a service is involved by whom it should be performed (Wetenschappelijke Raad voor het Regeringsbeleid 2000). In this respect, the Protocol (nr. 2) on Services of General Interest, accompanying the Lisbon Treaty, further complements this statement by recognizing:

> "[…] the essential role and the wide discretion of national, regional and local authorities in providing, commissioning and organising services of general economic interest as closely as possible to the needs of the users; the diversity between various services of general economic interest and the differences in the needs and preferences of users that may result from different geographical, social or cultural situations; [..]"

Despite this distant role of the EU, the European Commission (Commission) attempted to further clarify the various forms of SGIs in 2011 (European Commission 2011). The Commission considers SGIs to be "services that public authorities of the Member States classify as being of general interest and are therefore subject to specific public service obligations." These services can be divided into two groups; non-economic and economic activities. Services of general economic interest (SGEI) are seen as economic activities that deliver outcomes that benefit the overall public good that would not, or not sufficiently enough, be supplied by the market without public intervention. Such economic activities are subject to specific European legislation and are therefore covered by the internal market rules (i.e., Lisbon Treaty, free movement, state aid, competition, and public procurement rules.). Non-economic services of general interest (NESGI) are not bound to these sets of rules. Additionally, social services of general interest (SSGI) can also be either economic or noneconomic. This category includes "social security schemes covering the main risks of life, such as those linked to health, ageing and disability, and a range of other essential social services provided directly to the person, such as occupational training, rehabilitation and language training for immigrants."

As a consequence of these discretionary powers, member states have the power to exempt services from the internal market rules by labeling them as a noneconomic SGI ("Court of Justice of the European Union 2008, ECLI:EU:T:2008:29"). However, this is restricted by the manifest error test of the commission. In the Netherlands, it is left to the democratic processes to decide what kind of public interests should be safeguarded, and how it intends to promote these interests (WRR 2000). In addition, this process decides upon who should perform a certain service derived from the public interest. These questions are part of an older and broader debate on the extent of the state's responsibilities, and their relation with the market. However, it is clear that the influence of EU law is limited to situations in which the market is approached for the provision of SGIs.

The Performance of SGIs: Internalize or Externalize?

Dutch public authorities have various ways of performing SGIs. EU public procurement law adheres to this discretionary power by providing the legal basis for these alternative performance options. Over the past decade, many of these exemptions to public procurement law have been developed by the ECJ. Firstly, a public authority can decide to perform a service by using its own resources, which is completely "internal." This means, for instance, that it uses one of its own divisions to collect waste. Secondly, a public authority can entrust the performance of a service to an entity over which it exercises control similar to its own departments, and that entity carries out the essential part of its activities for the controlling public authority or authorities (also referred to as quasi in-house performance). In the Netherlands, this can be done on the basis of either private law (e.g., a Dutch *B.V.*, *Cooperatie* or *Stichting*) or public law (e.g., a Dutch *Openbaar Lichaam*, provided by the Dutch Inter-municipal Statutory Regulations Act) ("Court of Justice of the European Union" (1999, p. ECLI:EU:C:1999:562). Thirdly, a public authority can arrange the provision of a SGI by cooperating with other public authorities entirely within the public domain. Such performance is exempted from public procurement law, which is based on the criteria derived from the Commission/Germany jurisprudence ("Court of Justice of the European Union" 2009, ECLI:EU:C:2009:357). Fourthly, a public authority can choose to grant another public authority an exclusive right, after which that entity decides upon questions surrounding performance. Such a right can be, for instance, granted through a ministerial regulation, a local bylaw regulation, or is included in the statutory documents of a separate entity. Fifthly, public authorities can grant a concession for the performance of a service, according to *Directive 2014/23/EU*. Lastly, a public authority decides to completely externalize a service to a third party. To achieve the best quality-lowest price ratio, such externalization is often achieved through a transparent and competitive procedure.

Consequently, public authorities have multiple alternatives to internalize or externalize the provision of SGIs. This variety of legal alternatives is not problematic as such, because member states and their public authorities should be able to perform a service themselves in certain policy fields. On the one hand certain functions, such as the administration of justice or democratic decision making, may not be externalized, whilst on the other hand, building maintenance and food services can. More troublesome is to identify the status of services, which are not as "black and white" as the previous examples. The grey area of this categorization is where decisions on public service delivery cause difficulties. In relation to these services, balanced decision making is even more important to be able to achieve the best outcome for society.

New Public Procurement Directives

On 28 March 2014, the modernized EU public procurement directives, namely Directive 2014/23/EU, 2014/24/EU, and Directive 2014/25/EU, were published. The modernization of these directives was part of a grand-scale operation to restructure and reform the EU internal market, which is based on thoughts that aim to open up Europe, by removing internal barriers and enforcing cross-border competition. For the purpose of this contribution, it is essential to describe the recent European developments on this matter, because internal performance alternatives as exemptions to public procurement law are also under scrutiny.

These reforms were initiated by Monti in his report "A New Strategy for the Single Market" (Monti report), which strived to initiate a re-claiming process of the internal market. The Monti report identified the internal market's achievements, but ultimately noted its future challenges, and subsequently proposed possible actions in numerous areas of the EU, such as the free movement principles, public procurement, SSGIs, regional and industrial policy, and coordination of taxation policies. The report identified that these areas are the "building blocks for reconciliation between the single market and the social and citizens" dimension in the treaty logic of a highly competitive social market economy" (Monti 2010, p. 68). The vision brought forward by Monti, in relation to public procurement, clearly shows its importance; "EU public procurement law plays a key role in the creation and maintenance of the single market" (Monti 2010, p. 7).

After a long legislative process, the new directives have, therefore, been adopted by the European Parliament and Council. On the one hand, the public procurement directives intend to increase the efficiency of public spending to ensure the best possible procurement outcome in terms of value for money. This modernization aims to simplify rules and to provide further flexibility in applying these rules. On the other hand, it enables public authorities to put public procurement to better use and to thus achieve societal goals, such as the protection of the environment, stimulation of innovation, and the betterment of social inclusion (Janssen 2012).

The new "Classic" directive on public procurement includes new rules in relation to in-house procurement and public–public collaboration. These rules predominantly codify the existing exemptions based on case law of the ECJ. The codification itself exemplifies the importance of these exemptions to public procurement law by emphasizing the freedom public authorities have to internalize public service delivery (Bleeker and Manunza 2014). Article 12 of the recently adopted Classic directive codifies the jurisprudence line of Teckal and Commission/Hamburg, but leaves many questions unanswered. It does elucidate the percentage of commercial activities which a separate Teckal-like entity or noninstitutional collaboration is allowed to perform. This has been set at 20 %. Additionally, contracts awarded to a controlling "mother" entity or a controlled "sister" entity are included in this doctrine. The new directive also confirms that collaboration between public authorities does not necessarily have to involve services derived from the public interest, and as a result supportive services can be included. The most predominant change to the scope of this exemption is the acceptance of private capital, which the court had firmly rejected on earlier occasions ("Court of Justice of the European Union 2005, ECLI:EU:C:2005:5"). Finally, the commission's initiative to abolish the exclusive right exemption was taken out by the council, leaving a commonly used exemption in place.

Two conclusions can be drawn from these changes. First, no further guidance is provided on what can be identified as SGIs or their relation with public procurement law. Therefore, a standard European approach to this subject will remain absent in the future. Second, the changes made to the scope of this article, are perhaps the most important conclusion. Its scope has substantially widened, meaning that applying these exemptions to public procurement law will become easier in the future.

Explaining Internalization of SGI Delivery

As previously stated, internal performance of services, and especially public–public collaboration, has gained importance in recent times (European Commission 2011a). In the Netherlands, an increase of collaborations between (local) public authorities has occurred, which consists of 698 collaborations based on public law, and 1022 collaborations based on private law. Such collaboration within the public domain, can first of all be explained by a leading vision document of the former Dutch government, which is still being implemented. It demonstrates the thoughts of former Dutch minister, Piet Hein Donner, who advocated a "compact" government. The role of "compact" refers to a strong and small government. It focuses on more efficiency and lower administrative burdens by intensifying collaboration amongst public authorities, which has its effect especially on a decentralized level (Ministry of the Interior and Kingdom Relations 2011, p. 5). This desire for more collaboration can be explained by the need to spend public funds efficiently. More collaboration amongst public authorities for efficiency purposes becomes even more relevant in times of financial crisis. Additionally, the Lisbon Treaty has emphasized the role of regional and local self-governance, which enforces this development (Manunza 2010, p. 76).

Second, internalization of SGI delivery as a whole is influenced by the current views on the public and private divide. It is fair to say that member states have become more critical in relation to the role of the market as a performer of SGIs. The advantages of introducing competition into markets are not as commonly accepted, and thus applied throughout Europe, as they were in the 1990s. In those times, liberalization and privatization were introduced in various areas, and public procurement procedures were often introduced if public authorities decided to externalize services. Monti described this situation as "market fatigue," which represents a loss in confidence in the market and has, consequently, led to lower acceptance of the market and its actors involved. This is, to some extent, caused by the fact that the limitations of the market, and the services it can provide, have become more visible. In the Dutch public debate, the market is often seen as unfair and a cause of inequality. In this regard, Monti stated that those who propose, instead of oppose, are forced to defend their views on the liberalization of markets and the introduction of more competition. Such views enhance the idea that government performance is vital in order to safeguard public interests and can obstruct clear views on the advantages and disadvantages of performance alternatives (Monti 2010, p. 12).

Consequences: Performance Internalization in Four Dutch Markets

The internalization of SGI performance, notably described in the above paragraphs, and the loss of confidence in market performance, which often accompanies it, can be exemplified by assessing the waste collection, supportive services, public transport, and social support market. Public procurement law's exemptions play a significant role in these markets, in which despite the initial introduction of competition by ways of public procurement procedures, the performance of an SGI is internalized by a public authority, or is excluded by the legislature from competition. Waste collection and supportive services, such as IT, exemplify the state's discretionary power in relation to SGI performance, and the consistent application of these exemptions by Dutch courts. The cases of the public transport and social support consider situations in which the legislature (partially) reversed its obligatory tendering policy, after which internal performance can gain importance again. This situation can also be seen as an example of Monti's "market fatigue."

The Waste Sector: Courts Uphold Internal Performance Exemptions

In the Netherlands, municipalities have been granted the responsibility to perform the collection of household waste under Article 10.21 Section 1 Dutch Environmental Protection Act. In order to fulfill this duty, municipalities have, as previously described, various performance alternatives. In the past decade, the Dutch government has attempted to introduce, or further expand, competition in the waste management sector. It aimed to fully liberalize this market by 2050. The introduction of more competition is desired in order to maximize the positive effects for the environment at the lowest cost (VROM-rapport 2003, p. 5). Despite the fact that a greater part of the market is now in the hands of third parties, it can be argued that in recent years public authorities have limited their contribution to this liberalization. The collection of waste is historically performed by using the recourses of public authorities, which in 2007 accounted for 25 % of all cases. It is performed in alternative ways in 75 % of the Dutch municipalities. From this part, 35 % of these municipalities leave performance up to market parties (Van Ommeren and Vermont 2007, p. 2). The remainder is performed through a collaboration of public authorities. More recent studies discuss a similar situation in other European member states (Hulst and Van Montfort 2007; Dijkgraaf and Radius 2008) Hence, internal performance is substantially present in the waste collection market, which is intended to be entirely liberalized.

Market parties in this sector have not hesitated to file court proceedings against these internal performance alternatives by claiming that these contracts should have been tendered under European public procurement law. Three cases before Dutch courts illustrate such actions. In the first case of AVR/Westland, the High Court confirmed the Court of Appeal's ruling by granting the municipality of The Hague permission to join the public collaboration of local public authorities. This entity, called "HVC," was established to collect and dispose of household waste ("Court of Appeal's-Gravenshage 2009, ECLI:NL:GHSGRL2009:BK6928"). In the years before this, appellant AVR had been contracted for the waste disposal via a public procurement procedure. After the expiry of the contract, the government was allowed to internalize performance, based on the exclusive right exception. The second case involved a situation whereby the public authority of Friesland contracted Afvalsturing Friesland N.V. for their waste collection and disposal services. This local government was exempted from using a public procurement procedure for a different reason as it could rightfully rely on the in-house exception ("Court of Appeal Arnhem-Leeuwarden 2013, ECLI:NL:GHARL:2013:6675"). This in-house exception also led to proceedings before the Court of s-Hertogenbosch, which rejected the claims of appellant Shanks, relying on the fact that this exception was no longer right due to a substantial change in supervision of Attero-Zuid. Shanks was unable to sufficiently prove this, which resulted in the fact that this collaboration between municipalities could continue ("District Court's-Hertogenbosch" 2012, ECLI:NL:RBSHE:2012:BY1 110).

Despite intended liberalization, many municipalities chose to perform the collection of waste entirely within the public domain. Third parties tried, but were unsuccessful in their attempt, to break open these internal performance structures, because the Dutch courts have been consistent in assessing these legal exemptions to public procurement law. It also shows that due to the legal alternatives similar services are performed in different ways.

Supportive Services: Internal Performance Outside the Public Interest

Services that support the provision of SGIs, such as IT, can also be performed entirely within the public domain ("District Court Utrecht." 2009, ECLI:NL:RBUTR:2009:BG9524). Briefly noting them is thus justified in this context. In addition to IT, transport, graphic design, and educational services that support the state's functioning, are also increasingly internalized and are also part of the public debate (De Lange 2013, p. 3). From a public procurement law standpoint, the legality of such legal constructions was confirmed by the Court of Utrecht in relation to IT. In this case, Amsterdam, Rotterdam, The Hague, and Utrecht were able to rely on the quasi in-house exemption. This allowed them to continue their collaboration in the form of "Wigo4it," because it met the criteria of being "closely connected" and had proper "supervision." For that reason, the application of public procurement law exemptions must be seen in a broader sense. Services, in and outside, the public interest can be exempted from public procurement obligations, which is confirmed by the new public procurement directives.

Public Transport: Inconsistent Obligatory Tendering

The case of public transport exemplifies a partial drawback of competition. Public transport is often regulated through concessions as opposed to public contracts. These concessions grant a party the right to perform a mode of public transport for a specific route. Service concessions fall under the scope of the newly adopted Directive 2014/24/EU on concessions. Such competition allows third parties, as a rule of thumb, to compete for public transport concessions in the Netherlands.

The Dutch regulatory framework of this sector consists of the Passenger Transport Act 2000 (PTA), which was introduced to stimulate the use of public transport and to efficiently utilize public funds. In addition, the European PSO-regulation is in place and provides guidance on how decentralized governments ensure the quantity, quality, and safety of public transport for a reasonable price. The Dutch Public Transport Decree 2000 further explicates the obligations of such a competitive procedure. Under the PSO-regulation, local governments are still allowed to apply the in-house exemption to national public procurement rules. However, whilst reforming the PTA in 2010, the legislature decided that in the Netherlands local public authorities will be not be able to apply this exemption. Hence, public transport concessions had to be distributed by using a transparent and objective competitive procedure, and internalization was excluded as a performance alternative. Despite these reforms, another amendment of the PTA was passed by Dutch parliament in October 2012. This amendment exempted four major cities in the Netherlands (Amsterdam, The Hague, Utrecht, and Rotterdam) from the obligation to follow a competitive procedure whilst distributing public transport concessions. The discussion in the Dutch Senate clarified that it was intended to provide freedom of choice and local autonomy. This amendment allows these cities to apply the in-house exception, which leads to the fact that state owned companies, such as HTM in the Hague, RET in Rotterdam, GVB in Amsterdam, and GVU in Utrecht, can often continue to operate their services without being influenced by competition. In this regard, it is interesting to consider that the utilization of these concessions is often not economically viable and market parties are, therefore, compensated by the government. Despite this exemption, the milestone ruling of Altmark, in which the court ruled that subsidies granted to an undertaking providing public transport can be identified as state aid if the price is not the result of a competitive procedure or if the Altmark criteria are fulfilled, is still applicable ("Court of Justice of the European Union 2003, ECLI:EU:C:2003:415). An extensive analysis of this situation goes beyond the scope of this contribution, but it does show that state aid rules must nonetheless be complied with. To conclude, this change of legislation in the Netherlands has led to inconsistent obligatory tendering, to say the least, and exemplifies a call from the major cities to keep a broad discretionary power whilst deciding upon public service provision.

Social Support: Obligatory Tendering Pulled Back Entirely

In the healthcare market, a similar situation occurred regarding the performance of the Social Support Act 2006. This act incorporates a compensation duty, which means that local authorities have to compensate citizens for the provision of equipment or services in various areas related to the consequences of their impairments. Examples of possible compensation are, "assistance with running a household" and "means of transportation." Article 10 of the act obligated local governments to externalize the performance of these services via public procurement procedures. It is important to note that such a duty to tender is derived from EU public procurement law which identifies two types of services under the current directives: IIA and IIB services. For IIA services, a strict public procurement regime applies, and for the second, no specific duty to use public procurement procedures exists. The Dutch government stated that assistance with running a household was to be predominantly classified as "cleaning services," which led to a classification under IIA-services. Others claimed the contrary, that it should have been classified as an IIB-service. In 2010, the Dutch parliament adopted three proposals to change the Social Support Act 2006. The most important amendment abolished the duty for municipalities to use public procurement procedures. As a consequence, assistance with running a household is now classified as an IIB-service. The legality of this amendment can be questioned in light of European law. In this regard, the Commission responded to questions posed by the Dutch government and stated that most of these services should be performed by market parties after the use of public procurement procedures.

In the overall assessment of this sector, it is of importance to consider whether the healthcare market in general, and this sector in specific, can benefit from competition. The need to safeguard the basic principles of this market, namely quality, accessibility, and affordability, ensures a continuous debate in relation to this topic. The vehement discussions in the European Council and Parliament involving the reforms of the public procurement directives exemplify this. It is clear that the healthcare market is a particular market, whereby the clash of safeguarding public interests and competition is very clear (Canoy 2009). However, such a debate is less relevant for contractible cleaning services, which are able to benefit from competition.

Towards regulating the pre-procurement phase

As stated before, the public debate in relation to competition and the Dutch government's compact government policy influences the decision to externalize or internalize the performance of SGIs. Despite the possible advantages of external performance, public authorities and the legislature have full discretionary power to decide upon such performance questions and can go against initial or intended liberalization. The markets previously described have shown that the relation between public procurement law and public service provision is affected, making a new approach to the public procurement framework worth considering.

In response to these developments, it has been suggested to introduce a transparent and objective legal framework that governs this "internal vs. external" decision-making phase (Manunza 2010, p. 115). The introduction of such a pre-procurement test can result in an improved provision of public services, as it answers the question of *who is most suitable to perform a service*; the market or the state (Manunza and Berends 2011). Such an approach relies on the economic analyses of markets to determine who should perform a service. It has been suggested to take an approach in which "social welfare" is the key criterion to analyze whether the market or the government should perform an SGI (Manunza 2010, p. 117). Additionally, it is said that the legal dimension of public procurement law is often not aligned with the economic restrictive approach "towards public make-or-buy decisions" (Sánchez Graells 2011, p. 232).

Key Factors: Objective Criteria and Transparency

On a conceptual level, the framework regulating the pre-procurement phase should be characterized by principles of objectivity and transparency. First, this means that the prior comparison between state and market performance of a service, and the subsequent decision on public service delivery, should both be based on criteria which are objectively identified beforehand. Instead of solely focusing on a price comparison, the comparison should be based on quality. The quality comparison can still take into account the cost of performance, but should in largely be focused on what is best for society as a whole. This is also in line with the newly adopted public procurement directives which favor competition based on quality. The exact determination of these criteria goes beyond the scope of this contribution and will require further research. Second, the decision making of public authorities in the pre-procurement phase will require transparency. The advantage of transparency lies in the fact that market parties can foresee public procurement policy and adjust their market behavior accordingly (Manunza 2010, p. 117). Vice versa, the decision-making phase of a public authority is able to improve due to this transparency, ensuring that the goal of best-value for money is achieved. However, the extent of this transparency, when it would be required and how this would be embedded in a legal framework also requires more research.

The following aims to contribute to this research endeavor by discussing two distinct types of legal regulations, which can contribute to constructing a more transparent and objective framework for public procurement whilst deciding upon public service delivery. First, the Dutch PPA 2012 is considered, in which a move toward regulating the pre-procurement phase is present. Second, the US FAIR Act is discussed which regulates this phase extensively on a federal level in the USA.

Motivating Public Procurement Choices

The following considers the importance of the Dutch PPA 2012, which has introduced a further emphasis on motivating procurement choices for contracting authorities. This can be necessary in the call for tenders, the relevant documents or the proposed contract. However, two choices made before the start of a procedure can possibly impact the need to motivate the decision to internalize or externalize performance. According to article 1.4 PPA 2012, contracting authorities must base the choice for the type of procedure, and the choice for tenderers, or candidates in this procedure, on objective criteria. Such a motivation must be provided by the contracting authority upon the request of undertakings. This duty to motivate has the potential to improve the choice between internal or external performance, because it could force contracting authorities to examine which performance alternative is most suitable for the performance of their public tasks. In addition, article 1.4 PPA 2012 proposes to improve the decision-making process of contracting authorities by focusing on the "societal value" of tenders. Societal value is described as the proper allocation and possible saving of public funds in an economic sense. It is unclear what the exact meaning of this term is. The Dutch term "maatschappelijk" indicates a "social" notion in the Dutch language. However, the achievement of societal goals, such as social inclusion and sustainability, are seemingly not necessarily intended by this article. If a market party would decide to contest the internal performance of a service before a Dutch court in the future, the assessment of the court may be different than the cases previously described in the waste sector. Hence, due to this duty to motivate, not only legal considerations, but also economic consideration can potentially play a role in the court's assessment. The first ruling on this matter by a Dutch district court stated that article 1.4 PPA 2012 was to be interpreted as requiring the achievement of best-value for money, but did not delve further on the potential scope of this article ("District Court Noord-Nederland 2013, ECLI:NL:RBNNE:2013: 7100"). Nonetheless, a broader interpretation, based on the Explanatory Memorandum, could greatly improve the decision-making process of public authorities. Whether or not higher courts agree with this interpretation, and if judges are sufficiently equipped to scrutinize public procurement policy, is to be found out in the future.

Additionally, the introduction of the Commissie van Aanbestedingsexperts ("Committee of Public Procurement Experts") can play a role in the future in the emergence of interpretations relating to article 1.4 PPA 2012. Even though their advice is not binding, the committee aims to provide an alternative to costly litigation by providing advice and mediation for disputes between contracting authorities and applicants. Considering that committee consists of lawyers, public purchasers, and economists, their advices could contain a more economic approach instead of a purely legal perspective.

Transparency and Review Procedures

In addition to motivating public procurement choices, regulation from the USA can prove to be an inspiring example (Manunza 2010, pp. 116-118). In the USA, a different approach is taken by which the decision to externalize or internalize public service delivery on a federal level is extensively regulated by the US FAIR Act. It is best described as a *may the best man win* approach. It introduces the obligation to publish a list of all federal governmental activities, making the intentions of these agencies transparent. This list divides services into "inherently governmental functions" or "commercial services." Inherently governmental functions are those functions that are so intimately related to the public interest that they mandate performance by government employees. As a rule, these functions are performed by government officials and the delivery of commercial services is externalized.

The inherently governmental functions, according to the US FAIR Act, fall into two categories. The first being the act of governing, i.e., the discretionary exercise of government authority; and the second being monetary transactions and entitlements. In general, agencies have considerable discretion in determining whether particular functions are inherently governmental. Factors that should at least play a role in this analysis are listed as well. These factors contribute to the decision of governmental agencies to claim a function as "inherently governmental." They include, amongst other things; if an activity is already performed on the market, the degree to which official discretion would be limited and if a statutory restriction that defines an activity as inherently governmental is in place. Federal agencies are also required by law, to give "special consideration" to the performance of functions, "closely associated with the performance of inherently governmental functions." However, they are not prohibited from contracting out such functions.

If a service is considered to be of commercial nature, a "streamlined" or "standard" competitive procedure can be followed, according to Section 2 of the Act. In the streamlined competitive procedure, the governmental agency calculates, compares, and certifies costs based on the scope and requirements of the activity, in order to determine whether government agency performance or private sector performance is most efficient and suitable. In the standard competition process, tenderers compete against one another based on objective and transparent criteria such as, a demonstrated understanding of the government's requirements, costs, technical approaches, management capabilities, or personnel qualifications. Interestingly, the government agency itself can also submit a tender, which allows for comparison of public and private performing actors. Section 3 of this act allows for a challenge and review process. These are also in place to give third parties a role in this decision-making process. "Interested parties" are allowed to submit a challenge of an omission of a particular activity, or an inclusion of a particular activity on the published list. The scope of this article is broad as it allows private parties and unions to object to the classification of the list. Such procedures with elements of transparency and judicial review can be of interest when creating a more coherent public procurement approach.

Concluding Remarks

To conclude, Dutch public authorities have various alternatives for the performance of SGIs and supportive services. The European reforms in relation to the internal market will not change the discretionary power that public authorities have for this purpose, nor will it sufficiently clarify the exemptions to European public procurement law in relation to internal performance. If anything, it has mostly expanded the scope of in-house exemptions. The sectors discussed have exemplified the consequences of this freedom, whereby these authorities have to decide upon the organization of public services. It has been shown that this freedom can lead to inconsistent public procurement policy and a growing internalization of public service delivery, justifying a stronger research focus on this matter.

The hesitation of public authorities to externalize services can be seen in strong contrast with the previous period of extensive market performance. Finding the right balance between the two should be the goal of public authorities in order to secure the best performance of a public service. The legality of the performance alternatives from a public procurement law perspective, combined with the freedom to provide services, can lead to outcomes, which are not beneficial for society. To improve the democratic decision making in the pre-procurement phase, elements of the Dutch PPA 2012 and the US FAIR Act have been assessed. Integrating these elements, such as objectivity and enhanced transparency in an integrated framework approach, which includes the fundamental choice between different service delivery alternatives, can result in improved public service delivery. The goal of such a coherent legal framework should be to objectively identify the advantages of various performance modalities and to reach the best performance of a public service.

Acknowledgments The author wishes to thank Prof. Dr. E. R. Manunza, Dr. H. van Harten, and B. Jones BA for their valuable comments on earlier drafts of this contribution.

References

Bleeker, R. G. T., & Manunza, E. R. (2014). De Invloed van het Europees Recht op het Nederlandse Aanbestedingsrecht [The influence of European Law on Dutch public procurement law]. In A. S. Hartkamp, C. H. Sieburgh, L. A. D. Keus, J. S. Kortmann, & M. H. Wissink (Eds.), *De Invloed Van Het Europese Recht op het Nederlandse Privaatrecht* [The influence of European Law on Dutch Private Law] (Vol. 1, pp. 741–810). Deventer: Kluwer.

Canoy, M. (2009). Marktwerking in de Zorg; Ondernemende Zorg of Zorgende Ondernemers? [Competition in the healthcare sector; entrepreneurial care of caring entrepreneurs?] Inaugural Speech 6 February 2009 at the University of Tilburg. Tilburg, The Netherlands.

De Lange, R. (2013/04/13). Bedrijfsleven Boos over Valse Concurrentie Door Bijklussende Overheid [Businessworld angry about false competition of double dipping government], *Het Financieele Dagblad [Dutch Financial Times]*, pp. 5–6.

Dijkgraaf, E., & Radius, R. (2008). *The waste market: Institutional developments in Europe*. Dordrecht: Springer.

European Commission. (2008). Commission interpretative communication on the application of community law on public procurement and concessions to institutionalised PPP (Brussels 2008/C 91/02). Brussels, Belgium: European Commission.

European Commission. (2011). *A quality framework for services of general interest in Europe (Communication from the Commission to the European Parliament, the Council, the European Economic and Social Committee and the Committee of the Regions)*. Brussels: European Commission.

European Commission. (2011a). Commission Staff Working Paper Concerning the Application of EU Public Procurement Law to Relations between Contracting Authorities ("Public-Public Cooperation") (Brussels, 4.10.2011 SEC (2011) 1169 final). Brussels: European Commission.

Hulst, R., & Van Montfort, A. (2007). The Netherlands: Cooperation as the only viable strategy. In R. Hulst & A. Van Montfort (Eds.), *Inter-municipal cooperation in Europe* (Vol. 1, pp. 139–168). Dordrecht: Springer.

Janssen, W. A. (2012). Maatschappelijk Verantwoord Aanbesteden; Van een Instrumentele Naar een Procedurele Benadering van het Aanbestedingsrecht [Societally responsible public procurement; from a procedural to an instrumental approach of public procurement law]. *Tijdschrift Aanbestedingsrecht, 9*(1), 7–17.

Manunza, E. R. (2010). Naar Een Consistente en Doelmatige Regeling van de Markt voor Overheidsopdrachten [Towards Consistent and Efficient Regulation of the Public Procurement Market]. In J. M. Hebly, E. Manunza, & M. Scheltema (Eds.), *Beschouwingen Naar Aanleiding*

Van Het Wetsvoorstel Aanbestedingswet [Reflections on the Proposal for a Public Procurement Act] (Vol. 1, pp. 49–123). The Hague: Preadvies voor de Vereniging van Bouwrecht.

Manunza, E. R., & Berends, W. J. (2011). Social services of general interest and the EU public procurement rules. In U. Neergaard, E. Szyszczak, J. W. van de Gronden, & M. Krajewski (Eds.), *Social services of general interest in the EU, legal issues of services of general interest* (Vol. 1, pp. 347–384). The Hague: T.M.C. Asser Press.

Ministery of the Interior and Kingdom Relations. (2011). *Visiedocument "Bestuur en Bestuurlijke Inrichting: Tegenstellingen met Elkaar Verbinden" [Vision Document "Administration and Administrative Design: Connecting Opposites"]*. The Hague: Ministry of the Interior and Kingdom Relations.

Monti, M. (2010). *"A new strategy for the single market; at the service of Europe's economy and society." (Report to the President of the European Commission José Manuel Barroso)*. Brussels: European Commission.

Sánchez Graells, A. (2011). *Public procurement and the EU competition rules*. Oxford: Hart Publishing.

Van Ommeren, F. J., & Vermont, J. A. R. (2007). Uit- Aan- en Inbesteden in het Publiek- en Privaatrecht? De Uitbesteding van het Recht om Huishoudelijk Afval in te Zamelen. [Internalisation and externalisation in public and private law? The externalisation of the right to collect household waste]. *De Gemeentestem, 7266*(7), 29–37.

VROM-rapport. (2003). Toekomstig Afvalbeleid: Een Eerste Stap naar een Nieuwe Lange Termijnvisie voor het Afval Beleid [Future Waste Policy: A First Step towards a Long-Term Vision for Waste Policy]. The Hague, The Netherlands: Ministery of Infrastructure and Environment.

Wetenschappelijke Raad voor het Regeringsbeleid. (2000). *Het Borgen van Publiek Belang (Rapporten aan de Regering) [Safeguarding the Public Interest (Report to the Dutch Government, nr. 56)]*. The Hague: Sdu Uitgevers.

Willem A. Janssen LLM is a lecturer and PhD researcher in the Public Procurement Research Center and Utrecht Center for Regulation and Enforcement in Europe, University of Utrecht. His research interest is in procurement law and procurement policy.

Construction Procurers' Perceptions of Value for Money

Warren Staples

Introduction

"Value for money" (VFM) is recognized as an important component of the market-oriented thinking underpinning new public management (NPM) (Haque 1999; Diefenbach 2009; Luke et al. 2011) and has pervaded the externalization of public services in many jurisdictions (Alford and O'Flynn 2012). Australia state governments have externalized much of their public works design, construction and maintenance capability (Furneaux et al. 2008). Large-scale public infrastructure projects are politically, socially, and economically significant. For public sector organizations and agencies charged with procuring construction projects and roads projects, justifying "value for money" both externally to taxpayers and communities, and internally to authorizing and/or client departments within government is crucial but inherently challenging. This is particularly so given the multiplicity of objectives sought as part of projects outcomes (Love et al. 2008, 2010; McCabe et al. 2011) and the increasing complexity of projects (Flyvbjerg 2007, 2009).

The importance of the role of middle managers in implementing strategy is addressed in the private sector literature (Floyd and Woolridge 1992; Floyd and Lane 2000), and increasingly being recognized in the public sector, where the alignment of strategy between senior and middle managerial levels in public organizations is associated with better organizational performance (Andrews et al. 2009, 2012). Middle managers with backgrounds in architecture, building, and engineering undertake the associated construction procurement activities. Construction procurement activities undertaken by public agency project managers include tendering, evaluation, selection, and contract award and might also include project planning, and contract management post award. Further, they are responsible for implementing procurement strategy and receive little policy guidance detailing how to implement strategy via procurement (Staples and Dalrymple 2015). These processes

W. Staples (✉)
RMIT University, Melbourne, Australia
e-mail: warren.staples@rmit.edu.au

K. V. Thai (ed.), *International Public Procurement,* Public Administration, Governance and Globalization 14, DOI 10.1007/978-3-319-13434-5_12

are heavily reliant on the professional and technical expertise of those procuring. Bovaird (2006) notes that public sector organizations were increasingly appreciating that market relationships were socially constructed in the procurement process, and not simply a product of market conditions. These project managers are, therefore, central actors in designing procurement processes that construct markets and create public value (Moore 1995). The way in which procurers' perceive "value for money" has implications for the way markets are constructed and value delivered.

Combining this responsibility for the implementation of strategy with their expertise, these project managers become the arbiters of VFM and reflect community, political, and multiple government agency perspectives (treasury, cabinet and client department) of "value for money." How these managers perceive VFM is likely to influence how they procure. This chapter focuses on construction procurement by Australian state governments and provides qualitative insights into how these public managers perceive "value for money" within the context of their procurement work.

In Australia, Federal, State, and Territory government procurement policies' emphasize the pursuit of VFM but contain only a limited description of what VFM means. The South Australian Procurement Board (2011) outline in their strategic plan 2011–2013 the objective of establishing a practical guide for public authorities on what "value for money" in government means, which further highlights the ambiguous nature of "value for money" for those charged with delivering it. In a survey of 47 UK local authorities, "value for money" was perceived as the primary objective of purchasing by 89 % of the leaders of council, 84 % of chief executives, and 77 % of purchasing managers (Murray 2001). "Value for money" is frequently the objective and mantra of those spending public money (Murray 2001); however, there is little in the literature that elucidates what "value for money" means to the public sector beyond efficiency, economy, and effectiveness (Glendinning 1988). The key research questions addressed in this chapter are:

- First, to what extent is VFM an objective for those procuring construction projects? and
- Second, how do construction procurers' perceive VFM?

The chapter begins by highlighting "value for money" as a key plank of the market orientation espoused by NPM and describing the introduction of "value" based externalization procurement policy in Australia and the UK. It then highlights the interest in "value for money" from scholars in construction management and public management. An overview of the research design and the methods used to generate primary data is then provided. The findings and discussion shows the multi-dimensional nature of "value for money" and its inherent complexity on infrastructure projects. "Value for money" is viewed primarily as comprising "economy" and "efficiency" drivers with less emphasis placed upon "effectiveness" drivers. Finally, the chapter concludes by considering the pervasiveness of "value for money" discourse for those responsible construction procurement activities and across public organizations and state jurisdictions with Australia.

Literature Review

NPM related reform and the externalization of public services is an area that has received considerable coverage in the extent literature (Pollitt and Bouckaert 2011; Alford and O'Flynn 2012; Walsh 1995). "Value for money" encapsulates the market orientation of NPM that has been introduced globally and impacted all public service sectors (Diefenbach 2009). Boyne (1998) posited that in the UK its impact was felt most strongly at a local government level when subjected to compulsory competitive tendering (CCT) with a mandate for procuring and contracting on the basis of lowest cost. In both the UK and Victoria, Australia the emphasis on economy ("money") under CCT was replaced with "best value," retaining the competitive element of the market, but emphasizing "value," rather than lowest cost as the guiding principle governing the externalization and delivery of public services (Boyne 1998; Bovaird and Halachmi 2001; Boyne et al. 2002).

While "best value" has not been applied in the same manner within Australian state and federal governments as it was in Victorian local government. Table 1 highlights that the externalization discourse emphasizing "value" has resonated at the federal level of Australian government but also across all state jurisdictions. Further, it shows that there has been clearly articulated recognition that "value for money" does not equal lowest cost when externalizing public services (Department of Finance 2012).

Public procurement policy guidance provided by the UK government and the devolved parliaments of Northern Ireland, Scotland, and Wales has likewise emphasized the "value for money" (HM Treasury 2006; Wales Government 2010; Department of Finance 2012; Scotland Transforming Procurement: Accelerating Delivery 2010; Northern Ireland Public Procurement Policy (Version 10) 2012).

The concept of "value for money" in the public sector has attracted attention from scholars and practitioners interested in several related fields: construction procurement, public–private partnerships (PPPs), public management, and accountability/auditing. There is considerable evidence that value-based procurement approaches, rather than lowest cost, are important to those responsible for construction procurement (Kenley et al. 2000; Wong et al. 2000; Tookey et al. 2001; Kelly et al. 2002; Palaneeswaran et al. 2003; Kelly et al. 2004; Walraven and de Vries 2009).

There is an emerging focus on construction procurement by Australian state governments (Staples and Dalrymple 2011; McCabe et al. 2011; Love et al. 2010, 2008; Furneaux et al. 2008). Love et al. (2008) provide insight into the selection of procurement approaches by public sector clients highlighting the risk-averse nature of Western Australian State Government clients finding that uncertainty avoidance was a major factor in choosing predominantly, a traditional lump sum (TLS) approach. The perceived strength of a lump sum approach was that it provided cost certainty to the client and avoided the risk associated with cost escalation. Love et al. (2008) found that government perceived the capacity of the supply side to deliver nontraditionally as limited, and that cost certainty and the issues associated

Table 1 Value for money in Australian federal, state, and territory governments

Federal, state, or territory governments	Value for money policy guidance
Federal government	Achieving VFM is the core rule of the 2012 Commonwealth Procurement Rules (Department of Finance 2012). Approvers (definition) must be satisfied, after reasonable enquires, that the procurement achieves a VFM outcome. VFM in procurement requires: encouraging competitive and nondiscriminatory processes; using Commonwealth resources in an efficient, effective, economical, and ethical manner that is not inconsistent with the policies of the Commonwealth; decisions-making in an accountable and transparent manner; considering the risks; and conducting a process commensurate with the scale and scope of the procurement
Australian capital territory	Section22a, Procurement principle—VFM (1) A territory entity must pursue VFM in undertaking any procurement activity (2) VFM means the best available procurement outcome (3) In pursuing VFM, the entity must have regard to the following: (a) probity and ethical behavior, (b) management of risk, (c) open and effective competition, (d) optimizing whole of life costs, and (e) anything else prescribed by regulation
Federal, state, or territory governments	VFM policy guidance
New South Wales	"The government's procurement policy provides the framework for agencies to achieve VFM from their procurement while being fair, ethical, and transparent. Public sector expertise resources, facilities and products should be used in preference to engaging the private sector, subject to VFM considerations. Where the private sector is to be engaged, opportunities to gain government business are encouraged through effective competition." (New South Wales 2013)
Northern territory	There are five procurement principles underpinning the NT Governments Procurement Framework, of which the first is best VFM
Queensland	The Queensland State Procurement Policy is about maximizing VFM and reducing costs of procurement, linking agency procurement, and the priorities of government
South Australia	In the public sector, the purchase of goods and services opens us to public scrutiny; therefore, we must obtain value and behave appropriately when spending public money. The aim of the State Procurement Act (2004) is to make certain that government bodies: obtain VFM when they spend public money; treat all participants ethically and fairly; ensure probity, accountability, and transparency in procurement
Tasmania	Buyers must behave ethically and comply with a code of conduct. They must also enhance opportunities for local businesses by ensuring that suppliers that wish to do business with the government are given the opportunity to do so

Table 1 (continued)

Federal, state, or territory governments	Value for money policy guidance
Victoria	"The VGPB is committed to delivering VFM outcomes for Victoria, while also developing procurement capability, minimizing risk and enabling access to procurement opportunities for all businesses." (VGPB 2012)
Western Australia	WA Government Procurement (2013) states: "GP's aim is to ensure services are responsive to customers' needs and to provide VFM outcomes for government through goods, services, and human services procurement."

with probity and accountability were important elements of public sector procurement. The authors further commented that public clients are under increasing pressure to obtain "value for money" from the services and projects they deliver and are considering the procurement methods selected so as to obtain better "value for money." Love et al. (2008, p. 760) noted the sheer volume of criteria used to select priorities for projects and how this demonstrates the complexity of best value as a concept. The authors concluded that a "procurement framework should be able to guide the decision maker rather than provide a prescriptive solution." Staples and Dalrymple (2014) found there was a level of alignment between the strategic plans of Australian state governments and the construction projects pursued—if a project was not in the strategic plan then it would not be funded in the budget cycle. The authors also found that strategic plans have little impact on the way construction procurement is undertaken, and that this interpretative step is frequently the work of project managers who are located in centralized public works and roads agencies. Love et al. (2010) found that there was an inconsistent understanding of project objectives amongst public officers procuring construction projects, and they also reported that the public sector client made a point of stating that cost certainty was achieved with a TLS approach. The authors concluded that repeatedly using a TLS method is not an effective way to obtain "value for money."

The PPP literature attempts to define and assess "value for money" largely in financial measures to decide whether it is a viable procurement approach. The focus is on undertaking cost-benefit analyses to determine whether the PPP procurement route is financially advantageous (Nisar 2007) or promoting it as a delivery method (Grimsey and Lewis 2005). VFM over these longer contractual time periods is complex and riddled with uncertainty (Burger and Hawkesworth 2011). The idea that the procurement approach chosen is a driver of "value for money" is a view consistently held in the construction procurement literature (Walker and Hampson 2003, pp. 43–54), where "value for money" differs according to the project and procurement approach adopted (e.g., alliance projects, see MacDonald et al. 2012, 2013).

The goals of public procurement are frequently multiple and conflicting (Murray et al. 2012; Murray 2009b; Erridge 2007), adding complexity to the commissioning and delivery roles (Bovaird 2006), and requiring value laden judgments by those involved. Murray (2001) found that "value for money" was the primary goal for the

UK local government procurers, while Erridge and McIlroy (2002; cited in Erridge 2007) outlined three sometimes conflicting goals of public procurement (commercial, regulatory, and socioeconomic—see Table 2). Economy, efficiency and effectiveness are the commonly described dimensions of "value for money" (Glendinning 1988), however Erridge and McIroy (2002) describe these "value for money" goals as largely "commercial" goals, and that public procurement has important "regulatory" (competition, transparency, equality, and compliance) and "socioeconomic" goals (public interest, employment concerns, social exclusion, economic development, and environmental policy).

As governments have increasingly externalized services (Alford and O'Flynn 2012) the subsequent associated auditing activities have increased in importance and complexity (Gronlund et al. 2011). The accountability/auditing field focuses on the auditing of public sector expenditure to determine whether it has achieved "value for money" (Gronlund et al. 2011; Johnsen et al. 2001; English 2007). Gronlund et al. (2011) focused on the types of audits undertaken and described prominent "value for money" elements as efficiency, economy, and effectiveness.

Methods

A qualitative approach was adopted and data were generated from ten public sector agencies (five roads and five works) in five Australian States: New South Wales (NSW), Queensland (QLD), South Australia (SA), Victoria (VIC), and Western Australia (WA). These states were selected as they are the major investors in construction projects. Over $40 billion of infrastructure expenditure is outlined in the 2013–2014 state governments budgets (NSW 2013; QLD 2013; SA 2013; TAS 2013; VIC 2013; WA 2013). This investment comprises both the commissioning of new infrastructure and recurrent expenditure on existing projects.

Table 2 Competing strands of public procurement. (Adapted from Erridge and McIlroy (2002))

Strand	Key themes	Achieved through
Commercial	- Value for money - Economy - Efficiency - Effectiveness	- Competition/competitive tendering - Closer relationships with suppliers - Longer contracts - Facilities management
Regulatory	- Competition - Transparency - Equality - Compliance	- EU public procurement directives - HM treasury tendering procedures - Organizational tendering rules
Socio-economic	- Public interest - Employment concerns - Social exclusion - Economic development - Environmental policy	- Best value - Contract compliance - Transfer of undertakings (Protection of employment) (TUPE) - Green buying guides

Table 3 Scenario for construction works procurers: procuring value for money

A. The Department of Education wants to build a primary school in (a regional town). The project is estimated to cost $9.5 million • How would you procure in this case? • What would best value be in this case? • What government priorities that you would seek to advance? • Who would determine these priorities?
B. The policy changes decreeing that all schools should all have solar panels, which will reduce the running costs for hot water and electricity in conjunction with supporting environmental technologies (holding tanks for hot water, etc.). By installing the solar panels for this project the budget is exceeded by $600,000. • Which decision do you take? • Who would determine the priorities?

Data were collected using three approaches: (1) telephone interviews, (2) face-to-face interviews, and (3) document analysis. Telephone based semistructured interviews were undertaken with twelve participants drawn from five roads and five construction agencies states and ranged from 14–20 min in duration with participants. The telephone based interviews focused on "value for money" and provided contact information for potential participants in the face-to-face interview phase. In order to further explore "value for money," 37 (20 (C)onstruction and 17 (R)oads) project managers who were involved in the preparation, evaluation, and awarding of construction contracts through a tender process were interviewed face-to-face in their place of employment. These project managers had, on average, over 20 years of public sector procurement experience. The average duration of the interviews was 66 min (range: 44–123 min) and featured a mixture of open-ended and closed questions designed to explore perceptions of "value for money," and the extent to which it was an objective. Open-ended questions were used in a stem-plus-query design (Cavana et al. 2001, p. 139), which allowed room for other issues to emerge, and for the researcher to prompt and probe, based on the answers provided by participants. The pattern of the interview was designed to be a series of funnel sequences (Cavana et al. 2001) starting with a broad, unstructured, open-ended question: "I am very interested in VFM. Would you tell me about Value for Money?" Then we proceeded to two more structured questions directly related to the research questions. Firstly, a closed ended question, and secondly a directed but open question:

- To what extent is purchasing VFM an objective?
- What does VFM mean to your department?

These interviews were supplemented by analysis of procurement and construction procurement policy documents and a limited amount of observation during site visits for fieldwork. Scenarios and reflections on current procurement practice were then used to further probe the issues of VFM (See Table 3).

Policy, procedure, and process documents from all of the locations were analyzed to see what light they shed on VFM. Interviews were audio recorded and Nvivo software was used to manage the data and create broad bucket coding (Richards 2005; Bazeley 2007; Richards and Morse 2007). These broad bucket codes were then further analyzed in a manner consistent with what Strauss and Corbin (1998) described as axial coding following the steps laid out by Dey (1993) including reading and annotating, creating categories, assigning categories, linking data, making connections, and producing an account.

The nature of procurement undertaken by the sample cohort of project managers is strategic, complex, and focused on the delivery of best VFM outcomes. The project managers procuring infrastructure for state government agencies are highly experienced. Those procuring have either spent an overwhelming proportion of their career in the public sector or have been career civil servants. They have, on average, more than 20 years of experience in both the public sector environment and the procurement of infrastructure. Most project managers are degree qualified in the areas of architecture, construction, and engineering.

Results and Discussion

When asked about the extent to which "value for money" was an objective all of the 37 project managers interviewed responded that "value for money" was important. One roads project manager (SA) commented on the importance of "value for money":

> I think it's a very, very, very strong objective; it's probably the biggest factor in anything that we do—(R13 SA).

The responses from construction agency project managers also reflected the importance of "value for money". A works project manager (SA) stated:

> It's a major objective. All our tendering systems are really focused on doing just that [delivering value for money]. It seems obvious to me, sorry [Laughing]. I mean, I suppose it is obvious, but that's what we have been trying to do for years—(C9 SA).

The overwhelming response from project managers was that "value for money" is extremely important; a fundamental objective and the primary driver of their procurement work. This was illustrated by one project manager (WA) who stated:

> Oh look its critical [value for money], at the end of the day the Government is looking at the most effective and efficient means of expending the taxpayers' dollars—(C8).

The finding that "value for money" is the primary objective and driver of construction procurement within Australia state governments is consistent with Murray's (2001, 1999) findings on procurement in UK local government. That "value for money" was reported as the primary procurement objective suggests that "value for money" discourse is extremely pervasive within government institutions. Value based policy influencing the externalization of services (for example "best value") has not been implemented by Australian state governments as it was in UK local governments (Bovaird and Halachmi, 2001). Best value was pursued at a Local Government in Victoria between 1999 and 2008 (Victorian Government 1999).

There was a high level of similarity as to the importance of "value for money" reported by project managers from both roads and construction backgrounds. One works project manager explained this in terms of extracting the most out of public funds:

> [...] we're always looking for value for money, and we want to achieve that, get the most out of the money we've got to play with so to speak—(C14 NSW).

One roads project manager described "value for money" as being the total focus because it is a priority for because of societal desires and expectations:

> To what extent? About a hundred [percent]. It might be 101 [percent] actually. Because the public expect to get value for money. They not only expect to get it, they actually want to see we're getting it too—(R1 QLD).

There was little difference in the extent to which "value for money" was an objective for roads and construction works agencies. Further, there was little difference between the states, which suggests that there are institutional forces that prioritize "value for money" across jurisdictions and government agencies. The likeness of the responses from participants suggests that the neo-liberal rhetoric or discourse of "value for money" is embraced and espoused by both sides of politics in Australia, although its meaning can differ as to the relative emphasis placed on economy, efficiency, or effectiveness.

Under CCT "value for money" was viewed as primarily focusing about "economy" and procuring on the basis of lowest cost, while "best value" emphasized the 3E's "economy, efficiency, and effectiveness." In Australia, the terms "value for money" and "best value" are not strongly related to policy regimes of particular political parties as in the UK and are used interchangeably and synonymously by the project managers.

Perceptions of "Value for Money"

There were two major strands of findings about the project managers' perceptions of "value for money." First, the project managers commented extensively on the nature of "value for money," and second, they highlighted the complexity of "value for money" drivers that are considered when undertaking construction procurement.

They commented on "value for money" not being able to be universally defined, and "value for money" being a relative concept, echoing Glendinning (1988) who referred to attempts to define "value" in the economics literatures. Further, project managers commented extensively that "value for money" required interpretation by them as procurers, necessitating their judgment, and because of its relative nature it differed from project to project depending on several factors including: location, financial environment, and forward plans. As one procurer of roads projects commented:

We keep getting these discussions where people are trying to get a universal formula or calculation of what is value for money. I think value for money can change on a network depending on the section of the road you're talking about, the environment you're in, how much money is available, what your forward plans might be and so on, which makes it very difficult to come down and argue or demonstrate value for money—(R4 QLD).

One building procurer suggested government needed to take a location based perspective, particularly to regional projects, where greater cross-government collaboration was needed to both contemplate and coordinate the achievement of the planned impacts for regional communities.

If there is no universally applicable definition of "value for money," and the procurers professional expertise is crucial in creating public value (Moore 1995), then the procurers' role becomes even more central in implementing strategy (Floyd and Woolridge 1992; Floyd and Lane 2000). The nature of "value for money" as perceived by the project managers and their role in creating value creates challenges in the policy environment as how to provide appropriate guidance on procuring "value for money" (see Wales Government (2010) Community Benefits). It may also require creative thinking about how the tacit knowledge of procurers can be codified through policy and systems, and shared between project managers, and across institutions and jurisdictions.

There was only one project manager (SA) out of the 37 project managers and 12 project executives interviewed who offered an official definition of "value for money." This definition was focused on balancing price with achieving objectives:

> I can give you the official definition [of value for money] … the fulfilment of objectives for the lowest whole-of-life cost, maximisation of the objectives—(C17 SA).

Governments are now providing policy advice (see Table 1) to departments and procurers about what VFM is, but how this policy information is both used and perceived is worthy of further exploration.

Politically Value-Laden Judgments

Project managers were conscious of how the political environment could influence "value for money" on a project and the role of politicians in defining "value for money." One participant (NSW) commented on the overarching authorization that is needed from the political environment to legitimize interpretations of "value for money":

> Yeah value for money is really quite subjective and has to be driven from the top. Really from the top, and the ministers, at the higher levels. Ministers are there to decide what is value for money. Not us. We try to represent, to a large extent the minister has to be aware of what is value for money—(C14 NSW).

The implication of this desire for political authorization is that without it project managers may not feel empowered to use their skills in their procurement solutions.

The second major theme was focused on the drivers of "value for money" on a project, and highlights the multi-dimensional nature and complexity of "value for money" for those procuring construction projects. This supports the findings of scholars who detail the large amount of criteria upon which projects are procured (Love et al. 2008) where a multiplicity of objects are frequently sought (McCabe et al. 2011). "Value for money" was viewed as comprising many drivers and factors.

However, the evidence showed that project managers still predominantly view "value for money" through commercial "economy" and "efficiency" lenses (Erridge and McIlroy 2002). Further, "value for money" drivers that initially appear unrelated to commercial imperatives are frequently viewed as drivers of good commercial outcomes, be it (for instance: relational contracting, getting good design, etc.).

Another important finding was the plurality of institutional perspectives with government. Project managers noted that government departments: treasury, premier, cabinet, and client agencies all have an opinion on what "value for money" is. Frequently these departments have their own commercial agendas, but sometimes they are focused on the socioeconomic uses of a facility. Within works agencies there is a strong commercial incentive to listen, and develop good relationships with client departments, as the clients commission projects and works procures for them. This theme of listening to client departments was noticeably stronger in state jurisdictions where client departments are not mandate to procure through a centralized works department. In other words, the works agency needs good relationships with clients to ensure ongoing work that makes the works agency a viable entity within government.

Roads agencies both commission and procure projects and are then responsible for the maintenance and upkeep of the infrastructure procured. The connected nature of expertise within the domains, and the fact that they will be responsible for the ongoing maintenance may mean they are in a better position to make VFM judgments over issues of life cycle.

Conclusion

The findings reveal the multi-dimensional nature of "value for money" and its inherent complexity on infrastructure projects. "Value for money" is the major objective for the managers responsible for procuring buildings and roads construction projects on behalf of Australian state governments. It is viewed as the main driver of procurement activities by project managers responsible for construction procurement of over $40 billion of infrastructure expenditure outlined in the 2013–2014 Australian State and Territory Governments budgets. This is encapsulated in the response from one manager:

Oh, ultimately to me, it's [VFM] the objective–(C1 QLD).

The discourse of "value for money" has been powerful within Australian state governments but relies on interpretation by, and the expertise of project managers to translate into procurement strategy, highlighting opportunity for creative policy. This is further supported by the finding that only one project manager cited an official definition of "value for money" and the definition was sufficiently open ended that it required interpretation by a project manager to operationalize it through procurement. Project managers are, therefore, very important for these types of specialized procurement. The importance of the project manager's role is further enhanced by the perceptions of "value for money" expressed that believe it is a relative term that requires interpretation and judgment by project managers in order to operationalize the concept. The complexity of VFM was highlighted by project managers as they listed multiple drivers that can then be viewed as fitting into the auditing perspective of the 3Es or the Erridge and McIlroy (2002) three goals of procurement (commercial, regulatory, and socioeconomic). What is clear when you analyze the responses through these three lenses is that most of the drivers of "value for money" are commercial oriented goals viewed through economy and efficiency lenses. Far less consideration is given to socioeconomic goals or effectiveness drivers of VFM.

This may be because project managers believe that effectiveness and socioeconomic criteria are politically value laden and therefore require the approval/authorization from politicians. Further exacerbating the complexity was the finding that it was acknowledged by project managers that there were multiple institutional perspectives on "value for money." While these multiple institutional perspectives exist economy and efficiency remain the primary focus for those procuring.

References

Alford, J., & O'Flynn, J. (2012). *Rethinking public service delivery: Managing with external providers*. New York: Palgrave Macmillan.

Andrews, R., Boyne, G. A., Law, J., & Walker, R. M. (2009). Strategy, structure and process in the public sector: A test of the miles and snow model. *Public Administration, 84*(4), 732–749.

Andrews, R., Boyne, G. A., Meier, K. J., O'Toole, L. J. Jr., & Walker, R. M. (2012). Vertical strategic alignment and public service performance. *Public Administration, 90*(1), 77–98.

Bazeley, P. (2007). Qualitative data analysis with NVivo. Los Angeles: Sage.

Bovaird, T. (2006). Developing new forms of partnership with the 'market' in the procurement of public services. *Public Administration, 84*(1), 81–102.

Bovaird, T., & Halachmi, A. (2001). Performance measurement and best value: An international perspective. *International Journal of Business Performance Management, 3*(2/3/4), 119–134.

Boyne, G. A. (1998). Competitive tendering in local government: A review of theory and evidence. *Public Administration, 76*(4), 695–712.

Boyne, G. A., Gould–Williams, J. S., Law, J., & Walker, R. M. (2002). Best value—total quality management for local government? *Public Money & Management, 22*(3), 9–16.

Burger, P., & Hawkesworth, I. (2011). How to attain value for money: Comparing PPP and traditional infrastructure public procurement. *OECD Journal on Budgeting, 1*(1/1), 91–146. http://dx.doi.org/10.1787/budget-11-5kg9zc0pvq6j. Accessed 12 September 2012.

Cavana, R. Y., Delahaye, B. L., & Sekaran, U. (2001). *Applied business research: qualitative and quantitative methods. Milton, Queensland.* Australia: Wiley.

Department of Finance (2012). Commonwealth procurement rules: Achieving value for money. www.finance.gov.au/procurement/docs/cpr_commonwealth_procurement_rules_july_2012.pdf. Accessed 10 July 2012.

Dey, I. (1993). *Qualitative data analysis: A user friendly guide for social scientists*. London: Routledge.

Diefenbach, T. (2009). New public management in public sector organizations: The dark sides of managerialistic enlightenment. *Public Administration, 87*(4), 892–909.

English, L. (2007). Performance audit of Australian public private partnerships: Legitimising government policies or providing independent oversight?. *Financial Accountability & Management, 23*(3), 313–336.

Erridge, A. (2007). Public procurement, public value and the northern ireland unemployment pilot project. *Public Administration, 85*(4), 1023–1043.

Erridge, A., & McIlroy, J. (2002). Public procurement and supply management strategies. *Public Policy & Administration, 17*(1), 52–71

Floyd, S. W., & Lane, P. J. (2000). Strategizing throughout the organization: Managing role conflict in strategic renewal. *Academy of Management Review, 25*(1), 154–177.

Floyd, S. W., & Woolridge, B. (1992). Managing strategic consensus: The foundation of effective implementation. *Academy of Management Executive, 6*(4), 27–39.

Flyvbjerg, B. (2007). Policy and planning for large-infrastructure projects: Problems, causes, cures. *Environment and Planning B: Planning and Design, 34*(4), 578–597.

Flyvbjerg, B. (2009). Survival of the unfit test: Why the worst infrastructure gets built—and what we can do about it. *Oxford Review of Economic Policy, 25*(3), 344–367.

Furneaux, C. W., Brown, K., & Allan, D. (2008). Public values embedded in Australian public works procurement. *Public Money & Management, 28*(3), 167–172.

Glendinning, R. (1988). The concept of value for money. *International Journal of Public Sector Management, 1*(1), 42–50.

Grimsey, D., & Lewis, M. K. (2005). Are public private partnerships value for money?: Evaluating alternative approaches and comparing academic and practitioner views, *Accounting Forum, 29*(4), 345–378.

Grönlund, A., Svärdsten, F., & Öhman, P. (2011). Value for money and the rule of law: The (new) performance audit in Sweden. *International Journal of Public Sector Management, 24*(2), 107–121

Haque, M. S. (1999). Ethical tension in public governance: Critical impacts on theory-building. *Administrative Theory & Praxis, 21*(4), 468–473.

HM Treasury (2006). Value for money assessment guide. http://www.hm-treasury.gov.uk/d/vfm_assessmentguidance061006opt.pdf. Accessed 10 May 2012.

Johnsen, A., Meklin, P., Oulasvirta, L., & Vakkuri, J. (2001). Performance auditing in local government: An exploratory study of perceived efficiency of municipal value for money auditing in Finland and Norway. *European Accounting Review, 10*(3), 583–599.

Kelly, J., Morledge, R., & Wilkinson, S. (2002). Best value in construction. Oxford: Blackwell.

Kelly, J., Male, S., & Graham, D. (2004). Value management of construction projects. Oxford: Blackwell.

Kenley, R., London, K., & Watson, K. (2000). Strategic procurement in the construction industry: Mechanisms for public sector clients to encourage improved performance in Australia. *Journal of Construction Procurement, 6*(2), 4–19.

Love, P. E. D., Davis, P. R., Edwards, D. J., & Baccarini, D. (2008). Uncertainty avoidance: Public sector clients and procurement selection. *International Journal of Public Sector Management, 21*(7), 753–776.

Love, P. E. D., Davis, P. R., & Baccarini, D. (2010). Dismantling the public sector bastion: Evaluating capital works. *International Journal of Public Sector Management, 23*(3), 188–202.

Luke, B., Kearins, K., & Verreynne, M. L. (2011). The risks and returns of new public management: Political business. *International Journal of Public Sector Management, 24*(4), 325–355

MacDonald, C., Walker, D. H. T., & Moussa, N. (2012). Value for money in project alliances. *International Journal of Managing Projects in Business Volume, 5*(2), 311–324.

MacDonald, C., Walker, D. H. T., & Moussa, N. (2013). Towards a project alliance value for money framework. *Facilities, 31*(5/6), 279–309.

McCabe, A., Parker, R., & Brown, K. (2011). Social outcomes in the construction industry: The case of the Western Australian 'Percent for Art' policy. *Construction Management and Economics, 29*(9), 929–941.

Moore, M. H. (1995). *Creating public value: Strategic management in government*. Cambridge: Harvard University Press.

Murray, J. G. (1999). Local government demands more from purchasing. *European Journal of Purchasing & Supply Management, 5*(1), 33–42.

Murray, J. G. (2001). Improving purchasing's contribution—the purchasing strategy of buying council. *International Journal of Public Sector Management, 14*(5), 391–410.

Murray, J. G. (2009b). Public procurement strategy for accelerating the economic recovery. *Supply Chain Management: An International Journal, 14*(6), 429–434.

Murray, J. G., Erridge, A., & Rimmer, N. (2012). International lessons on austerity strategy. *International Journal of Public Sector Management, 25*(4), 248–259.

New South Wales (2013). NSW government procurement information. www.procurepoint.nsw.gov.au/policies/nsw-government-procurement-information Accessed 28 March 2013.

Nisar, T. M. (2007). Value for money drivers in public private partnership schemes, International Journal of Public Sector Management, 20(2), 147–156.

Northern Ireland Public Procurement Policy (Version 10) (2012). Northern Ireland public procurement policy (version 10). http://www.dfpni.gov.uk/index/procure ment-2/cpd/cpd-policy-and-legislation/ni-pp-policy/ni_public_pro curement_policy__version_10_.pdf. Accessed 28 March 2014.

NSW. (2013). NSW treasury 2013–2014 infrastructure statement. (budget paper no. 4). www.budget.nsw.gov.au/__data/assets/pdf_file/0018/25236/BP4_Infrastructure_Statement_2013–14_dnd.pdf. Accessed 20 August 2013.

Palaneeswaran, E., Kumaraswamy, M., & Ng, T. (2003). Targeting optimum value in public sector projects through 'best value'-focused contractor selection. *Engineering, Construction and Architectural Management, 10*(6), 418–431.

Pollitt, C., & Bouckaert, G. (2011). *Public management reform: A comparative analysis of new public management, governance and the neo-weberian state* (3rd ed.). Oxford: Oxford University Press.

QLD. (2013). Queensland state budget 2013–2014 capital statement—budget paper no. 3. http://www.budget. qld.gov.au/budget-papers/2013–14/bp3–2013–14.pdf Accessed 20 Aug 2013.

Richards, L. (2005). *Handling qualitative data: A practical guide*. London: Sage.

Richards, L., & Morse, J. M. (2007). *Readme first for a user's guide to qualitative methods* (2nd Vol.). Thousand Oaks: Sage.

Scottish Government Scotland (2010). *Scotland transforming procurement: Accelerating delivery*. Edinburgh: Author.

South Australia (2013). South Australia budget 2013–2014 budget paper 5: Capital investment statement. http://servicesa.cdn.on.net/docs/Budgetp5_201314.pdf. Ac-cessed 20 August 2013.

South Australia Procurement Board (2011). Strategic plan 2011–2013, government of South Australia. http://www.spb.sa.gov.au/site/news_publications/publications/spb_strategic_plan.aspx. Accessed 20 Jan 2014.

Staples, W. J., & Dalrymple, J. F. (2011). Exploring infrastructure procurement by Australian state governments. *International Journal of Managing Projects in Business, 4*(3), 512–523.

Staples, W. J., & Dalrymple, J. F. (2015). Construction procurement and state government strategy: Aligned or disconnected? *Australian Journal of Public Administration*. http://onlinelibrary.wiley.com/doi/10.1111/1467-8500.12114/abstract. Accessed 20 Jan 2015.

Strauss, A., & Corbin, J. (1998). *Basics of qualitative research: Techniques and procedures for developing grounded theory* (2nd ed.). Thousand Oaks: Sage.

TAS (2013). Tasmanian budget 2013–2014 budget paper no 1 the budget. http://www.sro.tas.gov.au/ domino/dtf/dtf.nsf/LookupFiles/2013–14-Budget-BP1.pdf/$file/2013–14-Budget-BP1.pdf Accessed 20 Aug 2013.

Tookey, J. E., Murray, M., Hardcastle, C., & Langford, D. (2001). Construction procurement routes: Re-defining the contours of construction procurement. *Engineering Construction & Architectural Management, 8*(1), 20–30.

Wales Government (2010). Community benefits: Delivering maximum value for the welsh pound. http://wales.gov.uk/docs/dpsp/publications/valuewales/100426commbenefitsen.pdf. Accessed 13 September 2013.

Walraven, A., & de Vries, B. (2009). "From demand driven contractor selection towards value driven contractor selection. *Construction Management and Economics, 27*(6), 597–604.

VGPB. (2012). Victorian government procurement. http://vgpb.vic.gov.au/domino/web_notes/vgpb/ procport.nsf?Open. Accessed 20 September 2013.

VIC. (2013). State government of victoria. (budget paper no. 4 state capital program). www.dtf.vic.gov.au/Publications/State-Budget-publications/Budget-Paper-No-4-State-Capital-Program. Accessed 20 Aug 2013.

Victorian Government (1999). Local government (best value principles) act 1999: Act No. 59/1999. www.legislation.vic.gov.au/Domino/Web_Notes/LDMS/PubStatbook.nsf/f932b66241ecf1b7ca256e92000e23be/63613d8633a76f3cca256e5b00213df1/$FILE/99–059a.pdf. Accessed 12 May 2012.

WA. (2013). Western Australian state budget papers 2013–14 treasurer's budget speech. http://www.treasury.wa.gov.au/cms/uploadedFiles/State_Budget/Budget_2013_14/2013–14_BP1.pdf?n = 9894. Accessed 20 Aug 2013.

WA Government Procurement (2013). WA government procurement. www.finance.wa.gov.au/cms/section.aspx?id = 454. Accessed 20 March 2014.

Walker, D., & Hampson, K. (2003). *Procurement strategies: A relationship-based approach*. Oxford: Blackwell Publishing.

Walsh, K. (1995). *Public services and market mechanisms: Competition, contracting and the new public management*. Houndmills: Macmillan.

Wong, C. H., Holt, G. D., & Cooper, P. A. (2000). Lowest price or value? Investigation of UK construction clients tender selection process. *Construction Management and Economics, 18*, 767–774.

Warren Staples Ph.D. is a lecturer in the School of Management, RMIT University, Australia. His teaching and research interests are in public management, public procurement, and corporate social responsibility

Part III
Preferential Public Procurement

The Reform to EU Utilities Procurement: Smart, Sustainable and Inclusive?

Eleanor Aspey

Introduction

As is common in countries across the world, one of the major concerns for the countries of the European Union (EU) in recent years has been recovery from the global financial crisis. In an attempt to help Europe on the road to recovery, President Barrosso announced in 2010 that the EU was setting out a new growth strategy for the coming decade, known as "Europe 2020" (European Commission 2010). The Europe 2020 strategy is based around three priorities: "smart" growth (developing innovation); "sustainable" growth (developing a greener and more resource efficient economy); and "inclusive" growth (improving employment and social cohesion). Seven flagship initiatives setting out specific goals are designed to be the primary means for achieving these aims, but they will need to be supported more widely through the EU legal regime (European Commission 2010).

Public procurement is mentioned throughout the 2020 strategy as a potential method for supporting the three 2020 growth priorities and was therefore a key area for development. In December 2011, the European Commission duly announced that they had begun the process of reforming the procurement regulatory regime applicable in the EU (European Commission 2011a). It was noted that public procurement had been set as one of the EU's 12 priority projects with which the commission aimed to "relaunch the single market for 2012," with improvement of the single market being seen by the EU as one of the most effective means of recovering from the financial crisis (European Commission 2011b). The commission set out three main aims for the procurement reform process: to simplify the rules and increase flexibility; to encourage access to public procurement for small- and medium-sized enterprises (SMEs); and to facilitate a "qualitative improvement in the use of public procurement" by ensuring greater consideration of social and green issues in procurement (European Commission 2011a). Based on these aims, in 2011 the

E. Aspey (✉)
University of Manchester, Manchester, UK
e-mail: eleanor.aspey@manchester.ac.uk

K. V. Thai (ed.), *International Public Procurement,* Public Administration, Governance and Globalization 14, DOI 10.1007/978-3-319-13434-5_13

commission set out three proposals for directives on public procurement: one revising public sector procurement, one revising utilities procurement, and an entirely new directive on concessions procurement. After a lengthy legislative process, the final versions of the three directives were adopted in February 2014 as Directive 2014/23/EU (concessions), Directive 2014/24/EU (public sector) and Directive 2014/25/EU (utilities sector—"the new Utilities Directive"). The directives are required to be implemented into national law by the Member States by 18 April 2016, with the previous directives remaining in force until that point.

This chapter focuses on the reform to procurement within the utilities sector. Although much smaller than the public sector, the utilities sector is still a significant sector of the EU economy, awarding approximately 10% of all procurement contracts in the EU each year, and 17% of the total contract value (PricewaterhouseCoopers, London Economics and Ecorys 2011, p. 5). It is also arguable that social and green concerns are of particular importance in the utilities sector. Many of the sectors (particularly energy, water, and transport) have great environmental impact, and there are also social and labour concerns given a recent growth amongst the utility sector for outsourcing to developing countries (Arrowsmith and Maund 2009, p. 445). There is therefore the potential for real impact on social and green issues through the regulation of procurement in this area, helping to boost "sustainable" and "inclusive" growth. This chapter will examine the extent to which the reforms to the EU utilities procurement regime support the aims of the 2020 strategy, providing procuring entities with opportunities for innovative, social, or green procurement.

The chapter will begin with an overview of the current EU regulatory regime on utilities procurement, providing a general background to the discussion of the reforms. We will then evaluate the relevant reforms in the new regime in light of the Europe 2020 aims, highlighting any positive changes and discussing any remaining constraints in the law and missed opportunities for improving procurement in this area. It will be shown that overall the reforms are a positive step, clarifying many of the issues which concerned utility procuring entities under the current law and showing the potential for green and social procurement in the EU in the future.

Overview of Current EU Utilities Procurement

The primary source of the EU's regulatory regime on procurement is the Treaty on the Functioning of the European Union (TFEU). While the treaty does not mention procurement explicitly, a number of the provisions do potentially have an impact on public and utilities contracts, with the most significant being the free movement provisions (covering the free movement of goods (Article 34 TFEU), freedom of establishment (Article 49 TFEU), and the freedom to provide services (Article 56 TFEU)). The treaty provisions set out predominantly negative obligations, prohibiting procuring authorities from setting requirements which discriminate, either directly or indirectly, against goods or services from another member state. Following Case C-324/98, *Telaustria Verlags GmbH v Telekom Austria AG* [2000] E.C.R. I-10745, however, the TFEU rules also impose some limited positive obligations relating to the transparency of the procurement proceedings, including a requirement that the contract be advertised.

The EU supports and expands upon the free movement provisions with secondary legislation which regulates procurement more directly, setting out more detailed rules relating to the conduct of the procurement process including precise rules on award procedures. For utilities, this regulation is currently found in Directive 2004/17/EC ("the 2004 Utilities Directive"), with the remedies for breach of the procurement rules being set out in Directive 92/13/EEC. The rules set out in this secondary legislation only apply to contracts over a set monetary threshold, revised every 2 years (the current thresholds can be found in Regulation 1336/2013). Under Article 40 of the 2004 Utilities Directive, utilities have a free choice between three award procedures; the open procedure (a strict tendering procedure in which no limit is set on the number of tenderers), the restricted procedure (a strict tendering procedure with a limited number of tenderers) and the negotiated procedure (a flexible procedure allowing discussion with potential suppliers, who may be limited by number).

The 2004 Utilities Directive covers three categories of body (see Art. 2(2)); contracting authorities (covering state, regional or local authorities or bodies covered by public law), public undertakings (companies subject to the dominant influence of a public authority), and private entities which operate on the basis of special or exclusive rights. Special or exclusive rights are defined as legislative, regulatory or administrative rights which limit the exercise of the specified utility activities to one or more entities and substantially affect the ability of other companies to carry out those activities (Art. 2(3)). The applicability of the TFEU free movement obligations to these private bodies is unclear and so the 2004 Utilities Directive also includes references to the same obligations in its text (e.g. a general principle of nondiscrimination is set out in Article 10), ensuring that the complete range of EU rules apply where the contract is over the threshold regardless of the type of procuring entity in question.

Regardless of which of the three categories above a procuring entity falls under, they will only be covered by the 2004 Utilities Directive when they carry out one of the activities listed in the Directive, and then only in relation to a contract awarded for the purpose of that activity. The relevant activities are listed in Arts. 3-7 of the Directive, and cover contracts in the fields of energy (the production, distribution and supply of gas, electricity and heat, and exploration and exploitation of oil, gas, coal and other solid fuels), water (the operation of a fixed network for the provision, transport or distribution of drinking water), transport (covering the operation of railway, tramway, trolley bus, bus or cable services, and airport and port terminal services), and postal services. For contracts for any other activities, contracting authorities and public undertakings will be covered by the comparable public sector procurement directive, Directive 2004/18/EC, while private bodies with special and exclusive rights will be fully unregulated. Connected to this, Article 12 of Directive 2004/18/EC explicitly excludes contracts for the utility activities set out above from the scope of that directive, meaning that contracting authorities or public undertakings which would otherwise be covered by the public sector rules are subject only to the 2004 Utilities Directive rules for procurement in those areas.

As regards the inclusion of green and social issues in procurement, important for the Europe 2020 agenda as discussed above, the current law is generally vague. The possibility of such issues often appears to be not considered at all or to be considered only as an afterthought. Some potential policies are clearly prohibited under the EU regime; for example, awarding a contract to a supplier on the basis that they promise to hire local unemployed labour clearly breaches the EU requirement of nondiscrimination on the basis of nationality. In most cases, however, it is simply not clear from the wording of the directive or from case law whether or not a particular policy is allowable. Implementing green or social policies therefore currently requires utilities to balance the possible risk of legal challenge against the potential benefits of the policy, a difficult balance to make given the lack of clarity in the law. The constraints under the current law are somewhat under-discussed in relation to the utilities sector, but Arrowsmith and Maund (2009) set out a discussion of the potential areas of concern in this sector. This author has also previously discussed the areas identified by procurement practitioners as having the most impact on labour issues in particular (Aspey 2012). The following section will discuss in more detail those areas of concern for green and social procurement which will be changed under the new Utilities Directive.

Key Areas of Reform

There are four major areas within the reform of the utilities regulatory regime in which changes to the law could potentially impact on the areas of the Europe 2020 strategy and green or social procurement. These are discussed below in the order in which they would generally arise in a procurement process. The section will begin by considering the impact of the introduction of a new award procedure for utilities, innovation partnerships. It will then discuss the amendments to the rules on setting the technical specifications of the product or service to be procured, before considering the changes to setting contractual conditions applicable on the winning tenderer and, finally, the criteria for awarding the contract.

Innovation Partnerships

Under the current law, there are no specific rules or guidance relating to developing innovative products or services; the assumption was that contracts for these purposes could be adequately provided for under the existing award procedures. Article 40(3)(b) of the 2004 Utilities Directive allows a contract which is purely for the purpose of research and development to be awarded without a prior call for competition but notes that this can only be done where the contract is not done with the aim of securing profit or recovering the costs of the research and development. A full competitive award procedure is therefore required where the contracting entity hopes to purchase the goods or services which have been researched at the end of the process (Apostal 2012, p. 220–221). The current system thus potentially requires two separate contracts for innovative products, one for research and one for the subsequent purchase, providing little benefit within the procurement process for developing new products rather than simply purchasing those which are already in existence.

To combat this problem, the new Utilities Directive sets out an innovation partnership procedure (Art. 49), which sets up a long-term structured partnership between the contracting entity and a private contractor covering both a research phase and subsequent purchase (provided the end product meets the required performance and cost levels) in one contract. Recital 59 of the new Utilities Directive notes that this procedure is intended to be used "[w]here a need for the development of an innovative product or service or innovative works and the subsequent purchase of the resulting supplies, services or works cannot be met by solutions already available on the market". Procurement of goods already on the market should therefore be completed by one of the existing award procedures and contracts for pure research and development remain one of the exemptions to the general rules and can be procured without a call for competition (see Art. 50(b) of the new Utilities Directive).

The innovation partnership is, as would be expected for a procedure designed to procure a currently unknown product or service, a relatively unstructured award procedure based on negotiations with the prospective partners. However, some guidance is provided in Article 49 as to the expected procurement process. Following Article 49(2), the process must be structured in successive stages which follow "the sequence of steps in the research and innovation process." While the article provides some examples of stages, including manufacturing, provision of services, and completion of works, it does not provide an exhaustive list or any more complete definition of research and innovation. Utilities would, therefore, appear free to structure the process as they wish so long as there are definite stages within that process. While the lack of clear guidelines may potentially deter some contracting entities from using the new procedure, the high level of discretion is preferable to strict guidelines overall, allowing contracting entities to tailor the stages to their particular requirements. Those which wish more guidance could perhaps follow the precommercial procurement guidelines designed by the European Commission for research and development unregulated by the procurement regime (European Commission 2007). Regardless of the number of stages used, targets must be set for the end of each stage and, based on the completion of those targets, utilities may choose to terminate the innovation partnership or reduce the number of partners at the end of each stage (Art. 49(2)).

The new Utilities Directive is, however, very vague on the requirements for the actual purchase stage. The only guidance given is that the value of the product or service should not be "disproportionate in relation to the investment for their development" (Art. 49(7)). Apostal notes that the provision is "poorly drafted", allowing not only a large amount of discretion in deciding value, but also not making it clear if there are any limits on the subsequent purchase, in theory allowing a contracting entity to decide to purchase the product or service only after it was commercially available on the market which would limit the utility of the provision (2012, p. 222). This vagueness is unfortunate as it may deter bidders from participating since they cannot necessarily guarantee either that it will be profitable or that they will have a definite customer for the product at the end of the process, as they would if the contracting entity was required to buy the final product.

Overall, the new innovation partnership procedure offers significant potential for developing innovative products and services and therefore supporting smart growth. Equally, it can potentially support the other Europe 2020 aims through the increased ability to innovate green and social products and services. However, the vagueness of the provision, particularly in regards to the subsequent purchase, may limit the uptake of the procedure in practice and it is regrettable that there was not greater detail provided in the directive.

Technical Specifications

The technical specifications of a contract set out exactly what it is that the utility wishes to buy. Under the 2004 Utilities Directive, these should set out the "required characteristics of a product or service" and for works contracts should also allow the relevant material, product or supply "to be described in a manner such that it fulfils the use for which it is intended by the contracting entity" (Art. 1, Annex XXI). These definitions are retained in Article 1, Annex VIII of the new Utilities Directive. The point at which the utility chooses what to buy offers significant potential for meeting the Europe 2020 aims by choosing innovative, green or socially sustainable products. Innovation in particular has always been encouraged at this stage by allowing the use of functional technical specifications which enable tenderers to suggest innovative methods of meeting the contracting entity's needs (Art. 34(3) 2004 Utilities Directive; see now Art. 60(3) new Utilities Directive). This section will focus on two potentially important areas for the Europe 2020 aims where the current law lacks clarity; setting requirements relating to the production methods of a product and requiring compliance with a particular product label.

Production Methods

The production process of a particular product may raise environmental or social concerns which a procuring entity may wish to change or minimise by setting certain production requirements. For example, an entity may wish to require that the product they purchase was produced by employees who benefited from certain labour guarantees. On the green side, the entity may wish to ensure that the product is produced in an environmentally sustainable manner. However, the extent to which procuring entities can set such production requirements is unclear under the 2004

Utilities Directive as the issue is not mentioned; the only guidance given relates to setting the requirements of the product or service itself, not the way in which it is made or provided.

The European Commission appeared to interpret the current law in a very conservative manner, effectively prohibiting the use of such production methods. Focusing on the statement in Annex XXI for works technical specifications, set out above, which requires that the specifications should allow the product to "fulfil the use for which it is intended," the commission suggests that production matters could therefore only be considered where they had a real practical impact on the characteristics of the product, whether visible or invisible (European Commission 2001a, p. 11; European Commission 2011c, p. 28). This would appear to prevent any social or green production requirement which will not physically change the product, such as fair trade standards, or where any physical change would be minimal and not impact the actual use of the product, for example, recycled paper. The European Commission has also suggested that setting social/labour requirements for the execution of the contract could be seen as an unlawful restriction on trade, as they would be difficult to apply only to the workforce working on the particular contract and might require a supplier's whole business to be changed (European Commission 2001b, p. 17). This would appear to apply equally to workforce requirements on production, suggesting they should be equally prohibited.

Kunzlik (2009), however, has argued that the reasoning of the European Commission is flawed. The commission states within its guidance that a requirement that electricity be sourced from environmentally friendly sources would be acceptable (European Commission 2001a, p. 11). This contradicts the Commission's own argument that production requirements must have an impact on product characteristics since green energy is indistinguishable at the point of consumption from energy generated from nonsustainable sources (Kunzlik 2009, p. 395). Given this and the 2004 Utilities Directive's silence on the issue, it is at least arguable that production requirements are allowable under the current law so long as they comply with the general principles of EU law (i.e., are transparent and nondiscriminatory) and they accurately define what the contracting authority wishes to buy, which may include a wish to purchase a sustainable product (McCrudden 2007, p. 542).

The reforms set out in the new Utilities Directive clarify the law and confirm that production requirements are allowed. Article 60(1) of the new Utilities Directive states that technical specifications:

> may also refer to the specific process or method of production or provision of the requested works, supplies or services or to a specific process for another stage of its life cycle *even where such factors do not form part of their material substance*, provided that they are linked to the subject-matter of the contract and proportionate to its value and its objectives (Emphasis added)

This suggests that the conservative interpretation of the European Commission, if it was ever valid, is no longer applicable as the production methods required do not have to impact on the actual substance of the product or service (and it is perhaps notable that the highlighted section of Article 60 above was not present in the original proposal by the commission, being added later by the council (European Parliament 2013). This supports the Europe 2020 aim of promoting sustainable growth by making it clear to contracting authorities that they are free to require that their goods and services are produced or provided in an environmentally sustainable manner. On this point it should also be noted that the technical specifications now clearly allow contracting authorities to set requirements for any point in a product's life cycle, which provides the potential for requirements to be set relating to environmentally sound disposal or recycling. It may also allow consideration of labour issues which arise when the product is sold at the various stages of the supply chain, rather than simply at manufacture, which is a key issue for many fair trade organisations.

The impact that the change will have on social production requirements, potentially important for the inclusive growth goal of Europe 2020, is less clear. The removal of the requirement that the production method must impact the characteristics of the product suggests that workforce criteria should be allowable just as environmental production requirements are, but the requirement in Article 60 that the production requirements be linked to the subject-matter of the contract could prove more problematic for social criteria. The issue previously highlighted by the European Commission that workforce requirements may require changes in the wider business still stands; it will be difficult for a supplier to change their workforce practices only in relation to the workforce working on the particular contract with the procuring entity both practically (e.g. identifying the relevant members of staff) and ethically (because one subsection of the workforce will now have higher working standards than the others). This may, therefore, prevent the use of social production requirements in practice.

Labelling Requirements

When setting out its requirements in the technical specifications, a procuring entity may wish to do so by reference to a particular product or service label, either nationally or internationally recognised. Doing so means the procuring entity does not have to either work out the precise requirements of the product itself or check that the tenders meet those requirements beyond checking that they have validly acquired the label, saving time and money. It is also especially useful when setting environmental or social requirements where the procuring entity may lack the relevant expertise to set particular requirements, and being able to rely on an accepted external standard will therefore enable the procuring entity to have greater certainty in the validity of the requirements.

Despite the benefits of using labelling requirements in technical specifications, in order to minimise the risk of national discrimination the current law only allows reference to environmental eco-labels which meet certain specified requirements set out in Article 34(6) of the 2004 Utilities Directive. The Article allows contracting entities to refer to the detailed specifications of "European or (multi-) national eco-labels, or … any other eco-label", either wholly or in part; it does not appear that they can simply refer to the label without also setting out the actual specifications. Equally, while contracting entities may state that any product or service which holds the requisite label is presumed to comply with the technical specifications, they must accept "any other appropriate means of proof" (Art. 34(6)) which the contracting authority must check is compliant with the label requirements. Taken together, these points remove many of the time benefits from using a label.

There is no provision within the 2004 Utilities Directive specifically for the use of any social- or labour-related labelling requirements. The issue was considered by the Court of Justice of the European Union (CJEU) under the comparable public sector provision (Art. 23, Directive 2004/18) in Case C-368/10, *European Commission v Kingdom of Netherlands* (judgment of 10 May 2012). Here, it was required that the product supplied to the contracting authority complied with the Max Havelaar and EKO labels, with a later clarification that labels which were based on equivalent or identical criteria would also be accepted. Consistent with the rules on eco-labels, the CJEU held requiring compliance with a label was unlawful; the actual requirements of the label had to be set out and compliance with the requirements checked.

Under the reformed law, the rules on labelling requirements are set out in Article 61 of the new Utilities Directive. This allows contracting entities to "require a specific label as means of proof that the works, supplies or services correspond to the required characteristics". This should generally remove the need to set out the detailed requirements of the label in full. Contracting entities are, however, required to accept all equivalent labels and it is not clear from the directive's wording who has the responsibility for proving equivalence. Arguably the responsibility would be best placed on the supplier, who has the best capability for showing how their product meets the requirements of the label and how they are equivalent, in which case this provision should ease the current burden on contracting authorities for examining compliance. Equally, Article 61(1) now only requires that a contracting authority accept other appropriate means of proving compliance from suppliers where that supplier can show they have "demonstrably no possibility of obtaining the specific label indicated by the contracting entity or an equivalent label within the time limits for reasons that are not attributable to that economic operator", which again should significantly limit the amount of time used checking compliance. This should therefore encourage contracting entities to use social and environmental labels more widely, boosting sustainable and inclusive growth in line with Europe 2020.

The main issue remaining with the reformed law is a limitation set out in Article 61(1)(a) which states that a label can only be required where "the label requirements *only* concern criteria which are linked to the subject-matter of the contract" (emphasis added). This may prevent reference to labels which consider a wide range of potential environmental and social concerns or those which are attached to businesses rather than products as there will be requirements within the label which are not specific to the particular contract awarded (see, e.g. the Fair Trade label, which has generic requirements in addition to product-specific; Fairtrade 2014). In such a situation, the law reverts back to the current situation; Article 61(2) states that contracting entities "shall not require the label as such" but should define the technical specification by reference to those parts of the label requirements which are relevant to the subject-matter. This may discourage contracting entities from considering labels in such situations, given the difficulty in sorting through potentially lengthy and complex social or environmental requirements to pick out the relevant issues, especially where they are not social or environmental experts themselves.

Contract Conditions

Contracting entities may wish to set out contractual conditions which set standards for the winning supplier to comply with over the course of the contract. They are beneficial for contracting entities as they allow a supplier's compliance with the particular standards in question to be checked throughout the contract performance period, unlike most other checks in a tender process (e.g. award criteria) which examine compliance only at that particular point in time (Aspey 2012, p. 306). Such conditions could potentially be useful for developing innovation over the course of a contract, and for ensuring compliance with green and social requirements.

The current law relating to the inclusion of contract conditions is set out in Article 38 of the 2004 Utilities Directive: "Contracting entities may lay down special conditions relating to the performance of the contract, provided that these are compatible with [Union] law … The conditions governing the performance of a contract may, in particular, concern social and environmental considerations". The main issues which arise here relate to the interpretation of the phrase "performance of the contract". The wording of the provision mirrors that of the public sector directive (see Art. 25, Directive 2004/18) which is generally taken to prohibit any conditions not related to contract performance (Arrowsmith 2005, p. 1280). However, if including contract conditions unrelated to the performance were allowable, this would be beneficial for social procurement in particular, enabling a contracting entity to be sure that good employment practices were being followed in the supplier's business as a whole. It would also allow conditions which, while not directly related to the contract performance, supported the wider goals of the contracting entity, e.g. conditions for the education and training of a particular sector of the population affected by the contract. Such conditions would, therefore, be very useful for the development of inclusive procurement under the Europe 2020 strategy.

Arrowsmith and Maund have argued, however, that the interpretation of "performance of the contract" should be more flexible for utilities (2009, p. 458). They suggest that if utilities cannot include contract conditions going beyond performance, they should logically be unable to exclude firms from the tendering process for reasons unrelated to contract performance, but this is in fact potentially allowable for utilities. Article 54 of the 2004 Utilities Directive states that contracting entities may exclude or select tenderers "according to objective rules and criteria", wording which is maintained in the reformed law (see Art. 78(1) new Utilities Directive). There is no link to the contract mentioned in this article and it would therefore appear lawful for a utility to exclude/select tenderers on the basis of more general matters applying to the whole business of the tenderer (and this appears to have been how UK utilities have interpreted the provision (Aspey 2012, p. 309)). This raises the illogical situation in which a utility can exclude a potential tenderer for an issue which they are not lawfully able to include in the contract. If this more liberal interpretation had been adopted in the reforms, it would have clarified the law and also provided further opportunities for boosting social and green procurement by enabling wider use of contract conditions.

The reform to the law, however, appears to confirm that the conservative view of the law is correct and conditions unrelated to performance are not allowable. Article 87 of the new Utilities Directive states that special conditions can be set by a contracting authority "provided that they are linked to the subject-matter of the contract". "Subject-matter" is given a relatively broad interpretation in Article 82(3) as anything which "relate[s] to the works, supplies or services to be provided under that contract in any respect and at any stage of their life cycle", but still clearly rules out conditions relating to a supplier's business as a whole. This potentially hinders opportunities for inclusive growth through boosting employment throughout the business. It also means the problem identified by Arrowsmith and Maund that utilities can potentially exclude suppliers for an issue they cannot legally include as a contract condition remains, and it is regrettable that the opportunity was not taken to link up the law in a coherent manner during the reform.

The reform does, however, have the benefit of clarifying what precisely is meant by performance through the reference to "subject-matter". The broad definition provided potentially also allows for conditions supporting the main contract, such as education/training requirements for those working on the contract, given that these can be seen as "relating" to the product or service procured. The definition in Article 80 is also widened from the definition in the 2004 Utilities Directive to add "innovation-related" and "employment-related" to social and environmental conditions in the list of allowable considerations, which may hopefully inspire utilities to include such conditions more commonly in the future.

Award Criteria

Issues of innovation and green or social concerns can also be included in the award criteria which are used to evaluate the tenders. This method allows the utility to balance the importance of the particular issue against other relevant issues such as cost and quality, enabling a relatively nuanced consideration of the different concerns. This is, therefore, a particularly good area for consideration of the Europe 2020 aims, enabling them to be balanced against the need for value for money which is equally important for developing economic growth.

The rules relating to award criteria are currently set out in Article 55 of the 2004 Utilities Directive. This allows utilities to award tenders on one of two grounds; lowest price or "most economically advantageous tender" (MEAT). Where MEAT is chosen as the basis of award, Article 55(1)(a) sets out a list of potential considerations such as technical merit and security of supply. Environmental characteristics are expressly included as a potential consideration. There is no mention of either social or innovative concerns but the CJEU held in Case C-513/99, *Concordia Bus Finland v Helsingen Kaupunki* [2002] ECR I-7213 that the list provided in the directive is nonexhaustive, therefore potentially allowing the inclusion of such issues in the award criteria.

Any award criteria included must, however, be "linked to the subject-matter of the contract" (Art. 55(1)(a), 2004 Utilities Directive), raising similar issues therefore as contract conditions. There is some debate over the meaning of "subject-matter" under the current law. Arnould, for example, suggests it should be given a narrow interpretation linking it to the technical specifications of the contract (and therefore suggesting production requirements could not be examined at this stage, see above) (2004, p. 192). Arrowsmith (2009, p. 238) takes a more liberal view, suggesting award criteria can be included for any issue which could lawfully be included as a contract condition and therefore enabling award criteria on a wider range of environmental and social issues. The new Utilities Directive clarifies this confusion by providing a definition of "subject-matter" in Article 82(3) which is also used for contract conditions, and which follows the definition used for technical specifications in Article 60(1). This definition allows award criteria to consider factors which are relevant at any stage of the life cycle, even where those factors do not form part of the material substance of the product. This provides a coherent approach across all stages in the procurement process and is broad enough to cover a wide range of possible considerations (though as with contract conditions, award criteria looking at the supplier's business as a whole will be prevented).

Another notable change to the award criteria system in the new Utilities Directive is the removal of lowest price as a separate criterion such that MEAT is now the only allowable award basis (Art. 82(1)). According to Recital 94 of the new Utilities Directive, the change was made to ensure the award criteria provisions were "presented in as simple and streamlined a way as possible". The notion of MEAT is, however, given an interpretation which makes it clear that financial concerns are still intended to be a major part of tender evaluation. Article 82(2) states that the MEAT should be identified "on the basis of the price or cost, using a cost-effectiveness approach, such as life-cycle costing … and may include the best price-quality ratio." Recital 95 emphasises that it is possible to award a tender "on the basis of either price or cost effectiveness only", making it clear that lowest price is still a viable award option. However, the change of wording of the article presents options such as life-cycle costing and price-quality analysis as the default, with price alone being an exception, which may well encourage the uptake of such forms of tender analysis more commonly and, correspondingly, increase the use of award criteria examining innovative, green and social issues. Supporting this, Article 82(2) has an amended list of suggested criteria which specifically lists social and environmental aspects and innovative characteristics as potentially relevant to quality.

One of the most important changes which will impact particularly on the sustainable growth aim of Europe 2020 is the introduction in Article 83 of a life-cycle costing system. This is specifically mentioned in Article 82(1) as a potential means of determining cost effectiveness. The system sets out two main types of costs which can be could be considered by utilities using the system when relevant; costs borne by the utility (Art. 83(1)(a)) and costs imputed to environmental externalities (Art. 83(1)(b)). The costs borne by the utility cover not only the acquisition costs but also use, maintenance and costs of disposal, which should help to deter contracting entities from choosing a nonsustainable product over a more sustainable option purely due to a lower initial purchase cost. Environmental externalities cover issues such as the cost of pollutant emissions. Article 83(1)(b) provides that these can be included only if their monetary value can be determined and verified in accordance with certain requirements set out in Article 83(2) based around nondiscrimination, transparency and accessibility. These requirements could potentially deter utilities from including the costs of such externalities in their tender evaluation, as they may lack the necessary expertise for determining a satisfactory system. However, Article 83(2)(a) notes that a system for repeated application can be used if it is non-discriminatory, which raises the possibility of having a system externally designed by a qualified body and then used for future tenders by the utilities, reducing the potential difficulties in this area. Overall, together with the inclusion of the costs borne by the utility over the life of the product being more clearly considered, the system in Article 83 appears to be a promising development for sustainable procurement.

Conclusion

The Europe 2020 growth strategy focuses on promoting smart, sustainable, and inclusive growth. This chapter has examined the impact of the proposed reforms to the EU utilities procurement regime on the development of those goals, particularly by improving the inclusion of innovative, green or social concerns in procurement. It can be seen that several of the reforms have the potential to improve the inclusion of such concerns. The most dramatic change is the inclusion of a completely new award procedure, the innovation partnership, which aims to help utilities work closely with a private partner to develop new products or services, and which is clearly linked to the Europe 2020 aim of smart growth. Other more subtle changes may have an equally important impact, however. In particular, the change to the definition of technical specifications which makes it clear that consideration of production and disposal issues is allowable should allow much greater consideration of green issues and boost sustainable growth, and will be well supported by the introduction of specific rules on life-cycle costing in award criteria. Equally, recognition of the benefits of allowing contracting entities to require compliance with certain product labels should ease the administrative burden of considering social and green issues and hopefully increase their use.

There are some issues with the reforms, however. The changes to the requirements for contractual conditions retains the problems the previous law had in examining issues related to a supplier's whole business. This not only prevents useful green and social conditions in such an area but also retains the difficulty in reconciling the law in this area with the ability to look at a supplier as a whole in exclusion/selection criteria. It is also unfortunate that the rules on innovation partnerships are not more precise, especially when regulating the final purchase of the innovative product or service, as this may hinder the actual uptake of the procedure significantly.

Overall, though, the reforms are a positive step, with many of the grey areas in the law clarified and greater flexibility for considering innovative, green and social issues in procurement. The procurement reforms should provide a valuable addition to the EU's overall mission to improve growth as set out in Europe 2020.

Notes

Section 2 of this chapter is based on the overview of EU procurement set out in Aspey, E. (2012) "Labour Considerations in EU Procurement: A Study of UK Utilities" *European Law Review* 37(3): 294–313, at 297–299.

References

Apostal, A. (2012). Pre-commerical procurement in support of innovation: Regulatory effectiveness? *Public Procurement Law, Review, 6,* 213–225.

Arnould, J. (2004). Secondary policies in public procurement: The innovations of the new directive. *Public Procurement Law Review, 13,* 187–197.

Arrowsmith, S. (2005). *The law of public and utilities procurement* (2nd edn.). London: Sweet and Maxwell.

Arrowsmith, S. (2009). Application of the EC treaty and directives to horizontal policies: A critical review. In S. Arrowsmith & P. Kunzlik (Eds.), *Social and environmental policies in EC procurement law: New directives and new directions* (pp. 147–248). Cambridge: Cambridge University Press.

Arrowsmith, S., & Maund, C. (2009). CSR in the utilities sector and the implications of EC procurement policy: A framework for debate. In S. Arrowsmith & P. Kunzlik (Eds.), *Social and environmental policies in ec procurement law: New directives and new directions* (pp. 436–478). Cambridge: Cambridge University Press.

Aspey, E. (2012). Labour considerations in EU procurement: A study of UK utilities. *European Law Review, 37*(3), 294–313.

European Commission. (2001a). *Interpretative communication of the commission on the community law applicable to public procurement and the possibilities for integrating environmental considerations into public procurement* (*COM* (*2001*) *274*). Luxembourg: Publications Office of the European Union.

European Commission. (2001b). *Interpretative Communication of the Commission on the Community Law Applicable to Public Procurement and the Possibilities for Integrating Social Considerations into Public Procurement* (*COM* (*2001*) *566*). Luxembourg: Publications Office of the European Union.

European Commission. (2007). *Pre-commercial procurement: Driving innovation to ensure sustainable high quality public services in Europe, (COM (2007) 799).* Luxembourg: Publications Office of the European Union.

European Commission. (2010). *Europe 2020: A strategy for smart, sustainable and inclusive growth* (*COM* (*2010*) *2020*). Luxembourg: Publications Office of the European Union.

European Commission. (2011a). *Modernising European public procurement to support growth and employment* (*IP/11/1580*). Luxembourg: Publications Office of the European Union.
European Commission. (2011b). *Twelve projects for the 2012 single market: Together for new growth* (*IP/11/469*). Luxembourg: Publications Office of the European Union.
European Commission. (2011c). *Buying green—a handbook on green public procurement* (2nd ed.). Luxembourg: Publications Office of the European Union.
European Parliament. (2013). Proposal for a directive of the European parliament and of the council on procurement by entities operating in the water, energy, transport and postal services sectors (COM (2011) 0895-4 column document, 2011/0439 (COD)). www.europarl.europa.eu/meetdocs/2009_2014/organes/imco/imco_20130905_1500.htm. Accessed 12 June 2014.
Fairtrade. (2014). Fairtrade standards. http://www.fairtrade.net/our-standards.html. Accessed 12 June 2014.
Kunzlik, P. (2009). The procurement of 'green' energy. In S. Arrowsmith & P. Kunzlik (Eds.), *Social and environmental policies in EC procurement law: New directives and new directions* (pp. 369–407). Cambridge: Cambridge University Press.
McCrudden, C. (2007). *Buying social justice: Equality, government procurement and legal change*. Oxford: Oxford University Press.
Pricewaterhouse Coopers, London Economics and Ecorys. (2011). Public procurement in Europe: Cost and effectiveness (report prepared for the European commission). http://ec.europa.eu/internal_market/publicprocurement/docs/modernising_rules/cost-effectiveness_en.pdf. Accessed 12 June 2014.

Eleanor Aspey Ph.D. is a lecturer in law at the School of Law, University of Manchester. Her research interests include administrative law and public procurement, particularly sustainable procurement

Stages of Development Towards Sustainable Public Procurement

Tünde Tátrai

Introduction

In interpreting sustainable public procurement, reference is made to the opinions of several stakeholders in order to underline the fact that market players today apply a substantially broader interpretation of sustainability in public procurement than 10 years ago. In the traditional sense, sustainability in public procurement means the assertion of green, social and economic criteria. We wish to question the commonplace according to which the assertion of sustainability criteria is an indicator of the advanced state of public procurement. We argue this in the sense that when a government or contracting authority is able to implement a truly sustainable public procurement policy, it is then the result of the interaction of several levels of development and a fortunate as well as successful strategy. We use the model by Telgen et al. (2007, p. 20) to demonstrate that truly sustainable public procurement is possible only above a certain level of development.

Accordingly, in the first half of this chapter, by laying the foundations for a theoretical background, the relationship between the level of development of public procurement and sustainability will be established. Then the misunderstandings, deficiencies and weaknesses will be presented, based on international examples, primarily those of the new European Union (EU) directives, owing to which the development of sustainable public procurement can at best be a long-term objective, against a background of legislation being renewed.

T. Tátrai (✉)
Corvinus University of Budapest, Budapest, Hungary
e-mail: tunde.tatrai@uni-corvinus.hu

K. V. Thai (ed.), *International Public Procurement,* Public Administration, Governance and Globalization 14, DOI 10.1007/978-3-319-13434-5_14

Sustainability and the Development of Public Procurement

In a traditional sense, we do understand the social, green and economic criteria of public procurement. This, however, does not mean that everyone attributes the same meaning to the above criteria. The framework of interpretation of sustainable public procurement keeps expanding, which does not mean that the understanding of life-cycle costing or the implications of the joint management of green and social criteria would be fully unambiguous for all. Several researchers point out that, in the course of applying sustainability criteria, attention should be paid to the balance between them (United Nations Environment Programme 2012).

The initiatives, which include public procurement carried out in the interest of sustainable development, the procurement of innovative goods and services or pre-commercial public procurement under the notion of sustainable procurement, have contributed to the broadening of sustainability. The reason behind this is that, from the viewpoint of policy, all these serve some kind of longer-term sustainability and yet frequently have only an obscure relationship with the true sustainability criteria. In their article on innovative public procurement Edler and Georghiou (2007) expressly call attention to the fact that "…a sophisticated risk-management are needed in order to cope with innovations in public services. A new cost-benefit rationale that translates into life-cycle costing and the criteria of the so-called Most Economically Advantageous Tender (MEAT) are needed to replace the lowest initial cost rationale" (Edler and Georghiou 2007, p. 950).

It is therefore not enough to give new names to the methods applied in traditional public procurement procedures; deeper analyses are needed in the course of their application to ensure that the assertion of sustainability criteria carries genuine added value.

The definition of sustainable public procurement is constantly evolving and changing; to get the overall picture, however, the novelties should not be disregarded. The subject matter of innovative public procurement, for instance, is at least as closely tied to that of sustainability as supporting SMEs, whose direct impact of reducing unemployment could even turn the preference given to SMEs into a social criterion. For example, Preuss (2009) handles the preference to SMEs and local companies under the economic criteria. The place of objectives, which are at times handled as social, at other times, as economic objectives, is not unambiguous. The simplification of the question, namely, applying it as a sustainability criterion is not enough. This is what Tátrai and Nyikos (2012) pointed at, in their case study analysing the interaction of objectives applied in public procurement arriving at the conclusion that these objectives frequently extinguish one another, i.e. they fail to reach the consequence for which the legislator built it into the regulatory environment in principle. The theoretical assertion of sustainable policy is therefore prevented by contradictory objectives damaging the perception of the credibility of the entire sustainability issue.

Approaches keep on changing, the subject matter is extending. For instance, in her Spanish case study, Medina-Arnáiz (2010) focuses on integrating gender equality into public procurement. Another good example is Coggburn (2004), who wrote about managerial values through green procurement. Preuss and Walker (2011) discussed the psychological barriers along the road to sustainable development from a public procurement point of view.

The initiatives broadening the above interpretation point out that public procurement itself by enhancing the contribution of the activity to sustainability can become a driver of both ethical and cultural issues and innovation or even economic development. The broad environment of interpretation that is taken as the basis when we analyse the levels of development in public procurement based on the Telgen et al's (2007) model with regard to sustainability. By way of a point of departure, it is worthwhile clarifying that the model intends to demonstrate the levels of development in public procurement whose highest (5-6-7) levels can be the closest levels with regard to sustainable public procurement according to our interpretation.

The different organisational structures, different regulatory, legislative and funding arrangements and different cultures are those aspects, which helped to elaborate a new model about the developments in public procurement.

The original model did not distinguish the distances between the stages, i.e. it did not consider that there were increasingly large leaps between the individual levels or stages of development. In this research our hypothesis was that a thinker who wished to create a higher-standard framework for public procurement would have an increasingly more difficult task. The essence of the seven-stage model is the followings:

Stage 1. Sourcing and delivery of goods and services
Stage 2. Compliance with legislation/regulation
Stage 3. Efficient use of public funds
Stage 4. Accountability
Stage 5. Value for money
Stage 6. Supporting of broader government policy objectives
Stage 7. Delivery of broader government objectives

Further, a few theoretical works related to sustainability selected by us will be identified and positioned within the seven-element model. The heart of this is the question whether sustainability means the path of development taken in the traditional sense, i.e. the more social, efficiency or green aspects are involved in procurement the more sustainable we are. Or, it is worthwhile to follow the logic of the seven-stage model offering a way towards achieving sustainable public procurement? We do not think that sustainable public procurement would presuppose fully developed, ethical, efficient, flexible and perfect public procurement environment but we do think that presumably in a cultural sense there is a strong relationship between the sustainable public procurement aspects of the individual levels and the maturity of public procurement in a state.

Stage 1. Sourcing and Delivery of Goods and Services
It is in the case of the first level that we can speak about an activity where the contracting authority would at all like to provide goods and services on time. In other words, we presume that genuine public procurement activity is taking place under relatively well organised conditions.

Stage 2. Compliance with Legislation
Compliance with legislation is conditional upon having the appropriate legal regulations at hand which can be complied with because it provides an efficient, transparent and innovative environment for the contracting authority. A good example of this is the opinion of McCrudden (2007).

"The use of public procurement to achieve increased compliance and its relationship to law is complex and multi-faceted. Whilst public procurement policy has assiduously tracked government policy more generally, government procurement law has generally lagged behind changes in policy developments, leaving lawyers and policy makers to either interpret the existing law to conform to the changing policy preferences, to change the existing law to reflect these preferences, or to restrict linking public procurement with the delivery of these policy preferences".

The policy level and the legislative level are built on one another according to McCrudden (2007), they cannot be envisaged without one another; a poor legislative work results ab ovo in a tremendous backlog for the legal environment.

Stage 3. Efficient Use of Public Funds
At the next level, available public funds are spent in the most efficient way possible. Parikka-Alhola and Nissinen (2012) brilliantly match the relationship between environmental aspects and the economically advantageous tender. Although their article points far beyond the issue of the efficient use of public funds, yet case studies unambiguously demonstrate that in order for a contracting authority to apply green criteria and the evaluation criteria related to the most economically advantageous tender, it is necessary that its set of conditions, the environment of public procurement, should ab ovo be about efficient use of public money. In order to be able to speak about life-cycle costing or green cost calculation, there must be transparent and efficient methods of spending public money available. Due to this, levels 3 and 4 presuppose the application of best value for money. That is, the availability of the appropriate information (Parikka-Alhola and Nissinen 2012, p. 44), the use of well-trained experts and transparent, unambiguous planning methodology are needed in the course of spending public moneys for the high-standard implementation of spending as well as the proper planning and administration of procurement. The article addresses the importance of developing the evaluation criteria, the clarification of the methodology and of the issue of weights in detail which can take place only if the purchaser knows what it has money for, how much, what is its degree of freedom in the course of spending its budget. The efficient use of public funds does not mean a perfect budgeting at government and contracting authority level but it does mean a secure, unambiguous environment also providing flexibility and freedom for a well prepared contracting authority where it can carry out its activities.

Stage 4. Accountability

The next level is that of transparency which presupposes the availability of as much and as useful information as possible both at government level for the policy maker and at the contracting authority's level. It is not surprising that the issue of accountability arises in relation to sustainability. Preuss (2009, p. 220) stated that "the strategic and transparent integration and achievement of a public sector organisation's social, environmental and economic goals in the systematic coordination of key inter-organisational commercial processes for improving the long-term performance of the organisation and the territorial base for which it is democratically accountable for, in line with overarching public policy priorities".

Incidentally, the article using the theoretical background of supply chain management highlights the role of transparency as well as the advantages based on a broader interpretation of procurement, namely: "the dissemination of sustainability, information within and beyond the local authority" (Preuss 2009, p. 219). Publicity, strategy, culture and risk management are regarded factors which support the development of public sector SCM.

Stage 5. Value for Money

An efficient and accountable public procurement environment is the precondition for any contracting authority to assert the best value for money criterion at the next level. In his article, Dimitri's (2013) point of departure is that the shift from a price-based set of evaluation criteria to the evaluation criteria of the most economically advantageous tender with a view to economic efficiency points towards best value for money (BVM). According to Dimitri (2013, p. 150), the reason is that "effective procurement can be a fundamental support to pursue fiscal, industrial and innovation policies by best employing the available financial resources effective procurement could be a crucial driver for the socio-economic development and growth of a state".

The application of the appropriate BVM approach is conditional upon good preparation and monitoring, and the latter is, as a matter of fact, a condition of the accountability condition at Level 4. The life-cycle perspective closely related to the subject matter is also discussed; understandably, an accurate specification, however, of the way in which a contracting authority is able to handle its preferences is a matter of designing public procurement. One of the most interesting set of issues in the economic aspect of sustainability is BVM whose genuine application requires much more penetrating preparation, specification of preference and planning provided that is what the contracting authority wants. Parikka-Alhola and Nissinen (2012) call attention to this when underlining in particular that "…due to the purchaser's preferences, not all of the relevant aspects may be taken into account or the weightings for different aspects may not relate to the true impact of such aspects. For example the durability, guarantees, opportunities for repairs and service upgrading opportunities, flexibility, which contributes to the environmental impact question but are not environmental impacts as such" (Parikka-Alhola and Nissinen 2012, p. 44).

So, the application of BVM means the first level of development where sustainability criteria can genuinely and unambiguously be met but their application can be rather multi-layered. Just because the MEAT criteria are applied, it is not yet certain the BVM methodology will be asserted, because all this needs to be aligned with the contents of the contract. Or, to start out from the previous example, just because a purchaser applies environmental criteria, it is not yet certain that the activity will have meaningful consequences which could be rated also from an environmental point of view. BVM is therefore a good basis for applying sustainability criteria, i.e. it is from this level of development that one can truly take into account the elements and consequences of sustainable public procurement.

Stage 6. Support for Broader Government Policy Objectives
The next level is when sustainability matures to such importance at governmental level that, as a policy objective, its application could bring advantages for the contracting authority. For this, however, it is necessary to make the objectives which the government intends to support unambiguous at this level of development. If ideas are formulated only at general level, contracting authorities will not understand exactly what target groups need to be preferred and for what reason, thus the government message can easily be misinterpreted.

McCrudden (2004) writes about how to use public procurement to achieve social outcomes. He describes the linkage of procurement to labour standards, international human rights norms, gender equality and employment. He states that we have to clarify "social procurement practices as a basis on which future legal and policy analyses can build" (McCrudden 2004, p. 266). If it is not clarified what we mean by social criteria, for instance, would we include support to SMEs and through it an increase in employment, we cannot even speak about a policy demand even in a general sense and the regulatory environment will also not be appropriate for those applying it, because they will not know which social criteria enjoy priority and which are the ones that do not. McCrudden (2004) also substantiates that the relationship between the legal and policy aspects and their juxtaposition are the conditions of ensuring sustainable public procurement.

Stage 7. Delivery of Broader Government Objectives
The highest level means the peak of the model where, theoretically, sustainable public procurement is fully implemented, because public procurement itself mediates the government's objectives. A good example of this is the article published by Kattel and Lember (2010) under International Public Procurement Conference 4 (2010), which handles public procurement as an industrial policy tool. The question is that "is it an option for developing countries? Is it advisable for developing countries to use public procurement efforts for development and should more developing countries join the WTO GPA?" (Kattel and Lember 2010, p. 368). Researchers believe that "using public procurement for development assumes high levels of policy capacity" (Kattel and Lember 2010, p. 368).

But there is a consequence, namely, that it is complicated for the developing countries to benefit from public procurement for innovation. The article by Kattel and Lember (2010) that triggered heated debate wished to outline an opportunity for breakthrough for developing countries concerning promoting innovation and development. They suggested four strategies for countries to design and implement public procurement policies in the context of economic development.

1. Public procurement as a level playing field, where the main goal is transparency, non-discrimination and free competition.
2. Discriminatory public procurement which is based on protectionism.
3. Public procurement for innovation where the competition is dependent on existing market competitiveness.
4. The soft public procurement measures option focuses on the policy capacity of the government and it can be used easily to start the learning-by-doing process.

Another good example is based on the article by Fisher (2013, p. 2) about the power of purchase, who asks questions about how sustainable development is to be achieved through procurement functions. She recognises that "sustainable public procurement is a strategic concern and political project" (p. 3). Fisher (2013) calls attention to the need to strike a balance between the objectives set; similarly, Tátrai and Nyikos (2012) also addresses the importance of exploring the contradictions between the objectives applied in relation to this aspect. Finally, Fisher effectively declares: "It is all too easy to focus on rules, regulations and legal technicalities; while obviously essential, they [sustainable development goals] need to be part of a bigger picture about sustainable development to enable government to achieve better things through sustainable public procurement" (p. 6).

The theoretical background is given for slightly improving the model by Telgen et al. (2007). The essence of the improvement is that in actual fact the model can also be evaluated from a sustainability point of view (Fig. 1).

The above point out that if approaching sustainability from another dimension, from another aspect, it can be defined that this is the buzzword capable of dynamising the development of public procurement and moving on to the next stages of development where we can have genuinely sustainable public procurement. Telgen et al. (2007) cited examples at Levels 5-6-7 which presuppose the existence of a legal and economic environment for public procurement that represents a higher standard and is carefully considered.

All this, however, does not mean that otherwise the non-sustainability criteria also develop the same way. Moreover, it is necessary to interpret the assertion of ethical forms of behaviour as part of sustainability. The distances between the individual grades or levels of development are increasingly large as they require changes in attitudes and much more extensive ways of thinking. That is why we modified or rather slightly supplemented the model by Telgen et al. (2007) by gradually increasing the individual scales thereby indicating that stepping on to the higher levels of development requires major changes in attitudes and, accordingly, it is more difficult to achieve such levels. In our view, therefore, any improvement in levels of development is more and more difficult.

At the same time, we accept the assumption that if we wish to make our public procurement genuinely sustainable, it will presumably be necessary to go through

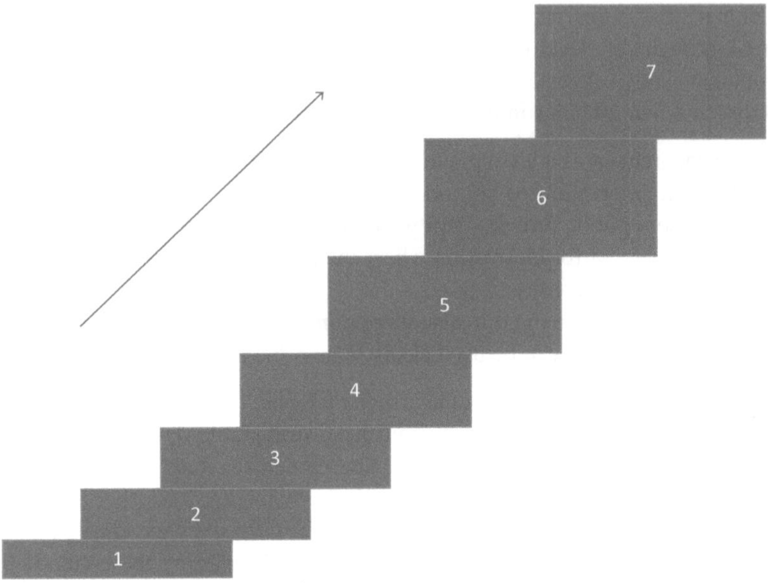

Fig. 1 Seven-stage model for sustainable public procurement. (Source: Based on Telgen et al. (2007))

the individual levels of development and will not immediately be able to conduct sustainable procedures by specifying objectives not in the traditional sense and including a couple of social or green elements. On that basis, a procedure which includes a green evaluation criterion cannot be regarded as sustainable because in order for this to be the case, a precondition should be met: generally, the maturity of the available public procurement regulatory system, the transparency of the assertion of green criteria and the enforcement of the value for money principle. That is why the understanding the logic of the model is essential, which is not yet shown for example in European statistics. It is unclear whether the statistical data concerning the appearance of green or social criteria in public procurement are truly meaningfully utilised or it is the contracting authority itself that sticks of an issue, such as the employment of unemployed strata using this as an evaluation criterion without monitoring performance to see whether the bidder really employs unemployed people.

In his article, Hettne (2013) holds a similar view: "Hence, the proposed Directives on public procurement show a possible way to foster innovation, improve the environment, public health and social conditions, but should not be seen as a particularly simple or highly efficient way. Sustainable procurement seems rather to be a complementary instrument to other policies in their field, which should be integrated in the overall Union policy" (Hettne 2013, p. 40).

Methods

Following the presentation of the theoretical background, we intend to evaluate the guidance needed for the achievement of the individual development levels primarily with respect to the new EU directives. Choosing from other international examples, we call attention to the environment of interpretation in which the final text evolved in the course of the enactment of the directives and what sort of consequences this will imply later.

Guide to Sustainability

The above shed some light on the new directions that can be detected in the interpretation of sustainable public procurement. While searching for new ways, we do not claim that every idea should be channelled into everyday practice. A conclusion, however, can be drawn. It is not enough to operate with phrases and goal identifications, it is much more important to develop the concrete environment of interpretation and not only at policy level well before the legislator creates it.

Let us review a few international examples concerning the interpretation of sustainability as well as what was done to assist in everyday practice and to interpret the law.

Let us take the UNEP definition as our point of departure: "Sustainable Procurement is a process whereby organisations meet their needs for goods, services, works and utilities in a way that achieves value for money on a whole life basis in terms of Procurement generating benefits not only to the organisation, but also to society and the economy, whilst minimising the appropriate balance between the 3 pillars of sustainable development i.e. economic, social and environmental" (United Nations Environment Programme 2012).

What makes this definition interesting? As UNEP has set up a separate guideline to ensure practical implementation. The guideline which supplements its set of rules includes separate interpreting provisions and accurate definitions. It addresses the application of eco-labels, contract management, the importance of monitoring just as much as the objectives and scope of sustainable public procurement policy. There is a separate part on training because it is exactly these added values which enhance the importance of assisting interpretation. If the procurement manager in everyday practice understands why a policy is born, how the procedure is to be administered and what kind of staff must be available, the purchaser will be able to follow the rules and implement the objectives specified therein.

Following the UNEP example, it is worth mentioning the revised World Trade Organization (WTO) Government Procurement Agreement which does not really show any substantial innovation. Yet, according to Tosoni (2013, p. 47), the "importance of the changes introduced in some key provisions should not be underestimated".

For example, technical specifications to promote conservation of natural resources or the protection of the environment can be used based on Art. I(u) (i) "technical specification means a tendering requirement that lays down the characteristics of goods or services to be procured, including quality, performance, safety and dimensions, or the processes and methods for their production or provision" (World Trade Organization 2014a).

According to Tosoni's point of view "GPA has clearly missed the opportunity to make a significant step forward for sustainable procurement" (Tosoni 2013, p. 48). For instance, the qualification criteria limit the possibility to promote sustainable development through public procurement. At the same time, WTO works on the Work Programme on Sustainable Procurement that should offer solutions and guidance on how to devise procurement procedures and performance more sustainable, and how to draw up sustainable development objectives in technical specification, qualification, evaluation and performance in detail.

It is expected that WTO shall follow a similar road, i.e. it intends to provide detailed assistance for the interpretation of its renewed, although not much altered set of rules. WTO has lagged somewhat behind in terms of the renewal of sustainability criteria; nevertheless, a separate Work Programme is expected to be developed on sustainable procurement and a different one for SMEs. It should be noted that a separate work programme is in the making on providing statistical data (World Trade Organization 2014b), which incidentally will serve as the basis for subsequent policy formation and with respect to which the EU set of regulations is lagging behind seriously (World Trade Organization 2011).

The EU Case

The new EU directives were adopted on 11 February 2014, whose sustainability aspects are summarised briefly based on the preamble. This reveals what goals and what subject matters are to be understood under sustainability based on the policy. Initially, the revision was undertaken for the following reasons:

The revision should "underpin a balanced policy which fosters demand for environmentally sustainable, socially responsible and innovative goods, services and works. This revision should also result in simpler and more flexible procurement procedures for contracting authorities and provide easier access for companies, especially SMEs" (European Commission, p. iii).

The renewal of the directives was preceded by serious preparation which made *inter alia* statistical data available on the basis of which it should be possible in principle to draw conclusions concerning the sustainable public procurement status of the individual member states. The following data should be underlined as examples:

…most (56 %) contracting authorities or entities were aware of their national action plans for green public procurement. The level of awareness in the UK, Norway and the Netherlands is above 80 %. In Sweden, Slovenia, Denmark, Cyprus, France, Belgium and Lithuania awareness ranges from 72 to 60 % (European Commission 2011, p. 80).

From a monitoring point of view, all this does not constitute green procedures; it is at best capable of indicating the European situation. Perhaps this can be regarded the greatest weakness of the stage of preparation, namely, that the new directives had to be drafted on the basis of few and frequently unrelated data or data of uncertain meaning. When there are no adequate data and sufficient information, it is not possible to achieve sustainable public procurement even in principle on the basis of the seven-stage model. Before drawing this conclusion, there is one more aspect that is worth calling attention to. In the course of preparation, the interaction of certain green, social and innovative criteria was also discussed, of which the evaluation report contained an expressly interesting summary (European Commission 2011).

The above statement is highly interesting, it calls attention to the fact that—based on preliminary surveys—many countries also have broader sustainable development policies which impose some environmental as well as social or innovation considerations on procurement at one or more level of public administration. Theoretical knowledge, the awareness of the close relationship between the criteria was given in order that the renewal of the directives takes place on an adequate theoretical basis. In spite of this, the output fails to show this.

The preamble to the directives refers to the Europe 2020 strategy several times, which is set out in the Commission Communication of 3 March 2010 entitled "Europe 2020, a strategy for smart, sustainable and inclusive growth". The strategy refers to public procurement in traces; we can see them on eight occasions, sometimes in relation to innovation, sometimes in relation to efficient public spending (see Table 1). No detailed information is, however, given on sustainable public procurement.

The directive does not include definitions; it refers to the subject matter of sustainability in relation to innovation and efficiency. The text mingles sustainable development and sustainable growth as goal definitions. Policy-level ideas fail to tie the details of the regulations of the subject matter leaving it to the discretion of the reader whether he/she can find the relationship between innovative partnership and sustainability, to cite an example. Or will it be seen whether the appearance of ethical elements have an added value in terms of the new directives on sustainability (new conflict of interest definition).

From this aspect, the directives formulate sustainability at European level simply and in many ways in an unworthy manner. It is not clear how the legislator intends to render European public procurement sustainable, whether it means sustainable development by it, or whether it regards innovation as a part of it. For the time being, we see an approximate solution at policy level but the regulatory environment does not help much in becoming the ground for ensuring sustainable development. If this is not there, additional levels of development can be hard to achieve which was detailed in the part on the theoretical background.

Of the few concrete issues, it is worth highlighting that the European directives envisage the interpretation of sustainability in a green, social, efficiency and innovation environment. All the help they provide in concretising it is that they indicate

Table 1 Topics included in broader policies integrating other policy objectives with procurement. (Source: European Commission (2011))

Specific topics	Environment	Social	Innovation
Anti-social dumping		x	
Biodiversity	x		
Chemical treatment	x		
Climate change, reduction of CO_2 emissions	x		
CSR (including human rights and ILO Core Labour Standards)	x	x	x
Energy efficiency and management, use of renewable energy	x		
Environmental technology	x		x
Green IT	x		x
High-tech, research and technology			x
Integration of people with disabilities		x	
Promotion of SMEs		x	
Sustainable development	x	x	x
Sustainable economic growth and employment	x	x	x
Sustainable farming and food	x	x	
Sustainable production and consumption	x	x	x
Sustainable timber	x	x	
Sustainable transport	x		
Waste management	x		

that it should not be mandatory to apply the sustainability criteria. For the time being, that is all the assistance for application.

The reserved contracts, which do not constitute anything novel from a social point of view, or the application of labels affecting both environmental and social elements or the reference to contract award criteria in relation to green and social criteria cannot be regarded as sufficient results. At the same time, it is a right approach that the issue of sustainability appears in relation to performance also:

"Article 70 Conditions for performance of contracts: Contracting authorities may lay down special conditions relating to the performance of a contract, provided that they are linked to the subject-matter of the contract within the meaning of Article 67(3) and indicated in the call for competition or in the procurement documents. Those conditions may include economic, innovation-related, environmental, social or employment-related considerations" (European Commission 2014).

The possibility to use looser rules with regard to social services reflects a different logic. There are two issues that should be underlined as concrete, well definable novelties in relation to sustainability: life-cycle costing (Article 68) and innovative partnerships (Article 31). The directive (European Commission 2014), however, fails to solve a number of practical problems occurring in the course of the application of life-cycle costing, for instance, how the contracting authority should make its calculations in establishing estimated value, but it does contain a list of costs, that is, specific items.

As to innovative partnerships—presumably according to the directive, one of the elements of sustainability is innovation—the question arises that if the contracting authority and the bidder develop something together and then the contracting authority requires the partner to compete again, why should the partner compete against others if so far they have been working on the joint project together. The directives mention PCP, i.e. pre-commercial procurement, as a positive example, in spite of the fact that there has only been negligible experience accumulating concerning PCP in Europe. The new type of procedure can be, for the time being, regarded as something unique, a novelty that really wishes to incorporate a novelty of procedural law and through this new ideas as well. The initiatives are praiseworthy, but the legislator is presumably going to meet additional information for implementation by the member states.

Successful sustainability is conditional upon not mixing growth with development and being innovative with the use of labels. The definition of sustainability criteria is needed with regard to technical content, eligibility criteria, evaluation criteria, the content of the contract and the condition of performance in order that market agents understand what is needed in order to administer their procedures in accordance with the sustainability criteria. The new directives address these elements only in part and contain genuine novelties only to a minor extent.

It could also serve demonstrative purposes if the subject matter of sustainability was handled in a uniform manner and not with varying content. The criteria applied in the text define the green, social and economic elements in a narrow sense as independent objectives rejecting even the simple interrelation that these objectives should also be aligned as their joint application could even lead to the levelling off of the objectives. The evaluation report drafted in the course of the preparation of the directives contained examples of such interrelations. We find it wanting that there is no interrelation between supporting SMEs and a decline in unemployment, there is no relationship between ethical public procurement and efficiency, the value-for-money approach and life-cycle costing. The theoretical background is relatively clear, which may provide a great deal of assistance to the legislator. If, however, there is no genuine assistance to those applying the law, it will not be possible to obtain the information needed for the individual member states to reach higher levels of sustainability. There are member states that will exceed the environment of interpretation in the directive taking their own experiences as the point of departure, but there are member states also that will expressly take the directives as the basis when managing the issue of sustainability.

In the course of analysing the sustainable elements of the directive, it is worth making a few statements to conceive what a European member state having to implement the directive needs to do.

- It will not remain at the level of principles.
- It will not wish to introduce trumped up social rules, for instance, try direct disbursement to subcontractors, although the directives contain this.
- It will not permit that innovation partnership should mean only that the contracting authority need not deal with conflict of interest if it wants to co-operate with an innovative partner.

- It will not allow that contracting authorities apply the employment of the unemployed as the only evaluation criterion which would make their procedure "social".
- It will not believe that requiring labelling systems would be amply sufficient for appearance in sustainability statistics.

The above ideas are only of an indicative value and wish to call attention to the misunderstandings and errors that can be conceived in the knowledge of the new European public procurement directives. We agree with Tosoni (2013, p. 48) that "further clarification is needed about how to practically implement sustainable procurement practices that are consistent both with the new Directives and GPA is welcomed".

Summary

In presenting literature, we specified several milestones which substantially exceed the interpretation of sustainable public procurement taken in the traditional sense. Based on the seven-stage model of Telgen et al. (2007) aimed at specifying the stages of development in public procurement, we establish that there was a great need for the appropriate development of the environment of interpreting sustainability in order that contracting authorities or the legislators be able to make progress in the course of implementation, that they should apply the value for money approach so that they should operate in an accountable and transparent manner and use public procurement gradually for better things. It is not possible to create sustainable procedures simply by applying a green or social criterion because the evaluation criteria, the technical content, the contractual obligations should serve more than just demonstrative purposes. The goal is to render the entire procurement process sustainable at the level of contracting authorities and to raise public procurement to the level of policy and its inclusion in sustainability strategies at government and international level.

Short of this, the seven-stage model pointed out that through the poor management of sustainability at regulatory level, ab ovo substantially less can be achieved because if it is not clear what a legislator wishes to achieve and in what manner, the solutions of those applying the law can only achieve levels 3-4-5 in a mixed way and these are the levels which contain some elements of sustainability. In our view, even the European Member States having an advanced procurement culture would only be able to reach stage 7, i.e. the level of sustainable procurement where public procurement genuinely becomes the engine of economic growth if they set up their own guidelines, help the contracting authorities and develop their practice taking into account their cultural differences and data. Every European Member State must pay the price for the weakness of a uniform public procurement policy. If therefore the foundations set by legal regulation are weak, high-standard performance cannot be expected, no matter how the same text is implemented by the member states or contracting authorities try to understand it.

References

Coggburn, J. D. (2004). Achieving managerial values through green procurement? *Public Performance and Managerial Review, 28*(2), 236–258.
Dimitri, N. (2013). Best value for money in procurement. *Journal of Public Procurement, 13*(2), 149–175.
Edler, J., & Georghiou, L. (2007). Public procurement and innovation—resurrecting the demand side. *Research Policy, 36,* 949–963.
European Commission. (2011). *Evaluation report impact and effectiveness of EU public procurement legislation.* [Online]. Available at http://ec.europa.eu/internal_market/publicprocurement/docs/modernising_rules/er853_1_en.pdf. Accessed 1 March 2014.
European Commission. (2014). Directive 2014/24/EU of the European Parliament and of the Council of 26 February 2014 on Public Procurement and Repealing Directive 2004/18/EC. Brussels, Belgium: European Commission.
Fisher, E. (2013). The power of purchase: Addressing sustainability through public procurement. European Procurement and Public Private Partnerships. *Law Review, 13*(1), 2–7.
Hettne, J. (2013). Sustainable public procurement and the single market—is there a conflict of interest? *European Procurement and Public Private Partnerships, 13*(1), 31–40.
Kattel, R., & Lember, V. (2010). Public procurement as an industrial policy tool: An option for developing countries? *Journal of Public Procurement, 10*(3), 368–404.
McCrudden, C. (2004). Using public procurement to achieve social outcomes. *Natural Resources Forum, 28,* 257–267.
McCrudden, C. (2007). *Corporate social responsibility and public procurement. research paper series.* (Working Paper No 9/2006). Oxford, UK: University of Oxford Faculty of Law Legal Studies.
Medina-Arnáiz, R. (2010). Integrating gender equality in public procurement: The Spanish case. *Journal of Public Procurement, 10*(4), 540–563.
Parikka-Alhola, K., & Nissinen, A. (2012). Environmental impacts and the most economically advantageous tender in public procurement. *Journal of Public Procurement, 12*(1), 43–80.
Preuss. L. (2009). Addressing sustainable development through public procurement: The case of local government. *Supply Chain Management: An International Journal, 14*(3), 213–223.
Preuss, L., & Walker, H. (2011). Psychological barriers in the road to sustainable development: Evidence from public sector procurement. *Public Administration, 89*(2), 493–521.
Tátrai, T., & Nyikos, G. (2012). The uses and abuses of public procurement in hungary. In G. L. Albano, K. F. Snider, & K. V. Thai (Eds.), *Charting a course in public procurement innovation and knowledge sharing* (pp. 29–53). Boca Raton: Pracademics Press.
Telgen, J., Harland, C., & Kinght, L. (2007). Public procurement in perspective. In L. Knight, C. Harland, J. Telgen, K. V. Thai, G. Callender, & K. McKen (Eds.), *Public procurement: International cases and commentary* (pp. 20–22). London: Routledge.
Tosoni, L. (2013). The impact of the revised WTO government procurement agreement on the EU procurement rules from a sustainability perspective. *European Procurement and Public Private Partnerships Law Review, 13*(1), 41–48.
United Nations Environment Programme. (2012). SPP implementation guidelines glossary and acronyms sustainable public procurement implementation guidelines—introducing UNEP's approach. Paris, France: UNEP DTIE Sustainable Consumption and Production Branch. [Online]. Available at www.unep.fr/scp. Accessed 1 March 2014.
World Trade Organization. (2011). The re-negotiation of the agreement on government procurement. [Online]. Available at http://www.wto.org/english/tratop_e/gproc_e/negotiations_e.htm. Accessed 1 March 2014.
World Trade Organization. (2014a). Agreement on government procurement. [Online]. Available at http://www.wto.org/english/tratop_e/gproc_e/gp_gpa_e.htm. Accessed 1 March 2014.
World Trade Organization. (2014b). Work programme on the collection and reporting of statistical data. [Online]. Available at http://www.wto.org/english/tratop_e/gproc_e/negotiations_e.htm. Accessed 1 March 2014.

Tünde Tátrai graduated as economist and lawyer, works currently as an associate professor in the Corvinus University of Budapest, Institute of Business Economics. She teaches electronic procurement, ethical procurement and public procurement.

Policy Implementation of Sustainable Public Procurement in China

Conghu Wang and Xiaoming Li

Introduction

Procurement is essential to the success of the whole supply chain (SC) because the purchased materials are the bases for any subsequent SC members to work on. Companies tend to focus on their own economic performance when dealing with purchasing (Simpson et al. 2002; Monczka et al. 2009). This typical behavior is understandable because companies have to spend their own money mostly for their own economic good in today's tough markets. In other words, only the shareholders have a legal claim on the purpose of the firm they own (Emiliani 2001; Weiss 2003), although the general public is a stakeholder (Freeman 1984), affected by the environmental and social achievement (or damage) of a firm. Environmental and social responsibilities can be viewed as externalities for companies in the private sector.

On the other hand, public procurement (PP) spends public money by government agencies to serve the general public. The general public is not only stakeholder but also shareholder (i.e., pays tax to contribute and own public money). Environmental and social responsibilities thus become internalities in PP. Moreover, as the most influential purchaser in a national economy, spending typically 15–30% of gross domestic product (GDP), the government can drive the market for sustainable products and services through its procurement policies and purchasing practices (United Nations 2012). Therefore, sustainability is constantly promoted and regulated by countries all over the world as shown for example in the Brundtland Report (1987). In particular, sustainable PP (SPP) has become a trend in new policy implementations (e.g., United Nations 2002).

C. Wang (✉)
School of Public Administration and Policy, Renmin University of China, Beijing, China
e-mail: wangconghu@ruc.edu.cn

X. Li
Department of Business Administration, Tennessee State University, Nashville, USA
e-mail: xli1@tnstate.edu

K. V. Thai (ed.), *International Public Procurement,* Public Administration, Governance and Globalization 14, DOI 10.1007/978-3-319-13434-5_15

On sustainable development, The United Nations Environment Programme (UNEP) and the United Nations Department of Economic and Social Affairs (UN-DESA) have thus far identified seven task forces, one of which is SPP (United Nations 2012). In essence, SPP extends the traditional focus on economy to include environment (i.e., green PP) and society (i.e., blue PP), as in the sustainable supply chain management literature. This triple bottom line in SPP indicates that PP provides legitimate value for money; PP covers environmental protection, including energy saving, water saving, material saving, air pollution control, recycling, and appropriate disposal; and PP protects human rights and employee safety, supports small- and medium-sized enterprises (SMEs) and community equity, and prevents labor discrimination.

Furthermore, different countries and regions must construct different public management systems because of their diverse political systems, distinct sociocultural forces, and various economic developments (McCourt 2008; Commission on Growth and Development 2008). This is particularly true for a developing country like China, given the fact that China has its own unique political and economic systems (Zhao et al. 2006). Research on how to promote SPP in China is warranted.

Thus, the purpose of our research is simple: promoting sustainable development by China's PP (CPP). Our research questions are fundamental "what" and "how" questions. Specifically, our contribution is threefold: We first summarize a suitable policy implementation model for CPP. Second, we develop central hypotheses for congruent implementation in China's sustainable PP (CSPP) and collect empirical feedback and evaluation from practice to prove them. In particular, we investigate policies, relationships between implementation agencies, and the purchasing process in CSPP. Third, we provide managerial and theoretical implications.

Literature Review

Implementation Theory

Implementation theory has always been focused on the Western Hemisphere, which accounts for close to 90% of all publications (Saetren 2005). As implementation research has evolved over the past 40 years, two schools of thought have emerged: top-down and bottom-up perspectives (e.g., Hill and Hupe 2002). The top-down perspective is "policy-centered" and assumes that policymakers can specify policy goals and set up certain mechanisms for successful implementation (e.g., Palumbo and Calista 1990, p. 13; Hill and Hupe 2002, pp. 41–51). Research in industrialized countries indicates that for congruent operation, the top-down implementation should emphasize the limitation of the number of links, centralization, and goal clarity (Pressman and Wildavsky 1973; Van Meter and Van Horn 1975; Mazmanian and Sabatier 1983): The longer the causality chains, the more numerous the reciprocal relationships among the links and the more complex implementation becomes. It is also more likely that policy goals become diluted and distorted. Moreover, centralization is a key factor. More direct lines of authority foster greater policy commitment, attention to rules, and adherence. Supervision and control can be exercised more straightforwardly when the relationship between formulator and implementer resembles a one-to-one relationship. Policy goals are supposed to be formulated in a way as uncontested as possible, clearly defined, and not too difficult to operationalize.

However, the top-down perspective draws the following major criticisms. First, the model either ignores or tries to eliminate the political aspects of implementation by treating it as a purely administrative process (e.g., Berman 1978). Second, the prescription nature fails to recognize implementation realities with multiple goals, vague language, and complex scenarios (May 2003). Third, top-downers neglect the reality of policy modification and distortion at the hands of street-level implementers, who typically are experts with better knowledge of true problems (Berman 1978; Elmore 1980).

These major criticisms on the top-down perspective cause the development of bottom-up perspective. The bottom-up perspective instead focuses on individuals and their behaviors, and makes the street-level bureaucrats central to the implementation (Howlett et al. 2009). The bottom-uppers also direct attention to the formal and informal relationships constituting the policymaking and implementing subsystems (Hill and Hupe 2002; Howlett et al. 2009). But, the bottom-up perspective does not provide satisfactory solutions, as its rejection towards the authority of policymakers is questionable in the standard political theory. It is also difficult to predict why coping strategies occur and what and how they vary.

Both the top-down perspective and the bottom-up perspective have valid arguments but also tend to ignore the portion of the implementation reality explained by the other. Some synthesizers have attempted to combine both perspectives. Key contributions include the backward-mapping approach (Elmore 1980), the ambiguity and conflict model (Matland 1995), and some iterative approaches (e.g., Thomas and Grindle 1990). But, there is no single comprehensive synthesis or unifying approach (Matland 1995), or too many case studies, not enough validation and replication (Goggin 1986).

China's Policy Implementation Model

China has a unitary state system, meaning that the central government has legitimate authority and credibility while local governments obey the central government (National People's Congress 1982). Moreover, the central government controls most tax revenue (Xiang 2002), and the Chinese culture features a strong authoritarian ideology (Sun and Yu 2010). So, policy implementation in China follows a top-down model (e.g., Palumbo and Calista 1990; Hill and Hupe 2002).

Under this top-down regulatory model, CPP has clear hierarchical tiers from top to bottom: central government, province, and prefecture-level city. Then, at each tier, the municipal government sets up the environment and resource for its administrative agency, including a supervisory agency (Wang and Li 2014). The separation between administration and supervision in CPP is required by the

Government Procurement Law of the People's Republic of China (GPL) (National People’s Congress 2002). Last, the administrative agency manages the whole purchasing process. Figure 1 summarizes the current policy implementation model with four layers for CPP; here the arrow shows the flow of influence.

However, due to unique reform and open policies, the development of CPP relies more on practices, also known as “crossing the river by feeling the stones” (Deng 1993, p. 224). CPP started after 1979 when China’s economy began to transit from central planning to market. Currently, characterized as dynamic and transient, institutions and mechanisms are still in the process of gradual improvement. Numerous organizational models for PP exist in different regions across China (Wang and Li 2014). First, the separation between administration and supervision is required by GPL but with divergent practices. This is mainly manifested in the various affiliations of procurement centers: financial departments, government agencies, state-owned asset management sectors, etc. Second, supervisory organizations are dispersed. In some places, construction projects, office supplies and services, and pharmaceuticals and medical devices belong to different procurement departments and different supervisory agencies; some areas are gradually integrating all PP into a single trading platform and considering a unified monitoring. Third, organizational structures and processes are different. In some places, the organizational structures are determined by the purchasing processes; other places set up organizational structures and processes in accordance with the goods and services purchased.

Moreover, transparency, one key element in PP, remainsa daunting task in Asia (Kim 2008). Transparency is a principle, a goal, and a tool because the publicized open procedures allow a wide variety of stakeholders to scrutinize public officials’

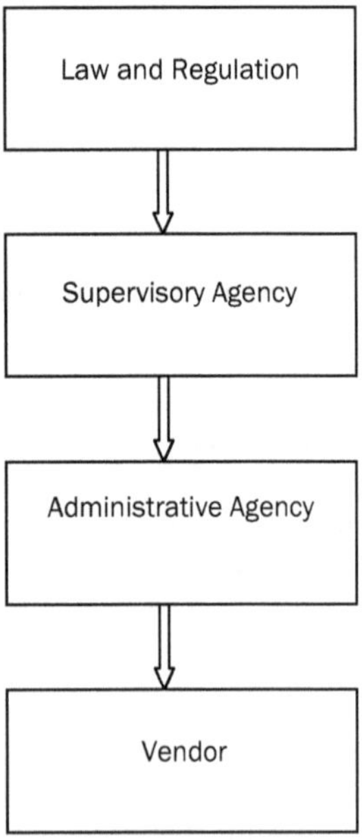

Fig. 1 A policy implementation model for CPP

and contractors' performance and decisions. This scrutiny helps keep officials and contractors accountable (OECD 2007) and serves as a vital ingredient for corruption control (Transparency International 2006), which is desperately needed in present-day China (Wang 2006). Although there has been an increase in data exposure of PP activities on the Internet, the scope is still very limited to online information bulletins and downloadable forms only (Wang 2006).

CSPP

To meet the need for CSPP, some laws and regulations have been issued to promote sustainable practice. Article 9 in GPL states that government procurement should endorse economic and societal development goals: protecting environment, supporting undeveloped and ethnic minority regions, and assisting SMEs. In the green PP, China's Ministry of Finance (MOF) and the National Development and Reform Commission (NDRC) jointly issued *the Opinions of Implementing Government Procurement of Energy Saving Products* in December 2004, giving these products certain priority; then, MOF and the Ministry of Environmental Protection (MEP) published a list of green product inventory in October 2006. Products in the list were required to meet the energy-saving standards and the environmental protection measures set by MEP. In March 2007 and August 2008, the list was expanded from 14 to 19 categories, from 444 to 760 enterprises; from 2979 to 7159 product models (Qiao and Wang 2011).

The blue PP, Article 36 of the Law on the Protection of Persons with Disabilities of the People's Republic of China (2008) states that PP should give priority to products and/or services from the welfare institutions of the disabled when other conditions are equivalent. MOF and the Ministry of Industry and Information Technology (2012) jointly issued the interim measures for promoting SMEs by allocating at least 30 % of the budget to them in PP.

However, actual implementation is still largely unacknowledged. Evaluation and feedback are greatly needed in order to advance CSPP. To this end, this chapter aims to provide meaningful insights from the angle of policy implementation. Results from our empirical study can be applied for further reform of CSPP policies and implementation in the near future.

Research Design and Method

Theoretical Framework

Through field study, we aim to investigate CSPP policies, relationships between implementation agencies, and the purchasing process under China's context of the top-down model. Applying literature results in implementation theory with China's context of the top-down model, we formulate the following hypotheses:

H1: Goal and criteria clarity enhances congruent implementation in CSPP.
H2: Centralized procurement enhances congruent implementation in CSPP.
H3: Information and evaluation transparency in the purchasing process enhances congruent implementation in CSPP.

In spring and summer 2012, we interviewed the chief official or manager in each organization unit at three layers: supervisory agency, administrative agency, and vendor. Table 1 lists the details of their units. These agencies represent three tiers of government: central government, province, and prefecture-level city. They are located within the following three representative environments:

- Balanced: central government and Beijing
- Conservative: Inner Mongolia and Luoyang
- Innovative: Shaoxing

Our intention was to study the same event from different key stakeholders in a systematic manner: data triangulation. The central government and the Beijing Municipal People's Government are located in Beijing, the capital of China and also the country's political and cultural center, representing a balanced environment. Inner Mongolia and Luoyang in Henan Province are in Inner China, representing underdeveloped regions. Shaoxing City has the country's oldest trading centre of public resources in the developed coastal regions, representing the frontier of China's reform.

We also interviewed sales managers at four major vendors: Lenovo, Huawei, Beijing Hyundai, and Midea. These are China's fortune 100 companies, representing industries in electronics, automobile, and office equipment. All together, we

Table 1 Organizations interviewed

	Supervisory agency (five interviewees)	Administrative agency (six interviewees)
Central government	Supervision office of government procurement of China's MOF	Procurement center of central government Procurement center of the People's Bank of China
Province	Supervision division of government procurement of Beijing Municipal Bureau of Finance Supervision division of government procurement of Inner Mongolia Bureau of Finance	Procurement center of Beijing Municipal Government Procurement center of Inner Mongolia Autonomous Region Government
Prefecture- level city	Supervision division of government procurement of Shaoxing Municipal Bureau of Finance Supervision division of government procurement of Luoyang Municipal Bureau of Finance	Trading center of Shaoxing Public Resource Procurement center of Luoyang Municipal Government

interviewed 15 chief personnel: 5 at supervisory agencies, 6 at administrative agencies, and 4 at vendor companies.

Our interviewing approach was guided by well-defined case study protocols (Eisenhardt 1989; Miles and Huberman 1994; Yin 2003): We conducted a focused and constrained multiple-case study in three areas: policy goals and criteria, relationships between implementation agencies, and the purchasing process. All interviews were conducted face-to-face, each lasting interview about 1 h. We maintained an open and pleasant interview environment to ensure trustworthiness: Participants did not avoid interview questions and responses were kept anonymous; open-ended questions allowed respondents to reflect on their experience; evidences from respondents at multiple organization units were used to support the same concept.

In particular, we followed a consistent interview guide. Our key interview questions include:

1. What is an appropriate implementation model of CSPP?
2. What are policy goals and implementation criteria in CSPP?
3. Who are the main implementation agencies in CSPP? Their organizational relationships? In particular, what is your view on centralized procurement in CSPP?
4. How to implement CSPP in the purchasing process, such as tendering, bidding, bid evaluation, contract awarding, contract execution, and after-sales service? What is the role of information and evaluation transparency?

To ensure rigorous data collection and analysis, we followed appropriate tests of construct validity, content validity, internal validity, external validity, and reliability (Eisenhardt 1989; Miles and Huberman 1994; Yin 2003). The construct validity determines whether the research measures what it is supposed to measure. The construct validity was established by examining multiple sources of evidences (five supervisory agencies, six administrative agencies, and four vendors) and letting interviewees review the case write-up. The content validity refers to the extent to which a measure represents adequate coverage for the construct domain or essence of the domain. The content validity was established by grounding our measures in existing literature and our interviews with key officials/managers. The internal validity focuses on causal effects. We built the internal validity by investigating logical consistency across supervisory agencies, administrative agencies, and vendors. The external validity looks at whether the findings can be extended to the populations and the settings of interest. We built the external validity by the cross-case analysis. Reliability demonstrates repeatability. We maintained reliability by a consistent, refined case study protocol.

After all interviews, the research team first conducted a within-case analysis; each interviewee represented one case–one organization. The detailed interview notes and our literature review articles were examined, and key findings were identified and tabled. This step involved numerous discussions and reviewing of texts and various tabular displays, resulting in an in-depth result of each interviewee's view on policy goals and criteria, relationships between implementation agencies, and the purchasing process. Next, a cross-case analysis was performed by using tabular displays to seek similarities and differences among interviewees. Because we studied the basics of policy goals and criteria, relationships between implementation agencies, and the purchasing processes, we found vast similarities and consistent patterns between interviewees. We also intermittently checked our interview notes to sharpen our constructs and interlinkages. With this iterative process, we were able to raise the abstraction level and our constructs' grounding in data was verified.

Data Analysis and Results

Implementation Model

All 15 interviewees strongly supported the top-down model, which is China's reality. CSPP has made substantial progress after 10 years of development, thanks to the vigorous promotion by MOF as a key administrative organization, close cooperation between the central government and local governments, and consistent regulations by the central government.

All interviewees concurred with our literature results: The central government is authoritative and controls most tax revenue whereas it is the custom for local government bureaucrats to follow orders and regulations from the top. The process thus is highly efficient. This authoritarian top-down model is still the best implementation model fitting China's reality for CSPP due to an urgent need in sustainable development (e.g., China is now the world's biggest CO_2 emitter, emitting more than one fourth of the world's total.). Although the bottom-up perspective seems more democratic, it is very time-consuming to reach any consensus for current divergent practice of CSPP, thus making it highly unproductive.

CSPP Policy Goals and Criteria

All 15 interviewees agreed that especially in the green procurement, the policy goal has been lucid. The green product inventory has been published for ten issues so far jointly by MOF, NDRC, MEP, and China Quality Certification Center. In 2012, the list detailed product brands, model numbers, and vendors' contact information. All governments must give priority to these published certified products. However, the blue PP has remained largely abstract legal provisions only: no apparent policy goal yet, no strong supervision from the central government, and not enough attention at administrative agencies. There is no certification standard and no product list in the blue PP. All 15 interviewees were aware that the green PP had been carried out much better than the blue PP.

On the next level, the implementation criteria guide how to implement specific purchasing based on policy goals. Examples include the proportion of green purchasing, the proportion of blue purchasing, bonus evaluation scores of sustainable products and services, and financial incentives on sustainable products and services.

In our interviews, the majority of officials at the supervisory agencies (three out of five) thought that the product inventory list was sufficient. There was no need for specific implementation criteria in different purchasing categories; moreover, a universal standard was not even appropriate. The administrative officials should have the discretionary right to make their own judgments. However, all six interviewees at the administrative agencies expressed the opposite opinion. They strongly suggested the need for concrete implementation criteria, especially in the evaluation scores and the score card calculation. The green product inventory list only requires that the green product should have the priority under the equivalence with conventional products. What if sustainable products have higher costs? How to balance sustainability and higher cost? How to award a higher score to sustainable products and services? There were no detailed guidelines so far, which caused difficult SPP implementation in practice. All four vendor managers agreed the need for concrete implementation standards, more control on the discretionary right of administration officials, and gradual improvement towards transparent evaluations on purchasing.

For future development and improvement, all 15 interviewees recommended more specified policy goals (especially in blue procurement). To increase operability, 12 interviewees (80 % of all 15 interviewed) recommended more concrete implementation criteria with product lists and bonus calculation methods for sustainable products and services by the central government.

Overall, our interview results support H1: Goal and criteria clarity enhances congruent implementation in CSPP.

CSPP Policy Implementation Agencies

All interviewees concurred that there are three major agencies in CSPP. Also, their relationships follow a top-down model: from supervisory agency to administrative agency to vendor, as illustrated in Fig. 1. Thirteen interviewees (87 % of interviewed) interviewees believed a strong organizational control in order to have a real impact on CSPP, and advocated a centralized PP center as the choice of the administrative agency. The centralized PP center should execute all PP, including office and general equipment, construction projects, medicines and medical devices, land transfers, and property transactions. Also, a unified supervisory agency should be established accordingly, responsible for all governance on PP. This supervisory agency has the administrative law enforcement power in inspection and oversight.

The proposed consolidated organizational structure by 13 interviewees suits pretty well to the People's Congress system in China—a unitary political regime, providing a unified model for deviating practices in current CPP. Thus, governments at three tiers (central, province, and prefecture-level city) can execute efficient and timely control on all public purchasing activities. Thanks to economies of scale, the procurement center can thoroughly accumulate all related skills and knowledge in CPP. Only two interviewees (13 % of interviewed) suggested keeping current decentralized purchasing, due to transient nature of current CPP. They emphasized caution against dramatic change in CSPP.

H2 is thus supported: Centralized procurement enhances congruent implementation in CSPP.

CSPP Purchasing Process

All 15 interviewees supported that CSPP had to be implemented into the purchasing process, including tendering, bidding, bid evaluation, contract awarding, contract execution, and after-sales service. Most important elements were bid evaluation (13 interviewees or 87 % of all 15 interviewees), followed by contract execution (10 interviewees or 67 %).

All five interviewees at supervisory agencies thought that CSPP had been implemented well in the purchasing process. But, all six interviewees at the administrative agencies thought differently that CSPP was not implemented as favorably as it should be; CSPP still largely remained at the policy level, not in the purchasing process, mostly due to economic self-interest at local governments, procurement centers, and vendors. All four interviewees at vendor companies agreed that CSPP had made progresses in saving energy, protecting environment, and supporting disadvantaged groups; however, CSPP in the purchasing process was still vague and abstract.

For future improvement, 14 interviewees (93 % of interviewed) proposed systematic transparency on the purchasing process. Tendering documents should be open to the public in advance; the administrative agency may solicit public comments or undertake an expert demonstration procedure by an independent, ad hoc committee of registered bid assessment experts of MOF in complex purchasing. Bid evaluation should be transparent including the evaluation process, the evaluation criteria, and evaluation resolutions. All these important documents should be published online to accept public scrutiny.

H3 is thus supported: Information and evaluation transparency in the purchasing process enhances congruent implementation in CSPP.

Discussion and Conclusion

All our interview results confirmed the literature results that China has a clear top-down model: CPP has a strong hierarchical structure from top to bottom and each upper tier has overriding influence on its lower tier. This top-down model determines that the policy itself should be authoritative, clear, and stable.

On the next level, our interview results showed that CSPP policy goals and criteria need to be lucid and specific. The green PP has achieved a much better outcome than has the blue PP because CSPP policy goals and criteria are clearer in the green PP than in the blue PP. This finding confirms the literature results from developed countries (Pressman and Wildavsky 1973; Van Meter and Van Horn 1975; Mazmanian and Sabatier 1983).

For actual implementation, our interview results validated two key elements: centralized procurement and information and evaluation transparency, which again confirm the literature results from developed countries (Pressman and Wildavsky 1973; Mazmanian and Sabatier 1983; Transparency International 2006; OECD 2007; Wang and Li 2014). Centralized PP suits China's unitary political regime and provides a unified model for deviating practices in current CPP. Also importantly, it promotes in-depth knowledge and skill development for each bureaucrat with clean evaluation and monitoring of each bureaucrat's performance, and can achieve economies of scale within each functional department and the overall PP. Information and evaluation transparency in CSPP remains a principle, a goal, and a tool because the open procedures permit general shareholders and stakeholders to examine CSPP's process, procedure, and performance. This examination keeps bureaucrats and PP vendors accountable.

Therefore, we summarize a favorable implementation framework under China's top-down model in Fig. 2. From top to bottom, the solid line arrows show the flow of influence; from bottom to top, the dotted line arrows show the flow of feedback and evaluation. Our major contribution is to collect empirical feedback and evaluation from practice to close the loop by making improvement suggestions at all four layers: The law and regulations should provide clear goals and specific criteria for congruent implementation; the supervisory agency needs to conduct unified and open oversight; the administrative agency should manage centralized purchasing for all public resources with transparency in the whole purchasing process; the vendor needs to register in the PP database and participate fairly in the transparent purchasing process.

Fig 2 A Favorable Top-Down Framework for CSPP

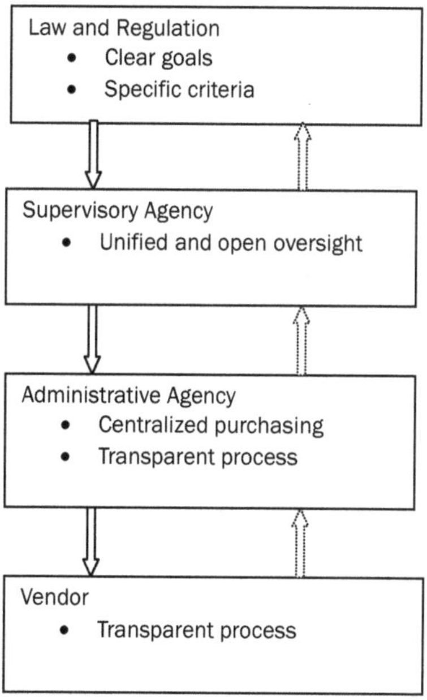

For managerial implications, we provide a framework for CSPP, as shown in Fig. 2. The framework can serve as a guideline to govern diversified practice of CSPP and as a foundation to further reform future CSPP in laws, regulations, and organizational setups and relations.

Acknowledgments The research is supported and funded by a National Natural Science Foundation of China research grant [No. 71273266].

References

Berman, P. (1978). The study of macro- and micro-implementation. *Public Policy, 26*(2), 157–184.

Commission on Growth and Development. (2008). *The growth report: Strategies for sustained growth and inclusive development*. Washington, DC: World Bank.

Deng, X. (1993). *Analects*. Beijing: Renmin Press.

Eisenhardt, K. (1989). Building theories from case study research. *Academy of Management Review, 14*(4), 532–550.

Elmore, R. F. (1980). Backward mapping: Implementation research and policy decisions. *Political Science Quarterly, 94*(4), 601–616.

Emiliani, M. L. (2001). A mathematical logic approach to the shareholder vs stakeholder debate. *Management Decision, 39*(8), 618–622.

Freeman, R. E. (1984). *Strategic management: A stakeholder approach*. Boston: Pitman Publishing.

Goggin, M. L. (1986). The 'too few cases/too many variables' problem in implementation research. *Western Political Quarterly, 39*, 328–347.

Hill, M., & Hupe, P. (2002). *Implementing public policy: Governance in theory and in practice*. Thousand Oaks: Sage.

Howlett, M., Ramesh, M., & Perl, A. (2009). *Studying public policy: Policy cycles and policy subsystems*. Oxford: Oxford University Press.

Kim, P. S. (2008). A daunting task in Asia: The move for transparency and accountability in the Asian public sector. *Public Management Review, 10*(4), 527–537.

Matland, R. E. (1995). Synthesizing the implementation literature: The ambiguity-conflict model of policy implementation. *Journal of Public Administration Research and Theory, 5*(2), 145–174.

May, P. J. (2003). Policy design and implementation. In G. Peter & J. Pierre (Eds.), *Handbook of public administration* (pp. 223–233). Thousand Oaks: Sage.

Mazmanian, D., & Sabatier, P. (1983). *Implementation and public policy*. Glenview: Scott.

McCourt, W. (2008). Public management in developing countries: From downsizing to governance. *Public Management Review, 10*(4), 467–479.

Miles, M. B., & Huberman, A. M. (1994). *Qualitative data analysis: An expanded sourcebook*. Thousand Oaks: Sage.

Monczka, P. M., Handfield, R. B., Giunipero, L. C., & Patterson, J. L. (2009). *Purchasing and supply chain management* (4th ed.). Florence: South-Western Cengage.

National People's Congress (1982). *The Constitution of the People's Republic of China*. Beijing, China: Author. http://www.gov.cn/gongbao/content/2004/content_62714.htm. Accessed 12 June 2014.

National People's Congress (2002). *The government procurement law of the People's Republic of China*. Beijing, China. http://www.gov.cn/english/laws/2005–10/08/content_75023.htm. Accessed 12 June 2014.

OECD (Organisation for Economic Co-Operation and Development). (2007). *Integrity in public procurement: Good practice from A to Z*. Paris: OECD Publishing.

Palumbo, D. J., & Calista, D. J. (1990). *Implementation and the policy process: Opening up the black box*. New York: Greenwood Press.

Pressman, J. L., & Wildavsky, A. B. (1973). *Implementation: How great expectations in Washington are dashed in Oakland*. Berkeley: University of California Press.

Qiao, Y., & Wang, C. (2011). Issues and challenges in implementing China's green public procurement program. *Journal of Environmental Protection, 2*(8), 1034–1045.

Saetren, H. (2005). Facts and myths about research on public policy implementation: Out-of-fashion, allegedly dead, but still very much alive and relevant. *Policy Studies Journal, 33*(4), 559–582.

Simpson, P. M., Siguaw, J. A., & White, S. C. (2002). Measuring the performance of suppliers: An analysis of evaluation processes. *Journal of Supply Chain Management, 38*(1), 29–41.

Sun, C., & Yu, B. (2010). Further understanding of the importance of China's centralized reality. *Cass Journal of Political Science, 4,* 33–42.

The Brundtland Commission (World Commission on Environment and Development). (1987). *Our common future*. http://www.un-documents.net/wced-ocf.htm. Accessed 12 June 2014.

Thomas, J. W., & Grindle, M. S. (1990). After the decision: Implementing policy reforms in developing countries. *World Development, 18*(8), 1163–1181.

Transparency International. (2006). *National integrity systems: Transparency international country study report*. Berlin: Transparency International.

United Nations (2002). *The world summit on sustainable development*. http://www.un.org/events/wssd/. Accessed 12 June 2014.

United Nations. (2012). *The Marrakech Process*. http://esa.un.org/marrakechprocess/tfsuspubproc.shtml. Accessed 12 June 2014.

Van Meter, D., & Van Horn, C. (1975). The policy implementation process: A conceptual framework. *Administration and Society, 6,* 445–488.

Wang, C. (2006). *Study in China's government procurement*. Beijing: Xiju Press.

Wang, C., & Li, X. (2014). Centralizing public procurement in China: Task environment and organizational structure. *Public Management Review, 16*(9), 900–921.

Weiss, J. W. (2003). *Business ethics: A stakeholder and issues management approach*. Mason: South-Western, Thomson Learning.

Xiang, H. (2002). China's financial system reform practice and proactive fiscal policy. *Economic Perspectives, 6,* 3–6.

Yin, R. K. (2003). *Case study research: Design and methods* (3rd ed.). Thousand Oaks: Sage.

Zhao, X., Flynn, B. B., & Roth, A. V. (2006). Decision sciences research in China: A critical review and research agenda—Foundations and overview. *Decision Sciences, 37*(4), 451–496.

Cong-hu Wang, JD, is an associate professor in School of Public Administration and Policy, Renmin University of China. His teaching and research interests are in public procurement, public administration, and public policy implementation.

Xiaoming Li, PhD, is an associate professor, Department of Business Administration, Tennessee State University. His teaching and research interests are in operations management and supply chain management.

The Role of Small and Medium-Sized Enterprises in a Sustainable Public Procurement System

Anna Górczyńska

The Role of SMEs in the EU Market

In a period of economic crisis, the promotion of small and medium-sized enterprises (SMEs) seems to be an important issue as they constitute almost 99 % of European enterprises and play a key role in economic growth.[1] The European Union (EU) still faces challenging economic conditions with an intensifying sovereign debt crisis in the euro zone, the spectre of double-dip recession looming in several countries, and faltering growth in the better performing ones. In this context, however, in 2012, SMEs retained their position as the backbone of the European economy: there are over 20.7 million such enterprises, which amount to more than 98 % of total businesses.

It is estimated that in 2012 SMEs accounted for 67 % of total employment in the European enterprises and 58 % of gross value added (GVA). The total SME employment of 87 million (29.6 % of total employment in European companies) played a substantial role in the European economy. For comparison, in Poland the total number of SMEs is estimated at 1.4 million, which corresponds to 99.8 % of the total number of companies in Poland. Polish SME employment amounts to 5.6 million (68.2 % of total employment in the private sector) and produces 51.5 % of GVA (European Commission 2012). However, the difficult economic environment continues to pose severe challenges to the sector of SMEs in all member states of the EU. The risk of decreased gross domestic product aggravates the economic situation of

[1] The commission gives the following definition of SMEs in Recommendation 2003/361/EC: (1) microenterprises—under 10 employees, a turnover of under € 2 million, an annual balance sheet total of under € 2 million; (2) small enterprises—under 50 employees, a turnover of under € 10 million, an annual balance sheet total of under € 10 million; (3) medium-sized enterprises—under 250 employees, a turnover of under 50 million, an annual balance sheet total of under € 43 million; www.ec.europa.eu/enterprise.

A. Górczyńska (✉)
Faculty of Law and Administration, University of Lodz, Lodz, Poland
e-mail: anna.gorczynska@interia.pl

K. V. Thai (ed.), *International Public Procurement*, Public Administration, Governance and Globalization 14, DOI 10.1007/978-3-319-13434-5_16

SMEs. Therefore the question arises whether it would be possible to promote SMEs by the public procurement system.

Thus, reasons should be presented for the special need for increasing SME participation in the public financing system. As mentioned above, SMEs are predominant in the market and justification for their wider participation in tendering could be motivated not only by their crucial role in the economy but also by their capacity for innovation, organizational simplicity, flexibility, and ability to quickly respond to the needs of the market. Secondly, the activity of SMEs in the procurement market would be profitable for those companies, leading to their higher revenues and economic growth (Hatzis 2009; Arrowsmith 2005; Arnould 2004; O'Brien 1993; Erridge 1998; Burgi 2007).

The public procurement system in the EU is of dual nature, meaning that contracts above a particular threshold are regulated by the EU legal system.[2] Contracts under the threshold remain outside the legal system of the EU and fall under the scope of national legislation (Case C-231/03 Coname [2005] ECR I-728, par. 20; case C-44/98 BASF [1999] ECR I-6269, par. 16; European Commission 2006).

The Member States are therefore able to implement measures to promote SMEs in their national public procurement systems. However, even in the case of under-the-threshold contracts, the member states have to take into consideration the basic rules of the common market which must be observed for all types of contracts. Some controversy arises regarding the implementation of legal measures favoring SMEs in above-the-threshold contracts. Thus, the problem of the legality of privileged treatment of SMEs such as, e.g., set-asides or other special preferences for contracts covered by EU directives has to be analyzed.

According to a 2008 analysis of the SME market (European Commission 2010b, p. 4) an estimated 60 % of above-the-threshold contracts were won by SMEs. In terms of the value of the contracts, this corresponds to a 33 % market share. However, both European (European Commission 2010b) and national reports (Council of Ministers 2008) list barriers to the access of SMEs to the EU market. The most significant ones are the following:

- Contracts too large for the capacity and financial standing of companies
- Lack of sufficient sources of information about participation possibilities for SMEs

[2] The thresholds are regulated in both directives on public procurement, but they have been amended several times in relation to the Government Procurement Agreement (GPA). The thresholds are recalculated by the commission every 2 years and the calculation is based on the average daily value of the Euro, expressed in Special Drawing Rights (SDRs). The current thresholds are as follows: € 134,000 for public supply and service contracts awarded by central government authorities; € 207,000 for public supply and service contracts awarded by contracting authorities, which are not central government authorities; certain products in the field of defence awarded by the central government authorities, certain services in the field of R&D, telecommunications, hotels and catering, transport by rail and waterway, provision of personnel, vocational training, investigation and security, certain legal and social services, certain sanitary, recreational, cultural and sports services; € 414,000 for supplies and services in the utilities sector; € 5,186,000 in the case of public works contracts in both classic and utilities sectors.

- Excessive financial requirements concerning guarantees and security related to participation in the award procedure and execution of contracts
- Insufficient time to prepare documents for the tendering procedure
- Excessive requirements, such as certificates
- High cost of obtaining such certificates as well as substantial financial burden including a tender security deposit, and providing security for the execution of the contract upon the request of the contractor
- Strict requirements for technical standards of the object of the contract
- Delayed payments from the contracting authority
- Sub-contracting instead of contracting, which limits the influence of SMEs on the execution of the object of the contract as well as their remuneration
- Unclear and ambiguous award criteria

During public consultations with SMEs, they pointed out that in order to facilitate SME access to public procurement, a change in the procurement culture of the contracting authorities is needed rather than legislative changes in the public procurement directives (European Commission 2008b).

The Principles of the Common Market and SMEs

In the public procurement system, the most important regulations refer to nondiscrimination and equal treatment of all enterprises. These rules, along with the fundamental freedoms of the common market, are the pillars of the EU legal system. These principles, derived from the Treaty of Functioning of the European Union (Article 18 of the Treaty on the Functioning of the European Union, OJ C 115), are also stated in the preamble and the text of the procurement directives.[3] The equal treatment principle means that all enterprises should be treated equally and all direct and indirect forms of discrimination are prohibited (Craing and Burca 2010; Arrowsmith 2005; Nielsen and Treumer 2005; Galster and Mik 1996; Cieśliński 2010; Sołtysińska 2006). Examples of different forms of discrimination are found in various judgements of the Court of Justice of the European Union (CJEU), which abolishes all forms of discrimination based on nationality and equivalent measures (Case C-260/04 Commission v. Italy [2007] ECR I-7083, par. 23; Case C-470/99 Universale Bau [2002] ECR I-11617, par. 91; joined Cases C-21/03 and C-34/03 [2005] Fabricom ECR I-1559, par. 27; Case C-264/99 Commission v. Italy [2000] I-4417; Case C-243/89 Commission v. Denmark [1999]; Case C-513/99 Concordia Bus Finland ECR [2002] I-7213; Case C-458/03 Parking Brixen [2005] ECR I-8612; Case C-410/04 ANAV [2006] ECR I-3303). Derogations from the fundamental freedoms are enumerated in the Treaty on the Functioning of the European Union (TFUE) (2012, Article 36) and refer to public interest exceptions such as,

[3] Article 2 of Directive 2004/18/EC and Article 10 of Directive 2004/17/EC provide that: "contracting authorities shall treat economic operators equally and non-discriminatorily and shall act in the transparent way."

among others, public morality, public security, and public health. The use of derogations is subjected to a number of conditions. No exceptions are given for the preferential treatment of SMEs. The provisions of the primary law of the EU have been interpreted and supplemented by the judgments of the CJEU. Even if the Treaty derogations are not applied, the CJEU has recognized that a measure does not infringe the principles of the Common Market if it can be justified on the basis of one of a number of other public interest grounds referred to as so-called mandatory requirements (Arrowsmith 2005). In the case of Cassis de Dijon (Case C-120/78 (Rewe-Zentral) [1979] ECR 649), the CJEU allowed for implementing measures, which were necessary to meet the mandatory requirements, particularly in the form of effective fiscal supervision, health care, fair trade, and consumer protection. This is a nonexhaustive list that the CJEU may extend if it considers it appropriate with a view to a particular public interest. However, the principle of overriding national interest should be interpreted narrowly. Such measures are also subject to the proportionality principle, which requires that any restriction on trade should be suitable to promote the objective sought and it should also be necessary to achieve that objective. The CJEU addressed the issue of mandatory requirements by analysis of the situation of SMEs, which were excluded from large-scale procurement contracts, but this fact did not allow the member state to adopt restrictions on the freedom to provide services by introducing national or regional preferences or special treatment of enterprises (Case C-360/89 Commission v. Italy [1992] ECR I-3401, par. 13, Case C-3/88, Commission v. Italy (Re Data Processing) [1989] ECR 4035).

The CJEU introduced criteria for the justification of nondiscriminatory restrictions with reference to an overriding public interest in the so-called Gebhard test (Case 55/94 Gebhard [1995] ECR I-4165). The test examines whether national measures can be applied based on an overriding public interest. The four conditions to be met are as follows: (1) the measures should be applied in a nondiscriminatory manner, (2) they must be justified by imperative requirements of public interest, (3) they should ensure the attainment of the objective which they pursue, and (4) they must not go beyond what is necessary to achieve this objective (Case 55/94 Gebhard [1995] ECR I-4165, par. 37). Once all criteria of the Gebhard test of proportionality are met, the measures can be treated as an overriding public interest and justified. However, it seems that national regulations favoring SMEs as set-asides do not fulfil all conditions of the Gebhard test and may not be treated as an overriding public interest ground (See also Sundstrand 2010).

Thus, it must be stated that the TFUE free movement rules shall be applied to the industrial policy of the EU and, in that sense, also to all regulations addressed to enterprises. With reference to the role of the state in the national economy, a distinction is made here between government as purchaser and government as regulator. The government in the role of a purchaser usually tries to promote industrial policies, while in its regulatory capacity the government is mainly interested in using the procurement policy as a tool (instrumentalization). However, the question still remains how the national discretion to implement horizontal policies is affected by the public procurement directives. The general principle, reflected in some CJEU rulings, that economic objectives cannot form the basis for justifying measures hindering access to the market, should be criticized.[4]

Another important aspect of legitimate forms of support for SMEs arises in the context of state aid for the presented types of economic activity. The CJEU considered this issue in the context of an Italian legal regulation which reserved 30% of supply contracts for enterprises established in the Mezzogiorno region (Case C-21/88 Du Pont de Nemours [1999] ECR I-889, see also S. Arrowsmith [2009]). It was argued that such state aid was permissible under TFEU exemptions from the general prohibition of state aid in the EU. The derogations of Article 105(3)(a) offer the possibility to authorize state aid by the commission if it is "given to promote the economic development of areas where the standard of living is abnormally low or where there is serious unemployment." However, in the aforementioned case the CJEU ruled that under the circumstances the measures to promote local enterprises and combat unemployment hindered community trade and could not be justified. In C-21/88 (Du Pont de Nemours), the CJEU precluded the use of procurement as a tool of regional policy because other forms of regional assistance, such as direct financial aid, are generally economically more efficient than procurement preferences. On the other hand, it can also be stated that under certain circumstances such measures could be in principle available, for example to circumvent a corrupt and inefficient bureaucracy as a means of distributing benefits (Stehman and Fernandez Martin 1991). In some other judgements (Case 94/99 ARGE Gewasserschtz v. Bundesministerium fur Land unad Forstwirtschaft [2000] p. I-11037), the CJEU stated that the principle of equal treatment would not be breached by tenderers subsidized by state aid that were able to submit a bid lower than that of others. However, the contracting authority could exclude such companies from the procedure in the case of illegal receipt of state aid.

The idea of free and unlimited competition is concretized by the best value for money principle in all tendering procedures. The contracting authorities are obliged to consider almost exclusively the economic aspects of bids and exemptions are interpreted strictly. The above remarks refer to an ideal form of the free market, but nowadays reality seems to be far more complicated. The member states are often tempted to use public procurement as a tool for their protectionist policies. In the past, numerous preferences for national products or services or for particular regions or national enterprises were directly introduced to national legal systems, but, finally, following interventions of the commission and then the CJEU, preferential treatment was abolished (Case C-275/98 (Unitron Scandinavia) ECR [1999]

[4] Arrowsmith (2009) presented the view that: "...such a general principle is too unsophisticated and needs to be nuanced. This so-called principle was first adopted to preclude economic objectives that were clearly incompatible with the scheme of the Treaty. It provides a neat way to encapsulate the principle that Treaty derogations cannot be used to justify objectives that are "mere" protectionism or objectives that merely address the board social or political consequences of inequality or economic decline in certain areas or activities. However, other policies that are economic in the sense of affecting industrial development—or, indeed, other financial or commercial interests of the state—should not be caught by a general principle that automatically precludes justification."

I-8291, par. 31-32; Case C-45/87 ECR [1988] I-4929, par. 26; Case C-3/88 (Re Data Processing) ECR [1989] p. 4035; Case C-16/98 ECR [2000], p. 111; Case C-225/98 [2000] p. 83; Górczyńska (2005)). Thus, as long as it was possible, the Member States overused their competences to introduce some noneconomic goals to the public procurement system. Some of those aspects, such as environmental protection or special preferences for the disabled, were lately implemented in the legal public procurement system. In this evolution of the strict interpretation of the economic principle of public procurement as its main and only aim, one can see the result of a European-wide debate on the possibility and limits of instrumentalization of public procurement. In general, some types of noneconomic objectives are legal and compliant with the TFEU fundamental freedoms. Thus, one could formulate an open question whether the legal system of public procurement in Europe is effective. The Member States in their national regulations for under-the-threshold contracts are not bound by European legislation, but they should apply all the basic rules of the Treaty (Hatzis 2009; Erridge 1998; for alternative view, see Arrowsmith 2009).[5] In this context, the question arises whether it would be possible to legalize those preferences which are used as a tool to combat unemployment and reduce economic fluctuations in the domestic market. The acceptance of some forms of promotion for domestic companies does not automatically mean hindering access to the domestic market. This can even constitute the legalization of a common practice and a form of removing obstacles to better access to public contracts for SMEs. A legal system which is inflexible and introduces excessively detailed regulation is ineffective and likely to be violated. In such a situation, the exigencies of economic life necessitate amendments to the legal system. Enforcement of legal regulations is often difficult for a variety of reasons, but one of the most important seems to be incompatibility with practice. Legal regulations without penalties attached are also ineffective, so it is of high importance to introduce rules with a possibility of imposing penalties, especially fines. As we have learned from the lesson of competition law, the legal system started to be effective when Regulation No. 1/2003 and Regulation No. 139/2004[6] came into force, introducing the involvement of national institutions and severe financial fines.

Soft Legal Regulations and SMEs

The role of SMEs in the public procurement system is not addressed in European legislation. The European Commission has published only guidelines referring to the promotion of SMEs, in which the importance of better access to public contracts

[5] This opinion is shared by Hatzis (2009) and Erridge (1998); an alternative view is presented by S. Arrowsmith and P. Kunzlik (2009), who stated that: "equal treatment in the procurement directives is different from the equal treatment derived from the Treaty."

[6] Council Regulation No 1/2003 of December 2002 on the implementation of the rules on competition laid down in Articles 81 and 82 of the Treaty [2003] OJ L001 P001; Council Regulation No 139/2004 of 20 January 2004 on the control of concentrations between undertakings [2004] OJ L24/1.

is pointed out.[7] In 2008 the European Commission adopted the "Small Business Act for Europe", (DG Enterprise and Industry 2004; DG Enterprise and Industry 2010; GHK 2010) which reflects the Commission's political will to recognize the central role of SMEs in the EU economy (European Commission 2008b). The act aims to improve the overall approach to entrepreneurship and to promote the growth of SMEs by helping them tackle the problems hampering their development. The new approach of the Commission to SMEs was presented in November 2011. The document presents a list of initiatives already taken and some proposed for the future. In the updated Small Business Act, new legislative initiatives are to be adopted, for example: a directive on e-invoicing, an optional cash accounting scheme, or the requirement for public authorities to pay within 30 days as a security guarantee for SMEs. It is also suggested that the administrative burden for SMEs accessing public procurement should be reduced and SMEs should have better opportunities for joint binding. The Commission will even seek, wherever possible, to exempt microenterprises from EU legislation or introduce a special regime in order to minimize the regulatory burden on them.

In helping SMEs benefit from the single market, the Member States are especially invited to fully implement the "European Code of Best Practices Facilitating Access by SMEs to Public Procurement Contracts," which was issued in 2008 (European Commission 2008a). The code is meant to assist public authorities in developing strategies and programmes facilitating SMEs' access to public procurement. The idea of the code was to create a more SME-friendly public procurement policy in the member states, which still needs to remain in conformity with EU principles. The Code points out that contracts can be divided into lots for better accessibility for SMEs. The splitting of a contract into lots must not lead to the avoidance of application of EU directives and the value of separate lots has to be added up to determine the level of EU legal requirements. Also the communication of the Commission of 13 April 2011 titled "The Single Market Act: Twelve levers to boost growth and confidence" (European Commission 2011) mentioned the importance of SMEs for the development of the common market. It was also stated that a revised and modernized public procurement legislative framework would make the award of public contracts more flexible and enable the contracts to be put to better use in support of other polices.

In 2011, proposals for new public procurement directives were adopted.[8] They were intended to reinforce the "Europe 2020 Strategy for smart, sustainable and inclusive growth" (European Commission 2010b). It was pointed out that public

[7] Council resolution on the action programme for SMEs, OJ 1986, C287/1; European Commission, draft resolution of the Council concerning the action programme for SMEs, COM (86) 445 final; European Commission 2000, "Promoting SMEs Participation in Public Procurement in the Community," COM (90) 166 final, p. 2; Council Decision 2000/819/EC on a multiannual programme for enterprise and entrepreneurship and in particular for small and medium-sized enterprises, OJ 2000, L 333/84.

[8] Proposal for a directive of the European Parliament and of the Council on public procurement, COM (2011) 896; proposal for a directive of the European Parliament and of the Council on procurement by entities operating in the water, energy, transport, and postal services, COM (2011)

procurement plays a key role in the Europe 2020 Strategy as one of the market-based instruments that promote the main goals of the strategy by improving the business environment and conditions for innovative business and encourage a wider use of green procurement. In 2014 three new directives were finally adopted[9] including numerous provisions formulated in the former proposals. The current, new legislative package of directives on public procurement is designed to reduce the administrative obstacles and costs related to tendering, make the procurement system more transparent and easier for SMEs, and encourage the use of e-procurement to simplify the process.

SME-Friendly Legal Provisions in the EU and Polish Legal Systems

Analysis of the current legislation leads to the conclusion that the European principles of equality prevent the application of clear preferences for the SME sector. An increase in the share of SMEs in public procurement may only take place by the application of transparent procedures, the reduction of the financial burden on the participants, and the implementation of training measures, which would ensure equal chances for all participants. In this context, the main SME friendly measures shall be presented, which are regulated by both European and domestic legal systems.

Subdividing Contracts into Lots

The public procurement directives allow contracts to be awarded in the form of separate lots (Article 9(5) of Directive 2004/18/EC and Article 17(6) (a) of Directive 2004/17/EC). This clearly facilitates SMEs' access to public procurement contracts and also broadens competition. However, the contracting authorities must respect the general legal rules concerning nondiscrimination and are not allowed to split contracts into lots to avoid the application of public procurement regulations on above-the-threshold contracts. The new directive 2014/24/EU on public procurement (Directive 2014/24/EU, Preamble 30) also mentions division into lots, which would make contracts more accessible for SMEs. This legal regulation even points out that if a contract is not subdivided into lots, the contracting authority will be obliged to provide a detailed explanation.

895; proposal for a directive of the European Parliament and of the Council on the award of concession contracts, COM (2011) 897.

[9] Directive 2014/24/EU of the European Parliament and of the Council of 26 February 2014 on public procurement and replacing the Directive 2004/18/EC (O.J.UE L 94/65); Directive 2014/25/EU of the European Parliament and of the Council of 26 February 2014 on procurement by entities operating in the water, energy, transport, and postal services and replacing the Directive 2004/17/EC (O.J. UE L 94/243); Directive 2014/23/EU of the European Parliament and of the Council of 26 February 2014 on the award of concession contracts (O.J. UE L 94/1).

Article 32 of the Polish Act on Public Procurement Law specifies the possibility to split a contract into lots for organizational, economic or technical reasons, or due to the financial capacity of the contracting authority. Thus, two options are possible: (1) tendering for lots or (2) each of the lots may be the object of a separate contract. Due to the fact that the value of the contract equals the aggregate value of all lots, individual lots are subject to the same procedure as the contract as a whole. The contracting authority may not split a contract into lots or understate its value with a view to avoiding the application of the provisions of law.

It should be pointed out that subdividing contracts into lots is in general positively received by SMEs as a measure, which allows many companies to be awarded contracts. However, a subdivided contract should be regulated at least at the level of specification of the object of the contract, so that also the qualification criteria should be adequate to the partial value and scope of the contract.

Subcontracting

SMEs are invited to act as subcontractors, even if it is economically optimal for them to win contracts for themselves. Subcontracting is usually regarded as less profitable for economic operators due to lower profits. However, in large-scale contracts, SMEs are not able to assume the position of main contractors or even bid jointly with other SMEs, so in such cases subcontracting may still provide them with good opportunities. Subject to national legislation, the contracting authorities may stipulate that the main contractor must not deal with its subcontractors on less favorable terms than those agreed upon the between the contracting authority and the main contractor. In this context, it is worth mentioning German legislation, where the contracting authority has to stipulate in the documentation that the successful tenderer may not impose less favorable conditions on its subcontractors than the conditions agreed with the main contractor, especially as far as payment arrangements are concerned.

The new directive 2014/24/EU on public procurement states that the member states may enable subcontractors to request direct payment by the contracting authority for the supplies, works, and services provided to the main contractor. This regulation is intended to increase the efficiency of protecting the payment interests of SMEs.

On the other hand, subcontracting cannot become the main form of facilitating access to the procurement market for SMEs. Polish legal regulations allow subcontractors to present their knowledge, experience, as well as appropriate technical potential and personnel capable of performing the contract. In some pathological award procedures, this may lead to instrumentalization of public procurement by, e.g., the common use of one curriculum, tools, and personnel by numerous enterprises. Thus, it should be noted that the positive effect of subcontracting could be decreased by manipulation and collusion of enterprises.

Subcontracting does not necessarily mean good performance of the contract and sufficient payment for the subcontractors as the general contractors often take advantage of their dominant position and impose rather unfavorable financial terms. The problem is of great importance, especially in the construction sector, as in Poland where the main award criterion is the lowest price. The tenderers often offer abnormally low bids, which theoretically should be rejected, but in practice it is a common form of combating one's competitors and a means of winning a contract. The negative consequences of the execution of contracts awarded close to the limit of profitability are, unfortunately, passed on to the subcontractors.

In Poland, civil agreements on the performance of a contract are concluded only between the contracting authority and the general contractor. All obligations between the general contractor and subcontractors are regulated by the civil code. In practice, this means that in the case of delayed payments or bankruptcy of the general contractor, all the subcontractors can do is to initiate civil law proceedings.

The recently adopted Polish "Act on the Payment of Outstanding Receivables of Enterprises for Selected Works Performed due to Awarded Public Contracts" is addressed specifically to the group of SMEs that executed motorway construction contracts. The act is designed to cover the claims of the SMEs that were subcontractors in large-scale road construction projects. As the act preferentially treats a particular sector and group of enterprises, it should be carefully examined to determine whether it is in conformity with equality of treatment and public aid rules.

Framework Agreements

Pursuant to Article 32 of Directive 2004/18/EC, and Article 14 and 40 (3)(i) of Directive 2004/17/EC, the contracting authorities can conclude a framework agreement with several economic operators, which is another possibility of promotion of SMEs. This is especially the case if a framework agreement involves a large number of economic operators and it is subdivided into lots or if contracts based on a framework agreement are awarded in the form of lots (European Commission 2008a, p. 9).

According to the Polish Act on Public Procurement, the contracting authority may conclude a framework agreement after conducting a procedure applying, as appropriate, the provisions concerning contract award by open procedure, restricted procedure, or negotiations with publication (Article 99). A framework agreement is defined as an agreement concluded between a contracting entity and one or more contractors. Its main aim is to establish terms and conditions, and especially prices, for public contracts that may be awarded in a particular period. As a result of concluding such an agreement, contracts may be awarded on a simplified basis and on terms not worse than those set down in the framework agreement. On the other hand, SMEs complain that once a framework agreement is concluded, they do not have any possibility of accessing the contract during the term of the agreement.

Functional Requirements in the Description of the Object of the Contract

One of the possible forms of the promotion of innovation in public procurement is defining technical specifications in terms of performance or functional requirements (Article 53(1) of Directive 2004/18/EC and Article 55(1) of Directive 2004/17/EC). The directives allow the contracting authority to specify the object of the contract not only in the form of enumerated requirements and a very detailed list of technical specifications and standards but also in the form of a general description. Thus, the aforementioned regulation allows enterprises to present a variety of technical solutions that are available in the marketplace. The bidders are not limited by the provisions of a technical specification, but can present new and innovative solutions which correspond to the needs of the contracting authority. This legal solution concerning description of the object of the contract may promote innovative SMEs, especially in the IT sector.

The second possibility to promote new and unknown products or services is offering variants. In such a case, the contracting authority has to specify in the contract documents the minimum requirements to be met by the variants and the form of their presentation.

Polish legal regulations allow for description of the object of the contract without referring to approvals, technical specifications, and reference systems (Article 30 of the Act of Public Procurement Law). The object of the contract is described by its functional character, while environmental impact characteristics may be also included. Such an approach can broaden the scope of contractors by allowing bids from companies, which find it difficult to define their products and methods in line with the existing standards and technical specifications, but are able to meet the expectations of the administration in terms of execution of the contract (Council of Ministers 2008, p. 39).

Consortia of Enterprises

The European regulations allow bids to be submitted by groups of enterprises often called consortia (Article 4 (2) of the Directive 2004/18/EC). Contracting authorities may not stipulate special conditions for participation of such groups in procurement procedures that would not be imposed on individual candidates. Consortia may not be required to assume a special legal form to submit a tender or a request to participate. However, the contracting authority may stipulate some special conditions for the performance of the contract by a group, which may require the group to assume a specific legal form once it has been awarded the contract. This provision should be applied to the extent that this change is necessary for the satisfactory performance of the contract. The new directive 2014/24/EU additionally stipulates that conditions for participation of groups of economic operators must be proportionate and justified by objective reasons (Directive 2014/24/EU of the European Parliament and of the Council on public procurement, (O.J.EU L 94/65), Preamble, article 16 and 71).

The EU legal system does not specify in detail how a consortium is to be established, so the legal form of cooperation between enterprises for the submission of a bid is up to the economic partners. Enterprises must establish a representation for the consortium and its scope, which is to be concretized at the level of the national legislation. A set of different provisions applies to the execution of the contract, in which the contracting authority may introduce the obligation to establish a special legal form, but only insofar as it is necessary for the satisfactory performance of the contract. Thus, economic operators are allowed to reject the proposal of the contracting authority to assume a specific legal form on the grounds of, e.g., additional expenditures or reciprocal payments. An interesting legal problem is connected with the admission of changes in a consortium's membership as well as the scope and period of such modifications. In the case of Makedoniko (Case C-57/01 Makedoniko, ECR [2003], p. I-1091), changes in the consortium were introduced after the award of the contract, but the Greek contracting authority excluded it from the procedure pursuant to national regulations.

The Court of Justice of the European Union has stated that the acceptability of changes in consortia shall be regulated by national legislation. Abolishment of changes in consortium membership may be based on the requirement of effectiveness of the award of contracts, which could be breached by changes introduced to the technical potential, financial standing, or reliability of the contractor (Brown 2003).

In the Polish legal system, contractors may bid for a contract jointly (Article 23 of the Act on Public Procurement Law) by establishing a consortium. Consortia are structured similarly to private partnerships. The contractors, who are parties to a written agreement, shall be jointly and severally responsible for the execution of the consortium agreement and contributing security to ensure the proper performance of the agreement. The regulation allows for shared responsibility for the execution of a contract. Once one of the members of the consortium has presented the required qualifications and technical and financial capacity, the whole consortium is deemed to meet that requirement of the contracting authority. However, all consortium members are evaluated separately in respect of exclusion from the contract award procedure. The possibility to establish a consortium can encourage SMEs to conclude this type of an agreement for joint application in tendering procedures. In practice, many questions arise, e.g., How to attract companies to conclude an agreement? How to arrange risk sharing? and How to formulate common economic objectives? Companies in good financial standing are not usually interested in forming a consortium, which would imply sharing the remuneration. However, it is an attractive solution for companies in less advantaged financial or technical standing or for groups of companies in which each partner can meet only part of the requirements.

Abolishment of Discrimination Against Contractors on the Grounds of Their Qualifications

According to the directives, the criteria for financial and economic activity and for technical ability need to be related and proportionate to the subject matter of the contract (Article 44(2) of Directive 2004/18/EC). The idea of proportionate selection criteria is very important for SMEs, as contracting authorities that set the capacity and ability levels too high exclude many of them from participation.

European legislation on public procurement allows an economic operator to rely on the economic and financial capacity and technical ability of other companies for proving compliance with the capacity and ability levels required by the contracting authority (Article 47(2) (3) (4) and article 52(1) of Directive 2004/18/EC and article 53 (4) (5) and article 54 (4)(5) of Directive 2004/17/EC). It should be mentioned that the economic operator must prove that it will have at its disposal the resources necessary for the execution of the contract. A group of economic operators may rely on the capacity of all its members. It is even possible for a group to also rely on the capacity of entities that are not its members. The *Code of Best Practices* (European Commission 2008a, p. 8) indicates that it is advisable for contracting authorities to draw attention to this possibility in the contract notice or even in a prior contract notice in order to give enterprises more time to prepare for joint bidding. The aforementioned provisions are aimed to facilitate the formation of groups of independent contractors, especially in the case of complex contracts.

An important obstacle to SME participation in public procurement is posed by disproportionate financial guarantees required by the contracting authority. Also unjustified and prolonged retention of resources in the form of, e.g., participation guarantee of an economic operator, should be avoided. In Polish legislation, the amount of a participation guarantee may not exceed 3 % of the value of the procurement contract.

The contracting authority may exclude candidates and tenderers from a procedure, thus eliminating time-consuming procedures that would otherwise involve many enterprises not meeting the selection criteria such as adequate financial standing or professional and technical qualifications. The contracting authority is bound to exclude form the procedure all those who have been convicted by a final judgement, which refers to, e.g., participation in a criminal organization, corruption, fraud to the detriment of the financial interests of the EU and money laundering. Also excluded are enterprises falling under the following categories: bankruptcy, offences concerning professional conduct, nonpayment of taxes and social security contributions, breach of environmental regulations and serious misinterpretation of certain documents (Article 45(1) and (2) of the Directive 2004/18/EC). However, in their domestic legal systems the member states can decide about the conditions of those exclusions and sustainability checks. The national law regulates the details, the scope of the required documents, and their form.

In the new legislative package, it is additionally stressed that the contracting authority should be given the possibility to exclude candidates or tenderers for violation of environmental and social obligations, including accessibility for disabled persons, or other forms of grave professional misconduct, such as violations of competition rules or of intellectual property rights (Directive 2014/24/EU on public procurement, Preamble 34 and 35). The new legislation is also intended to introduce the possibility for economic operators to adopt compliance measures aimed at remedying the consequences of criminal offences or misconduct and effectively preventing further occurrences of misbehavior. These measures may especially consist of personnel and organizational measures, such as staff reorganization, implementation of reporting and control systems, or the creation of an internal audit structure. In the case of implementation of such measures, the economic operator should no longer be excluded on these grounds. It should be added that the aforementioned regulation would strengthen the position of tenderers, but in extreme situations this can prevent exclusion of contractors who have committed a crime or grave misconduct.[10]

In the new Directive 2014/24/EU on public procurement (Preamble 31 and 32), the importance of simplifying the information obligation is presented as a measure increasing SMEs opportunities for being awarded contracts. It provides for the mandatory acceptance of self-declarations as evidence for selection purposes. The production of documentary evidence is intended to be facilitated by a standardized document, the so-called European Procurement passport, which is a proof of the absence of grounds for exclusion. The proposal also intends to introduce a limitation on the requirements for participants. The directive contains an exhaustive list of possible conditions for participation in procurement procedures. It states that such conditions should be restricted to those that are appropriate to ensure that the candidate or tenderer has the capacity and ability to perform the contract to be awarded. An example of an SME-friendly solution is the provision that turnover requirements must be limited to three times the estimated contract value (except in duly justified cases).

In Polish contract award procedures, the contracting authority may request contractors supply declarations or documents necessary to conduct tendering procedures (Article 25 of Act on Public Procurement Law). Declarations or documents proving compliance with conditions for participation in the procedures and conformity of the supplies, services, or construction works offered should be indicated by the contracting authority in a contract notice, a specification of essential terms of the contract or an invitation to submit tenders. The 2009 amendment of the Act on Public Procurement Law introduced another regulation important for SMEs. The contractor may prove compliance with the contracting authority's requirements not only by ownership of technical equipment, employment of qualified personnel, or presentation of documents proving its financial standing but also by proving that it

[10] In Polish amendments to the Act on Public Procurement Law, a new provision on exclusion from the procedure is going to be adopted (Article 24 (1b)), which is in opposition to the proposed directive. According to the proposed regulations, the contractor shall be obligatorily excluded from the procedure and all future contracts if a large-scale contract (with a value of € 20–10 million) has been annulled by the contracting authority due to nonperformance of at least 5 % of the value of the contract.

has these at its disposal. Thus, the bidder is allowed to present a written obligation from another enterprise to provide the required equipment or human resources. The aforementioned legal solution is aimed to encourage SME participation in tendering procedures by easing the strict requirement of ownership of equipment or employment of personnel. However, this solution has also been criticized by contracting authorities because of cases of abuse. In practice, in an extreme situation very small enterprises could participate in tenders without authorization to perform specific activities, knowledge, experience, appropriate technical and personnel potential as well as economic and financial standing if only they can present proof that they have these at their disposal from other companies. This could create collusion between the enterprises aimed at price fixing or division of the market. Moreover, in this way companies which cannot participate themselves in the procedure due to exclusion from contract award could in practice execute the contract. The conditions of exclusion from the award procedure are enumerated in Article 24 of the Act on Public Procurement Law, which presents a list of categories of excluded contractors, including enterprises that caused damage by failing to perform a contract, contractors in arrears with the payment of taxes, other charges or social and health insurance contributions, or both natural and legal persons who have been sentenced by a final judgment for an offence committed in connection with contract award or for other offences (e.g., bribery, offences against economic turnover or environment, or any offence committed with the aim of gaining financial profits).

e-Procurement

The main idea of e-procurement stipulated in the directives is to promote cheap and fast communication and transparent award procedures (Article 1(7), (13), Article 33, Article 42(1), (4), (5), Article 54 of Directive 2004/18/EC; Article 1(5), (6), (12), Article 15, Article 48(1), (4), (5), Article 54; and Article 56 of Directive 2004/17/EC). All member states have introduced national public procurement websites to enable search for contracts notices as a result of implementation of a Europe-wide strategy for the development of e-procurement (European Commission 2004) and the declaration to promote procurement by electronic means presented in the Digital Agenda for Europe (European Commission 2010a). However, in many countries it is still difficult for tenderers to monitor notices and receive relevant information. In that context, the following measures can be suggested to increase e-procurement: publication of all public procurement notices online, creation of a single centralized website for public procurement, free access to notices, a multifunctional search engine, the possibility for SMEs to receive alerts of notices in their field of economic activity, direct downloading of contract notices and tender documents, and an electronic tendering facility enabling the contracting authority to receive bids electronically ensuring the integrity of information, confidentiality, and appropriate access (European Commission 2008a, p. 11).

One of the main aims of the new legislative package (Directive 2014/24/EU of the European Parliament and of the Council on public procurement, Preamble 33) is to promote e-procurement in terms of the entire award procedure. The commission also intends to manage a mandatory electronic system called e-Certis, which is aimed to facilitate exchange of certificates and other documentary evidence required by contracting authorities.

The promotion of e-procurement could be illustrated by the idea of creation of a public procurement information platform, which would provide a unified pan-European system creating an aggregation of tender notices linking open data and semantic web technologies. This platform requires a multistep method to deal with the requirements of the public procurement sector and the open government data initiative: (1) modelling the unstructured information included in public procurement notices, (2) supplementing that information with the existing product classification systems and the linked data vocabularies, and (3) publishing relevant information extracted from the notices according to the linking-open-data approach. Public procurement notices contain a variety of data such as type of contract, region, duration, total amount, and target enterprise. Various methods can be applied to expand user queries, facilitate access to information, and provide more accurate information. Expanded user queries can involve extra time in the process of retrieving notices. Moreover, the platform is also supposed to be especially relevant to SMEs that want to tender in the EU, easing access to information on notices and fostering SME participation in cross-border public procurement procedures across Europe (Alvarez 2012, p.12).

The Act on Public Procurement Law in Poland enables e-procurement, but the actual application of the legal possibilities is insufficient (Górczyńska 2011). The act regulates electronic auctions as well as electronic communication for procurement procedures, but those measures are applied relatively rarely. It is believed that e-procurement and the use of electronic communication can deliver economic savings, eliminate errors, and reduce waste. The main problems are related to the national regulations on electronic signature and the extended process of adoption of the new act on electronic signature, which is meant to reduce administrative burden on the development of e-commerce and e-procurement. In 2011, only 651 electronic auctions were organized on the electronic auction platform managed by the Polish Office of Public Procurement.[11] In comparison with Portugal, where almost all tendering procedures are conducted by e-procurement, Polish legislation requires significant changes to make electronic procurement attractive for contracting authorities and contractors. The currently discussed amendments aim to implement a 3-step program of e-procurement promotion (elimination of legal obstacles to increase the use of electronic auctions and electronic communication, development of the electronic auction platform and a fully electronic procurement procedure). It

[11] According to the data provided by the Public Procurement Office (2011), electronic bidding accounted for merely 0.17 % of all procurements in 2010 (as compared to previous years: 2009—0.16 %, 2008—0.05 %).

is planned to introduce a fully electronic tendering procedure for almost all tenders within 4 years.

Best Value for Money as the Main Award Criterion

The contracting authority can encourage SME participation in tenders by adopting award criteria such as the economically most advantageous offer rather than the price-only criterion. Employing the principle of the economically most advantageous offer, the contracting authority can evaluate, besides the the price, also additional criteria, such as after-sale services, technical assistance, technical merit, functional characteristics, cost-effectiveness, running costs, or even quality or innovative solutions. In the aforementioned form of contract award, life-cycle costs are taken into consideration along with the direct cost of purchasing goods.

The new directives directly formulate the rules for life-cycle costs of the products, services, or works. The life-cycle covers all stages of the existence of the object of the procedure. The costs to be taken into account include direct monetary expenses or external environmental costs that are to be calculated under the common European methodology. However, it should be observed that the application of life-cycle costs may imply additional costs and sometimes even barriers for SMEs. However, the use of different life-cycle cost methodologies detracts from the generally positive assessment of the proposed legislation. In the absence of one common European methodology for life-cycle cost calculation, the contracting authorities will be obliged to accept offers based on different methods as long as the contractor can prove that his method fulfils the requirements enumerated in the directive and is comparable with the methodology adopted by the contracting authority. This regulation can lead to higher costs and a longer period of preparation of documents, and even to numerous appeals resulting from potentially discriminatory treatment of contractors. Thus, the application of this regulation entails problems with the recognition and comparability of life-cycle cost methods.

Conclusions

The benefits of SME participation in public procurement can be divided into benefits for the contracting authority and benefits for the economy and society. The benefits for the administration are lower costs of goods and services, better quality, flexibility, and specialization. The benefits for the economy and society include greater competition in the market, innovation, lower unemployment, and economic growth. The main disadvantage for SMEs is the relatively high cost of participation in the public procurement market (Vengrauskas et al. 2008).

Based on a general assessment of the public procurement market, the conclusion can be drawn that public procurement rules directly or indirectly addressing SMEs do not distort competition in the common market. The Member States are allowed to introduce measures or even SME-friendly policies for the award of under-the-threshold contracts. However, national legislation must respect the principles of state aid. In that context, it could be still disputable whether SMEs can benefit from state aid, a social clause, or innovation promotion. Noneconomic aspects can be included at the various stages of the procedure by implementation of environmentally friendly solutions or a social clause with preferences for persons threatened with social exclusion. Other provisions, e.g., regarding combating unemployment, can be adopted in the execution phase of the contract.

The question still remains whether SMEs could be the object of state aid in the form of procurement preferences. SMEs are the main business beneficiaries of the EU structural funds. The main forms of state aid, such as preferential loans, tax relief, consultancy, and training, are addressed to micro-companies. This has been sometimes criticized as support should be rather addressed to high technology sectors and multinational corporations. On the other hand, SMEs are especially active in biotechnology, IT science, electronics, environmental protection, green technologies, sophisticated technical services, consulting, and legal advisory services as well as in so-called creative sectors which combine business with art and culture and even computer games. However, venture capital and private equity funds seem to be a good form of supporting new and creative enterprises and may be a far more effective form of public spending. Otherwise, structural funds would be distributed in an ineffective way and without added value.

In the proposed amendment to the Polish Act on Public Procurement Law, numerous measures are introduced to enable wider access of SMEs to the public procurement market. The Act on Public Procurement Law does not stipulate any preferences for SMEs as regards awarding public contracts. In the official justification, it is stated that many barriers faced by SMEs in terms of access to public contracts have already been removed by appropriate provisions in the proposed amendment. The main problems are probably connected with insufficient knowledge about SME-friendly regulations among enterprises and contracting authorities (Government of Poland 2011, p. 76).

The final version of the amendments to the Polish Act on Public Procurement Law refers to some particular measures aimed to promote SMEs (Government of Poland 2011, p. 77). The most important ones include splitting bids into lots, the requirement that subcontracting specifications should precisely define conditions of participation for subcontractors, and the possibility to impose an obligation on concessionaires of public works to award 30 % of their contracts to subcontractors. According to the assumptions formulated in the justification of the proposed amendment, the main trends in the development of public procurement in Poland are connected with increased participation of SMEs in public procurement, increased demand for innovative products, environmentally friendly solutions in public procurement, increased implementation of electronic measures in the procurement system, and inclusion of social clauses in award procedures.

In reference to the presented analysis of legality of any preferences for SMEs in the procurement market, some remarks should be made on the relationship between

SMEs and various possible violations of the law, which may not be justified. The level of risk of illegal arrangements between the contracting authority and the contractors, as well as between private bidders, still remains significant. It should be mentioned that contracting authorities should have more possibilities to exert influence on subcontracting. Despite the generally positive role of subcontracting in the public procurement system, it is in practice often reported that subcontracting can be a method of distributing collusive gains and often reduces the quality of contract performance, which is lower than that declared by the main contractor. The national regulations of the member states or the guidelines implemented by the contracting authorities themselves are aimed to minimize the aforementioned risk by some measures, including: abolishment of subcontracting for very innovative bids which require technical merit and highly qualified personnel, obligatory requirement of self-performance of contracts based on intellectual property rights, and a mandatory requirement included in the contract notice to present a list of subcontractors.

One of the possible solutions for combating corruption could be a higher level of involvement of the bidders who were not awarded the contract in its execution. In this context, splitting contracts into lots seems to be a viable method of combating fraud.

The legal system regulating public procurement both on the European and national levels seems to be still ineffective in ensuring the best value for money. Numerous amendments to the current legislation, the new legislative package of the procurement directives from 2014, and almost 200 judgements of the Court of Justice referring to the various aspects of the issue still remain insufficient to fully implement the common market. The system is overregulated and sometimes does not correspond to economic practice. In this author's view, the public procurement system should be deregulated, especially in the face of the economic crisis and the rapid development of non-European economies resulting in worldwide competition. European legislation should govern the main aspects of the procedures, leaving greater discretionary powers to the contracting authorities, which should be assisted by the purchasing institutions in all member states. Direct responsibility of political decisionmakers and the contracting authorities for award procedures should not only be implemented but also efficiently executed in the case of breach of substantial elements of contract awards. However, the most important aspect of combating fraud, corruption, and all illegal arrangements is increased control of the execution of contracts as the main source of corruption, bribery and various forms of illegal behavior.

References

Alvarez, J. M. (2012). Towards a Pan-European E-procurement platform to aggregate, publish and search public procurement notices powered by linked open data: The MOLDEAS approach. *International Journal of Software Engineering and Software Engineering, 22*(3), 365–383.

Arnould, J. (2004). Secondary policies in public procurement: The innovations of the new directives. *Public Procurement Law Review, 13,* 163–187.

Arrowsmith, S. (2005). *The law of public and utilities procurement*. Andover: Sweet and Maxwell.
Arrowsmith, S. (2009). Application of the EC treaty and directives to horizontal policies: A critical overview. In S. Arrowsmith & P. Kunzlik (Eds.), *Social and environmental policies in EC procurement law* (pp. 147–248). Cambridge: Cambridge University Press.
Brown, A. (2003). Post-tendering changes in the membership of a bidding consortium: Case C-57/01. *Public Procurement Law Review, 12,* 52–74.
Burgi, M. (2007). Small and medium sized enterprises and procurement law—European legal framework and German experiences. *Public Procurement Law Review, 16,* 262–284.
Cieśliński, A. (2010). *Wspólnotowe Prawo Gospodarcze*. Warszawa 2006, CH Beck.
Council of Ministers. (2008). *The new approach to public procurement: Public procurement and small and medium-sized enterprises, innovation and sustainable development*. Warsaw: Council of Ministers.
Craig, P., & Burca, G. (2010). *EC law: Text, cases and materials*. Oxford: Oxford University Press.
DG Enterprise and Industry. (2004). *The access of SMEs to public procurement contracts* (Final Report). Brussels, Belgium, European Commission.
DG Enterprise and Industry. (2010). *Evaluation of SMEs access to public procurement markets in the EU* (Final report). Brussels: DG Enterprise and Industry.
Erridge, A. (1998). Involvement of SMEs in public procurement. *Public Procurement Law Review, 7,* 22–37.
European Commission. (2000). *Promoting SMEs participation in public procurement in the community* (Council decision 2000/819/EC on a multiannual programme for enterprise and entrepreneurship and in particular for small and medium-sized enterprises). Brussels: European Commission.
European Commission. (2004). *Action plan for the implementation of the legal framework for electronic public procurement*. Brussels: European Commission.
European Commission. (2006). *Interpretative communication on the community law applicable to contract awards not or not fully subject to the provisions of the public procurement directives*. Brussels: European Commission.
European Commission. (2008a). *European code of best practices facilitating access by SMEs to public procurement contracts*. Brussels: European Commission.
European Commission. (2008b). *'Think small first': A small business act for Europe*. Brussels: European Commission.
European Commission. (2010a). *Digital agenda for Europe*. Brussels: European Commission.
European Commission. (2010b). *Europe 2020 strategy for smart, sustainable and inclusive growth*. Brussels: European Commission.
European Commission. (2011). *The single market act: Twelve levers to boost growth and confidence*. Brussels: European Commission.
European Commission. (2012). Treaty on the functioning of the European Union. http://eur-lex.europa.eu/legal-content/EN/TXT/?uri=CELEX:12012E/TXT.
Galster, J., & Mik, C. (1996). *Podstawy Europejskiego prawa Wspólnotowego. Zarys Wykładu* (pp. 187–198). Warszawa: Scholar Publishing.
GHK. (2010). *Evaluation of SMEs' access to public procurement markets in the EU: Final report*. (Executive Summary). Brussles: Author.
Górczyńska, A. (2005). Zasady Wspólnotowego Prawa Zamówień Publicznych. In M. Królikowska-Olczak (Ed.), *Prawo Europejskie w Systemie Polskiej Gospodarki* (pp. 23–53). Warszawa: Difin.
Górczyńska, A. (2011). Electronic public procurements. In P. Nowak (Ed.), *Innovations 2011. Modern Administration of the Łódzkie Voivodeship* (pp. 29–40). Lodz: Urząd Marszałkowski Województwa Łódzkiego.
Government of Poland. (2011). *Amendments to Polish act on public procurement law* (p. 76). Warsaw: Government of Poland.
Hatzis, N. (2009). The legality of SME development policies under EC procurement law. In S. Arrowsmith & P. Kunzlik (Eds.), *Social and environmental policies in EC procurement law* (pp. 246–267). Cambridge: Cambridge University Press.

Nielsen, R., & Treumer, S. (2005). *The new public procurement directives*. Copenhagen: DJOF Publishing.

O'Brien, G. (1993). Public procurement and small and medium sized enterprises. *Public Procurement Law Review, 2*, 76–89.

Public Procurement Office. (2011). *The report on functioning of the public procurement system in Poland in 2010*. Warsaw, Poland, Public Procurement Office Press.

Sołtysińska, A. (2006). *Europejskie Prawo Zamówień Publicznych*. Kraków: Zakamycze.

Stehmann, O., & Fernandez Martin, J. (1991). Product market integration versus regional cohesion in the community. *European Law Review, 16*, 216–235.

Sundstrand, A. (2010). *Set-asides for small and medium sized enterprises*. Paper presented at the 1st interdisciplinary symposium on public procurement, June 6th–7th, Rome, Villa Mondragone, Italy.

Vengrauskas, V., Gineitiene, Z., Serpytis, K., & Girdenis, J. (2008). The role of small and medium sized enterprises in the Lithuanian public procurement market. *Public Administration, 19*(3), 29–35.

Anna Górczyńska PhD is an assistant professor, is chair of the European Economic Law, and director of the Centre for Public Procurement and Public-Private Partnership, Faculty of Law and Administration, University of Lodz, Poland. Her research interests are in public procurement law, public-private partnership, European economic law, competition law, regional policy, structure funds of the EU, e-administration, ICT, and sports law.

Index

A
Accountability, 3, 15, 24, 27, 77, 146, 150, 196, 216, 242, 273
financial, 79, 85, 86
importance of, 17
issue of, 275

B
Best value for money (BVM), 7, 231, 275, 319
achievements of, 232
main award criterion, 317

C
China, 5, 7, 288–298
collaborative public procurement in, 210
policy implementation model, 289–291
Collaborative procurement, 203, 206, 208–210, 213, 215–217
institutional arrangements for, 204
survival of, 211
Commercial cards, 3, 57, 58, 60, 84
Commercial cards, 213
Consortia, 7, 312
of enterprises, 311
Conspiracies governance, 5
Construction, 4, 34–37, 42, 145–152, 156, 169, 238, 239
procurement, 6, 237–239, 241, 243–245
Contract management, 2, 13–17, 23–26, 237, 279
Control, 71, 75, 77–80, 85, 211, 223, 291, 295
Co-production, 4, 231
Corruption, 3, 5, 7, 19, 184, 195, 313, 319
Costarica, 2, 3, 13–18, 21, 24–26
Customers' preferences, 4, 134

D
Defense acquisition, 89–94, 97, 99, 100, 105–107, 123
Defense research
centers, 90
framework, 92, 102, 207
mapping, 102, 107, 123
topics, 3, 99, 100, 106, 111, 123
Discrete Choice Experiment (DCE), 4, 130,134

E
Efficiency, 1–4, 6, 13, 19, 22, 57, 78, 90, 183, 196, 204, 213, 247, 273, 283
E-government, 26, 27
Enforcement, 183, 195, 197, 199, 278, 295, 306
E-procurement, 2, 7, 15, 16, 22, 23, 26, 196, 315, 316
Equity, 1, 203, 288, 318
European Union (EU), 5–7, 89, 90, 162, 222, 255, 271, 301
collaborative public procurement, 208–210
directives, 162, 208, 271, 279, 280, 302, 307
public procurement law, 222, 223, 225, 229

F
Fairness, 1, 6, 132, 133

G
Glenview, 33–36, 39, 40, 55
Global competition, 1

K. V. Thai (ed.), *International Public Procurement,* Public Administration, Governance and Globalization 14, DOI 10.1007/978-3-319-13434-5

Government cost savings, 36, 57, 58, 60, 65, 70, 174

I

India, 5, 203–205, 211–216
- collaborative purchasing, 211
- comparative situation, 214
- competition case law position, 213
- competition law position, 212
- procurement rule position, 212

Infrastructure, 19, 94, 146, 150, 162, 196, 197, 237

Innovation, 21, 27, 94, 207, 255, 264, 281, 311
- contract management, 26
- partnerships, 258–260
- public procurement, 2–4

Innovative procurement, 2, 3, 272

Institutional and non-institutional cooperation, 225

Intergovernmental, 36, 39, 48, 51–55

J

Joint procurement, 204, 205

Joint purchasing agreements, 205–210, 213, 215, 216

L

Lots, 7, 307–310, 318, 319

M

Make-or-buy decision, 230

Merlink, 3, 18, 19, 26

Mixed purchasing, 36, 43, 53

Municipal procurement, 3, 4, 230

Municipal Partnering Initiative (MPI), 3, 31

Municipal Waste Services (MWS), 4, 129

N

National
- economic interests, 1
- procurement platform, 16

Network, 5, 53, 129, 183–187, 195, 198, 199, 245

P

Partial price selection, 159, 163

Pooled procurement, 5, 37, 203

Preferential public procurement, 6

Pre-procurement phase, 221, 222, 230, 231

Pricing
- component selection, 4, 146, 150, 157–159, 160, 163
- for public purchase, 4, 169, 175
- price-setting practices, 172
- regulation, 168–171, 175

Public procurement regulation, 147, 168, 308

Process efficiency, 57, 225

Procurement, 4–6, 16, 22, 41, 145, 198, 206, 279, 287, 318
- cycle, 3, 17, 18, 20, 24
- savings, 14
- system, 7, 8, 169, 199, 302, 306, 308, 319

Project alliance, 150, 162

Public contracting, 13, 25, 208

Public private partnership (PPP), 3, 106, 172, 178, 239

Public procurement law, 6, 206, 211, 221–230, 233, 315, 318
- EU, 222, 223, 225, 229

Public sector organizations, 237, 238

Purchasing cards, 57, 58, 61, 62, 69–74, 77–80, 84, 85
- impact of, 64

R

Reform, 2, 7, 196, 197, 222, 224, 256, 265, 291
- key areas of, 258
- European, 233

Regulation, 5, 8, 162, 168–171, 291, 304, 306, 311, 319
- pricing, 170–176
- procurement, 196, 203, 256

Sanctions, 94

S

Small and medium-sized enterprises (SMEs), 255, 288, 301–303
- role of, 7
- principles of, 303–306

Socioeconomic objectives, 1, 2

Subcontracting, 309, 310, 318, 319
- effects of, 309

Sustainable/sustainability, 7, 271–273, 276, 279–284, 295, 313
- guide to, 279
- interpretation of, 284
- procurement, 7, 27, 205, 272, 279, 280, 284

public procurement, 7, 8, 271, 272, 276–281
purchasing, 205

T

Thailand, 5, 183, 185, 186, 188, 198
Transparency, 1, 4, 13, 27, 196, 198, 232–234, 267, 296
advantage of, 231
objectives of, 15
principles of, 150, 163

U

Utilities, 7, 169, 256–268
of electricity, 204

V

Value for money (VFM), 2, 6, 133, 237, 238, 243–248, 273, 275, 279, 305
concept of, 239
Value-for-customer, 4, 131, 132
in public procurement, 133

MIX
Papier aus verantwortungsvollen Quellen
Paper from responsible sources
FSC® C105338

If you have any concerns about our products,
you can contact us on
ProductSafety@springernature.com

In case Publisher is established outside the EU,
the EU authorized representative is:
Springer Nature Customer Service Center GmbH
Europaplatz 3, 69115 Heidelberg, Germany

Printed by Libri Plureos GmbH
in Hamburg, Germany